PENGUIN BOOKS

Orwell and the Dispossessed

'One of the most influential English writers of the twentieth century' Robert McCrum, *Observer*

'A prophet who thought the unthinkable and spoke the unspeakable, even when it offended conventional thought' Peter Grosvenor, *Daily Express*

'He saw through everything because he could also see through himself. Many writers and journalists have tried to imitate his particular kind of clarity without possessing anything like his moral authority' Peter Ackroyd, *The Times*

'Orwell's innocent eye was often devastatingly perceptive . . . a man who looked at his world with wonder and wrote down exactly what he saw, in admirable prose' John Mortimer, *Evening Standard*

'Matchlessly sharp and fresh . . . The clearest and most compelling English prose style this century' John Carey, *Sunday Times*

'It is impossible not to be elated by his literary and political writing -- and enraged by what he was up against . . . the most lovable of writers, someone whose books can make the reader long for his company' Geoffrey Wheatcroft, *Spectator*

'His intellectual honesty was a virtue . . . it wasn't just the amount of truth he told but the way he told it, in prose transmuted to poetry by the pressure of his dedication' Clive James, *New Yorker*

'The finest English essayist of his century . . . He made it his business to tell the truth at a time when many contemporaries believed that history had ordained the lie . . . His work endures, as lucid and vigorous as the day it was written' Paul Gray, *Time*

ERIC ARTHUR BLAIR (George Orwell) was born in 1903 in India, where his father worked for the Civil Service. The family moved to England in 1907 and in 1917 Orwell entered Eton, where he contributed regularly to the various college magazines. From 1922 to 1927 he served with the Indian Imperial Police Force in Burma, an experience that inspired his first novel, *Burmese Days* (1934). Several years of poverty followed. He lived in Paris for two years before returning to England, where he worked successively as a private tutor, schoolteacher and bookshop assistant, and contributed reviews and articles to a number of periodicals. *Down and Out in Paris and London* was published in 1933. In 1936 he was commissioned by Victor Gollancz to visit areas of mass unemployment in Lancashire and Yorkshire, and *The Road to Wigan Pier* (1937) is a powerful description of the poverty he saw there. At the end of 1936 Orwell went to Spain to fight for the Republicans and was wounded. *Homage to Catalonia* is his account of the civil war. He was admitted to a sanatorium in 1938 and from then on was never fully fit. He spent six months in Morocco and there wrote *Coming Up for Air*. During the Second World War he served in the Home Guard and worked for the BBC Eastern Service from 1941 to 1943. As literary editor of *Tribune* he contributed a regular page of political and literary commentary, and he also wrote for the *Observer* and later for the *Manchester Evening News*. His unique political allegory, *Animal Farm*, was published in 1945, and it was this novel, together with *Nineteen Eighty-Four* (1949), which brought him world-wide fame.

George Orwell died in London in January 1950. A few days before, Desmond MacCarthy had sent him a message of greeting in which he wrote: 'You have made an indelible mark on English literature . . . you are among the few memorable writers of your generation.'

PETER DAVISON is Research Professor of English at De Montfort University, Leicester. He was born in Newcastle upon Tyne in 1926 and studied for a London External BA (1954) by correspondence course. He edited an Elizabethan text for a London MA (1957) and then taught at Sydney University, where he gained a Ph.D. He was awarded a D.Litt. and an Hon. D. Arts by De Montfort University in 1999. He has written and edited fifteen books as well as the Facsimile Edition of the manuscript of *Nineteen Eighty-Four* and the twenty volumes of Orwell's *Complete Works* (with Ian Angus and Sheila Davison). He is a Past-President of the Bibliographical Society, whose journal he edited for twelve years. He was made an OBE in 1999 for services to literature.

PETER CLARKE is Professor of Modern British History and Master of Trinity Hall, Cambridge. His books on twentieth-century Britain include *A Question of Leadership: Gladstone to Blair* and volume nine of the *Penguin History of Britain: Hope and Glory, Britain 1900–1990*. He is a regular reviewer for the *Sunday Times* and other publications.

Orwell and the Dispossessed

Down and Out in Paris and London
in the Context of Essays, Reviews and Letters selected from
The Complete Works of George Orwell

Edited by Peter Davison
Introduction by Peter Clarke

PENGUIN BOOKS

PENGUIN CLASSICS

UK | USA | Canada | Ireland | Australia
India | New Zealand | South Africa

Penguin Books is part of the Penguin Random House group of companies
whose addresses can be found at global.penguinrandomhouse.com.

Penguin
Random House
UK

This collection first published in 2001
Reissued in Penguin Classics 2020
001

The texts in this collection are taken from *The Complete Works of George Orwell*,
published by Martin Secker & Warburg Ltd (vols. 1–9 1986, vols. 10–20 1998).
Down and Out in Paris and London previously published in Penguin Books 1940 and 1989.
Some material previously published in different form, in *The Collected Essays, Journalism and
Letters of George Orwell*, Vols. 1–4, in Penguin Books 1970

Set in 10/12.5 pt Monotype Columbus
Typeset by Rowland Phototypesetting Ltd, Bury St Edmunds, Suffolk
Printed and bound in Great Britain by Clays Ltd, Elcograf S.p.A.

A CIP catalogue record for this book is available from the British Library

ISBN: 978–0–241–41800–0

www.greenpenguin.co.uk

MIX
Paper from
responsible sources
FSC® C018179

Penguin Random House is committed to a
sustainable future for our business, our readers
and our planet. This book is made from Forest
Stewardship Council® certified paper.

Contents

Introduction

Orwell is one of the great English writers of the twentieth century. To adapt a phrase that became famous in 1940, one could claim that he found a unique register in which to 'speak for England'. The England he spoke for was a nation notoriously preoccupied with 'class' – it was 'two nations', as Orwell acknowledged, ruefully but also hopefully. It is hardly surprising, then, that his published work dwells on class so frequently and fruitfully, or that this theme provides more than enough to fill the present volume with a diverse and distinctive selection of his writings.

What made Orwell unique was not his preoccupation with class: it was his ability to instil the topic with compelling human interest. It was commonplace for left-wing intellectuals in the 1930s to discover class as the key to the social and political crises of their day. Marxism seemed an attractive ideology in a world sliding from an economic slump into dictatorship and war. In an ossified and schematic form, and with tenuous fidelity to the insights of the historical Marx, Marxist economic determinism offered a textbook analysis of what was wrong with bourgeois society. It simultaneously explained why capitalism was bound to fail, why it fostered imperialism abroad and fascism at home, why it could not be reformed but only replaced, and why the proletariat was the appointed agent of revolutionary transformation. What distinguished Orwell was that he had so little use for the proletariat as a category – viewed distantly through the wrong end of a telescope – and instead insisted on discovering for himself the realities of how the poor lived.

Class has been conceptualized in many different ways. In his sweeping historical analysis, *Class in Britain*, David Cannadine suggests that a (misleadingly) similar language of class in fact discloses the persistent rivalry of three implicit models of the social structure. One is a continuously ranked hierarchy, making sense of social inequalities by locating individuals on rungs of a ladder. Another is a triadic structure of upper, middle and lower orders, which implicitly makes a middle or middling class the key mediating group. The third is a polarized, adversarial and self-conscious dichotomy between the oppressors and the oppressed, the exploiters and the exploited – clearly the form of class consciousness on which Marxism seizes in identifying class struggles as the motor of history.[1]

Here is a robust, versatile and useful taxonomy of class. Tested against it, Orwell is open to the stricture that 'when he tried to describe the social structure of his native land, his efforts were disappointingly confused, and dismally commonplace'.[2] The trouble is that, like many others, he slid between the different categories in this conceptual scheme, sometimes dwelling on the historic chain of hierarchy, while at other times discriminating finely between the social gradations of the middle classes, as in his famous self-identification as 'lower-upper-middle class'. And yet – with an incoherence that is bound to offend the canons of clear-cut social analysis – he reverts time and again to a split between 'us' and 'them' as the prevailing sense in which he understood class.

Orwell did so, however, not in a top-down, theory-driven way but as bottom-up lived experience. Historically, this is what saved him. One result was that he was not at the mercy of an *a priori* concept of class, like many of his left-wing contemporaries who constructed their understanding of the world in conformity with a prefabricated design and found themselves increasingly in denial about its structural flaws. Orwell's house of class had been built brick by brick, with tolerance for curious nooks and crannies. Thus it is hardly adequate to speak simply of the weakness of his theoretical understanding of class: this was exactly what liberated him from idealization of the proletariat and from the illusion that a rigorous class analysis was all that was necessary for political salvation.

Instead, he relied upon immersion and intuition. His immersion in the daily struggle of actual working-class life gave him a kind of first-hand experience very different from the abstractions of 'the class struggle'. His intuition as an imaginative writer guided him in developing a language and a literary genre in which he could carry reports between 'two nations', divided as much by mutual incomprehension as they undoubtedly were by material differences.

Orwell became a foreign correspondent in the class war. He could never forget that he was an Old Etonian roughing it; he did not really believe that his immersion would be permanent. The tools of his trade remained the notebook and the typewriter, with his writing as the ultimate objective and justification of his 'down-and-out' adventures. In a review printed in this volume, he makes the point that there were very few books 'which come from genuine workers and present a genuinely working-class outlook'. Yet he claimed: 'If all of them could get their thoughts on to paper, they would change the consciousness of our race.'[3]

Vicariously, Orwell became the voice of the inarticulate, of 'a normally silent multitude'. For though individuals might be able to talk well enough, the process of writing introduced alien conventions and inhibitions that thwarted effective communication. Orwell realized his own vocation as a writer in using his acquired skills to translate the experience of the poor into a truth that would live on the page.

Down and Out in Paris and London was his first triumph, in more senses than one. 'As for the truth of my story,' he writes in the preface to the French edition, 'I think I can say that I have exaggerated nothing except in so far as all writers exaggerate by selecting.'[4] In fact, Orwell took rather more liberties than he publicly acknowledged at the time, as we can now see. The annotations printed below in a friend's copy of *Down and Out* supply some illustrative detail of his methods.[5] Some episodes are transposed, collapsed or conflated. Some of the marginal notes – 'This all happened', 'Quite true' – may perversely raise doubts about the veracity of the rest.

Plainly, Orwell should not be relied upon, still less held accountable, for the literal accuracy of his reporting. Nor can his accounts of low life and degradation be regarded as representative of contemporary working or living conditions, even in the depths of the slump. Many working-class people, whose trades escaped structural unemployment, enjoyed the 1930s as an era of rising living standards, as historians have long made clear. Orwell's gallery of engaging or exotic characters, eking out an existence on the brink of destitution, plainly cannot serve as a proxy for the working class as a whole, either in France or Britain. But to pursue such a line of criticism risks missing the point entirely.

Orwell gives us poverty with a human face. His concern in these pages was not with the swathe of upwardly mobile workers whose consumption patterns prefigured the 'affluent society' of the postwar period – though he wrote elsewhere, notably in his novel *Coming Up for Air*, of this emerging, suburbanized, homogenized, Americanized England. Still less did Orwell's quest lead him to depict the immiserization of a solidaristic proletariat as a school of heroic resistance presaging the overthrow of capitalism. The individuals whom he describes are neither stock figures nor two-dimensional emblems of the oppressed and dangerous classes.

Instead, Orwell shows us people essentially much like ourselves – but down on their luck. At times he makes this explicit. 'The mass of the rich and the poor are differentiated by their incomes and nothing else, and the average millionaire is only the average dishwasher dressed in a new suit,' he tells us, and then confides: 'Everyone who has mixed on equal terms with the poor knows this quite well.'[6] But most of us, as he well knows, have not done this, and therefore we do not know it; that is the whole trouble, and it is no good simply telling us. The challenge for Orwell's art is to show us.

Hence his characteristic indirect strategies. By catching our attention with an anecdote, by seizing on an unexpected detail, by enlisting our sympathies in small things, he wins our credence in building up the big picture. The poor are not dull or uninteresting in his account; they are not extras in a drama where only the rich have speaking parts. Their stories will sometimes make your hair stand on end, and even if you can hardly believe that it is all true, you rarely doubt that these are real people. Orwell conveys a palpable sense of recognition: that we have met people like this even though we may never have lived ourselves in such circumstances. Only having secured the ground of our shared intuitions about particular individuals and experiences does he venture any generalizations; and these, rather than sticking out as didactic intrusions, carry the persuasive force of germane common sense.

Because Orwell's best work is so easy to read, it does not mean that it was easy to write. His overflowing wastepaper-basket, his pile of rejection slips, his burnt draft novels of the early 1930s, all testify to his own painful apprenticeship. But with the publication of *Down and Out in Paris and London* we can identify the voice of a maturing writer who was finding his *métier*. This was literally the beginning of the career of George Orwell

(rather than a struggling writer hitherto known only as Eric Blair).
Deceptively simple in style and exposition, none of it was as artless as it
seemed.

In analysing Orwell's literary strategy in this way, of course, we are
simply turning his own critical method back upon himself. 'The Art of
Donald McGill', reprinted here, was a pioneer exercise in analysing one
example of popular culture – British seaside postcards – that had simply
been taken for granted. If this was worth doing, then the art of George
Orwell is surely also worth exploration, as is well attested today by the
burgeoning interest in his literary oeuvre, captured in the magnificent
twenty volumes of *The Complete Works of George Orwell*, the source for this
selection.

What needs to be remembered is that Orwell is, above all, a political
writer. In making this point, I will cite below some of his introductory
comments from a lecture which is not reprinted here, 'Culture and Democracy', in which he offered some unusually explicit comments on the
relationship of class to politics, as he saw it. The lecture dates from
November 1941; it was given as part of a series organized by the Fabian
Society and was subsequently published in a version to which Orwell
objected; so the text itself may not represent him faithfully.[7] But the
substance of his remarks may be worth retrieval in framing the concerns
and explicating the sub-text of many of the pieces collected in *Orwell and
the Dispossessed*.

By 1941 Orwell was famous as the author of *The Lion and the Unicorn*.
It was, of course, a tract for the times: making its immediate case with
half an eye upon sceptical American readers who needed persuading that
Britain was indeed fighting for democracy. It was also, as a thousand
subsequent acts of plagiarism testify, a moving affirmation of English
patriotism. The right can happily make a cliché of 'the old maids biking
to Holy Communion through the mists of the autumn mornings' while
the left prefer to relish the image of 'a family with the wrong members in
control'.[8] What is crucial is the tension between Orwell's long-held sense
of the stupid injustice of the British class system and his commitment, at
this moment of crisis, to 'my country right or left'.[9] Yet he did not abandon
a left-wing analysis that gave priority to class in favour of a patriotic
version that edited class divisions out of the story.

It was through democracy that Orwell sought to resolve these conflicting emphases. Rather than simply restricting democracy to mean 'a form of society in which power is in the hands of the common people', Orwell pointed to another sense, in contrast with totalitarianism, as 'a form of society in which there is considerable respect for the individual, a reasonable amount of freedom of thought, speech and political organization, and what one might call a certain decency in the conduct of the government'. The point was, as he put it, 'I don't need to debunk the first definition' since the common people were plainly not in power; but, he continued, 'particularly in left-wing circles, I think it is necessary to say that democracy in the other sense – freedom of speech, respect for the individual and all the rest of it – does have a reality, an importance, which cannot be made away with by mere juggling with words.'[10]

It is, in fact, Orwell's rejection of crude class determinism that is the key to his political position. Whereas it was a conventional Marxist ploy to 'unmask' the capitalist realities behind western democratic rhetoric, Orwell went further:

Nothing is easier, particularly if you have a screen of battleships between you and danger, than to prove in words or on paper that there is no real difference between totalitarianism and 'bourgeois' democracy. I haven't the slightest doubt that each of my readers has said that. I have said it frequently . . . Everybody knows that line of thought. It is impossible to go into a left-wing gathering anywhere without hearing it put forward. But I think it is necessary to recognize that it is not only nonsense, but nonsense that can only be uttered by people who have a screen of money and ships between themselves and reality.[11]

This passage works on several levels. It turns a more sophisticated class analysis back upon the left-wing intelligentsia itself, virtually accusing it of its own kind of false consciousness. Moreover, there is a visceral quality in Orwell's antipathy towards the stereotyped reflexes – 'political correctness' would be an anachronistic term – that he found among his own ostensible political allies on the left. He was certainly an awkward comrade. And it is easy to see how he achieved an international reputation as the author of a critique of totalitarianism, first in *Animal Farm* and then in *Nineteen Eighty-Four*.

Orwell's ironical fate was to be hailed by the political right in the cold-war era. Today it is easier to make sense of his abiding concerns. The nub of his argument was that, so long as formal democracy survived, the possibility of beneficial change remained open; and that unless, in the wider sense, democratic values survived, change would be for the worse. The somewhat imprecise phrase for which he persistently groped in identifying these values was 'a certain decency'. Though explicitly disclosed during the Second World War, it was a humanist perspective long apparent in Orwell's earlier dispatches from the class war. It would be false, therefore, to suppose that he retreated in any significant way from his indictment of the way that the poor were condemned to live in a supposedly civilized society. The range of his writings in this volume, extending into the late-1940s, shows him as alert and unforgiving in this respect, as in the days when he was himself down and out.

Peter Clarke

1. David Cannadine, *Class in Britain* (Yale University Press, 1998), esp. pp. 19–20.
2. Cannadine, p. 144.
3. See p. 228, below.
4. See p. 221, below.
5. See pp. 60–61, below.
6. See p. 152, below.
7. See *CW*, XIII/*884* and *885*.
8. *CW*, XII/*763*.
9. The title of an essay published in the autumn of 1940, *CW*, XII/*694*, reproduced in *Orwell's England* in this series.
10. *CW*, XIII/*885*.
11. *Ibid.*

Editorial Note

In the main, the items reproduced here are given in the chronological order in which they were written or published. However, the order of events is sometimes better represented by not following this practice. It will be obvious, from dates and item numbers, where the chronological order has not been followed. Letters are typewritten unless stated otherwise. The titles used for Orwell's essays and articles are not always his own but this distinction is not noted unless there is a special reason to do so.

All the items are drawn from *The Complete Works of George Orwell*, edited by Peter Davison, assisted by Ian Angus and Sheila Davison (Secker & Warburg, 1998). Some explanatory headnotes and many footnotes have been added, amplified and modified. The *Complete Works* did not provide biographical notes of authors of books reviewed but, for this selection, these have been added if the author had a link with Orwell or if they might illuminate the context of Orwell's review. Item numbers from the original edition are given in italics within square parentheses, and a list of volumes in which these items can be found is given in the Further Reading.

Where the text was in some way obscure, the original edition does not modify but marks the word or passage with a superior degree sign (°); in most instances such passages have been silently corrected in this edition but in a few instances the degree sign has been retained, for example, where one of Orwell's idiosyncratic spellings occurs: e.g., 'agressive' or 'adress'.

References to items in the *Complete Works* are generally given by volume, forward slash and item number in italic: e.g.: XV/*1953*; page references to *CW* are given similarly except that the page number is in roman: XII/387; page references to this present volume are given as 'p. 57'; references are also made to the companion three volumes: *Orwell in Spain*, *Orwell and Politics* and *Orwell's England*. References to *Down and Out in Paris and London* are given to this edition by page and, within square brackets, by the *CW* volume number (IV) and page (the page numbers in *CW* and Penguin Twentieth-Century Classics are identical for the text): e.g., p. 101 [IV/49].

The following works are designated by abbreviated forms:

Complete Works and *CW*: *The Complete Works of George Orwell*, edited by Peter Davison assisted by Ian Angus and Sheila Davison, 20 vols. (1998); volume numbers are given in roman numerals, I to XX. Vols. X–XX of a second, enlarged and amended, edition are being published in paperback from September 2000.

CEJL: *The Collected Essays, Journalism and Letters of George Orwell*, edited by Sonia Orwell and Ian Angus, 4 vols. (1968; paperback, 1970)

Crick: Bernard Crick, *George Orwell: A Life* (1980; 3rd edn, 1992)

A Literary Life: P. Davison, *George Orwell: A Literary Life* (1996)

Orwell Remembered: Audrey Coppard and Bernard Crick, eds., *Orwell Remembered* (1984)

Remembering Orwell: Stephen Wadhams, ed., *Remembering Orwell* (1984)

S&A, *Unknown Orwell*: Peter Stansky and William Abrahams, *The Unknown Orwell* (1972)

S&A, *Transformation*: Peter Stansky and William Abrahams, *Orwell: The Transformation* (1979)

Shelden: Michael Shelden, *Orwell: The Authorised Biography* (1991)

The Thirties: Malcolm Muggeridge, *The Thirties* (1940; 1971); reviewed by Orwell, XII/615

A fuller reading list is given in Further Reading.

Peter Davison,
De Montfort University, Leicester

Acknowledgements

George Orwell's (Eric Blair's) work is the copyright of the Estate of the late Sonia Brownell Orwell. Most of the documents in this edition are held by the Orwell Archive (founded by Sonia Orwell in 1960) at University College London. Gratitude is expressed to the Archive, and particularly its Archivist, Gill Furlong, for the help given the editor. Thanks are also gratefully extended to the Henry W. and Albert A. Berg Collection, The New York Public Library, and the Astor, Lennox and Tilden Foundations, for permission to reproduce Orwell's letter to Leonard Moore of 19 November 1932; and to the British Broadcasting Corporation for 'Answering You' and 'The Proletarian Writer'.

Over thirty years ago it was my privilege to spend a day at the Shakespeare Institute, Birmingham, with two colleagues discussing the presentation of the New Penguin Shakespeare series (to which I contributed editions of *1* and *2 Henry IV*) with the great typographer and designer, Hans Schmoller. Now I am indebted to his daughter, Monica, for sensitive and expert guidance in the preparation of these four volumes for this new Penguin series. I am most grateful, and delighted that, as it were, 'my end is in my beginning', if I might adapt Mary, Queen of Scots, and T. S. Eliot.

'This is . . . a book for those who want to see the notorious "two-nations" of England made into one.'

(Orwell, Foreword to *The End of the 'Old School Tie'* by T. C. Worsley)

'I was told that an impassable gulf divided the Rich from the Poor; I was told that the Privileged and the People formed Two Nations, governed by different laws, influenced by different manners, with no thoughts or sympathies in common; with an innate inability of mutual comprehension. I believed that if this were indeed the case, the ruin of our common country was at hand . . .'

(Charles Egremont in *Sybil*, by Benjamin Disraeli, 1845,
Book IV, ch. 8 (1998), 245)

'[The people of England] no longer believe in any innate difference between the governing and the governed classes of this country. They are sufficiently enlightened to feel they are victims. Compared with the privileged classes of their own land, they are in a lower state than any other population compared with its privileged classes. All is relative, my lord, and believe me, the relations of the working classes of England to its privileged orders are relations of enmity, and therefore of peril.'

(A Chartist delegate to Lord Valentine, *Sybil*, p. 227)

Foreword to The End of the 'Old School Tie' *by*
T. C. Worsley
May 1941[1]

The Searchlight Books[2] have been planned to deal with the immediate
rather than the distant future. Certain problems, however, are bound to
arise in an urgent form as soon as the war is over and are likely to be dealt
with in some shoddy makeshift way unless they are thought out in detail
beforehand. Of these the educational problem is the most important, and
T. C. Worsley's book is a preliminary sketch towards its solution.

What he says will not please the defenders of the existing system.
Neither will it please the more 'advanced' experimentalists or the people
who imagine that nothing can ever be achieved in England unless we rip
down the whole social structure and build again from the bottom. The
subjects he deals with in most detail are the need for some kind of uniform
educational system for all children up to the age of eleven, as a basis for
genuine democracy, and the special position of the Public Schools. He is
not so uncompromisingly hostile to the Public Schools as most people of
Left-wing opinions. He recognizes that much of the trouble in the England
of the last twenty years has come from the divorce between toughness
and intelligence, leaving us on the one hand with an official and military
class who do their duty according to their lights but whose lights are still
those of the pre-1914 world, and on the other hand with an intelligentsia
who can see what is happening but lack all training for action. Part of his
theme is the importance of not simply attacking the Public Schools, but
of trying to incorporate what is good in them in a new system set free
from class privilege.

The one thing certain about the British educational system is that if we
do not ourselves change it after the war, it will be because Hitler is
changing it for us. Indeed it is changing already, thanks to the dispersal

of the child population, the impoverishment of the middle classes and the ever-growing need of the age for technicians. It is in our power to decide whether the change shall be made consciously, as part of a movement towards full democracy, or haphazardly, with vested interests of all kinds fighting rearguard actions and holding up the course of history. This is, therefore, a book for those who want to see the notorious 'two-nations'[3] of England made into one, and with as short a transition stage as possible. It is written for the general public, but educational specialists will find much in it to interest them.

1. This book was first printed in April 1941 but 'destroyed by enemy action' (bombing). It was reset in May and published in June 1941. Orwell dated his Foreword May 1941.

2. Searchlight Books were planned by Fredric Warburg (1898–1980), Tosco Fyvel (1907–1985) and Orwell during the summer of 1940 'in the lush garden of Scarlett's Farm', the home of the Warburgs near Twyford, Berkshire: 'while German bombs . . . began to fall on London; and while above our heads . . . the Spitfires and Hurricanes of the RAF accomplished their decisive air victory of the war, we talked about the future' (Tosco Fyvel, *George Orwell: A personal memoir* (1982), 106; ch. 10 gives a good account of the genesis of the series). Seventeen Searchlight Books were planned; nine were published in 1941 and two in 1942; the remainder did not appear. Orwell began the series with *The Lion and the Unicorn* (XII/763; and see, in this series, *Orwell's England* for part I, and *Orwell and Politics* for parts II and III). He also wrote forewards for two books, this one and Joyce Cary's *The Case for African Freedom*.

3. Orwell is referring to the novel, *Sybil*, by Benjamin Disraeli (1845) in which Charles Egremont says, 'I was told that an impassable gulf divided the Rich from the Poor; I was told that the Privileged and the People formed Two Nations, governed by different laws, influenced by different manners, with no thoughts or sympathies in common; with an innate inability of mutual comprehension. I believed that if this were indeed the case, the ruin of our common country was at hand . . .' (245) Egremont, a member of the landlord class with a set of chambers in Albany, Piccadilly, discovers how people live in a rural slum, Marney, 'where penury and disease fed upon the vitals of a miserable population', and an industrial town, Wodgate. Disraeli paints both in the worst light. Thus, of the people of Wodgate, he writes: 'It is not that the people are immoral, for immorality implies some forethought; or ignorant, for ignorance is relative; but they are animals; unconscious; their minds a blank; and their worst actions only the impulse of a gross or savage instinct. There are many in this town who are ignorant of their very names; very few who can spell them. It is rare that you meet with a young person who knows his own age; rarer to find the boy who has seen a book, or the girl who has seen a flower' (51 and 164). Orwell, in his descent into 'the lower depths', has much in common with Egremont.

From Burma to Paris

*George Orwell served in the Indian Imperial Police in Burma from 1922
until 1927. He returned to England on leave on 12 July 1927 and, having
left his ship in Marseilles and travelled home through France, arrived back
in England in August. While on holiday with his family in Cornwall in
September he decided not to return to Burma. His resignation took effect from
1 January 1928 and entailed the loss of almost £140 (approximately £5,500
in today's values). By the time he left Burma he was earning £696 a year
(roughly £28,000 today), to which were added bonuses for learning Hindi,
Burmese and Shaw-Karen. He would not earn nearly that much again in the
next fourteen years until he joined the BBC in 1941 (£640). It is likely,
from what we know of clothes he had made for him on his return' and the
style in which he lived for most of his time in Paris, that he had saved a fair
amount of his pay. During the rest of his leave he rented a cheap room in the
Portobello Road in Notting Hill, London W11. He began to make expeditions
to the East End of London in the autumn of 1927. The order of the events
in* Down and Out in Paris and London *should therefore be reversed;
indeed, the proof of the title-page, printed before he had chosen the name
'George Orwell' and when he wished to be known completely anonymously,
has 'Confessions of a Down and Out in London and Paris by X'. In the
spring of 1928, Orwell went to Paris and took a room at 6 rue du Pot de
Fer in the Fifth Arrondissement, a working-class district near Monge Métro
station. He set himself to becoming a writer and had a modest success in
getting articles into small-circulation, left-wing journals. He also wrote
either one or two novels and a number of short stories, none of which survive.
The article reproduced here, 'Unemployment' (translated from the French
version by Janet Percival and Ian Willison), is one of three from 'An Inquiry
into "Civic Progress" in England: The Plight of the British Workers',
published by* Le Progrès Civique *in 1928 and 1929. A second article, 'A
Day in the Life of a Tramp', is reprinted in a companion volume in this
series,* Orwell's England. *For each he was paid 225 francs (about £1.80
– some £70 in today's values). He also wrote articles on John Galsworthy,
the exploitation of the Burmese people and on censorship in England, for
French journals. An article on the French journal* Ami du Peuple, *written
in Paris and published in English in* G.K.'s Weekly, *29 December 1928,*

is reproduced below. The Complete Works *print all the articles, with their French originals. The article on unemployment printed here was also published on 29 December 1928 and is the first in the series on the plight of British workers. These articles draw on Orwell's experiences soon after his return from Burma and before he went to Paris. The very short paragraphs are not typical of Orwell. Orwell wrote in English (in a version that has not survived) and the French translator, Raoul Nicole, is almost certainly responsible for breaking Orwell's prose into short bites. For about ten weeks in the late autumn of 1929, Orwell worked as a dish-washer and kitchen porter in a luxury hotel and restaurant in Paris. This was the only time he was seriously poor and served as the basis for the Paris section of* Down and Out.[2]

1. See *A Literary Life*, 36.
2. Ibid., 34, and, generally, Crick, 172–4; S&A, *Unknown Orwell*, 213–16; Shelden, 135–43.

[82]

'Unemployment'
Le Progrès Civique, *29 December 1928*

The prices and measurements given in French in the original have been retained, despite a certain incongruity (with old-style English equivalents where helpful), so that where the original French uses English denominations, such as shillings, this will be clear. There were twenty shillings to a pound (so a shilling corresponds to 5p). For approximate contemporary values, multiply by forty. There were 124 francs to the £ when Orwell was in Paris.

England! Unemployment! You cannot speak of one without raising the ghost of the other.

Unemployment is one of the realities of postwar English life; it is also the reward given to the British worker for his war service.

Before the war, unemployment was certainly not unknown, but the relatively small number of the unemployed was of negligible significance. They constituted what could be termed 'the reserve army of labour', and acted as a brake on the over-rapid rise in wages; they were also sometimes used as stopgaps when there was a labour shortage.

At that time the economic mechanism ran, or at least seemed to run, fairly smoothly.

Public opinion viewed things calmly, assuming that the machinery could never go far wrong.

But war came and suddenly everything did go wrong. Competition, the very foundation of modern trade, which forces the industrialists from one country into cut-throat rivalry with those of another, was to blame. In all competition there must be a winner and a loser. Before the war England was the winner; today she is the loser. That, in a nutshell, was the cause of all the trouble.

***[1]

The war put an end to England's industrial supremacy. The countries which did not fight, notably America, gained possession of most of her export markets for their own profit. But, even worse, the rest of the world was becoming industrialised more quickly than she was.

The very fact that she had led the way in the race to industrialise told against her.

Her capital was tied up in obsolete machinery, which was unsuited to new methods, but which had cost too much to allow it to be scrapped.

Other countries, which had started later in the race, were better equipped for modern needs. England's main industries, coal and steel, are among those which have suffered most.

At the present time, the coal mines are the hardest hit. They are in such a deplorable state that many of them can only be run at a loss under the present system.

In England, the system of dual property rights in the mining regions gives rise to an enormous waste of fuel, labour and machinery.

Exorbitant rates are paid to the owners of the ground under which the coal seams lie. In addition, each mine is devoured by its own collection of hangers-on: the shareholders, whose demands for dividends push up the price of coal accordingly.

Given all these disadvantages, can we be surprised that English coal no longer finds a market?

To remedy this state of affairs, the capitalists have attempted to force the miners to work for inadequate wages. Their efforts here have failed, but in the meantime Polish coal is selling at a price some 10 or 15 francs [1s 8d or 2s 6d] below the lowest price which England can offer under the present system.

It is the same in steelworks and cotton mills. Today England is paying dearly for her former industrial supremacy.

Result: one and a quarter million, one and a half million, sometimes nearly two million unemployed in England.

With one or two million people starving in a country, there is a threat of imminent revolution, so it was realised from the outset that the state had a duty to come to the aid of the unemployed.

With the end of the war there came an end to the misleading and short-lived prosperity of wartime. The soldiers returning home had been told that they had been fighting for civilisation and for a country 'fit for heroes to live in', as Lloyd George put it;[2] in short, that postwar England would be an Eldorado where riches would go hand in hand with a higher standard of living.

Alas! As Eldorado did not materialise, it was necessary to think up something at once, before the ex-servicemen had time to find out that they had been deceived and realised that, in the end, they had fought for nothing after all.

And that is why the Government rushed through the Unemployment Insurance Act in 1920; under this act any worker in regular employment could choose to pay a sum of money which would indemnify him should he lose his job. These payments would give him the right to claim benefit in the case of forced unemployment – a wise precaution against the starvation and revolution which would inevitably result.

Here is a brief summary of the clauses of this act:

Each week the workers pay a premium of 3 francs for men and 2 francs 50 for women. In return, if they have made at least thirty payments, they can, if necessary, draw the special unemployment benefit.

This benefit amounts to an allowance of 18 shillings (110 francs) a week for a total of twenty-six weeks of unemployment. This period can be extended in certain exceptional circumstances.

Besides this, if the unemployed man is married, he receives a weekly allowance of 5 shillings (30 francs) for his wife, and of 1 shilling (6 francs) for each of his children. For unemployed women and young persons under twenty-one the allowances are even smaller.

It should be pointed out straightaway that this has nothing at all to do with charity. It is, in fact, a kind of insurance, and the majority of workers receive nothing in return for their payments.

It must be added that these subsidies for the unemployed have become an absolute necessity as a result of a decline in the English economy for which the workers are by no means responsible.

It is also worth noting that the unemployment benefits do not err on the side of generosity.

One shilling per week is not much to keep a child on. Even with 18 shillings a week a grown man has difficulty in making ends meet.

This needs to be stressed, because there is a ridiculous story in the Conservative press which states that unemployment is due only to the laziness and the greed of the workers.

According to this story, the sole aim of the British worker is to avoid all tiring labour in order to live in idleness on his 18 shillings a week.

And the inventors of this story have coined the word 'dole' for unemployment benefits.[3]

'Dole' is a wicked word, an expression full of disdain evoking the idea of money paid out by charity to unworthy scroungers.

The belief that the unemployed represent a veritable army of sybarites enjoying themselves on money begged from the charity of the taxpayers is widely held by the comfortably-off in England.

In fact, the lot of the unemployed is in reality far from enviable. How, after all, can one live on 18 shillings a week? The reply is simple: one does not live, one just avoids dying.

Take, for example, the case of an unemployed married man with a wife and two young children. His total weekly income amounts to 25 shillings (150 francs).

Could anyone believe for a minute that he could buy many luxuries with this sum, and that the poor devil would not prefer any job, however arduous, which would bring in more?

A poor family, in the situation I have just described, lives herded together in one room in some stinking slum in London, Manchester, or perhaps some Welsh mining town.

They probably pay 7 shillings (42 francs) a week in rent alone. The remainder must suffice to feed and keep four people.

Given this sort of income, what can their meals consist of? Bread and tea, tea and bread, week in, week out.

This is wretched sustenance: bad bread, white and lacking nutriment, and very strong tea is the staple diet for very poor people in England.

In winter, it is almost impossible to heat the one shabby room properly. The man cannot afford to buy tobacco. Beer is out of the question.

Even the children's milk is rationed. Spare clothes and the less essential pieces of furniture make their way one by one to the pawnbroker's. Dismal day follows dismal day without bringing an end to unemployment.

So 'idleness in luxury', as the Conservative newspapers say in righteous indignation, turns out to mean, on closer inspection, 'a state of near starvation'.

* * *

It may be that the unemployed man is single. Then he will take up residence in one of the enormous barracks known as 'lodging-houses' reserved for very poor people. By doing this he will be able to save a shilling or two on his weekly rent.

These lodging-houses are run by large companies, which make a significant income for them.

The lodgers sleep in enormous dormitories where thirty or forty campbeds – like those of soldiers – are lined up about three feet apart (90 centimetres).

They spend their days in underground kitchens, built under the street, where they can cook their food, if they have any, in a frying pan on a coke fire.

Most of the unmarried down-and-outs in England – the unemployed, beggars, newspaper-sellers and the like – live in these lodging houses; overcrowded, insanitary, comfortless places. The beds, usually revoltingly filthy, are crawling with vermin.

And it is here that the unemployed man takes his meals, consisting of bread and tea. He sits in a blank stupor in front of the fire for those long hours when he is not searching for some kind of work.

Apart from this constantly frustrating search for work, he has nothing at all to do. One can understand that in his situation he desperately hopes to work, to accomplish any task at all, however disgusting and poorly paid, for this completely empty existence, with no entertainment or distraction of any kind – and where hunger is never far away – is one of monotony and crushing boredom.

The unemployed man has just about enough money to meet the essential necessities of life, and the idleness which is forced upon him is a hundred times worse than the worst possible task.

Moreover his unemployment benefit will not be paid to him for ever, and even collecting it is not exactly easy.

He has to go to the Labour Exchange every day to see if there is any work and must often wait there for several hours before anyone has time to attend to him.

To draw his weekly allowance, he has to appear in person and again wait around. Thus one can see at any hour of the day long queues of shabbily dressed, haggard men crowding round the doors of the Labour Exchange. Passers-by look at them with pity or contempt. The officials whose job it is to pay them are at pains to make them aware of the inferiority of their situation. They will not let the unemployed forget for a minute that they are outcasts, living at public expense, who must therefore behave humbly and submissively in all circumstances. The officials are within their rights in refusing payment if the unemployed present themselves drunk or even smelling of drink.

Then comes the dreaded day when the 'dole' runs out. The twenty-six weeks have passed and the unemployed man, still with no work, finds himself with no money either.

What can he do now? Perhaps he has saved a few shillings which will carry him on for a day or two longer. He could give up his four-franc bed and spend his nights in the open, reduce his meals to the bare minimum which will just allow him to stay alive. What is the use? If the longed-for job does not materialise, he must make the choice between begging, stealing, or dying of poverty.

He will probably decide to beg. He will ask for money in the street or else he will seek the assistance reserved for paupers from the local rates under the terms of the Poor Law. Perhaps he will have himself admitted to the workhouse where the poor, treated more or less like prisoners, are kept at public expense.

If he is lucky he will obtain, under that same law, a weekly payment of 10 shillings (62 francs), on which he will have to exist as best he can.

He could also become a 'tramp', and wander up and down the country looking for work on the way and seeking bed and board in a different workhouse[4] every night.

But there are so many of these unfortunate creatures that the whole edifice of the Poor Law is in danger of crumbling. It was conceived to cope with normal conditions, and cannot bear the additional weight of the thousands of jobless who, since they no longer receive unemployment pay, are often obliged to go on being supported by the community.

In South Wales, where the failure of the pits has thrown half a million men onto the streets, the relief funds for the needy paid from the local rates have now gone bankrupt.

* * *

These are the conditions of unemployment in England. To remedy this state of affairs, the present Conservative government has done nothing except make optimistic pronouncements.

At the beginning of this year, when Mr Baldwin[5] was asked to make subsidies from the public purse on behalf of South Wales, the Prime Minister replied that he was 'counting on private charity' to help the miners deep in destitution.

Tentative projects were proposed aimed at creating an artificial demand for labour by undertaking wide-scale public works, such as the building of roads or canals, but as it would have needed new taxes to set up the project, nothing very much has been achieved.

The mass emigration of the unemployed has also been encouraged, but the conditions offered were not very attractive. What is more, Canada and Australia have their own industrial problems to solve, just like their mother country.

They have no use at the moment for surplus English miners, and have made this quite clear to the miners themselves.

Thus it seems unlikely that emigration will smooth over the difficulty.

The government has striven to hide its mistakes by varnishing the truth. The official unemployment statistics have been drawn up quite deliberately to give an erroneous impression. They only count the *insured* unemployed, omitting the tens of thousands of people who have never had a regular job since the war. Wives and children supported by the jobless do not appear in these lists either.

The real number of those in need is thus grossly underestimated. The Conservative press avoids mentioning unemployment as much as possible: when it is mentioned, it is with dismissive allusions to the 'dole' and to the laziness of the working classes.

So the comfortably-off middle-class Englishman, who knows nothing – and prefers to know nothing – of the life of the poor, learns nothing which might shake him out of his complacent indifference.

And how, we ask, will all this end? What solution can be envisaged?

One thing alone seems certain. Efforts will be made to prevent most of these poor creatures from actually dying of hunger. For example, no government would dare to make a stand against half-a-million starving miners. Whatever happens, to avoid revolution they will make sure that the unemployed can receive subsidies from somewhere.

But apart from that, any great improvement seems impossible. Unemployment is a by-product of capitalism and large-scale industrial competition. As long as this state of affairs persists, poverty will hold the workers in thrall, now in one country, now in another.

For the moment, the English worker is the scapegoat. He will no doubt continue to suffer until there is a radical change in the present economic system.

Meanwhile his only real hope is that one day a government will be elected which has sufficient strength and intelligence to bring about the change.

E.-A. BLAIR[6]

1. These 'spacers' appear in the original French text. They *may* indicate Orwell's original paragraphing.
2. David Lloyd George (1863–1945; Earl Lloyd George of Dwyfor, 1945) was Liberal Chancellor of the Exchequer, 1905–15, and Prime Minister, 1916–22. He proved an effective wartime leader and after the war, unsuccessfully advocated a reasonable peace settlement with Germany. In a speech at Wolverhampton on 24 November 1918, two weeks after the Armistice, he posed the question, 'What is our task?' It was, he said, 'To make Britain a fit country for heroes to live in.' The old-age pension was once often familiarly known as one's 'Lloyd-George'.

3. 'Dole' as a gift of food or money goes back at least to the fourteenth century. It is used by Langland (anything but a 'Conservative' writer) in *Piers Plowman*. Its pejorative use, especially in the twentieth century, is ironic, because employees as well as employers contribute to unemployment insurance, which is the source of unemployment benefits. The idea was first put forward in England by Lloyd George, a Liberal, in his budget for 1909, which the House of Lords rejected.

4. The French text renders 'workhouse' as *l'asile* and adds the English word, in italics in parentheses, immediately after. Several words are given in both English and the closest French equivalent, or simply in English in italics. Thus, 'tramp' appears in italics and also translated as *vagabond*.

5. Stanley Baldwin (1867–1947; Earl Baldwin, 1937) was Conservative Prime Minister three times, 1923–4, 1924–9 (when Orwell wrote this article) and 1935–7. He successfully negotiated the crisis occasioned by the abdication of King Edward VIII on 11 December 1936, but much of the blame for Britain's failure to prepare adequately for the Second World War is often laid at his door.

6. The pen-name 'George Orwell' was first used in January 1933 for *Down and Out in Paris and London*, but it was not regularly used for reviews and articles and so on until December 1936. Unless the pen-name is used, the form used for individual publications is given at the end of each item – E.-A. Blair, E. A. Blair, Eric Blair, E. A. B., E. B., and typographic variants. For much of his time at the BBC (1941–3) he was known as Eric Blair.

---

[80]

'A Farthing Newspaper'
G. K.'s Weekly, *29 December 1928*[1]

The *Ami du Peuple* is a Paris newspaper. It was established about six months ago, and it has achieved something really strange and remarkable in the world where everything is a 'sensation', by being sold at ten centimes, or rather less than a farthing the copy. It is a healthy, full-size sheet, with news, articles and cartoons quite up to the usual standard, and with a turn for sport, murders, nationalist sentiment and anti-German propaganda. Nothing is abnormal about it except its price.

Nor is there any need to be surprised at this last phenomenon, because the proprietors of the *Ami du Peuple* have just explained all about it, in a huge manifesto which is pasted on the walls of Paris wherever billsticking is not *défendu*. On reading this manifesto one learns with pleased surprise that the *Ami du Peuple* is not like other newspapers, it was the purest public spirit, uncontaminated by any base thoughts of gain, which brought it to birth. The proprietors, who hide their blushes in anonymity, are emptying their pockets for the mere pleasure of doing good by stealth. Their objects, we learn, are to make war on the great trusts, to fight for a lower cost of living, and above all to combat the powerful newspapers which are strangling free speech in France. In spite of the sinister attempts of these other newspapers to put the *Ami du Peuple* out of action, it will fight on to the last. In short, it is all that its name implies.

One would cheer this last stand for democracy a great deal louder, of course, if one did not happen to know that the proprietor of the *Ami du Peuple* is M. Coty, a great industrial capitalist,[2] and also proprietor of the *Figaro* and the *Gaulois*. One would also regard the *Ami du Peuple* with less suspicion if its politics were not anti-radical and anti-socialist, of the goodwill-in-industry, shake-hands-and-make-it-up species. But all that is beside the point at this moment. The important questions, obviously, are these: Does the *Ami du Peuple* pay its way? And if so, how?

The second question is the one that really matters. Since the march of progress is going in the direction of always bigger and nastier trusts, any departure is worth noticing which brings us nearer to that day when the newspaper will be simply a sheet of advertisement and propaganda, with a little well-censored news to sugar the pill. It is quite possible that the *Ami du Peuple* exists on its advertisements, but it is equally possible that it makes only an indirect profit, by putting across the sort of propaganda wanted by M. Coty and his associates. In the above mentioned manifesto, it was declared that the proprietors might rise to an even dizzier height of philanthropy by giving away the *Ami du Peuple* free of charge. This is not so impossible as it may sound. I have seen a daily paper (in India) which was given away free for some time with apparent profit to its backers, a ring of advertisers who found a free newspaper to be a cheap and satisfactory means of blowing their own trumpet. Their paper was rather above the average Indian level, and it supplied, of course, just such news as they themselves approved, and no other. That obscure Indian paper forecast the logical goal of modern journalism; and the *Ami du Peuple* should be noticed, as a new step in the same direction.

But whether its profits are direct or indirect, the *Ami du Peuple* is certainly prospering. Its circulation is already very large, and though it started out as a mere morning paper it has now produced an afternoon and late evening edition. Its proprietors speak with perfect truth when they declare that some of the other papers have done their best to crush this new champion of free speech. These others (they, too, of course, acting from the highest altruistic motives) have made a gallant attempt to [have] it excluded from the newsagents' shops, and have even succeeded as far as the street-corner kiosks are concerned. In some small shops, too, whose owners are socialists, one will even see the sign 'Ici on ne vend pas *l'Ami du Peuple*' exhibited in the windows. But the *Ami du Peuple* is not worrying. It is sold in the streets and the cafés with great vigour, and it is sold by barbers and tobacconists and all kinds of people who have never done any newsagency before. Sometimes it is simply left out on the boulevard in great piles, together with a tin for the two-sou pieces, and with no attendant whatever. One can see that the proprietors are determined, by hook or by crook, to make it the most widely-read paper in Paris.

And supposing they succeed – what then? Obviously the *Ami du Peuple* is going to crowd out of existence one or more of the less prosperous papers – already several are feeling the pinch. In the end, they will presumably either be destroyed, or they will survive by imitating the tactics of the *Ami du Peuple*. Hence every paper of this kind, whatever its intentions, is the enemy of free speech. At present France is the home of free speech, in the Press if not elsewhere. Paris alone has daily papers by the dozen, nationalist, socialist, and communist, clerical and anti-clerical, militarist and anti-militarist, pro-semitic and anti-semitic. It has the *Action Française*, a Royalist paper and still one of the leading dailies, and it has *Humanité*, the reddest daily paper outside Soviet Russia. It has *La Libertà*, which is written in Italian and yet may not even be sold in Italy, much less published there. Papers are printed in Paris in French, English, Italian, Yiddish, German, Russian, Polish, and languages whose very alphabets are unrecognizable by a western European. The kiosks are stuffed with papers, all different. The Press combine, about which French journalists are already grumbling, does not really exist yet in France. But the *Ami du Peuple*, at least, is doing its gallant best to make it a reality.

And supposing that this kind of thing is found to pay in France, why should it not be tried elsewhere? Why should we not have our farthing, or at least our half-penny newspaper in London? While the journalist exists merely as the publicity agent of big business, a large circulation, got by fair means or foul, is a newspaper's one and only aim. Till recently various of our newspapers achieved the desired level of 'net sales' by the simple method of giving away a few thousand pounds now and again in football competition prizes. Now the football competitions have been stopped by law, and doubtless some of the circulations have come down with an ugly bump. Here, then, is a worthy example for our English Press magnates. Let them imitate the *Ami du Peuple* and sell their papers at a farthing. Even if it does no other good whatever, at any rate the poor devils of the public will at last feel that they are getting the correct value for their money.

E. A. BLAIR

1. This was Orwell's first writing to be published professionally in England. 'G. K.' was G. K. Chesterton (1874–1936), essayist, biographer, novelist and poet, remembered particularly for his comic verse, the Father Brown detective stories (1911–35) and *The Man Who Was Thursday* (1908). He was converted to Roman Catholicism in 1922. He founded his weekly in 1925 and edited it until his death, when it was taken over by Hilaire Belloc; see *214, n. 1.* See Crick, 192; S&A, *Unknown Orwell,* I, 215. For the journal, see *G. K.'s Weekly: an Appraisal* by Brocard Sewell [1995?].

2. François Coty (1874–1934) built a famous perfumery business, the name of which long outlasted its founder, and became one of France's wealthiest men. He subsidized *L'Ami du Peuple* and *Gaulois,* both of which pursued nationalist and anti-left policies. The title *L'Ami du Peuple* was, ironically, that of the inflammatory radical newspaper edited by Jean-Paul Marat (1743–93), so influential in the cause of the French Revolution.

[105]

Review of Hunger and Love *by Lionel Britton;* Albert Grope *by F.O. Mann*
The Adelphi, *April 1931*

Hunger and Love is not so much a novel as a kind of monologue upon poverty. Its central character, Arthur Phelps, is a youth of promise, born in the slums. He begins life as an errand boy on twelve shillings a week, then works his way up to be an assistant in a bookshop; when he has partially educated himself and attained an income of twenty-seven shillings a week, the war intervenes and finishes him. He is not a very nice youth, but he is as nice as you could expect him to be on twenty-seven shillings a week; and the peculiar merit of the book is that it does approach life from the twenty-seven-shilling-a-week angle. Most fiction is written by the well-fed, about the well-fed, for the well-fed. This is the ill-fed man's version; the world as it appears to an unskilled workman – a workman, necessarily, with enough brains to grasp what is happening to him. There are plenty of these men about nowadays, and they are thinking night and day of the world they live in. This (it will also do to illustrate Mr. Britton's curious style) is the way in which they think:

The little meannesses they subject you to, the incessant degradation, foulness – collar on jugular, little toe twisted ankylosed [*sic*] through pressure of shoe, get up in morning no bath, wear clothes till rot with body sweat, drain stink sink stink w.c. stink live in sleep in work in, mean little jobs consume life activity: can you go through life and be unaware of this great foul disease of humanity?

Such thoughts recur and recur – a sort of mental eczema, a perpetual restless irritation over mean things. To the well-fed it seems cowardly to complain of tight boots, because the well-fed live in a different world – a world where, if your boots are tight, you can change them; their minds are not warped by petty discomfort. But below a certain income the petty crowds the large out of existence; one's preoccupation is not with art or religion, but with bad food, hard beds, drudgery and the sack. 'Culture and love and beauty are so *damned* silly when you're out of work.' Serenity is impossible to a poor man in a cold country, and even his active thoughts will go in more or less sterile complaint.

This is a thing that wants remembering, and the virtue of *Hunger and Love* is that it rubs in the irritating, time-wasting nature of poverty; the nasty, squalid little things which by their cumulative effect make life on less than two pounds a week radically different from life on even three or four pounds. Arthur Phelps can hardly live an hour without being reminded that the world means to starve him. He wants comfort and cleanliness; he gets a stuffy slum bedroom, and fat men coughing into his plate in cheap eating houses. He wants leisure; he gets sixty or seventy hours a week at dull, unnecessary work. He wants knowledge; he gets a board school 'education',[1] and thereafter peeps into textbooks when the boss is not looking. He wants love, but love costs money; he gets moments with half-witted shop-girls, or prostitutes. However much he struggles he flounders back into his poverty, like a sheep floundering into mud. As a social document, with its insistence on mean, recurrent troubles, this book is entirely sound.

Having said this, however, one must add that as a novel *Hunger and Love* is almost worthless. Obviously the thing to do with such important material – the world of an intelligent poor man – was to make it into a memorable story. Instead of this we have a book that is one long digression, telling, certainly, the truth about life, but making no attempt to be readable. The tricks of style, and particularly the repetitions, become very tiresome after a few chapters. (It must be several hundred times that Mr. Britton reminds us that the earth moves round the sun at 18.5 miles a second – this apropos of man's tininess amid the universe; it is worth knowing, but one does not want to read it every two pages.) No doubt Mr. Britton would say that his object was to tell the truth, not to compose an elegant novel; but even so, truth is not served by leaving out commas. A writer with any sense of selection would have cut this book down from 700 pages to 200, and lost nothing. If Mr. Britton had done this, while keeping a firm hold on the realities of his subject, *Hunger and Love* might have been a first-rate book instead of merely an unusual one. Still, it *is* unusual.

It is a far cry from *Hunger and Love* to *Albert Grope*. *Albert Grope* is also the story of a man born and bred in the slums, but these are picturesque slums, not the smelly variety. *Hunger and Love* is compounded of discontent and astronomy, with perhaps a touch of James Joyce; *Albert Grope* is Dickens – rather diluted. The hero begins life as a shop-boy, sets up as a bookseller, then as an advertising agent, and ends moderately rich and happily married. He is very like a faded portrait of David Copperfield, which is perhaps what the author intended. The pleasant and simple nature of the hero, and the eccentric characters whom he meets, are described with a competence worthy of something more original.

ERIC BLAIR

1. A basic education for everyone was established in 1870 by the Elementary Education Act, organized through local School Boards. Fees could be charged but these were almost completely abolished in 1891.

[110]

To Dennis Collings
Thursday night [27 August 1931]   *Handwritten*

[A lodging-house in Southwark Bridge Road]

Dear Dennis,[1]

Please excuse pencil & bad writing, as I am writing this in a lodging house. It is a 7d[2] kip – & looks it, I may say – in Southwark, & I believe the only one at the price in London. We go down for the hopping tomorrow morning: 2d tram to Bromley, & hike the rest.

I have had an interesting 2 days camping in Trafalgar Square. It has, at this time of year, a floating population of 200 or so. You can make yourself fairly comfortable against the north wall & can get tea all day long, as a coffee shop nearby will give you boiling water free or 1d for a billyful (billies are called 'drums' by the way). I was there all yesterday & was to have spent the night in St Martin's Church, but as you had to queue up for an hour to get a decent place we decided to stay in the square. You take my tip & *never* sleep in Trafalgar Square. We were tolerably comfortable till midnight, except that once in 5 or 10 minutes the police came round waking those who were asleep & making anyone who was sitting on the ground stand up. Every ten minutes it would be, 'Look out, mates, 'ere comes the flattie (policemen). Take up thy bed & walk' etc.[3] And then the police: 'Now then, get off of that. If you want to sit, sit on the benches' etc. There were only benches for 40 out of the 200, but we got *some* rest, as we kipped down again the moment the policeman had passed. After midnight the cold was glacial. Perhaps a dozen people managed to sleep, the rest walked the streets, with an occasional sit-down for a rest – this for 4 consecutive hours. At 4 am someone managed to get hold of a big pile of newspaper posters & brought them along to use as blankets. ''Ere y'are, mate tuck in the fucking eiderdown. Don't we look like fucking parsons in these 'ere surplices? 'Ere, I got "Dramatic appeal from the Premier" round *my* neck. That ought to warm yer up, oughtn't it?' etc. We made ourselves into large newspaper parcels, & were comparatively warm, tho' still not warm enough to sleep, apart from the police. I doubt whether more than 10 or 20 of the 200 people slept a wink during the night. At 5 we all went to Stewart's coffee shop in St Martin's Lane, where it is understood that you can sit from 5 am to 9 am for a 2d cup of tea – or even for less, for often 2 or 3 fellows who had only 2d between them clubbed together & shared a cup of tea. You were allowed to sleep with your head on the table till 7 am, after which the proprietor woke you up. This is the absolutely regular routine of Trafalgar Square 'sleepers'. Two of the fellows I was with had had 7 consecutive weeks of it & some people do it all the year round. They make up the sleepless night by naps during the morning. The rules about what you may & may not do in Trafalgar Square are curious, & should interest you as an anthropologist. Till noon you can do what you like (even shave in the fountains) except that the police wake you if they see you asleep. From noon to 9 pm you can sit on the benches or the pedestals of the statues, but are moved on if you sit on the ground. After 9 pm you are also moved on from the pedestals of the statues. Between 9 pm & midnight the police wake those who are asleep every 5 minutes, after midnight every half hour. For all this no ostensible reason.

About 8 pm last night a woman came up crying bitterly. It appeared that she was a tart & someone had poked her & then cleared off without paying the fee, which was 6d. It appeared that of the dozen or so women among the 200 in the square, half were prostitutes; but they were the prostitutes of the unemployed, & usually earn so little that they have to spend the night in the Square. 6d. is the usual fee, but in the small hours when it was bitter cold they were doing it for a cigarette. The prostitutes live on terms of perfect amity with the other down & out women. In Stewart's coffee shop this morning, however, an old girl who had slept in Covent Garden was denouncing 2 tarts, who had earned enough to get a few hours in bed & then a good breakfast. Each time they ordered another cup of tea she was yelling, 'There's another fuck! That's for that fucking negro you let on for a tanner' etc.

Today went much as yesterday & tonight, as we have a long day before us, I decided on getting a bed. My mates have gone to St Martin's Church, preferring to spend their money on a meat breakfast. This place is an apalling° squalid cellar, as hot as hell & the air a sort of vapour of piss, sweat & cheese. A pale youth, some kind of labourer but looking consumptive, keeps declaiming poetry in front of the fire. Evidently he is genuinely fond of it. You should hear him declaiming:

> A voice so thrilling ne'er was 'eard
> In Ipril from the cuckoo bird,
> Briking the silence of the seas
> Beyond the furthest 'Ebrides etc.[4]

Also speaks of himself as 'sicklied o'er with the pile cast of care'.[5] I should love to hear him recite 'O holy hope & high humility'. I have met other curious types of whom I will write to you when I have time. Also about the prevalence of homosexuality in London, & stowaways. The songs I have heard this time are 'Alleluia, I'm a bum', which I believe is American. Also one about

> Tap, tap, tapetty-tap,
> I'm a perfect devil for that,
> Tapping 'em 'ere, tapping 'em there,
> I've been tapping 'em everywhere.

Tap = beg. Perhaps an old music hall song?

I hope this letter has not been too inconsequent & illegible. I will write when I have further news & a more comfortable place to write in. If you don't hear within a fortnight it probably will mean I've been pinched for begging, as the mates I'm going with are hardened 'tappers' & not above petty theft.

Yours

Eric A Blair

1. Dennis Collings (1905–) was a friend of Orwell's from the time the Blair family moved to Southwold in 1921; Collings's father became the Blair family doctor. Collings grew sisal in Mozambique, 1924–7; read anthropology at Cambridge, 1928–31; and was appointed assistant curator of the Raffles Museum, Singapore, when he joined the Colonial Service in 1934. That year he married Eleanor Jaques (d. 1962), whom Orwell also knew well. He contributed to *Orwell Remembered* (76–83), and see Shelden, 156, 192. A later letter to Dennis Collings, dated 4 September 1931, sent while Orwell was hop-picking, is printed in X/227–8. Orwell uses his experience in Trafalgar Square in ch. 3 of *A Clergyman's Daughter* (1935). Its heroine, Dorothy Hare, spends several nights there when poverty-stricken.
2. 7d ≐ seven pence in pre-metric currency, a fraction less than 3p, perhaps £1.00 in contemporary values. The letter 'd' stands for the Latin, *denarius* (plural *denarii*).

3. Jesus told the man who had been waiting by the Pool of Bethesda for thirty-eight years for a cure, 'Rise, take up thy bed, and walk' (John 5:8).

4. A rough variant of the second four lines of stanza 2 of Wordsworth's poem 'The Solitary Reaper' (with 'April' for 'spring-time' and 'Beyond' for 'Among').

5. *Hamlet*, II.ii: 'pale cast of thought'.

[*111, 113*]

Hop-Picking Diary

25.8.31: On the night of the 25th I started off from Chelsea with about 14/– in hand, and went to Lew Levy's kip in Westminster Bridge Road. It is much the same as it was three years ago, except that nearly all the beds are now a shilling instead of ninepence. This is owing to interference by the L.C.C.[1] who have enacted (in the interests of hygiene, as usual) that beds in lodging houses must be further apart. There is a whole string of laws of this type relating to lodging houses,* but there is not and never will be a law to say that the beds must be reasonably comfortable. The net result of this law is that one's bed is now three feet from the next instead of two feet, and threepence dearer.

26.8.31: The next day I went to Trafalgar Square and camped by the north wall, which is one of the recognized rendezvous of down and out people in London. At this time of year the square has a floating population of 100 or 200 people (about ten per cent of them women), some of whom actually look on it as their home. They get their food by regular begging rounds (Covent Garden at 4 am. for damaged fruit, various convents during the morning, restaurants and dustbins late at night etc.) and they manage to 'tap' likely-looking passers by for enough to keep them in tea. Tea is going on the square at all hours, one person supplying a 'drum',[2] another sugar and so on. The milk is condensed milk at 2½d[3] a tin. You jab two holes in the tin with a knife, apply your mouth to one of them and blow, whereupon a sticky greyish stream dribbles from the other. The holes are then plugged with chewed paper, and the tin is kept for days, becoming

---

* For instance, Dick's café in Billingsgate. Dick's was one of the few places where you could get a cup of tea for 1d, and there were fires there so that anyone who had a penny could warm himself for hours in the early mornings. Only this last week the L.C.C. closed it on the ground that it was unhygienic [Orwell's note].

coated with dust and filth. Hot water is cadged at coffee shops, or at night boiled over watchmen's fires, but this has to be done on the sly, as the police won't allow it. Some of the people I met on the square had been there without a break for six weeks, and did not seem much the worse, except that they are all fantastically dirty. As always among the destitute, a large proportion of them are Irishmen. From time to time these men go home on visits, and it appears that they never think of paying their passage, but always stow away on small cargo boats, the crews conniving.

I had meant to sleep in St Martin's Church, but from what the others said it appeared that when you go in you are asked searching questions by some woman known as the Madonna, so I decided to stay the night in the square. It was not so bad as I expected, but between the cold and the police it was impossible to get a wink of sleep, and no one except a few hardened old tramps even tried to do so. There are seats enough for about fifty people, and the rest have to sit on the ground, which of course is forbidden by law. Every few minutes there would be a shout of 'Look out, boys, here comes the flattie!' and a policeman would come round and shake those who were asleep, and make the people on the ground get up. We used to kip down again the instant he had passed, and this went on like a kind of game from eight at night till three or four in the morning. After midnight it was so cold that I had to go for long walks to keep warm. The streets are somehow rather horrible at that hour; all silent and deserted, and yet lighted almost as bright as day with those garish lamps, which give everything a deathly air, as though London were the corpse of a town. About three o'clock another man and I went down to the patch of grass behind the Guards' parade ground, and saw prostitutes and men lying in couples there in the bitter cold mist and dew. There are always a number of prostitutes in the square; they are the unsuccessful ones, who can't earn enough for their night's kip. Overnight one of these women had been lying on the ground crying bitterly, because a man had gone off without paying her fee, which was sixpence. Towards morning they do not even get six-pence, but only a cup of tea or a cigarette. About four somebody got hold of a number of newspaper posters, and we sat down six or eight on a bench and packed ourselves in enormous paper parcels, which kept us fairly warm till Stewart's café in St Martin's Lane opened. At Stewart's you can sit from five till nine for a cup of tea (or sometimes three or four people even share a cup between them) and you are allowed to sleep with your head on the table till seven; after that the proprietor wakes you. One meets a very mixed crowd there – tramps, Covent Garden porters, early business people, prostitutes – and there are constant quarrels and fights. On this occasion an old, very ugly woman, wife of a porter, was violently abusing two prostitutes, because they could afford a better breakfast than she could. As each dish was brought to them she would point at it and shout accusingly, 'There goes the price of another fuck! *We* don't get kippers for breakfast, do we, girls? 'Ow do you think she paid for them doughnuts? That's that there negro that 'as 'er for a tanner' etc. etc., but the prostitutes did not mind much.

27.8.31: At about eight in the morning we all had a shave in the Trafalgar Square fountains, and I spent most of the day reading *Eugénie Grandet*, which was the only book I had brought with me. The sight of a French book produced the usual remarks – 'Ah, French? That'll be something pretty warm, eh?' etc. Evidently most English people have no idea that there are French books which are not pornographic. Down and out people seem to read exclusively books of the Buffalo Bill type. Every tramp carries one of these, and they have a kind of circulating library, all swapping books when they get to the spike.[4]

That night, as we were starting for Kent the next morning, I decided to sleep in bed and went to a lodging house in the Southwark Bridge Road. This is a sevenpenny kip, one of the few in London, and looks it. The beds are five feet long, with no pillows (you use your coat rolled up), and infested by fleas, besides a few bugs. The kitchen is a small, stinking cellar where the deputy sits with a table of flyblown jam tarts etc. for sale a few feet from the door of the lavatory. The rats are so bad that several cats have to be kept exclusively to deal with them. The lodgers were dock workers, I think, and they did not seem a bad crowd. There was a youth among them, pale and consumptive looking but evidently a labourer, who was devoted to poetry. He repeated

> A voice so thrilling ne'er was 'eard
> In Ipril from the cuckoo bird,
> Briking the silence of the seas
> Beyond the furthest 'Ebrides

with genuine feeling. The others did not laugh at him much.

28.8.31: The next day in the afternoon four of us started out for the hop-fields. The most interesting of the men with me was a youth named Ginger, who is still my mate when I write this. He is a strong, athletic youth of twenty six, almost illiterate and quite brainless, but daring enough for anything. Except when in prison, he has probably broken the law every day for the last five years. As a boy he did three years in Borstal, came out, married at eighteen on the strength of a successful burglary, and shortly afterwards enlisted in the artillery. His wife died, and a little while afterwards he had an accident to his left eye and was invalided out of the service. They offered him a pension or a lump sum, and of course he chose the lump sum and blued it in about a week. After that he took to burglary again, and has been in prison six times, but never for a long sentence, as they have only caught him for small jobs; he has done one or two jobs which brought him over £500. He has always been perfectly honest towards me, as his partner, but in a general way he will steal anything that is not tied down. I doubt his ever being a successful burglar, though, for he is too stupid to be able to foresee risks. It is all a great pity, for he could earn a decent living if he chose. He has a gift for street selling, and has had a lot of jobs at selling on commission, but when he has had a good day he bolts instantly with the takings. He is a marvellous hand at picking up bargains and can always, for instance, persuade the butcher to give him a pound of eatable meat for twopence, yet at the same time he is an absolute fool about money, and never saves a halfpenny. He is given to singing songs of the Little Grey Home in the West type, and he speaks of his dead wife and mother in terms of the most viscid sentimentality. I should think he is a fairly typical petty criminal.

Of the other two, one was a boy of twenty named Young Ginger, who seemed rather a likely lad, but he was an orphan and had had no kind of upbringing, and lived the last year chiefly on Trafalgar Square. The other was a little Liverpool Jew of eighteen, a thorough guttersnipe. I do not know when I have seen anyone who disgusted me so much as this boy. He was as greedy as a pig about food, perpetually scrounging round dust-bins, and he had a face that recalled some low-down carrion-eating beast. His manner of talking about women, and the expression of his face when he did so, were so loathsomely obscene as to make me feel almost sick. We could never persuade him to wash more of himself than his nose and a small circle round it, and he mentioned quite casually that he had several different kinds of louse on him. He too was an orphan, and had been 'on the toby' almost from infancy.

I had now about 6/−, and before starting we bought a so-called blanket for 1/6d[5] and cadged several tins for 'drums'. The only reliable tin for a drum is a two-pound snuff tin, which is not very easy to come by. We had also a supply of bread and margarine and tea, and a number of knives and forks etc., all stolen at different times from Woolworth's. We took the twopenny tram as far as Bromley, and there 'drummed up' on a rubbish dump, waiting for two others who were to have joined us, but who never turned up. It was dark when we finally stopped waiting for them, so we had no chance to look for a good camping place, and had to spend the night in long wet grass at the edge of a recreation ground. The cold was bitter. We had only two thin blankets between the four of us, and it was not safe to light a fire, as there were houses all round; we were also lying on a slope, so that one rolled into the ditch from time to time. It was rather humiliating to see the others, all younger than I, sleeping quite soundly in these conditions, whereas I did not close my eyes all night. To avoid being caught we had to be on the road before dawn, and it was several hours before we managed to get hot water and have our breakfast.

29.8.31: When we had gone a mile or two we came to an orchard, and the others at once went in and began stealing apples. I had not been prepared for this when we started out, but I saw that I must either do as the others did or leave them, so I shared the apples; I did not however take any part in the thefts for the first day, except to keep guard. We were going more or less in the direction of Sevenoaks, and by dinner time we had stolen about a dozen apples and plums and fifteen pounds of potatoes. The others also went in and tapped whenever we passed a baker's or a teashop, and we got quite a quantity of broken bread and meat. When we stopped to light a fire for dinner we fell in with two Scotch tramps who had been stealing apples from an orchard nearby, and stayed talking with them for a long time. The others all talked about sexual subjects, in a revolting manner. Tramps are disgusting when on this subject, because their poverty cuts them off entirely from women, and their minds consequently fester with obscenity. Merely lecherous people are all right, but people who would like to be lecherous, but don't get the chance, are horribly degraded by it. They remind me of the dogs that hang enviously round while two other dogs are copulating. During the conversation Young Ginger related how he and some others on Trafalgar Square had discovered one of their number to be a 'Poof', or Nancy Boy. Whereupon they had instantly fallen upon him, robbed him of 12/6d, which was all he had, and spent it on themselves. Evidently they thought it quite fair to rob him, as he was a Nancy Boy.

We had been making very poor progress, chiefly because Young Ginger and the Jew were not used to walking and wanted to stop and search for scraps of food all the time. On one occasion the Jew even picked up some chipped potatoes that had been trodden on, and ate them. As it was getting on in the afternoon we decided to make not for Sevenoaks but for Ide Hill spike, which the Scotchmen had told us was better than it is usually represented. We halted about a mile from the spike for tea, and I remember that a gentleman in a car nearby helped us in the kindest manner to find wood for our fire, and gave us a cigarette each. Then we went on to the spike, and on the way picked a bunch of honeysuckle to give to the Tramp Major. We thought this might put him in a good temper and induce him to let us out next morning, for it is not usual to let tramps out of the spike on Sundays. When we got there however the Tramp Major said that he would have to keep us in till Tuesday morning. It appeared that the Workhouse Master was very keen on making every casual do a day's work, and at the same time would not hear of their working on Sunday; so we should have to be idle all Sunday and work on Monday. Young Ginger and the Jew elected to stay till Tuesday, but Ginger and I went and kipped on the edge of a park near the church. It was beastly cold, but a little better than the night before, for we had plenty of wood and could make a fire. For our supper, Ginger tapped the local butcher, who gave us the best part of two pounds of sausages. Butchers are always very generous on Saturday nights.

30.8.31: Next morning the clergyman coming to early service caught us and turned us out, though not very disagreeably. We went on through Sevenoaks to Seal, and a man we met advised us to try for a job at Mitchell's farm, about three miles further on. We went there, but the farmer told us that he could not give us a job, as he had nowhere where

we could live, and the Government inspectors had been snouting round
to see that all hop-pickers had 'proper accommodation'. (These inspectors,* by the way, managed to prevent some hundreds of unemployed
from getting jobs in the hop-fields this year. Not having 'proper accommodation' to offer to pickers, the farmers could only employ local people,
who lived in their own houses.) We stole about a pound of raspberries
from one of Mitchell's fields, and then went and applied to another farmer
called Kronk, who gave us the same answer; we had five or ten pounds
of potatoes from his fields, however. We were starting off in the direction
of Maidstone when we fell in with an old Irishwoman, who had been
given a job by Mitchell on the understanding that she had a lodging in
Seal, which she had not. (Actually she was sleeping in a toolshed in
somebody's garden. She used to slip in after dark and out before daylight.)
We got some hot water from a cottage and the Irishwoman had tea with
us, and gave us a lot of food that she had begged and did not want; we
were glad of this, for we had now only 2½d left, and none too much
food. It had now come on to rain, so we went to a farmhouse beside the
church and asked leave to shelter in one of their cowsheds. The farmer
and family were just starting out for evening service, and they said in a
scandalised manner that of course they could not give us shelter. We
sheltered instead in the lych-gate of the church, hoping that by looking
draggled and tired we might get a few coppers from the congregation as
they went in. We did not get anything, but after the service Ginger
managed to tap a fairly good pair of flannel trousers from the clergyman.
It was very uncomfortable in the lych-gate, and we were wet through and
out of tobacco, and Ginger and I had walked twelve miles; yet I remember
that we were quite happy and laughing all the time. The Irishwoman (she
was sixty, and had been on the road all her life, evidently) was an
extraordinarily cheerful old girl, and full of stories. Talking of places to
'skipper' in, she told us that one cold night she had crept into a pigsty
and snuggled up to an old sow, for warmth.

When night came on it was still raining, so we decided to find an
empty house to sleep in, but we went first to buy half a pound of sugar
and two candles at the grocer's. While I was buying them Ginger stole

* Appointed by the Labour Government [Orwell's note].

three apples off the counter, and the Irishwoman a packet of cigarettes. They had plotted this beforehand, deliberately not telling me, so as to use my innocent appearance as a shield. After a good deal of searching we found an unfinished house and slipped in by a window the builders had left open. The bare floor was beastly hard, but it was warmer than outside, and I managed to get two or three hours' sleep. We got out before dawn, and by appointment met the Irishwoman in a wood nearby. It was raining, but Ginger could get a fire going in almost any circumstances, and we managed to make tea and roast some potatoes.

1.9.31: When it was light the Irishwoman went off to work, and Ginger and I went down to Chambers' farm, a mile or two away, to ask for work. When we got to the farm they had just been hanging a cat, a thing I never heard of anyone doing before. The bailiff said that he thought he could give us a job, and told us to wait; we waited from eight in the morning till one, when the bailiff said that he had no work for us after all. We made off, stealing a large quantity of apples and damsons, and started along the Maidstone road. At about three we halted to have our dinner and make some jam out of the raspberries we had stolen the day before. Near here, I remember, they refused at two houses to give me cold water, because 'the mistress doesn't allow us to give anything to tramps'. Ginger saw a gentleman in a car picnicking nearby, and went up to tap him for matches, for he said, that it always pays to tap from picnickers, who usually have some food left over when they are going home. Sure enough the gentleman presently came across with some butter he had not used, and began talking to us. His manner was so friendly that I forgot to put on my cockney accent, and he looked closely at me, and said how painful it must be for a man of my stamp etc. Then he said, 'I say, you won't be offended, will you? Do you mind taking this?' 'This' was a shilling, with which we bought some tobacco and had our first smoke that day. This was the only time in the whole journey when we managed to tap money.

We went on in the direction of Maidstone, but when we had gone a few miles it began to pour with rain, and my left boot was pinching me badly. I had not had my boots off for three days and had only had about eight hours sleep in the last five nights, and I did not feel equal to another night in the open. We decided to make for West Malling spike, which was about eight miles distant, and if possible to get a lift part of the way.

I think we hailed forty lorries before we got a lift. The lorry drivers will not give lifts nowadays, because they are not insured for third party risks and they get the sack if they have an accident. Finally we did get a lift, and were set down about two miles from the spike, getting there at eight in the evening. Outside the gates we met an old deaf tramp who was going to skipper in the pouring rain, as he had been in the spike the night before, and they would confine him for a week if he came again. He told us that Blest's farm nearby would probably give us a job, and that they would let us out of the spike early in the morning if we told them we had already got a job. Otherwise we should be confined all day, unless we went out 'over the wall' – i.e. bolted when the Tramp Major was not looking. Tramps often do this, but you have to cache your possessions outside, which we could not in the heavy rain. We went in, and I found that (if West Malling is typical) spikes have improved a lot since I was last in.* The bathroom was clean and decent, and we were actualy° given a clean towel each. The food was the same old bread and marg, though, and the Tramp Major got angry when we asked in good faith whether the stuff they gave us to drink was tea or cocoa.† We had beds with straw palliasses and plenty of blankets, and both slept like logs.

In the morning they told us we must work till eleven, and set us to scrubbing out one of the dormitories. As usual, the work was a mere formality. (I have never done a stroke of real work in the spike, and I have never met anybody who has.) The dormitory was a room of fifty beds, close together, with that warm, faecal stink that you never seem to get away from in the workhouse. There was an imbecile pauper there, a great lump of about sixteen stone, with a tiny, snouty face and a sidelong grin. He was at work very slowly emptying chamberpots. These workhouses seem all alike, and there is something intensely disgusting in the atmosphere of them. The thought of all those grey-faced, ageing men living a very quiet, withdrawn life in a smell of W.Cs, and practising homosexuality, makes me feel sick. But it is not easy to convey what I mean, because it is all bound up with the smell of the workhouse.

At eleven they let us out with the usual hunk of bread and cheese, and

---

* No: a bit worse if anything [Orwell's note].
† To this day I don't know which it was [Orwell's note].

we went on to Blest's farm, about three miles away; but we did not get there till one, because we stopped on the way and got a big haul of damsons. When we arrived at the farm the foreman told us that he wanted pickers and sent us up to the field at once. We had now only about 3d left, and that evening I wrote home asking them to send me 10/–; it came two days later, and in the mean time we should have had practically nothing to eat if the other pickers had not fed us. For nearly three weeks after this we were at work hop-picking, and I had better describe the different aspects of this individually.

2.9.31 to 19.9.31: Hops are trained up poles or over wires about 10 feet high, and grown in rows a yard or two apart. All the pickers have to do is to tear them down and strip the hops into a bin, keeping them as clean as possible of leaves. In practice, of course, it is impossible to keep all the leaves out, and the experienced pickers swell the bulk of their hops by putting in just as many leaves as the farmer will stand for. One soon gets the knack of the work, and the only hardships are the standing (we were generally on our feet ten hours a day), the plagues of plant lice, and the damage to one's hands. One's hands get stained as black as a negro's with the hop-juice, which only mud will remove,* and after a day or two they crack and are cut to bits by the stems of the vines, which are spiny. In the mornings, before the cuts had reopened, my hands used to give me perfect agony, and even at the time of typing this (October 10th) they show the marks. Most of the people who go down hopping have done it every year since they were children, and they pick like lightning and know all the tricks, such as shaking the hops up to make them lie loose in the bin etc. The most successful pickers are families, who have two or three adults to strip the vines, and a couple of children to pick up the fallen hops and clear the odd strands. The laws about child labour are disregarded utterly, and some of the people drive their children pretty hard. The woman in the next bin to us, a regular old-fashioned East Ender, kept her grand-children at it like slaves. – 'Go on, Rose, you lazy little cat, pick them 'ops up. I'll warm your arse if I get up to you' etc. until the children, aged from 6 to 10, used to drop down and fall asleep on the ground. But they liked the work, and I don't suppose it did them more harm than school.

---

* Or hop-juice, funnily enough [Orwell's note].

As to what one can earn, the system of payment is this. Two or three times a day the hops are measured, and you are due a certain sum (in our case twopence) for each bushel you have picked. A good vine yields about half a bushel of hops, and a good picker can strip a vine in about 10 minutes, so that theoretically one *might* earn about 30/– by a sixty hour week. But in practice this is quite impossible. To begin with, the hops vary enormously. On some vines they are as large as small pears, and on others hardly bigger than peas; the bad vines take rather longer to strip than the good ones – they are generally more tangled – and sometimes it needs five or six of them to make a bushel. Then there are all kinds of delays, and the pickers get no compensation for lost time. Sometimes it rains (if it rains hard the hops get too slippery to pick), and one is always kept waiting when changing from field to field, so that an hour or two is wasted every day. And above all there is the question of measurement. Hops are soft things like sponges, and it is quite easy for the measurer to crush a bushel of them into a quart if he chooses. Some days he merely scoops the hops out, but on other days he has orders from the farmer to 'take them heavy', and then he crams them tight into the basket, so that instead of getting 20 bushels for a full bin one gets only 12 or 14 – i.e. a shilling or so less. There was a song about this, which the old East End woman and her grandchildren were always singing:

> Our lousy hops!
> Our lousy hops!
> When the measurer he comes round,
> Pick 'em up, pick 'em up off the ground!
> When he comes to measure
> He never knows where to stop;
> Ay, ay, get in the bin
> And take the fucking lot!

From the bin the hops are put into 10-bushel pokes which are supposed to weigh a hundredweight and are normally carried by one man. It used to take two men to hoist a full poke when the measurer had been taking them heavy.

With all these difficulties one can't earn 30/– a week or anything near it. It is a curious fact, though, that very few of the pickers were aware how little they really earned, because the piece-work system disguises the low rate of payment. The best pickers in our gang were a family of gypsies, five adults and a child, all of whom, of course, had picked hops every year since they could walk. In a little under three weeks these people earned exactly £10 between them – i.e., leaving out the child, about 14/– a week each. Ginger and I earned about 9/– a week each, and I doubt if any individual picker made over 15/– a week. A family working together can make their keep and their fare back to London at these rates, but a single picker can hardly do even that. On some of the farms nearby the tally, instead of being 6 bushels to the shilling, was 8 or 9, at which one would have a hard job to earn 10/– a week.

When one starts work the farm gives one a printed copy of rules, which are designed to reduce a picker more or less to a slave. According to these rules the farmer can sack a picker without notice and on any pretext whatever, and pay him off at 8 bushels a shilling instead of six – i.e. confiscate a quarter of his earnings. If a picker leaves his job before the picking is finished, his earnings are docked the same amount. You cannot draw what you have earned and then clear off, because the farm will never pay you more than two thirds of your earnings in advance, and so are in your debt till the last day. The binmen (i.e. foremen of gangs) get wages instead of being paid on the piecework system, and these wages cease if there is a strike, so naturally they will raise Heaven and earth to prevent one. Altogether the farmers have the hop-pickers in a cleft stick, and always will have until there is a pickers' union. It is not much use to try and form a union, though, for about half the pickers are women and gypsies, and are too stupid to see the advantages of it.

As to our living accommodation, the best quarters on the farm, ironically enough, were disused stables. Most of us slept in round tin huts about 10 feet across with no glass in the windows, and all kinds of holes to let in the wind and rain. The furniture of these huts consisted of a heap of straw and hop-vines, and nothing else. There were four of us in our hut, but in some of them there were seven or eight – rather an advantage, really, for it kept the hut warm. Straw is rotten stuff to sleep in (it is much more draughty than hay) and Ginger and I had only a blanket each, so we suffered agonies of cold for the first week; after that we stole enough pokes to keep us warm. The farm gave us free firewood, though not as much as we needed. The water tap was 200 yards away, and the latrine the same distance, but it was so filthy that one would have walked a mile sooner than use it. There was a stream where one could do some laundering, but getting a bath in the village would have been about as easy as buying a tame whale.

The hop-pickers seemed to be of three types: East Enders, mostly costermongers, gypsies, and itinerant agricultural labourers with a sprinkling of tramps. The fact that Ginger and I were tramps got us a great deal of sympathy, especially among the fairly well-to-do people. There was one couple, a coster and his wife, who were like a father and mother to us. They were the kind of people who are generally drunk on Saturday nights and who tack a 'fucking' on to every noun, yet I have never seen anything that exceeded their kindness and delicacy. They gave us food over and over again. A child would come to the hut with a saucepan: 'Eric, mother was going to throw this stew away, but she said it was a pity to waste it. Would you like it?' Of course they were not really going to have thrown it away, but said this to avoid the suggestion of charity. One day they gave us a whole pig's head, ready cooked. These people had been on the road several years themselves, and it made them sympathetic – 'Ah, I know what it's like. Skippering in the fucking wet grass, and then got to tap the milkman in the morning before you can get a cup of tea. Two of my boys were born on the road' etc. Another man who was very decent to us was an employee in a paper factory. Before this he had been vermin-man to —, and he told me that the dirt and vermin in—'s kitchens, even [their headquarters], passed belief. When he worked at—'s branch in T— Street,[6] the rats were so numerous that it was not safe to go into the kitchens at night unarmed; you had to carry a revolver. After I had mixed with these people for a few days it was too much fag to go on putting on my cockney accent, and they noticed that I talked 'different'. As usual, this made them still more friendly, for these people seem to think that it is especially dreadful to 'come down in the world'.

Out of about 200 pickers at Blest's farm, 50 or 60 were gypsies. They are curiously like oriental peasants – the same heavy faces, at once dull and sly, and the same sharpness in their own line and startling ignorance outside it. Most of them could not read even a word, and none of their children seemed ever to have gone to school. One gypsy, aged about 40, used to ask me such questions as, 'How far is Paris from France?' 'How many days' journey by caravan to Paris?' etc. A youth, aged twenty, used to ask this riddle half a dozen times a day. – 'I'll tell you something you can't do?' – 'What?' – 'Tickle a gnat's arse with a telegraph pole.' (At this, never-failing yells of laughter.) The gypsies seem to be quite rich, owning caravans, horses etc. yet they go on all the year round working as itinerant labourers and saving money. They used to say that our way of life (living in houses etc.) seemed disgusting to them, and to explain how clever they had been in dodging the army during the war. Talking to them, you had the feeling of talking to people from another century. I often heard a gypsy say, 'If I knew where so and so was, I'd ride my horse till it hadn't a shoe left to catch him' – not a 20th century metaphor at all. One day some gypsies were talking about a noted horse-thief called George Bigland, and one man, defending him, said: 'I don't think George is as bad as you make out. I've known him to steal Gorgias' (Gentiles') horses, but he wouldn't go so far as to steal from one of us.'

The gypsies call us Gorgias and themselves Romanies, but they are nicknamed Didecais (not certain of spelling). They all knew Romany, and occasionally used a word or two when they didn't want to be understood. A curious thing I noticed about the gypsies – I don't know whether it is the same everywhere – was that you would often see a whole family who were totally unlike one another. It almost seems to countenance the stories about gypsies stealing children; more likely, though, it is because it's a wise child etc.

One of the men in our hut was the old deaf tramp we had met outside West Malling spike – Deafie, he was always called. He was rather a Mr F.'s aunt[7] in conversation, and he looked just like a drawing by George Belcher,[8] but he was an intelligent, decently educated man, and no doubt would not have been on the road if he could hear. He was not strong enough for heavy work, and he had done nothing for years past except odd jobs like hopping. He calculated that he had been in over 400 different spikes. The other man, named Barrett, and a man in our gang named George, were good specimens of the itinerant agricultural labourer. For years past they had worked on a regular round: Lambing in early spring, then pea-picking, strawberries, various other fruits, hops, 'spud-grabbing', turnips and sugar beet. They were seldom out of work for more than a week or two, yet even this was enough to swallow up anything they could earn. They were both penniless when they arrived at Blest's farm, and I saw Barrett work certainly one day without a bite to eat. The proceeds of all their work were the clothes they stood up in, straw to sleep on all the year round, meals of bread and cheese and bacon, and I suppose one or two good drunks a year. George was a dismal devil, and took a sort of worm-like pride in being underfed and overworked, and always tobying from job to job. His line was, 'It doesn't do for people like us to have fine ideas.' (He could not read or write, and seemed to think even literacy a kind of extravagance.) I know this philosophy well, having often met it among the dishwashers in Paris. Barrett, who was 63, used to complain a lot about the badness of food nowadays, compared with what you could get when he was a boy. – 'In them days we didn't live on this fucking bread and marg, we 'ad good solid tommy. Bullock's 'eart. Bacon dumpling. Black pudden. Pig's 'ead.' The glutinous, reminiscent tone in which he said 'pig's 'ead' suggested decades of underfeeding.

Besides all these regular pickers there were what are called 'homedwellers'; i.e. local people who pick at odd times, chiefly for the fun of it. They are mostly farmers' wives and the like, and as a rule they and the regular pickers loathe one another. One of them, however, was a very decent woman, who gave Ginger a pair of shoes and me an excellent coat and waistcoat and two shirts. Most of the local people seemed to look on us as dirt, and the shopkeepers were very insolent, though between us we must have spent several hundred pounds in the village.

One day at hop-picking was very much like another. At about a quarter to six in the morning we crawled out of the straw, put on our coats and boots (we slept in everything else) and went out to get a fire going – rather a job this September, when it rained all the time. By half past six we had made tea and fried some bread for breakfast, and then we started off for work, with bacon sandwiches and a drum of cold tea for our dinner. If it didn't rain we were working pretty steadily till about one, and then we would start a fire between the vines, heat up our tea and knock off for half an hour. After that we were at it again till half past five, and by the time we had got home, cleaned the hop juice off our hands and had tea, it was already dark and we were dropping with sleep. A good many nights, though, we used to go out and steal apples. There was a big orchard nearby, and three or four of us used to rob it systematically, carrying a sack and getting half a hundredweight of apples at a time, besides several pounds of cobnuts. On Sundays we used to wash our shirts and socks in the stream, and sleep the rest of the day. As far as I remember I never undressed completely all the time we were down there, nor washed my teeth, and I only shaved twice a week. Between working and getting meals (and that meant fetching everlasting cans of water, struggling with wet faggots, frying in tin-lids etc.) one seemed to have not an instant to spare. I only read one book all the time I was down there, and that was a Buffalo Bill. Counting up what we spent I find that Ginger and I fed ourselves on about 5/- a week each, so it is not surprising that we were constantly short of tobacco and constantly hungry, in spite of the apples and what the others gave us. We seemed to be forever doing sums in farthings to find out whether we could afford another half ounce of shag or another two-pennorth of bacon. It wasn't a bad life, but what with standing all day, sleeping rough and getting my hands cut to bits, I felt a wreck at the end of it. It was humiliating to see that most of the people there looked on it as a holiday – in fact, it is because hopping is regarded as a holiday that the pickers will take such starvation wages. It gives one an insight into the lives of farm labourers too, to realise that according to their standards hop-picking is hardly work at all.

One night a youth knocked at our door and said that he was a new picker and had been told to sleep in our hut. We let him in and fed him in the morning, after which he vanished. It appeared that he was not a picker at all, but a tramp, and that tramps often work this dodge in the hopping season, in order to get a kip under shelter. Another night a woman who was going home asked me to help her get her luggage to Wateringbury station. As she was leaving early they had paid her off at eight bushels a shilling, and her total earnings were only just enough to get herself and family home. I had to push a perambulator, with one eccentric wheel and loaded with huge packages, two and a half miles through the dark, followed by a retinue of yelling children. When we got to the station the last train was just coming in, and in rushing the pram across the level crossing I upset it. I shall never forget that moment – the train bearing down on us, and the porter and I chasing a tin chamberpot that was rolling up the track. On several nights Ginger tried to persuade me to come and rob the church with him, and he would have done it alone if I had not managed to get it into his head that suspicion was bound to fall on him, as a known criminal. He had robbed churches before, and he said, what surprised me, that there is generally something worth having in the Poorbox. We had one or two jolly nights, on Saturdays, sitting round a huge fire till midnight and roasting apples. One night, I remember, it came out that of about fifteen people round the fire, everyone except myself had been in prison. There were uproarious scenes in the village on Saturdays, for the people who had money used to get well drunk, and it needed the police to get them out of the pub. I have no doubt the residents thought us a nasty vulgar lot, but I could not help feeling that it was rather good for a dull village to have this invasion of cockneys once a year.

19.9.31: On the last morning, when we had picked the last field, there was a queer game of catching the women and putting them in the bins. Very likely there will be something about this in the *Golden Bough*. It is evidently an old custom, and all harvests have some custom of this kind attached to them. The people who were illiterate or therabouts° brought their tally books to me and other 'scholars' to have them reckoned up, and some of them paid a copper or two to have it done. I found that in quite a number of cases the farm cashiers had made a mistake in the addition, and invariably the mistake was in favour of the farm. Of course the pickers got the sum due when they complained, but they would not have if they had accepted the farm cashier's reckoning. Moreover, the farm had a mean little rule that anyone who was going to complain about his tally book had to wait till all the other pickers had been paid off. This meant waiting till the afternoon, so that some people who had buses to catch had to go home without claiming the sum due to them. (Of course it was only a few coppers in most cases. One woman's book, however, was added up over £1 wrong.°)

Ginger and I packed our things and walked over to Wateringbury to catch the hop-pickers' train. On the way we stopped to buy tobacco, and as a sort of farewell to Kent, Ginger cheated the tobacconist's girl of fourpence, by a very cunning dodge. When we got to Wateringbury station about fifty hoppers were waiting for the train, and the first person we saw was old Deafie, sitting on the grass with a newspaper in front of him. He lifted it aside, and we saw that he had his trousers undone and was exhibiting his penis to the women and children as they passed. I was surprised – such a decent old man, really; but there is hardly a tramp who has not some sexual abnormality. The Hoppers' train was ninepence cheaper than the ordinary fare, and it took nearly five hours to get us to London – 30 miles. At about 10 at night the hop-pickers poured out at London Bridge station, a number of them drunk and all carrying bunches of hops; people in the street readily bought these bunches of hops, I dont know why. Deafie, who had travelled in our carriage, asked us into the nearest pub and stood us each a pint, the first beer I had had in three weeks. Then he went off to Hammersmith, and no doubt he will be on the bum till next year's fruit-picking begins.

On adding up our tally book, Ginger and I found that we had made just 26/– each by eighteen days' work. We had drawn 8/– each in advances (or 'subs' as they are called), and we had made another 6/– between us by selling stolen apples. After paying our fares we got to London with about 16/– each. So we had, after all, kept ourselves while we were in Kent and come back with a little in pocket; but we had only done it by living on the very minimum of everything.

19.9.31 to 8.10.31: Ginger and I went to a kip in Tooley Street, owned by Lew Levy who owns the one in Westminster Bridge Road. It is only sevenpence a night, and it is probably the best sevenpenny one in London. There are bugs in the beds, but not many, and the kitchens, though dark and dirty, are convenient, with abundant fires and hot water. The lodgers are a pretty low lot – mostly Irish unskilled labourers, and out of work at that. We met some queer types among them. There was one man, aged 68, who worked carrying crates of fish (they weigh a hundredweight each) in Billingsgate market. He was interested in politics, and he told me that on Bloody Sunday in '88 he had taken part in the rioting and been sworn in as a special constable on the same day. Another old man, a flower seller, was mad. Most of the time he behaved quite normally, but when his fits were on he would walk up and down the kitchen uttering dreadful beast-like yells, with an expression of agony on his face. Curiously enough, the fits only came on in wet weather. Another man was a thief. He stole from shop counters and vacant motor cars, especially commercial travellers' cars, and sold the stuff to a Jew in Lambeth Cut. Every evening you would see him smartening himself up to go 'up West'. He told me that he could count on £2 a week, with a big haul from time to time. He managed to swoop the till of a public house almost every Christmas, generally getting £40 or £50 by this. He had been stealing for years and only been caught once, and then was bound over. As always seems the case with thieves, his work brought him no good, for when he got a large sum he blued it instantly. He had one of the ignoblest faces I ever saw, just like a hyena's; yet he was likeable, and decent about sharing food and paying debts.

Several mornings Ginger and I worked helping the porters at Billingsgate. You go there at about five and stand at the corner of one of the streets which lead up from Billingsgate into Eastcheap. When a porter is having trouble to get his barrow up, he shouts 'Up the 'ill!' and you spring forward (there is fierce competition for the jobs, of course) and shove the barrow behind. The payment is 'twopence an up'. They take on about one shover-up for four hundredweight, and the work knocks it out of your thighs and elbows, but you don't get enough jobs to tire you out. Standing there from five till nearly midday, I never made more than 1/6d. If you are very lucky a porter takes you on as his regular assistant, and then you make about 4/6d a morning. The porters themselves seem to make about £4 or £5 a week. There are several things worth noticing about Billingsgate. One is that vast quantities of the work done there are quite unnecessary, being due to the complete lack of any centralised transport system. What with porters, barrowmen, shovers-up etc, it now costs round about £1 to get a ton of fish from Billingsgate to one of the London railway termini. If it were done in an orderly manner, by lorries, I suppose it would cost a few shillings. Another thing is that the pubs in Billingsgate are open at the hours when other pubs are shut. And another is that the barrowmen at Billingsgate do a regular traffic in stolen fish, and you can get fish dirt cheap if you know one of them.

After about a fortnight in the lodging house I found that I was writing nothing, and the place itself was beginning to get on my nerves, with its noise and lack of privacy, and the stifling heat of the kitchen, and above all the dirt. The kitchen had a permanent sweetish reek of fish, and all the sinks were blocked with rotting fish guts which stank horribly. You had to store your food in dark corners which were infested by black beetles and cockroaches, and there were clouds of horrible languid flies everywhere. The dormitory was also disgusting, with the perpetual din of coughing and spitting – everyone in a lodging house has a chronic cough, no doubt from the foul air. I had got to write some articles, which could not be done in such surroundings, so I wrote home for money and took a room in Windsor Street near the Harrow Road. Ginger has gone off on the road again. Most of this narrative was written in the Bermondsey public library, which has a good reading room and was convenient for the lodging house.

NOTES.

New words (i.e. words new to me) discovered this time.

Shackles...............broth or gravy.

Drum, a.................a billy can. (With verb to drum up meaning to light a fire.)

Toby, on the ....on the tramp. (Also to toby, and a toby, meaning a tramp. *Slang Dictionary* gives the toby as the highroad.)

Chat, a ....a louse. (Also chatty, lousy. *S.D.* gives this but not a chat.)

Get, a ....? (Word of abuse, meaning unknown.)[10]

Didecai, a ....a gypsy.

Sprowsie, a..........a sixpence.

Hard-up...............tobacco made from fag ends. (*S.D.* gives a hard-up as a man who collects fag ends.)

Skipper, to............to sleep out. (*S.D.* gives a skipper as a barn.)

Scrump, to...........to steal.

Knock off, to.......to arrest.

Jack off, to...........to go away.

Jack, on his..........on his own.

Clods ....coppers.

Burglars' slang.

A stick, or a cane...........a jemmy. (*S.D.* gives stick.)

Peter, a............................a safe. (In *S.D.*)

Bly,* a ....an oxy-acetylene blowlamp.

---

* I forgot to mention that these lamps are hired out to burglars. Ginger said that he had paid £3.10.0 a night for the use of one. So also with other burglars' tools of the more elaborate kinds. When opening a puzzle-lock, clever safe-breakers use a stethoscope to listen to the click of the tumblers [Orwell's note].

Use of the word 'tart' among the East Enders. This word now seems absolutely interchangeable with 'girl', with no implication of 'prostitute'. People will speak of their daughter or sister as a tart.

Rhyming slang. I thought this was extinct, but it is far from it. The hop-pickers used these expressions freely: A dig in the grave, meaning a shave. The hot cross bun, meaning the sun. Greengages, meaning wages. They also used the abbreviated rhyming slang, e.g. 'Use your twopenny' for 'Use your head'. This is arrived at like this: Head, loaf of bread, loaf, twopenny loaf, twopenny.

Homosexual vice in London. It appears that one of the great rendezvous is Charing Cross underground station. It appeared to be taken for granted by the people on Trafalgar Square that youths could earn a bit this way, and several said to me, 'I need never sleep out if I choose to go down to Charing Cross.' They added that the usual fee is a shilling.

1. London County Council.
2. Orwell gives the meanings of some 'new words' he uses, such as 'drum', at the end of his diary.
3. 2½d = two and a half pence in pre-metric currency, approximately 1p – roughly 35p at today's values.
4. A spike is a casual ward or workhouse to accommodate vagrants. For Orwell's essay 'The Spike', April 1931, see X/*104*.
5. 6/– and 1/6d = six shillings and one shilling and sixpence in pre-metric currency: 30p and 7½p today (perhaps about £11 and £2.50 at current values).
6. Names deleted on legal grounds.
7. Mr F.'s aunt is the aunt of Flora Finching's deceased husband in *Little Dorrit* by Dickens. Left in Flora's care, she was known simply as 'Mr F.'s Aunt'. Her major characteristics are described as 'extreme severity and grim taciturnity; sometimes interrupted by a propensity to offer remarks in a deep warning voice, which, being totally uncalled for by anything said by anybody, and traceable to no association of ideas, confounded and terrified the mind'. One interjection might have had special appeal for Orwell, who had lived at Henley-on-Thames as a child: 'Mr F.'s Aunt, after regarding the company for ten minutes with a malevolent gaze, delivered the following fearful remark. "When we lived at Henley, Barnes's gander was stole by tinkers" ' (ch. 13).
8. George Belcher (1875–1947) was a Royal Academician. His books of drawings included *Characters* (1922), *Taken from Life* (1929) and *Potted Char* (1933).
9. About £35 today.
10. Presumably the contemporary 'git' (roughly, as in 'you git,' an ignorant fool). Compare the Scots, 'gyte' (pronounced 'git'), formerly used for a child.

*For a short article based on the Hop-Picking Diary, see 'Hop-Picking', X/
233–5; see also ch. 2 of Orwell's novel,* A Clergyman's Daughter *(1935).*

---

[135]

Unpublished essay, 'Clink'
[*August 1932*]

*The events narrated in 'Clink'¹ started on Saturday, 12 December 1931 (or
possibly a week later). The text is printed from Orwell's typescript. See
Richard Rees,* George Orwell: Fugitive from the Camp of Victory, *144.*

This trip was a failure, as the object of it was to get into prison, and I did
not, in fact, get more than forty eight hours in custody; however, I am
recording it, as the procedure in the police court etc. was fairly interesting.
I am writing this eight months after it happened, so am not certain of any
dates, but it all happened a week or ten days before Xmas 1931.

I started out on Saturday afternoon with four or five shillings, and went
out to the Mile End Road, because my plan was to get drunk and
incapable, and I thought they would be less lenient towards drunkards in
the East End. I bought some tobacco and a 'Yank Mag'² against my
forthcoming imprisonment, and then, as soon as the pubs opened, went
and had four or five pints, topping up with a quarter bottle of whisky,
which left me with twopence in hand. By the time the whisky was low in
the bottle I was tolerably drunk – more drunk than I had intended, for it
happened that I had eaten nothing all day, and the alcohol acted quickly
on my empty stomach. It was all I could do to stand upright, though my
brain was quite clear – with me, when I am drunk, my brain remains clear
long after my legs and speech have gone. I began staggering along the
pavement in a westward direction, and for a long time did not meet any
policemen, though the streets were crowded and all the people pointed
and laughed at me. Finally I saw two policemen coming. I pulled the
whisky bottle out of my pocket and, in their sight, drank what was left,
which nearly knocked me out, so that I clutched a lamp-post and fell
down. The two policemen ran towards me, turned me over and took the
bottle out of my hand.

THEY: 'Ere, what you bin drinking? (*For a moment they may have thought it was a case of suicide.*)

I: Thass my boll whisky. You lea' me alone.

THEY: Coo, 'e's fair bin bathing in it! – What you bin doing of, eh?

I: Bin in boozer 'avin' bit o' fun. Christmas, ain't it?

THEY: No, not by a week it ain't. You got mixed up in the dates, you 'ave. You better come along with us. We'll look after yer.

I: Why sh'd I come along you?

THEY: Jest so's we'll look after you and make you comfortable. You'll get run over, rolling about like that.

I: Look. Boozer over there. Less go in 'ave drink.

THEY: You've 'ad enough for one night, ole chap. You best come with us.

I: Where you takin' me?

THEY: Jest somewhere as you'll get a nice quiet kip with a clean sheet and two blankets and all.

I: Shall I get drink there?

THEY: Course you will. Got a boozer on the premises, we 'ave.

All this while they were leading me gently along the pavement. They had my arms in the grip (I forget what it is called) by which you can break a man's arm with one twist, but they were as gentle with me as though I had been a child. I was internally quite sober, and it amused me very much to see the cunning way in which they persuaded me along, never once disclosing the fact that we were making for the police station. This is, I suppose, the usual procedure with drunks.

When we got to the station (it was Bethnal Green, but I did not learn this till Monday) they dumped me in a chair & began emptying my pockets while the sergeant questioned me. I pretended, however, to be too drunk to give sensible answers, & he told them in disgust to take me off to the cells, which they did. The cell was about the same size as a Casual Ward cell (about 10 ft. by 5 ft. by 10 ft. high), but much cleaner & better appointed. It was made of white porcelain bricks, and was furnished with a W.C., a hot water pipe, a plank bed, a horsehair pillow and two blankets. There was a tiny barred window high up near the roof, and an electric bulb behind a guard of thick glass was kept burning all night. The door was steel, with the usual spy-hole and aperture for serving food through. The constables in searching me had taken away my money, matches, razor, and also my scarf – this, I learned afterwards, because prisoners have been known to hang themselves on their scarves.

There is very little to say about the next day and night, which were unutterably boring. I was horribly sick, sicker than I have ever been from a bout of drunkenness, no doubt from having an empty stomach. During Sunday I was given two meals of bread and marg. and tea (spike quality), and one of meat and potatoes – this, I believe, owing to the kindness of the sergeant's wife, for I think only bread and marg, is provided for prisoners in the lock-up. I was not allowed to shave, and there was only a little cold water to wash in. When the charge sheet was filled up I told the story I always tell, viz. that my name was Edward Burton,[3] and my parents kept a cake-shop in Blythburgh, where I had been employed as a clerk in a draper's shop; that I had had the sack for drunkenness, and my parents, finally getting sick of my drunken habits, had turned me adrift. I added that I had been working as an outside porter at Billingsgate, and having unexpectedly 'knocked up' six shillings on Saturday, had gone on the razzle. The police were quite kind, and read me lectures on drunkenness, with the usual stuff about seeing that I still had some good in me etc. etc. They offered to let me out on bail on my own recognizance, but I had no money and nowhere to go, so I elected to stay in custody. It was very dull, but I had my 'Yank Mag', and could get a smoke if I asked the constable on duty in the passage for a light – prisoners are not allowed matches, of course.

The next morning very early they turned me out of my cell to wash, gave me back my scarf, and took me out into the yard and put me in the Black Maria. Inside, the Black Maria was just like a French public lavatory, with a row of tiny locked compartments on either side, each just large enough to sit down in. People had scrawled their names, offences and the lengths of their sentences all over the walls of my compartment; also, several times, variants on this couplet –

> Detective Smith knows how to gee;
> Tell him he's a cunt from me.

('Gee' in this context means to act as an agent provocateur.) We drove round to various stations picking up about ten prisoners in all, until the

Black Maria was quite full. They were quite a jolly crowd inside. The compartment doors were open at the top, for ventilation, so that you could reach across, and somebody had managed to smuggle matches in, and we all had a smoke. Presently we began singing, and, as it was near Christmas sang several carols. We drove up to Old Street Police Court singing –

> Adeste, fideles, laeti triumphantes,
> Adeste, adeste ad Bethlehem, etc.

which seemed to me rather inappropriate.

At the police court they took me off and put me in a cell identical with the one at Bethnal Green, even to having the same number of bricks in it – I counted in each case. There were three men in the cell beside myself. One was a smartly dressed, florid, well-set-up man of about thirty five, whom I would have taken for a commercial traveller or perhaps a bookie, and another a middle-aged Jew, also quite decently dressed. The other man was evidently a habitual burglar. He was a short rough-looking man with grey hair and a worn face, and at this moment in such a state of agitation over his approaching trial that he could not keep still an instant. He kept pacing up and down the cell like a wild beast, brushing against our knees as we sat on the plank bed, and exclaiming that he was innocent – he was charged, apparently, with loitering with intent to commit burglary. He said that he had nine previous convictions against him, and that in these cases, which are mainly of suspicion, old offenders are nearly always convicted. From time to time he would shake his fist towards the door and exclaim 'Fucking toe-rag! Fucking toe-rag!', meaning the 'split' who had arrested him.

Presently two more prisoners were put into the cell, an ugly Belgian youth charged with obstructing traffic with a barrow, and an extraordinary hairy creature who was either deaf and dumb or spoke no English. Except this last all the prisoners talked about their cases with the utmost freedom. The florid, smart man, it appeared, was a public house 'guv'nor' (it is a sign of how utterly the London publicans are in the claw of the brewers that they are always referred to as 'governors', not 'landlords'; being, in fact, no better than employees), & had embezzled the Christmas Club money. As usual, he was head over ears in debt to the brewers, and no doubt had taken some of the money in hopes of backing a winner. Two of the subscribers had discovered this a few days before the money was due to be paid out, and laid an information. The 'guv'nor' immediately paid back all save £12, which was also refunded before his case came up for trial. Nevertheless, he was certain to be sentenced, as the magistrates are hard on these cases – he did, in fact, get four months later in the day. He was ruined for life, of course. The brewers would file bankruptcy proceedings and sell up all his stock and furniture, and he would never be given a pub licence again. He was trying to brazen it out in front of the rest of us, and smoking cigarettes incessantly from a stock of Gold Flake packets he had laid in – the last time in his life, I dare say, that he would have quite enough cigarettes. There was a staring, abstracted look in his eyes all the time while he talked. I think the fact that his life was at an end, as far as any decent position in society went, was gradually sinking into him.

The Jew had been a buyer at Smithfields for a kosher butcher. After working seven years for the same employer he suddenly misappropriated £28, went up to Edinburgh – I don't know why Edinburgh – and had a 'good time' with tarts, and came back and surrendered himself when the money was gone. £16 of the money had been repaid, and the rest was to be repaid by monthly instalments. He had a wife and a number of children. He told us, what interested me, that his employer would probably get into trouble at the synagogue for prosecuting him. It appears that the Jews have arbitration courts of their own, & a Jew is not supposed to prosecute another Jew, at least in a breach of trust case like this, without first submitting it to the arbitration court.

One remark made by these men struck me – I heard it from almost every prisoner who was up for a serious offence. It was, 'It's not the prison I mind, it's losing my job.' This is, I believe, symptomatic of the dwindling power of the law compared with that of the capitalist.

They kept us waiting several hours. It was very uncomfortable in the cell, for there was not room for all of us to sit down on the plank bed, and it was beastly cold in spite of the number of us. Several of the men used the W.C., which was disgusting in so small a cell, especially as the plug did not work. The publican distributed his cigarettes generously, the constable in the passage supplying lights. From time to time an extraordinary clanking noise came from the cell next door, where a youth who had stabbed his 'tart' in the stomach – she was likely to recover, we heard – was locked up alone. Goodness knows what was happening, but it sounded as though he were chained to the wall. At about ten they gave us each a mug of tea – this, it appeared, not provided by the authorities but by the police court missionaries – and shortly afterwards shepherded us along to a sort of large waiting room where the prisoners awaited trial.

There were perhaps fifty prisoners here, men of every type, but on the whole much more smartly dressed than one would expect. They were strolling up and down with their hats on, shivering with the cold. I saw here a thing which interested me greatly. When I was being taken to my cell I had seen two dirty-looking ruffians, much dirtier than myself and presumably drunks or obstruction cases, being put into another cell in the row. Here, in the waiting room, these two were at work with note-books in their hands, interrogating prisoners. It appeared that they were 'splits', and were put into the cells disguised as prisoners, to pick up any information that was going – for there is complete freemasonry between prisoners, and they talk without reserve in front of one another. It was a dingy trick, I thought.

All the while the prisoners were being taken by ones & twos along a corridor to the court. Presently a sergeant shouted 'Come on the drunks!' and four or five of us filed along the corridor and stood waiting at the entrance of the court. A young constable on duty there advised me –

'Take your cap off when you go in, plead guilty and don't give back answers. Got any previous convictions?'

'No.'

'Six bob you'll get. Going to pay it?'

'I can't, I've only twopence.'

'Ah well, it don't matter. Lucky for you Mr Brown isn't on the bench this morning. Teetotaller he is. He don't half give it to the drunks. Coo!'

The drunk cases were dealt with so rapidly that I had not even time to notice what the court was like. I only had a vague impression of a raised platform with a coat of arms over it, clerks sitting at tables below, and a railing. We filed past the railing like people passing through a turnstile, & the proceedings in each case sounded like this –

'Edward-Burton-drunk-and-incapable-Drunk?-Yes-Six-shillings-move-on-NEXT!'

All this in the space of about five seconds. At the other side of the court we reached a room where a sergeant was sitting at a desk with a ledger.

'Six shillings?' he said.

'Yes.'

'Going to pay it?'

'I can't.'

'All right, back you go to your cell.'

And they took me back and locked me in the cell from which I had come, about ten minutes after I had left it.

The publican had also been brought back, his case having been postponed, and the Belgian youth, who, like me, could not pay his fine. The Jew was gone, whether released or sentenced we did not know. Throughout the day prisoners were coming and going, some waiting trial, some until the Black Maria was available to take them off to prison. It was cold, and the nasty faecal stench in the cell became unbearable. They gave us our dinner at about two o'clock – it consisted of a mug of tea and two slices of bread and marg. for each man. Apparently this was the regulation meal. One could, if one had friends outside get food sent in, but it struck me as damnably unfair that a penniless man must face his trial with only bread and marg. in his belly; also unshaven – I, at this time, had had no chance of shaving for over forty eight hours – which is likely to prejudice the magistrates against him.

Among the prisoners who were put temporarily in the cell were two friends or partners named apparently Snouter and Charlie, who had been arrested for some street offence – obstruction with a barrow, I dare say. Snouter was a thin, red-faced, malignant-looking man, and Charlie a short, powerful, jolly man. Their conversation was rather interesting.

CHARLIE: Cripes, it ain't 'alf fucking cold in 'ere. Lucky for us ole Brown ain't on to-day. Give you a month as soon as look at yer.
SNOUTER (bored, and singing):

> Tap, tap, tapetty-tap,
> I'm a perfect devil at that;
> Tapping 'em 'ere, tapping 'em there,
> *I* bin tapping 'em everywhere

CHARLIE: Oh, fuck off with yer tapping! Scrumping's what yer want this time of year. All them rows of turkeys in the winders, like rows of fucking soldiers with no clo'es on – don't it make yer fucking mouth water to look at 'em. Bet yer a tanner I 'ave one of 'em afore tonight.

SNOUTER: What's 'a good? Can't cook the bugger over the kip-'ouse fire, can you?

CHARLIE: Oo wants to cook it? I know where I can flog (sell) it for a bob or two, though.

SNOUTER: 'Sno good. Chantin's the game this time of year. Carols. Fair twist their 'earts round, I can, when I get on the mournful. Old tarts weep their fucking eyes out when they 'ear me. I won't 'alf give them a doing this Christmas. I'll kip indoors if I 'ave to cut it out of their bowels.

CHARLIE: Ah, *I* can sling you a bit of a carol. 'Ymns, too. (He begins singing in a good bass voice) –

> Jesu, lover of my soul,
> Let me to thy bosom fly –

THE CONSTABLE ON DUTY (looking through the grille): Nah then, in 'ere, nah then! What yer think this is? Baptist prayer meeting?

CHARLIE (in a low voice as the constable disappears): Fuck off, pisspot. (He hums) –

> While the gathering waters roll,
> While the tempest still is 'igh!

You won't find many in the 'ymnal as I can't sling you. Sung bass in the choir my last two years in Dartmoor, I did.

SNOUTER: Ah? Wassit like in Dartmoor now? D'you get jam now?

CHARLIE: Not jam. Gets cheese, though, twice a week.

SNOUTER: Ah? 'Ow long was you doing?

CHARLIE: Four year.

SNOUTER: Four years without cunt – Cripes! Fellers inside'd go 'alf mad if they saw a pair of legs (a woman), eh?

CHARLIE: Ah well, in Dartmoor we used to fuck old women down on the allotments. Take 'em under the 'edge in the mist. Spud-grabbers they was – ole trots seventy year old. Forty of us was caught and went through 'ell for it. Bread and water, chains – everythink. I took my Bible oath as I wouldn't get no more stretches after that.

SNOUTER: Yes, you! 'Ow come you got in the stir lars' time then?

CHARLIE: You wouldn't 'ardly believe it, boy. I was narked – narked by my own sister! Yes, my own fucking sister. My sister's a cow if ever there was one. She got married to a religious maniac, and 'e's so fucking religious that she's got fifteen kids now. Well, it was 'im put 'er up to narking me. But I got it back on 'em *I* can tell you. What do you think I done first thing, when I come out of the stir? I bought a 'ammer, and I went round to my sister's 'ouse and smashed 'er piano to fucking matchwood. I did. 'There', I says, 'that's what you get for narking me! You mare', I says etc. etc. etc.

This kind of conversation went on more or less all day between these two, who were only in for some petty offence & quite pleased with themselves. Those who were going to prison were silent and restless, and the look on some of the men's faces – respectable men under arrest for the first time – was dreadful. They took the publican out at about three in the afternoon, to be sent off to prison. He had cheered up a little on learning from the constable on duty that he was going to the same prison as Lord Kylsant.[4] He thought that by sucking up to Lord K. in jail he might get a job from him when he came out.

I had no idea how long I was going to be incarcerated, & supposed that it would be several days at least. However, between four and five o'clock they took me out of the cell, gave back the things which had been confiscated, and shot me into the street forthwith. Evidently the day in custody served instead of the fine. I had only twopence and had had nothing to eat all day except bread and marg., and was damnably hungry; however, as always happens when it is a choice between tobacco and food, I bought tobacco with my twopence. Then I went down to the Church Army shelter in the Waterloo Road, where you get a kip, two meals of bread and corned beef and tea and a prayer meeting, for four hours work at sawing wood:

The next morning I went home,[5] got some money, and went out to Edmonton. I turned up at the Casual Ward about nine at night, not downright drunk but more or less under the influence, thinking this would lead to prison – for it is an offence under the Vagrancy Act for a tramp to come drunk to the Casual Ward. The porter, however, treated me with great consideration, evidently feeling that a tramp with money enough to buy drink ought to be respected. During the next few days I made several more attempts to get into trouble by begging under the noses of the police, but I seemed to bear a charmed life – no one took any notice of me. So, as I did not want to do anything serious which might lead to investigations about my identity etc., I gave it up. The trip, therefore, was more or less of a failure, but I have recorded it as a fairly interesting experience.

1. Clink is a cant word for a prison, from the Clink, one-time prison in the London borough of Southwark, dating from the sixteenth century.

2. Orwell referred to pulp magazines known as Yank Mags in his essay 'Raffles and Miss Blandish' (pp. 335–70, below). They were sold at three old pence a copy (approximately 1p). He provided this footnote: 'They are said to have been imported into this country as ballast, which accounted for their low price and crumpled appearance. Since the war the ships have been ballasted with something more useful, probably gravel.' See also 'Boys' Weeklies', below.

3. When choosing a pseudonym for the publication of *Down and Out in Paris and London*, Orwell told Leonard Moore that he always used the name P. S. Burton; see letter to Leonard Moore [19 November 1932], below. Blythburgh is a mile or so inland from Southwold.

4. Lord Kylsant (1863–1937), a Conservative MP, Chairman of the Royal Mail Steam Package Company, and with large shipbuilding interests, was sentenced to twelve months' imprisonment in 1931 for circulating a false prospectus. His personal guilt was never entirely established in the public mind.

5. His lodgings at 2 Windsor Street, Paddington, near St Mary's Hospital. The house has been demolished; part of the estate is illustrated in John Thompson, *Orwell's London* (1984), 31.

[141]

'Common Lodging Houses'
New Statesman & Nation, *3 September 1932*

Common lodging houses, of which there are several hundred in London, are night-shelters specially licensed by the L.C.C. They are intended for people who cannot afford regular lodgings, and in effect they are extremely cheap hotels. It is hard to estimate the lodging-house population, which varies continually, but it always runs into tens of thousands, and in the winter months probably approaches fifty thousand. Considering that they house so many people and that most of them are in an extraordinarily bad state, common lodging houses do not get the attention they deserve.

To judge the value of the L.C.C. legislation on this subject, one must realise what life in a common lodging house is like. The average lodging house ('doss house', it used to be called) consists of a number of dormitories, and a kitchen, always subterranean, which also serves as a sitting-room. The conditions in these places, especially in southern quarters such as Southwark or Bermondsey, are disgusting. The dormitories are horrible fetid dens, packed with anything up to a hundred men, and furnished with beds a good deal inferior to those in a London casual ward. Normally these beds are about 5 ft 6 in. long by 2 ft 6 in. wide, with a hard convex mattress and a cylindrical pillow like a block of wood; sometimes, in the cheaper houses, not even a pillow. The bed-clothes consist of two raw-umber-coloured sheets, supposed to be changed once a week, but actually, in many cases, left on for a month, and a cotton counterpane; in winter there may be blankets, but never enough. As often as not the beds are verminous, and the kitchens invariably swarm with cockroaches or black beetles. There are no baths, of course, and no room where any privacy is attainable. These are the normal and accepted conditions in all ordinary lodging houses. The charges paid for this kind of accommodation vary between 7d and 1/1d a night. It should be added that, low as these charges sound, the average common lodging house brings in something like £40 net profit a week to its owner.

Besides the ordinary dirty lodging houses, there are a few score, such as the Rowton Houses and the Salvation Army hostels, that are clean and decent. Unfortunately, all of these places set off their advantages by a discipline so rigid and tiresome that to stay in them is rather like being in jail. In London (curiously enough it is better in some other towns) the common lodging house where one gets both liberty and a decent bed does not exist.

The curious thing about the squalor and discomfort of the ordinary lodging house is that these exist in places subject to constant inspection by the L.C.C. When one first sees the murky, troglodytic cave of a common lodging-house kitchen, one takes it for a corner of the early nineteenth century which has somehow been missed by the reformers; it is a surprise to find that common lodging houses are governed by a set of minute and (in intention) exceedingly tyrannical rules. According to the L.C.C. regulations, practically everything is against the law in a common lodging house. Gambling, drunkenness, or even the introduction of liquor, swearing, spitting on the floor, keeping tame animals, fighting – in short, the whole social life of these places – are all forbidden. Of course, the law is habitually broken, but some of the rules are enforceable, and they illustrate the dismal uselessness of this kind of legislation. To take an instance: some time ago the L.C.C. became concerned about the closeness together of beds in common lodging houses, and enacted that these must be at least 3 ft apart. This is the kind of law that is enforceable, and the beds were duly moved. Now, to a lodger in an already overcrowded dormitory it hardly matters whether the beds are 3 ft apart or 1 ft; but it does matter to the proprietor, whose income depends upon his floor space. The sole real result of this law, therefore, was a general rise in the price of beds. Please notice that though the space between the beds is strictly regulated, nothing is said about the beds themselves – nothing, for instance, about their being fit to sleep in. The lodging-house keepers can, and do, charge 1/– for a bed less restful than a heap of straw, and there is no law to prevent them.

Another example of L.C.C. regulations. From nearly all common lodging houses women are strictly excluded; there are a few houses specially for women, and a very small number – too small to affect the general question – to which both men and women are admitted. It follows that any homeless man who lives regularly in a lodging house is entirely cut off from female society – indeed, cases even happen of man and wife being separated owing to the impossibility of getting accommodation in the same house. Again, some of the cheaper lodging houses are habitually raided by slumming parties, who march into the kitchen uninvited and hold lengthy religious services. The lodgers dislike these slumming parties intensely, but they have no power to eject them. Can anyone imagine such things being tolerated in a hotel? And yet a common lodging house is only a hotel at which one pays 8d a night instead of 10/6d. This kind of petty tyranny can, in fact, only be defended on the theory that a man poor enough to live in a common lodging house thereby forfeits some of his rights as a citizen.

One cannot help feeling that this theory lies behind the L.C.C. rules for common lodging houses. All these rules are in the nature of inter-ference-legislation – that is, they interfere, but not for the benefit of the lodgers. Their emphasis is on hygiene and morals, and the question of comfort is left to the lodging-house proprietor, who, of course, either shirks it or solves it in the spirit of organised charity. It is worth pointing out the improvements that could actually be made in common lodging houses by legislation. As to cleanliness, no law will ever enforce that, and in any case it is a minor point. But the sleeping accommodation, which is the important thing, could easily be brought up to a decent standard. Common lodging houses are places in which one pays to sleep, and most of them fail in their essential purpose, for no one can sleep well in a rackety dormitory on a bed as hard as bricks. The L.C.C. would be doing an immense service if they compelled lodging-house keepers to divide their dormitories into cubicles and, above all, to provide comfortable beds; for instance, beds as good as those in the London casual wards. And there seems no sense in the principle of licensing all houses for 'men only' or 'women only', as though men and women were sodium and water and must be kept apart for fear of an explosion; the houses should be licensed for both sexes alike, as they are in some provincial towns. And the lodgers should be protected by law against various swindles which the proprietors and managers are now able to practise on them. Given these conditions, common lodging houses would serve their purpose, which is an important one, far better than they do now. After all, tens of thousands of unemployed and partially employed men have literally no other place in which they can live. It is absurd that they should be compelled to choose, as they are at present, between an easy-going pigsty and a hygienic prison.[1]

ERIC BLAIR

1. A fortnight after the publication of this article, a letter to the editor of the *New Statesman & Nation* by Theodore Fyfe, of Cambridge, was published. He described himself as an architect who had worked for the London County Council on the construction of a 'lodging home of the better kind'. He thought that the LCC's management of common lodging houses ('a festering sore', until they took over) 'worthy of all praise' and concluded: 'They would be the first to admit that much more might be done, but . . . the common lodging house is not the only evil under the sun.' On 19 October 1932, Orwell expressed his annoyance to Eleanor Jaques at not having seen Fyfe's letter, so that he might respond to it; it was not until she had sent it to him in her letter of 13 December 1932 that he saw what Fyfe had written.

[148]

After returning from Paris at the end of 1929, Orwell endured 'several years of fairly severe poverty' (as he described it, XII / 613). He eked out a living by private tutoring and teaching in two private schools: The Hawthorns at Hayes, Middlesex (April 1932 to July 1933) and Frays College, Uxbridge, Middlesex, in the autumn of 1933. He gave up teaching when he became seriously ill with pneumonia just before Christmas 1933. He then lived with his parents at Southwold until he became a part-time assistant at Booklovers' Corner, 1 South End Road, Hampstead, from October 1934 to January 1936 (when he made his journey to Wigan and the north). His experience of teaching is reflected in A Clergyman's Daughter *(1935) and bookshops feature in* Keep the Aspidistra Flying *(1936). See Crick, 218–78; Shelden, 169–72, 193–200 and 212–17. For Orwell's earnings from 1922 to 1945, tabulated against sources, see* A Literary Life, *32 and 92–3.*

To Leonard Moore
Sat.[1] [19 November 1932]   Handwritten

'The Hawthorns', Church Rd, Hayes, Mdx.

Dear Mr Moore,[2]

Many thanks for your letter. I sent off the proof with the printer's queries on it yesterday. I made a few alterations & added one or two footnotes, but I think I arranged it so that there would be no need of 'over-running'. I will send on the other proof as soon as possible.

As to a pseudonym, the name I always use when tramping etc. is P. S. Burton,[3] but if you don't think this sounds a probable kind of name, what about

> Kenneth Miles,
> George Orwell,
> H. Lewis Allways.

I rather favour George Orwell.[4]

I would rather not promise to have the other book[5] ready by the summer. I could certainly do it by then if I were not teaching, but in this life I can't *settle* to any work, & at present particularly I am rushed off my feet. I have got to produce a school play, & I have not only had to write it, but I have got to do all the rehearsing &, worst of all, make most of the costumes. The result is that I have practically no leisure.

I should like very much to come out & see you & Mrs Moore some time. I can get to Gerrards Cross quite easily from here, but I have unfortunately forgotten your home adress.° Perhaps you could let me know it? I could come over some Sunday afternoon – Sunday the 4th Dec., for instance, if you would be at home then?

Yours sincerely

Eric A. Blair

P.S. [at top of letter] As to the *title* of the book. Would 'The Confessions of a Dishwasher' do as well? I would *rather* answer to 'dishwasher' than 'down & out',[6] but if you and Mr G.[7] think the present title best for selling purposes, then it is better to stick to it.

1. This undated letter, as for a number of others, can be placed from the receipt stamp used in Moore's office.

2. Orwell was introduced to the man who became his literary agent, Leonard Moore, by Mabel Fierz, who, with her husband, Francis, befriended Orwell. The agency was called Christy & Moore. Moore lived at Gerrard's Cross in Buckinghamshire and Orwell sometimes visited him there. Early versions of *Down and Out in Paris and London* were rejected (including by T. S. Eliot on behalf of the publisher Jonathan Cape). Orwell gave up but Mabel Fierz took the manuscript to Leonard Moore who passed it to Victor Gollancz. Gollancz became Orwell's first publisher. See *A Literary Life*, 31. Moore died in January 1959.

3. In 'Clink', see above, Orwell had the name Edward Burton put down on the charge sheet and he used the name Burton for a character in his play 'King Charles II' (see X/*154*).

4. In the BBC radio broadcast about the magazine *The Adelphi*, first transmitted 6 July 1958, and produced by Rayner Heppenstall, Sir Richard Rees recalled Orwell's fear that if his real name appeared in print 'an enemy might get hold of [it] and work some kind of magic on it'. In *George Orwell: Fugitive from the Camp of Victory*, Rees elaborated on this: Orwell had told him that it 'gave him an unpleasant feeling to see his real name in print because "how can you be sure your enemy won't cut it out and work some kind of black magic on it?" Whimsy, of course; but even Orwell's genuine streak of old-fashioned conventionality sometimes bordered on whimsy and you could not always be quite certain if he was serious or not' (44).

5. *Burmese Days.*

6. Writing to Eleanor Jaques on 18 November 1932 (X/*147*), Orwell told her that Gollancz wished to call the book 'Confessions of a Down & Out'. He went on: 'I am protesting against this as I don't answer to the name of down & out, but I will let it go if he thinks seriously that it is a taking title.'

7. Victor Gollancz (1893–1967; Kt., 1965) was educated at Oxford and taught at Repton for two years. There his introduction of a class on civics brought him into conflict with the headmaster, Dr Geoffrey Fisher (later Archbishop of Canterbury). He was sacked in 1918

and then worked on minimum-wage legislation and edited 'The World Today' series for Oxford University Press. In 1921 he joined Benn Brothers, publishers of trade journals and a few books. He became managing director of a separate company, Ernest Benn Ltd, in 1923, which he developed successfully. In October 1927 he established his own publishing house, issuing sixty-four books in his first year, the first of which was Susan Glaspell's *Brook Evans*. He had been born into an orthodox Jewish family and was a member of the Labour Party but later described himself as a Christian Socialist. His best-known achievement was the formation of the Left Book Club in 1936; under this imprint Orwell's *The Road to Wigan Pier* was published in March 1937. Orwell and Gollancz fell out over the latter's refusal to publish *Homage to Catalonia* and *Animal Farm*, and Orwell's publisher became Martin Secker and Warburg (in particular Fredric Warburg). However, they continued to collaborate on a number of projects, notably the alleviation of hunger in Europe after the 1939–45 War. See *Gollancz; The Story of a Publishing House, 1928–1978*, by Sheila Hodges (1978). Gollancz's daughter, Livia, was particularly helpful to the editor in making available the Gollancz archives.

---

[157]

Publication of Down and Out in Paris and London

Down and Out in Paris and London *was published in London by Victor Gollancz on 9 January 1933; 1,500 copies were printed. Later in the month, 500 additional copies were printed. A third impression (date unknown) of 1,000 copies followed; none were remaindered. The type was distributed on 13 February 1934. Harper & Brothers, in New York, published 1,750 copies on either 30 June 1933, according to Ian Willison, or 25 July 1933, according to Miss Herdman of Harper; see X/181 and 177A. A review appeared in* Books *(US) on 30 July, making the July date more likely. According to Willison, the type was also distributed on 13 February 1934; 383 copies were remaindered. A French translation by R. N. Raimbault and Gwen Gilbert,* La Vache enragée,[1] *with a preface by Panaït Istrati,[2] was published by Gallimard, in Paris, on 2 May 1935. This edition of 5,500 copies had not been sold out by March 1953. Orwell wrote an introduction for the French edition; see pp. 221–2, below. Penguin Books published a paper-bound edition of 55,000 copies on 18 December 1940. The contemporary French translation has the title* Dans la dèche *(an expression Arnold Bennett uses to describe destitution in the French-influenced English in the Paris scenes of* The Old Wives' Tale *(1908): 'Is he also in the ditch?' III.vi.3).*

Orwell's knowledge of The People of the Abyss *(1903) by Jack London is well established. Whether he knew the work of the Czech–German Egon Erwin Kisch, in* Der Rasende Reporter *(1925), is uncertain. It is a series of short pieces on factual topics connected by thematic cross-references. The first is 'Unter den Obdachlosen von Whitechapel' (Among the Homeless of Whitechapel), an account of a night spent in a Salvation Army hostel in the East End of London.³ What was factual, what autobiographical, and what fictitious in* Down and Out in Paris and London *was noted by Orwell in a copy of the book given to his friend Brenda Salkeld (1900–1999; at the time gym teacher at St Felix School, Southwold. They remained friends throughout Orwell's life). She and Michael Shelden, who located the book, kindly made these annotations available. The book is inscribed: 'To Brenda, with best wishes – Eric A Blair 28.12.32.' There are sixteen annotations, keyed here by chapter and page number (CW, vol. I page number given in square brackets):*

II, 72 [7]: para 'Listen, then': 'Not autobiography. The fellow really did talk like this, tho'.'

III, 75 [12]: first para: 'Succeeding chapters not actually autobiography, but drawn from what I have seen.'

IV, 81 [20]: para 'It was now absolutely necessary': 'This is a fairly accurate portrait except for the name.'

V, 84 [24]: para 2, against 'Bouillon Zip': 'Bouillon Kub⁴ – changed for fear of libel.'

V, 84 [24]: para 'The room was an attic': 'All this fairly exact description of actual happenings.'

VI, 89 [32]: 'Boris would contribute': 'Exaggerated: but I have seen people living in just this fashion.'

VII, 91 [36]: opening lines: 'This all happened.'

VIII, 97 [44]: para 'It was through one of these Russian refugees': 'This happened very much as described.'

X, 104 [54]: opening lines: 'All as exact as I could make it.'

XV, 125 [82]: start of Valenti's story: 'He did tell me this story, tho' not so consecutively.'

XIX, 137 [100]: opening lines: 'All the following is an entirely accurate description of the restaurant.'

XXIII, 153 [123]: para 'Roucolle died, aged seventy-four': 'More or less true, I believe.'

XXIV, 156 [127]: para 'Sleeping in the saloon': 'Quite true.'

XXIV, 157 [128]: para 'I was outside in the street': 'This incident is invented to explain trip, but all the experiences described hereafter are authentic.'

XXVI, 166 [141]: para 'He led the way': 'Called the "Ramblers' Rest" – High Church organisation.'

XXIX, 180 [160]: para 'An old public school boy': 'He wasn't actually an O.E,⁵ but from some other well-known school, I forget which.'

1. The title is idiomatic: 'manger de la vache enragée' means 'to suffer great hardship', or – more appropriately, with reference to Orwell's book – 'to rough it'. *La Vache enragée* was also the title of a satiric monthly journal published in Paris in 1896, for which Toulouse-Lautrec designed a poster.

2. Panaït Istrati (Gherassim Istrati, 1884–1935), Romanian author and translator, wrote in, and translated into, French. He was encouraged by Romain Rolland (1866–1944), who dubbed him 'a Balkan Gorki'. In 1927 he travelled in the USSR, and in 1929 published *Vers l'autre flamme*, three volumes written in collaboration with two others. According to the French translation of the *Small Soviet Encyclopédie Littéraire* (Moscow, 1966), it misrepresented Soviet life to such an extent, because of Istrati's petit-bourgeois conception of liberty, that Rolland and 'all true friends of the USSR' turned their backs on him (from *L'Arc*, Aix-en-Provence, 1983, 86/7, translated from Russian into French by Arthur Rubinstein and Jean Riere, 138). Istrati translated several novels by Upton Sinclair and William Faulkner for French publishers. In his preface to *La Vache enragée*, he makes a number of comparisons between Gorki and Orwell. He concludes that Orwell's book makes one think, makes one meditate on life's griefs, just as does a novel by Balzac, but without one's having to endure Balzac's tedious detail. Istrati died three weeks before *La Vache enragée* appeared.

3. See Keith B. Williams, 'The Will to Objectivity: Egon Erwin Kisch's *Der Rasende Reporter*', *Modern Language Review*, 85 (1990), 92–106, an early draft of which was kindly given to the editor by its author. See also Dieter Schlenstedt, *Egon Erwin Kisch: Leben und Werk* (Berlin, 1985); for *Der Rasende Reporter*, see edition published by Verlag Kiepenheuer und Witsch (Cologne, 1983).

4. Bouillon Kub was soup in granulated cube form based on beef essence. A famous advertisement of about the time Orwell was writing showed the red cube against a bull's head. The Bibliothèque des Arts Décoratifs, Paris, has a copy, and a colour illustration is in Attilio Rosi, *Posters* (Milan, 1966; London, 1969), dated 1930, though it bears the date 1931 next to the name of the designer, Leonatto Cappiello. The poster also appeared in the background in Truffaut's film *Le Dernier Métro* (1980), set in German-occupied Paris.

5. Old Etonian.

Down and Out in Paris and London

O scathful harm, condicion of poverte!
CHAUCER

Down and Out in Paris and London

A NOTE ON THE TEXT

Down and Out in Paris and London was first published by Gollancz on 9 January 1933 and by Harper & Brothers in New York on 30 June of that year. A French translation – of considerable importance in the establishment of the text of this edition – was made by R. N. Raimbault and Gwen Gilbert, entitled *La Vache enragée*, and published by Gallimard, 8 May 1935. Unmarked page proofs (the Proof) of the first London edition came to light some forty years later. They carry the date, 1932, on the title-page, the title is given as *Confessions of a Down and Out in London and Paris*, and the author simply as 'X'. Eric Blair's choice of the name 'George Orwell' stems from his letter of 19 November 1932 to his agent, Leonard Moore. This edition is based on the first London edition amended in the light of *La Vache enragée*, a translation which Orwell greatly admired, in contrast to that of *Burmese Days*, which he described as 'VERY BAD'. (There is a second translation into French, *Dans la dèche à Paris et à Londres*, by Michel Petris, 1982, which sticks much more closely to the English-language edition.)

Victor Gollancz, who encouraged Orwell as a writer and published his first books, was very cautious of running up against the law, a danger even more prevalent for publishers at that time than it is today. It was not so very long before the publication of *Down and Out in Paris and London* that Henry Vizetelly[1] had been jailed for publishing the novels of Emile Zola, an experience that ruined his health. On 1 July 1932 Orwell told his agent what Gollancz required:

Names are to be changed, swearwords etc. cut out, and there is one passage which is to be either changed or cut out. It's a pity, as it is about the only good bit of writing in the book, but he says the circulation libraries would not stand for it.

That 'good bit of writing' (Charlie's story, chapter II) was not, in the event, lost, though it was evidently modified. On 6 July 1932 Orwell told Leonard Moore, 'I have crossed out or altered the phrases that seemed to show too definitely what was happening & perhaps like this it might pass inspection.' Evidently it did, though no details have survived. (Leonard Moore's last surviving letter to Orwell, written a couple of months before Orwell's death, requested the cutting of 140 lines from the Spanish translation of *Nineteen Eighty-Four* which, it was feared, would strike the Argentinian authorities as immoral.) The Proof shows that there was a further glossing-over of swearwords and a couple of interesting passages of rewriting. On page 114, lines 27–8, 'he farted loudly, a favourite Italian insult' was changed to 'delivered a final insult in the same manner as Squire Western in *Tom Jones*'. On page 125, lines 17–18, 'Hôtel——, after some famous prostitute who was born in the quarter, I expect' had to be changed to 'Hôtel Suzanne May, after some famous prostitute of the time of the Empire'. The Proof also shows that Orwell added three more footnotes.

The publishers of *La Vache enragée* (the title is idiomatic French for being destitute and was used for a short-lived humorous journal published in Paris in 1896) were less inhibited than Gollancz was forced to be. The English edition, the translators explained, had had to resort to dashes for many swearwords (some quite mild) but they had restored these words in full in the light of the author's indications. Orwell's French was good, but where he used French in his English text the translators sometimes made this more colloquial. In addition, Orwell added explanatory footnotes for the French readers, evidently in answer to questions posed by the translators, and they themselves added footnotes (explaining, for example, the meanings of public houses and public schools and that traffic in England drove on the left and not, as in France, on the right).

This variety of material enables something of the original tone of Orwell's book to be recovered, but it is not always possible to make clear-cut decisions as to what to include and what to leave out. It is not always plain which are Orwell's additional footnotes to the French translation (moreover, for this edition, they have to be translated back into English),[2] and the filling in of blanks presents a number of problems. Thus, on page 168, line 7, the English edition has a dash, the French has 'sacrées', but the Proof has 'f—'. The French here, and elsewhere, is not an equivalent of what is suggested by the Proof – e.g., page 170, line 22, where the Proof again has 'f—', while the French has 'sale' ('filthy'). Blanks in the English text may be replaced in French by obscenities, remarkably mild expressions, or by nothing at all. Among words introduced into the French text are: sale, dingo, chier, foutre, sacré cochon, couillons-là, sacr . . . , salauds-là, vache.

This edition is circumspect in completing blanks, not out of prurience, but on grounds of textual uncertainty; only those footnotes are added which can reasonably be assigned to Orwell; and the more colloquial French of *La Vache enragée* has been adopted in the light of Orwell's approval of the French translation and bearing in mind his wish that Spanish names in *Homage to Catalonia* should be regularized in any later editions. A full explanation of what has been done will be found in the Textual Note to the *Complete Works* edition, I/217–30 (Secker and Warburg, 1986). That edition also gives footnotes found in the French edition that are not included here.

1. Henry Vizetelly (1820–94), publisher who established the Mermaid Series of Dramatists and published translations of Dostoievski, Flaubert, Tolstoy and Zola, some of which are still in print. His publication of Zola's *La Terre*, though 'amended', led to his being charged with obscenity in 1889; he was fined and jailed. Imprisonment is thought to have been one cause of his death.

2. Footnotes from the French translation and any editorial comments are indicated by an asterisk in the text. The numbered footnotes are Orwell's and the square brackets within the text appear in the first edition and are, presumably, what Orwell wanted.

I

The Rue du Coq d'Or, Paris, seven in the morning. A succession of furious, choking yells from the street. Madame Monce, who kept the little hotel opposite mine, had come out onto the pavement to address a lodger on the third floor. Her bare feet were stuck into sabots and her grey hair was streaming down.

Madame Monce: '*Sacrée salope!* How many times have I told you not to squash bugs on the wallpaper? Do you think you've bought the hotel, eh? Why can't you throw them out of the window like everyone else? *Espèce de traînée!*'

The woman on the third floor: 'Va donc, eh! vieille vache!'

Thereupon a whole variegated chorus of yells, as windows were flung open on every side and half the street joined in the quarrel. They shut up abruptly ten minutes later, when a squadron of cavalry rode past and people stopped shouting to look at them.

I sketch this scene, just to convey something of the spirit of the Rue du Coq d'Or. Not that quarrels were the only thing that happened there – but still, we seldom got through the morning without at least one outburst of this description. Quarrels, and the desolate cries of street hawkers, and the shouts of children chasing orange-peel over the cobbles, and at night loud singing and the sour reek of the refuse-carts, made up the atmosphere of the street.

It was a very narrow street – a ravine of tall leprous houses, lurching towards one another in queer attitudes, as though they had all been frozen in the act of collapse. All the houses were hotels and packed to the tiles with lodgers, mostly Poles, Arabs and Italians. At the foot of the hotels were tiny *bistros*, where you could be drunk for the equivalent of a shilling. On Saturday nights about a third of the male population of the quarter was drunk. There was fighting over women, and the Arab navvies who lived in the cheapest hotels used to conduct mysterious feuds, and fight them out with chairs and occasionally revolvers. At night the policemen would only come through the street two together. It was a fairly rackety place. And yet amid the noise and dirt lived the usual respectable French shopkeepers, bakers and laundresses and the like, keeping themselves to themselves and quietly piling up small fortunes. It was quite a representative Paris slum.

My hotel was called the Hôtel des Trois Moineaux. It was a dark, rickety warren of five storeys, cut up by wooden partitions into forty rooms. The rooms were small and inveterately dirty, for there was no maid, and Madame F., the *patronne*, had no time to do any sweeping. The walls were as thin as matchwood, and to hide the cracks they had been covered with layer after layer of pink paper, which had come loose and housed innumerable bugs. Near the ceiling long lines of bugs marched all day like columns of soldiers, and at night came down ravenously hungry, so that one had to get up every few hours and kill them in hecatombs. Sometimes when the bugs got too bad one used to burn sulphur and drive them into the next room; whereupon the lodger next door would retort by having *his* room sulphured, and drive the bugs back. It was a dirty place, but homelike, for Madame F. and her husband were good sorts. The rent of the rooms varied between thirty and fifty francs a week.

The lodgers were a floating population, largely foreigners, who used to turn up without luggage, stay a week and then disappear again. They were of every trade – cobblers, bricklayers, stonemasons, navvies, students, prostitutes, rag-pickers. Some of them were fantastically poor. In one of the attics there was a Bulgarian student who made fancy shoes for the American market. From six to twelve he sat on his bed, making a dozen pairs of shoes and earning thirty-five francs; the rest of the day he attended lectures at the Sorbonne. He was studying for the Church, and books of theology lay face-down on his leather-strewn floor. In another room lived a Russian woman and her son, who called himself an artist. The mother worked sixteen hours a day, darning socks at twenty-five centimes a sock, while the son, decently dressed, loafed in the Montparnasse cafés. One room was let to two different lodgers, one a day worker and the other a night worker. In another room a widower shared the same bed with his two grown-up daughters, both consumptive.

There were eccentric characters in the hotel. The Paris slums are a gathering-place for eccentric people – people who have fallen into solitary, half-mad grooves of life and given up trying to be normal or decent. Poverty frees them from ordinary standards of behaviour, just as money frees people from work. Some of the lodgers in our hotel lived lives that were curious beyond words.

There were the Rougiers, for instance, an old ragged, dwarfish couple who plied an extraordinary trade. They used to sell postcards on the Boulevard St Michel. The curious thing was that the postcards were sold in sealed packets as pornographic ones, but were actually photographs of châteaux on the Loire; the buyers did not discover this till too late, and of course never complained. The Rougiers earned about a hundred francs a week, and by strict economy managed to be always half starved and half drunk. The filth of their room was such that one could smell it on the floor below. According to Madame F., neither of the Rougiers had taken off their clothes for four years.

Or there was Henri, who worked in the sewers. He was a tall, melancholy man with curly hair, rather romantic-looking in his long sewerman's boots. Henri's peculiarity was that he did not speak, except for the purposes of work, literally for days together. Only a year before he had been a chauffeur in good employ and saving money. One day he fell in love, and when the girl refused him he lost his temper and kicked her. On being kicked the girl fell desperately in love with Henri, and for a fortnight they lived together and spent a thousand francs of Henri's money. Then the girl was unfaithful; Henri planted a knife in her upper arm and was sent to prison for six months. As soon as she had been stabbed the girl fell more in love with Henri than ever, and the two made up their quarrel and agreed that when Henri came out of jail he should buy a taxi and they would marry and settle down. But a fortnight later the girl was unfaithful again, and when Henri came out she was with child. Henri did not stab her again. He drew out all his savings and went on a drinking-bout that ended in another month's imprisonment; after that he went to work in the sewers. Nothing would induce Henri to talk. If you asked him why he worked in the sewers he never answered, but simply crossed his wrists to signify handcuffs, and jerked his head southward, towards the prison. Bad luck seemed to have turned him half-witted in a single day.

Or there was R., an Englishman, who lived six months of the year in Putney with his parents and six months in France. During his time in France he drank four litres of wine a day, and six litres on Saturdays; he had once travelled as far as the Azores, because the wine there is cheaper than anywhere in Europe. He was a gentle, domesticated creature, never rowdy or quarrelsome, and never sober. He would lie in bed till midday, and from then till midnight he was in his corner of the *bistro*, quietly and methodically soaking. While he soaked he talked, in a refined, womanish voice, about antique furniture. Except myself, R. was the only Englishman in the quarter.

There were plenty of other people who lived lives just as eccentric as these: Monsieur Jules, the Roumanian, who had a glass eye and would not admit it, Fureux the Limousin stonemason, Roucolle the miser – he died before my time, though – old Laurent the rag-merchant, who used to copy his signature from a slip of paper he carried in his pocket. It would be fun to write some of their biographies, if one had time. I am trying to describe the people in our quarter, not for the mere curiosity, but because they are all part of the story. Poverty is what I am writing about, and I had my first contact with poverty in this slum. The slum, with its dirt and its queer lives, was first an object-lesson in poverty, and then the background of my own experiences. It is for that reason that I try to give some idea of what life was like there.

11

Life in the quarter. Our *bistro*, for instance, at the foot of the Hôtel des Trois Moineaux. A tiny brick-floored room, half underground, with wine-sodden tables, and a photograph of a funeral inscribed '*Crédit est mort*'; and red-sashed workmen carving sausage with big jack-knives; and Madame F., a splendid Auvergnat peasant woman with the face of a strong-minded cow, drinking Malaga all day 'for her stomach'; and games of dice for *apéritifs*; and songs about 'Les Fraises et Les Framboises', and about Madelon, who said, '*Comment épouser un soldat, moi qui aime tout le régiment?*'; and extraordinarily public love-making. Half the hotel used to meet in the *bistro* in the evenings. I wish one could find a pub in London a quarter as cheery.

One heard queer conversations in the *bistro*. As a sample I give you Charlie, one of the local curiosities, talking.

Charlie was a youth of family and education who had run away from home and lived on occasional remittances. Picture him very pink and young, with the fresh cheeks and soft brown hair of a nice little boy, and lips excessively red and wet, like cherries. His feet are tiny, his arms abnormally short, his hands dimpled like a baby's. He has a way of dancing and capering while he talks, as though he were too happy and too full of life to keep still for an instant. It is three in the afternoon, and there is no one in the *bistro* except Madame F. and one or two men who are out of work; but it is all the same to Charlie whom he talks to, so long as he can talk about himself. He declaims like an orator on a barricade, rolling the words on his tongue and gesticulating with his short arms. His small, rather piggy eyes glitter with enthusiasm. He is, somehow, profoundly disgusting to see.

He is talking of love, his favourite subject.

'*Ah, l'amour, l'amour! Ah, que les femmes m'ont tué!* Alas, *messieurs et dames*, women have been my ruin, beyond all hope my ruin. At twenty-two I am utterly worn out and finished. But what things I have learned, what abysses of wisdom have I not plumbed! How great a thing it is to have acquired the true wisdom, to have become in the highest sense of the word a civilised man, to have become *raffiné, vicieux*,' etc. etc.

'*Messieurs et dames*, I perceive that you are sad. *Ah, mais la vie est belle* – you must not be sad. Be more gay, I beseech you!

> Fill high ze bowl vid Samian vine,
> Ve vill not sink of semes like zese!

'*Ah, que la vie est belle!* Listen, *messieurs et dames*, out of the fullness of my experience I will discourse to you of love. I will explain to you what is the true meaning of love – what is the true sensibility, the higher, more refined pleasure which is known to civilised men alone. I will tell you of the happiest day of my life. Alas, but I am past the time when I could know such happiness as that. It is gone for ever – the very possibility, even the desire for it, are gone.

'Listen, then. It was two years ago; my brother was in Paris – he is a lawyer – and my parents had told him to find me and take me out to dinner. We hate each other, my brother and I, but he preferred not to disobey my parents. We dined, and at dinner he grew very drunk upon three bottles of Bordeaux. I took him back to his hotel, and on the way I bought a bottle of brandy, and when we had arrived I made my brother drink a tumblerful of it – I told him it was something to make him sober. He drank it, and immediately he fell down like somebody in a fit, dead drunk. I lifted him up and propped his back against the bed; then I went through his pockets. I found eleven hundred francs, and with that I hurried down the stairs, jumped into a taxi, and escaped. My brother did not know my address – I was safe.

'Where does a man go when he has money? To the *bordels*, naturally. But you do not suppose that I was going to waste my time on some vulgar debauchery fit only for navvies? Confound it, one is a civilised man! I was fastidious, *exigeant*, you understand, with a thousand francs in my pocket. It was midnight before I found what I was looking for. I had fallen in with a very smart youth of eighteen, dressed *en smoking* and with his hair cut *à l'américaine*, and we were talking in a quiet *bistro* away from the boulevards. We understood one another well, that youth and I. We talked of this and that, and discussed ways of diverting oneself. Presently we took a taxi together and were driven away.

'The taxi stopped in a narrow, solitary street with a single gas-lamp flaring at the end. There were dark puddles among the stones. Down one side ran the high blank wall of a convent. My guide led me to a tall, ruinous house with shuttered windows, and knocked several times at the door. Presently there was a sound of footsteps and a shooting of bolts, and the door opened a little. A hand came round the edge of it; it was a large, crooked hand, that held itself palm upwards under our noses, demanding money.

'My guide put his foot between the door and the step. "How much do you want?" he said.

'"A thousand francs," said a woman's voice. "Pay up at once or you don't come in."

'I put a thousand francs into the hand and gave the remaining hundred to my guide; he said good night and left me. I could hear the voice inside counting the notes, and then a thin old crow of a woman in a black dress put her nose out and regarded me suspiciously before letting me in. It was very dark inside; I could see nothing except a flaring gas-jet that illuminated a patch of plaster wall, throwing everything else into deeper shadow. There was a smell of rats and dust. Without speaking, the old woman lighted a candle at the gas-jet, then hobbled in front of me down a stone passage to the top of a flight of stone steps.

'"*Voilà!*" she said; "go down into the cellar there and do what you like. I shall see nothing, hear nothing, know nothing. You are free, you understand – perfectly free."

'Ah, *messieurs*, need I describe to you – *forcément*, you know it yourselves – that shiver, half of terror and half of joy, that goes through one at these moments? I crept down, feeling my way; I could hear my breathing and the scraping of my feet on the stones, otherwise all was silence. At the bottom of the stairs my hand met an electric switch. I turned it, and a great electrolier of twelve red globes flooded the cellar with a red light. And behold, I was not in a cellar, but in a bedroom, a great rich garish bedroom, coloured blood red from top to bottom. Figure it to yourselves, *messieurs et dames!*

Red carpet on the floor, red paper on the walls, red plush on the chairs, even the ceiling red; everywhere red, burning into the eyes. It was a heavy, stifling red, as though the light were shining through bowls of blood. At the far end stood a huge square bed, with quilts red like the rest, and on it a girl was lying, dressed in a frock of red velvet. At the sight of me she shrank away and tried to hide her knees under the short dress.

'I had halted by the door. "Come here, my chicken," I called to her.

'She gave a whimper of fright. With a bound I was beside the bed; she tried to elude me, but I seized her by the throat – like this, do you see? – tight! She struggled, she began to cry out for mercy, but I held her fast, forcing back her head and staring down into her face. She was twenty years old, perhaps; her face was the broad dull face of a stupid child, but it was coated with paint and powder, and her blue, stupid eyes, shining in the red light, wore that shocked, distorted look that one sees nowhere save in the eyes of these women. She was some peasant girl, doubtless, whom her parents had sold into slavery.

'Without another word I pulled her off the bed and threw her onto the floor. And then I fell upon her like a tiger! Ah, the joy, the incomparable rapture of that time! There, *messieurs et dames*, here is what I would expound to you; *voilà l'amour!* There is the true love, there is the only thing in the world worth striving for; there is the thing beside which all your arts and ideals, all your philosophies and creeds, all your fine words and high attitudes, are as pale and profitless as ashes. When one has experienced love – the true love – what is there in the world that seems more than a mere ghost of joy?

'More and more savagely I renewed the attack. Again and again the girl tried to escape; she cried out for mercy anew, but I laughed at her.

'"Mercy!" I said, "do you suppose I have come here to show mercy? Do you suppose I have paid a thousand francs for that?" I swear to you, *messieurs et dames*, that if it were not for that accursed law that robs us of our liberty, I would have murdered her at that moment.

'Ah, how she screamed, with what bitter cries of agony. But there was no one to hear them; down there under the streets of Paris we were as secure as at the heart of a pyramid. Tears streamed down the girl's face, washing away the powder in long dirty smears. Ah, that irrecoverable time! You, *messieurs et dames*, you who have not cultivated the finer sensibilities of love, for you such pleasure is almost beyond conception. And I too, now that my youth is gone – ah, youth! – shall never again see life so beautiful as that. It is finished.

'Ah yes, it is gone – gone for ever. Ah, the poverty, the shortness, the disappointment of human joy! For in reality – *car en réalité*, what is the duration of the supreme moment of love? It is nothing, an instant, a second perhaps. A second of ecstasy, and after that – dust, ashes, nothingness.

'And so, just for one instant, I captured the supreme happiness, the highest and most refined emotion to which human beings can attain. And in the same moment it was finished, and I was left – to what? All my savagery, my passion, were scattered like the petals of a rose. I was left cold and languid, full of vain regrets; in my revulsion I even felt a kind of pity for the weeping girl on the floor. Is it not nauseous, that we should be the prey of such mean emotions? I did not look at the girl again; my sole thought was to get away. I hastened up the steps of the vault and out into the street. It was dark and bitterly cold, the streets were empty, the stones echoed under my heels with a hollow, lonely ring. All my money was gone, I had not even the price of a taxi fare. I walked back alone to my cold, solitary room.

'But there, *messieurs et dames*, that is what I promised to expound to you. That is Love. That was the happiest day of my life.'

He was a curious specimen, Charlie. I describe him, just to show what diverse characters could be found flourishing in the Coq d'Or quarter.

III

I lived in the Coq d'Or quarter for about a year and a half. One day, in summer, I found that I had just four hundred and fifty francs left, and beyond this nothing but thirty-six francs a week, which I earned by giving English lessons. Hitherto I had not thought about the future, but I now realised that I must do something at once. I decided to start looking for a job, and – very luckily as it turned out – I took the precaution of paying two hundred francs for a month's rent in advance. With the other two hundred and fifty francs, besides the English lessons, I could live a month, and in a month I should probably find work. I aimed at becoming a guide to one of the tourist companies, or perhaps an interpreter. However, a piece of bad luck prevented this.

One day there turned up at the hotel a young Italian who called himself a compositor. He was rather an ambiguous person, for he wore side whiskers, which are the mark either of an apache or an intellectual, and nobody was quite certain in which class to put him. Madame F. did not like the look of him, and made him pay a week's rent in advance. The Italian paid the rent and stayed six nights at the hotel. During this time he managed to prepare some duplicate keys, and on the last night he robbed a dozen rooms, including mine. Luckily he did not find the money that was in my pockets, so I was not left penniless. I was left with just forty-seven francs – that is, seven and ten-pence.

This put an end to my plans of looking for work. I had now got to live at the rate of about six francs a day, and from the start it was too difficult to leave much thought for anything else. It was now that my experiences of poverty began – for six francs a day, if not actual poverty, is on the fringe of it. Six francs is a shilling, and you can live on a shilling a day in Paris if you know how. But it is a complicated business.

It is altogether curious, your first contact with poverty. You have thought so much about poverty – it is the thing you have feared all your life, the thing you knew would happen to you sooner or later; and it is all so utterly and prosaically different. You thought it would be quite simple; it is extraordinarily complicated. You thought it would be terrible; it is merely squalid and boring. It is the peculiar *lowness* of poverty that you discover first; the shifts that it puts you to, the complicated meanness, the crust-wiping.

You discover, for instance, the secrecy attaching to poverty. At a sudden stroke you have been reduced to an income of six francs a day. But of course you dare not admit it – you have got to pretend that you are living quite as usual. From the start it tangles you in a net of lies, and even with the lies you can hardly manage it. You stop sending clothes to the laundry, and the laundress catches you in the street and asks you why; you mumble something, and she, thinking you are sending the clothes elsewhere, is your enemy for life. The tobacconist keeps asking why you have cut down your smoking. There are letters you want to answer, and cannot, because stamps are too expensive. And then there are your meals – meals are the worst difficulty of all. Every day at meal-times you go out, ostensibly to a restaurant, and loaf an hour in the Luxembourg Gardens, watching the pigeons. Afterwards you smuggle your food home in your pockets. Your food is bread and margarine, or bread and wine, and even the nature of the food is governed by lies. You have to buy rye bread instead of household bread, because the rye loaves, though dearer, are round and can be smuggled in your pockets. This wastes you a franc a day. Sometimes, to keep up appearances, you have to spend sixty centimes on a drink, and go correspondingly short of food. Your linen gets filthy, and you run out of soap and razor-blades. Your hair wants cutting, and you try to cut it yourself, with such fearful results that you have to go to the barber after all, and spend the equivalent of a day's food. All day you are telling lies, and expensive lies.

You discover the extreme precariousness of your six francs a day. Mean disasters happen and rob you of food. You have spent your last eighty centimes on half a litre of milk, and are boiling it over the spirit lamp. While it boils a bug runs down your forearm; you give the bug a flick with your nail, and it falls plop! straight into the milk. There is nothing for it but to throw the milk away and go foodless.

You go to the baker's to buy a pound of bread, and you wait while the girl cuts a pound for another customer. She is clumsy, and cuts more than a pound. *'Pardon, monsieur,'* she says, 'I suppose you don't mind paying two sous extra?' Bread is a franc a pound, and you have exactly a franc. When you think that you too might be asked to pay two sous extra, and would have to confess that you could not, you bolt in panic. It is hours before you dare venture into a baker's shop again.

You go to the greengrocer's to spend a franc on a kilogram of potatoes. But one of the pieces that make up the franc is a Belgian piece, and the shopman refuses it. You slink out of the shop, and can never go there again.

You have strayed into a respectable quarter, and you see a prosperous friend coming. To avoid him you dodge into the nearest café. Once in the café you must buy something, so you spend your last fifty centimes on a glass of black coffee with a dead fly in it. One could multiply these disasters by the hundred. They are part of the process of being hard up.

You discover what it is like to be hungry. With bread and margarine in your belly, you go out and look into the shop windows. Everywhere there is food insulting you in huge, wasteful piles; whole dead pigs, baskets of hot loaves, great yellow blocks of butter, strings of sausages, mountains of potatoes, vast Gruyère cheeses like grindstones. A snivelling self-pity comes over you at the sight of so much food. You plan to grab a loaf and run, swallowing it before they catch you; and you refrain, from pure funk.

You discover the boredom which is inseparable from poverty; the times when you have nothing to do and, being underfed, can interest yourself in nothing. For half a day at a time you lie on your bed, feeling like the *jeune squelette* in Baudelaire's poem. Only food could rouse you. You discover that a man who has gone even a week on bread and margarine is not a man any longer, only a belly with a few accessory organs.

This – one could describe it further, but it is all in the same style – is life on six francs a day. Thousands of people in Paris live it – struggling artists and students, prostitutes when their luck is out, out-of-work people of all kinds. It is the suburbs, as it were, of poverty.

I continued in this style for about three weeks. The forty-seven francs were soon gone, and I had to do what I could on thirty-six francs a week from the English lessons. Being inexperienced, I handled the money badly, and sometimes I was a day without food. When this happened I used to sell a few of my clothes, smuggling them out of the hotel in small packets and taking them to a second-hand shop in the Rue de la Montagne St Geneviève. The shopman was a red-haired Jew, an extraordinarily disagreeable man, who used to fall into furious rages at the sight of a client. From his manner one would have supposed that we had done him some injury by coming to him. '*Merde!*' he used to shout, '*you* here again? What do you think this is? A soup kitchen?' And he paid incredibly low prices. For a hat which I had bought for twenty-five shillings and scarcely worn he gave five francs, for a good pair of shoes five francs, for shirts a franc each. He always preferred to exchange rather than buy, and he had a trick of thrusting some useless article into one's hand and then pretending that one had accepted it. Once I saw him take a good overcoat from an old woman, put two white billiard-balls into her hand, and then push her rapidly out of the shop before she could protest. It would have been a pleasure to flatten the Jew's nose, if only one could have afforded it.

These three weeks were squalid and uncomfortable, and evidently there was worse coming, for my rent would be due before long. Nevertheless, things were not a quarter as bad as I had expected. For, when you are approaching poverty, you make one discovery which outweighs some of the others. You discover boredom and mean complications and the beginnings of hunger, but you also discover the great redeeming feature of poverty: the fact that it annihilates the future. Within certain limits, it is actually true that the less money you have, the less you worry. When you have a hundred francs in the world you are liable to the most craven panics. When you have only three francs you are quite indifferent; for three francs will feed you till tomorrow, and you cannot think further than that. You are bored, but you are not afraid. You think vaguely, 'I shall be starving in a day or two – shocking, isn't it?' And then the mind wanders to other topics. A bread and margarine diet does, to some extent, provide its own anodyne.

And there is another feeling that is a great consolation in poverty. I believe everyone who has been hard up has experienced it. It is a feeling of relief, almost of pleasure, at knowing yourself at last genuinely down and out. You have talked so often of going to the dogs – and well, here are the dogs, and you have reached them, and you can stand it. It takes off a lot of anxiety.

IV

One day my English lessons ceased abruptly. The weather was getting hot and one of my pupils, feeling too lazy to go on with his lessons, dismissed me. The other disappeared from his lodgings without notice, owing me twelve francs. I was left with only thirty centimes and no tobacco. For a day and a half I had nothing to eat or smoke, and then, too hungry to put it off any longer, I packed my remaining clothes into my suitcase and took them to the pawnshop. This put an end to all pretence of being in funds, for I could not take my clothes out of the hotel without asking Madame F.'s leave. I remember, however, how surprised she was at my asking her instead of removing the clothes on the sly, shooting the moon being a common trick in our quarter.

It was the first time that I had been into a French pawnshop. One went through grandiose stone portals (marked, of course, '*Liberté, Égalité, Fraternité*' – they write that even over the police stations in France) into a large bare room like a school classroom, with a counter and rows of benches. Forty or fifty people were waiting. One handed one's pledge over the counter and sat down. Presently, when the clerk had assessed its value, he would call out, '*Numéro* such and such, will you take fifty francs?' Sometimes it was only fifteen francs, or ten, or five – whatever it was, the whole room knew it. As I came in the clerk called with an air of offence, '*Numéro 83* – here!' and gave a little whistle and a beckon, as though calling a dog. *Numéro 83* stepped to the counter; he was an old bearded man, with an overcoat buttoned up at the neck and frayed trouser-ends. Without a word the clerk shot the bundle across the counter – evidently it was worth nothing. It fell to the ground and came open, displaying four pairs of men's woollen pants. No one could help laughing. Poor *Numéro 83* gathered up his pants and shambled out, muttering to himself.

The clothes I was pawning, together with the suitcase, had cost over twenty pounds, and were in good condition. I thought they must be worth ten pounds, and a quarter of this (one expects quarter value at a pawnshop) was two hundred and fifty or three hundred francs. I waited without anxiety, expecting two hundred francs at the worst.

At last the clerk called my number: '*Numéro 97!*'

'Yes,' I said, standing up.

'Seventy francs?'

Seventy francs for ten pounds' worth of clothes! But it was no use arguing; I had seen someone else attempt to argue, and the clerk had instantly refused the pledge. I took the money and the pawnticket and walked out. I had now no clothes except what I stood up in – the coat badly out at elbow – an overcoat, moderately pawnable, and one spare shirt. Afterwards, when it was too late, I learned that it is wiser to go to a pawnshop in the afternoon. The clerks are French, and, like most French people, are in a bad temper till they have eaten their lunch.

When I got home, Madame F. was sweeping the *bistro* floor. She came up the steps to meet me. I could see in her eye that she was uneasy about my rent.

'Well,' she said, 'what did you get for your clothes? Not much, eh?'

'Two hundred francs,' I said promptly.

'*Tiens!*' she said, surprised; 'well, *that's* not bad. How expensive those English clothes must be!'

The lie saved a lot of trouble, and, strangely enough, it came true. A few days later I did receive exactly two hundred francs due to me for a newspaper article, and, though it hurt to do it, I at once paid every penny of it in rent. So, though I came near to starving in the following weeks, I was hardly ever without a roof.

It was now absolutely necessary to find work, and I remembered a friend of mine, a Russian waiter named Boris, who might be able to help me. I had first met him in the public ward of a hospital, where he was being treated for arthritis in the left leg. He had told me to come to him if I were ever in difficulties.

I must say something about Boris, for he was a curious character and my close friend for a long time. He was a big, soldierly man of about thirty-five, and had been good-looking, but since his illness he had grown immensely fat from lying in bed. Like most Russian refugees, he had had an adventurous life. His parents, killed in the Revolution, had been rich people, and he had served through the war in the Second Siberian Rifles, which, according to him, was the best regiment in the Russian Army. After the war he had first worked in a brush factory, then as a porter at Les Halles, then had become a dishwasher, and had finally worked his way up to be a waiter. When he fell ill he was at the Hôtel Scribe, and taking a hundred francs a day in tips. His ambition was to become a *maître d'hôtel*, save fifty thousand francs, and set up a small, select restaurant on the Right Bank.

Boris always talked of the war as the happiest time of his life. War and soldiering were his passion; he had read innumerable books of strategy and military history, and could tell you all about the theories of Napoleon, Kutuzof, Clausewitz, Moltke and Foch. Anything to do with soldiers pleased him. His favourite café was the Closerie des Lilas in Montparnasse, simply because the statue of Marshal Ney stands outside it. Later on, Boris and I sometimes went to the Rue du Commerce together. If we went by Metro, Boris always got out at Cambronne station instead of Commerce, though Commerce was nearer; he liked the association with General Cambronne, who was called on to surrender at Waterloo, and answered simply, '*Merde!*'

The only things left to Boris by the Revolution were his medals and some photographs of his old regiment; he had kept these when everything else went to the pawnshop. Almost every day he would spread the photographs out on the bed and talk about them:

'*Voilà, mon ami!* There you see me at the head of my company. Fine big men, eh? Not like these little rats of Frenchmen. A captain at twenty – not bad, eh? Yes, a captain in the Second Siberian Rifles; and my father was a colonel.

'*Ah, mais, mon ami*, the ups and downs of life! A captain in the Russian Army, and then, piff! the Revolution – every penny gone. In 1916 I stayed a week at the Hôtel Edouard Sept; in 1920 I was trying for a job as night watchman there. I have been night watchman, cellarman, floor scrubber, dishwasher, porter, lavatory attendant. I have tipped waiters, and I have been tipped by waiters.

'Ah, but I have known what it is to live like a gentleman, *mon ami*. I do not say it to boast, but the other day I was trying to compute how many mistresses I have had in my life, and I made it out to be over two hundred. Yes, at least two hundred . . . Ah, well, *ça reviendra.* Victory is to him who fights the longest. Courage!' etc. etc.

Boris had a queer, changeable nature. He always wished himself back in the army, but he had also been a waiter long enough to acquire the waiter's outlook. Though he had never saved more than a few thousand francs, he took it for granted that in the end he would be able to set up his own restaurant and grow rich. All waiters, I afterwards found, talk and think of this; it is what reconciles them to being waiters. Boris used to talk interestingly about hotel life:

'Waiting is a gamble,' he used to say; 'you may die poor, you may make your fortune in a year. You are not paid wages, you depend on tips – ten per cent. of the bill, and a commission from the wine companies on champagne corks. Sometimes the tips are enormous. The barman at Maxim's, for instance, makes five hundred francs a day. More than five hundred, in the season . . . I have made two hundred francs a day myself. It was at a hotel in Biarritz, in the season. The whole staff, from the manager down to the *plongeurs*, was working twenty-one hours a day. Twenty-one hours' work and two and a half hours in bed, for a month on end. Still, it was worth it, at two hundred francs a day.

'You never know when a stroke of luck is coming. Once when I was at the Hôtel Royal an American customer sent for me before dinner and ordered twenty-four brandy cocktails. I brought them all together on a tray, in twenty-four glasses. "Now, *garçon*," said the customer (he was drunk), "I'll drink twelve and you'll drink twelve, and if you can walk to the door afterwards you get a hundred francs." I walked to the door, and he gave me a hundred francs. And every night for six days he did the same thing; twelve brandy cocktails, then a hundred francs. A few months later I heard he had been extradited by the American Government – embezzlement. There is something fine, do you not think, about these Americans?'

I liked Boris, and we had interesting times together, playing chess and talking about war and hotels. Boris used often to suggest that I should become a waiter. 'The life would suit you,' he used to say; 'when you are in work, with a hundred francs a day and a nice mistress, it's not bad. You say you go in for writing. Writing is bosh. There is only one way to make money at writing, and that is to marry a publisher's daughter. But you would make a good waiter if you shaved that moustache off. You are tall and you speak English – those are the chief things a waiter needs. Wait till I can bend this accursed leg, *mon ami*. And then, if you are ever out of a job, come to me.'

Now that I was short of my rent, and getting hungry, I remembered Boris's promise, and decided to look him up at once. I did not hope to become a waiter so easily as he had promised, but of course I knew how to scrub dishes, and no doubt he could get me a job in the kitchen. He had said that dishwashing jobs were to be had for the asking during the summer. It was a great relief to remember that I had after all one influential friend to fall back on.

v

A short time before, Boris had given me an address in the Rue du Marché des Blancs Manteaux. All he had said in his letter was that 'things were not marching too badly', and I assumed that he was back at the Hôtel Scribe, touching his hundred francs a day. I was full of hope, and wondered why I had been fool enough not to go to Boris before. I saw myself in a cosy restaurant, with jolly cooks singing love-songs as they broke eggs into the pan, and five solid meals a day. I even squandered two francs fifty on a packet of Gauloises Bleu, in anticipation of my wages.

In the morning I walked down to the Rue du Marché des Blancs Manteaux; with a shock, I found it a slummy back street as bad as my own. Boris's hotel was the dirtiest hotel in the street. From its dark doorway there came out a vile sour odour, a mixture of slops and synthetic soup – it was Bouillon Zip, twenty-five centimes a packet. A misgiving came over me. People who drink Bouillon Zip are starving, or near it. Could Boris possibly be earning a hundred francs a day? A surly *patron*, sitting in the office, said to me, Yes, the Russian was at home – in the attic. I went up six flights of narrow, winding stairs, the Bouillon Zip growing stronger as one got higher. Boris did not answer when I knocked at his door, so I opened it and went in.

The room was an attic ten feet square, lighted only by a skylight, its sole furniture a narrow iron bedstead, a chair, and a washhandstand with one game leg. A long S-shaped chain of bugs marched slowly across the wall above the bed. Boris was lying asleep, naked, his large belly making a mound under the grimy sheet. His chest was spotted with insect bites. As I came in he woke up, rubbed his eyes, and groaned deeply.

'Name of Jesus Christ!' he exclaimed, 'oh, name of Jesus Christ, my back! Curse it, I believe my back is broken!'

'What's the matter?' I exclaimed.

'My back is broken, that is all. I have spent the night on the floor. Oh, name of Jesus Christ! If you knew what my back feels like!'

'My dear Boris, are you ill?'

'Not ill, only starving – yes, starving to death if this goes on much longer. Besides sleeping on the floor, I have lived on two francs a day for weeks past. It is fearful. You have come at a bad moment, *mon ami.*'

It did not seem much use to ask whether Boris still had his job at the Hôtel Scribe. I hurried downstairs and bought a loaf of bread. Boris threw himself on the bread and ate half of it, after which he felt better, sat up in bed, and told me what was the matter with him. He had failed to get a job after leaving the hospital, because he was still very lame, and he had spent all his money and pawned everything, and finally starved for several days. He had slept a week on the quay under the Pont d'Austerlitz, among some empty wine barrels. For the past fortnight he had been living in this room, together with a Jew, a mechanic. It appeared (there was some complicated explanation) that the Jew owed Boris three hundred francs, and was repaying this by letting him sleep on the floor and allowing him two francs a day for food. Two francs would buy a bowl of coffee and three rolls. The Jew went to work at seven in the mornings, and after that Boris would leave his sleeping-place (it was beneath the skylight, which let in the rain) and get into the bed. He could not sleep much even there, owing to the bugs, but it rested his back after the floor.

It was a great disappointment, when I had come to Boris for help, to find him even worse off than myself. I explained that I had only about sixty francs left and must get a job immediately. By this time, however, Boris had eaten the rest of the bread and was feeling cheerful and talkative. He said carelessly:

'Good heavens, what are you worrying about? Sixty francs – why, it's a fortune! Please hand me that shoe, *mon ami*. I'm going to smash some of those bugs if they come within reach.'

'But do you think there's any chance of getting a job?'

'Chance? It's a certainty. In fact, I have got something already. There is a new Russian restaurant which is to open in a few days in the Rue du Commerce. It is *une chose entendue* that I am to be *maître d'hôtel*. I can easily get you a job in the kitchen. Five hundred francs a month and your food – tips, too, if you are lucky.'

'But in the meantime? I've got to pay my rent before long.'

'Oh, we shall find something. I have got a few cards up my sleeve. There are people who owe me money, for instance – Paris is full of them. One of them is bound to pay up before long. Then, think of all the women who have been my mistress! A woman never forgets, you know – I have only to ask and they will help me. Besides, the Jew tells me he is going to steal some magnetos from the garage where he works, and he will pay us five francs a day to clean them before he sells them. That alone would keep us. Never worry, *mon ami*. Nothing is easier to get than money.'

'Well, let's go out now and look for a job.'

'Presently, *mon ami*. We shan't starve, don't you fear. This is only the fortune of war – I've been in a worse hole scores of times. It's only a question of persisting. Remember Foch's maxim: "*Attaquez! Attaquez! Attaquez!*"'

It was midday before Boris decided to get up. All the clothes he now had left were one suit, with one shirt, collar and tie, a pair of shoes almost worn out, and a pair of socks all holes. He had also an overcoat which was to be pawned in the last extremity. He had a suitcase, a wretched twenty-franc cardboard thing, but very important, because the *patron* of the hotel believed that it was full of clothes – without that, he would probably have turned Boris out of doors. What it actually contained were the medals and photographs, various odds and ends, and huge bundles of love-letters. In spite of all this Boris managed to keep a fairly smart appearance. He shaved without soap and with a razor-blade two months old, tied his tie so that the holes did not show, and carefully stuffed the soles of his shoes with newspaper. Finally, when he was dressed, he produced an ink-bottle and inked the skin of his ankles where it showed through his socks. You would never have thought, when it was finished, that he had recently been sleeping under the Seine bridges.

We went to a small café off the Rue de Rivoli, a well-known rendezvous of hotel managers and employees. At the back was a dark, cave-like room where all kinds of hotel workers were sitting – smart young waiters, others not so smart and clearly hungry, fat pink cooks, greasy dishwashers, battered old scrubbing-women. Everyone had an untouched glass of black coffee in front of him. The place was, in effect, an employment bureau, and the money spent on drinks was the *patron*'s commission. Sometimes a stout, important-looking man, obviously a restaurateur, would come in and speak to the barman, and the barman would call to one of the people at the back of the café. But he never called to Boris or me, and we left after two hours, as the etiquette was that you could only stay two hours for one drink. We learned afterwards, when it was too late, that the dodge was to bribe the barman; if you could afford twenty francs he would generally get you a job.

We went to the Hôtel Scribe and waited an hour on the pavement, hoping that the manager would come out, but he never did. Then we dragged ourselves down to the Rue du Commerce, only to find that the new restaurant, which was being redecorated, was shut up and the *patron* away. It was now night. We had walked fourteen kilometres over pavement, and we were so tired that we had to waste one franc fifty on going home by Metro. Walking was agony to Boris with his game leg, and his optimism wore thinner and thinner as the day went on. When we got out of the Metro at the Place d'Italie he was in despair. He began to say that it was no use looking for work – there was nothing for it but to try crime.

'Sooner rob than starve, *mon ami*. I have often planned it. A fat, rich American – some dark corner down Montparnasse way – a cobblestone in a stocking – bang! And then go through his pockets and bolt. It is feasible, do you not think? I would not flinch – I have been a soldier, remember.'

He decided against the plan in the end, because we were both foreigners and easily recognised.

When we had got back to my room we spent another one franc fifty on bread and chocolate. Boris devoured his share, and at once cheered up like magic; food seemed to act on his system as rapidly as a cocktail. He took out a pencil and began making a list of the people who would probably give us jobs. There were dozens of them, he said.

'Tomorrow we shall find something, *mon ami*, I know it in my bones. The luck always changes. Besides, we both have brains – a man with brains can't starve.

'What things a man can do with brains! Brains will make money out of anything. I had a friend once, a Pole, a real man of genius; and what do you think he used to do? He would buy a gold ring and pawn it for fifteen francs. Then – you know how carelessly the clerks fill up the tickets – where the clerk had written *"en or"* he would add *"et diamants"* and he would change "fifteen francs" to "fifteen thousand". Neat, eh? Then, you see, he could borrow a thousand francs on the security of the ticket. That is what I mean by brains . . .'

For the rest of the evening Boris was in a hopeful mood, talking of the times we should have together when we were waiters together at Nice or Biarritz, with smart rooms and enough money to set up mistresses. He was too tired to walk the three kilometres back to his hotel, and slept the night on the floor of my room, with his coat rolled round his shoes for a pillow.

VI

We again failed to find work the next day, and it was three weeks before the luck changed. My two hundred francs saved me from trouble about the rent, but everything else went as badly as possible. Day after day Boris and I went up and down Paris, drifting at two miles an hour through the crowds, bored and hungry, and finding nothing. One day, I remember, we crossed the Seine eleven times. We loitered for hours outside service doorways, and when the manager came out we would go up to him ingratiatingly, cap in hand. We always got the same answer: they did not want a lame man, nor a man without experience. Once we were very nearly engaged. While he spoke to the manager Boris stood straight upright, not supporting himself with his stick, and the manager did not see that he was lame. 'Yes,' he said, 'we want two men in the cellars. Perhaps you would do. Come inside.' Then Boris moved, and the game was up. 'Ah,' said the manager, 'you limp. *Malheureusement—*'

We enrolled our names at agencies and answered advertisements, but walking everywhere made us slow, and we seemed to miss every job by half an hour. Once we very nearly got a job swabbing out railway trucks, but at the last moment they rejected us in favour of Frenchmen. Once we answered an advertisement calling for hands at a circus. You had to shift benches and clean up litter, and, during the performance, stand on two tubs and let a lion jump through your legs. When we got to the place, an hour before the time named, we found a queue of fifty men already waiting. There is some attraction in lions, evidently.

Once an agency to which I had applied months earlier sent me a *petit bleu*, telling me of an Italian gentleman who wanted English lessons. The *petit bleu* said 'Come at once' and promised twenty francs an hour. Boris and I were in despair. Here was a splendid chance, and I could not take it, for it was impossible to go to the agency with my coat out at elbow. Then it occurred to us that I could wear Boris's coat – it did not match my trousers, but the trousers were grey and might pass for flannel at a short distance. The coat was so much too big for me that I had to wear it unbuttoned and keep one hand in my pocket. I hurried out, and wasted seventy-five centimes on a bus fare to get to the agency. When I got there I found that the Italian had changed his mind and left Paris.

Once Boris suggested that I should go to Les Halles and try for a job as a porter. I arrived at half-past four in the morning, when the work was getting into its swing. Seeing a short fat man in a bowler hat directing some porters, I went up to him and asked for work. Before answering he seized my right hand and felt the palm.

'You are strong, eh?' he said.

'Very strong,' I said untruly.

'*Bien.* Let me see you lift that crate.'

It was a huge wicker basket full of potatoes. I took hold of it, and found that, so far from lifting it, I could not even move it. The man in the bowler hat watched me, then shrugged his shoulders and turned away. I made off. When I had gone some distance I looked back and saw *four* men lifting the basket onto a cart. It weighed three hundredweight, possibly. The man had seen that I was no use, and taken this way of getting rid of me.

Sometimes in his hopeful moments Boris spent fifty centimes on a stamp and wrote to one of his ex-mistresses, asking for money. Only one of them ever replied. It was a woman who, besides having been his mistress, owed him two hundred francs. When Boris saw the letter waiting and recognised the handwriting, he was wild with hope. We seized the letter and rushed up to Boris's room to read it, like a child with stolen sweets. Boris read the letter, then handed it silently to me. It ran:

My Little Cherished Wolf,

With what delight did I open thy charming letter, reminding me of the days of our perfect love, and of the so dear kisses which I have received from thy lips. Such memories linger for ever in the heart, like the perfume of a flower that is dead.

As to thy request for two hundred francs, alas! it is impossible. Thou dost not know, my dear one, how I am desolated to hear of thy embarrassments. But what wouldst thou? In this life which is so sad, trouble comes to everyone. I too have had my share. My little sister has been ill (ah, the poor little one, how she suffered!) and we are obliged to pay I know not what to the doctor. All our money is gone and we are passing, I assure thee, very difficult days.

Courage, my little wolf, always the courage! Remember that the bad days are not for ever, and the trouble which seems so terrible will disappear at last.

Rest assured, my dear one, that I will remember thee always. And receive the most sincere embraces of her who has never ceased to love thee, thy

Yvonne.

This letter disappointed Boris so much that he went straight to bed and would not look for work again that day.

My sixty francs lasted about a fortnight. I had given up the pretence of going out to restaurants, and we used to eat in my room, one of us sitting on the bed and the other on the chair. Boris would contribute his two francs and I three or four francs, and we would buy bread, potatoes, milk and cheese, and make soup over my spirit lamp. We had a saucepan and a coffee-bowl and one spoon; every day there was a polite squabble as to who should eat out of the saucepan and who out of the coffee-bowl (the saucepan held more), and every day, to my secret anger, Boris gave in first and had the saucepan. Sometimes we had more bread in the evening, sometimes not. Our linen was getting filthy, and it was three weeks since I had had a bath; Boris, so he said, had not had a bath for months. It was tobacco that made everything tolerable. We had plenty of tobacco, for some time before Boris had met a soldier (the soldiers are given their tobacco free) and bought twenty or thirty packets at fifty centimes each.

All this was far worse for Boris than for me. The walking and sleeping on the floor kept his leg and back in constant pain, and with his vast Russian appetite he suffered torments of hunger, though he never seemed to grow thinner. On the whole he was surprisingly gay, and he had vast capacities for hope. He used to say seriously that he had a patron saint who watched over him, and when things were very bad he would search the gutter for money, saying that the saint often dropped a two-franc piece there. One day we were waiting in the Rue Royale; there was a Russian restaurant near by, and we were going to ask for a job there. Suddenly Boris made up his mind to go into the Madeleine and burn a fifty-centime candle to his patron saint. Then, coming out, he said that he would be on the safe side, and solemnly put a match to a fifty-centime stamp, as a sacrifice to the immortal gods. Perhaps the gods and the saints did not get on together; at any rate, we missed the job.

On some mornings Boris collapsed in the most utter despair. He would lie in bed almost weeping, cursing the Jew with whom he lived. Of late the Jew had become restive about paying the daily two francs, and, what was worse, had begun putting on intolerable airs of patronage. Boris said that I, as an Englishman, could not conceive what torture it was to a Russian of family to be at the mercy of a Jew.

'A Jew, *mon ami*, a veritable Jew! And he hasn't even the decency to be ashamed of it. To think that I, a captain in the Russian Army – have I ever told you, *mon ami*, that I was a captain in the Second Siberian Rifles? Yes, a captain, and my father was a colonel. And here I am, eating the bread of a Jew. A Jew . . .

'I will tell you what Jews are like. Once, in the early months of the war, we were on the march, and we had halted at a village for the night. A horrible old Jew, with a red beard like Judas Iscariot, came sneaking up to my billet. I asked him what he wanted. "Your honour," he said, "I have brought a girl for you, a beautiful young girl only seventeen. It will only be fifty francs." "Thank you," I said, "you can take her away again. I don't want to catch any diseases." "Diseases!" cried the Jew, "*mais, monsieur le capitaine*, there's no fear of that. It's my own daughter!" That is the Jewish national character for you.

'Have I ever told you, *mon ami*, that in the old Russian Army it was considered bad form to spit on a Jew? Yes, we thought a Russian officer's spittle was too precious to be wasted on Jews . . .' etc. etc.

On these days Boris usually declared himself too ill to go out and look for work. He would lie till evening in the greyish, verminous sheets, smoking and reading old newspapers. Sometimes we played chess. We had no board, but we wrote down the moves on a piece of paper, and afterwards we made a board from the side of a packing-case, and a set of men from buttons, Belgian coins and the like. Boris, like many Russians, had a passion for chess. It was a saying of his that the rules of chess are the same as the rules of love and war, and that if you can win at one you can win at the others. But he also said that if you have a chessboard you do not mind being hungry, which was certainly not true in my case.

VII

My money oozed away – to eight francs, to four francs, to one franc, to twenty-five centimes; and twenty-five centimes is useless, for it will buy nothing except a newspaper. We went several days on dry bread, and then I was two and a half days with nothing to eat whatever. This was an ugly experience. There are people who do fasting cures of three weeks or more, and they say that fasting is quite pleasant after the fourth day; I do not know, never having gone beyond the third day. Probably it seems different when one is doing it voluntarily and is not underfed at the start.

The first day, too inert to look for work, I borrowed a rod and went fishing in the Seine, baiting with blue-bottles. I hoped to catch enough for a meal, but of course I did not. The Seine is full of dace, but they grew cunning during the siege of Paris, and none of them has been caught since, except in nets. On the second day I thought of pawning my overcoat, but it seemed too far to walk to the pawnshop, and I spent the day in bed, reading the *Memoirs of Sherlock Holmes*. It was all that I felt equal to, without food. Hunger reduces one to an utterly spineless, brainless condition, more like the after-effects of influenza than anything else. It is as though one had been turned into a jellyfish, or as though all one's blood had been pumped out and lukewarm water substituted. Complete inertia is my chief memory of hunger; that, and being obliged to spit very frequently, and the spittle being curiously white and flocculent, like cuckoo-spit. I do not know the reason for this, but everyone who has gone hungry several days has noticed it.

On the third morning I felt very much better. I realised that I must do something at once, and I decided to go and ask Boris to let me share his two francs, at any rate for a day or two. When I arrived I found Boris in bed, and furiously angry. As soon as I came in he burst out, almost choking:

'He has taken it back, the dirty thief! He has taken it back!'

'Who's taken what?' I said.

'The Jew! Taken my two francs, the dog, the thief! He robbed me in my sleep!'

It appeared that on the previous night the Jew had flatly refused to pay the daily two francs. They had argued and argued, and at last the Jew had consented to hand over the money; he had done it, Boris said, in the most offensive manner, making a little speech about how kind he was, and extorting abject gratitude. And then in the morning he had stolen the money back before Boris was awake.

This was a blow. I was horribly disappointed, for I had allowed my belly to expect food, a great mistake when one is hungry. However, rather to my surprise, Boris was far from despairing. He sat up in bed, lighted his pipe and reviewed the situation.

'Now listen, *mon ami*, this is a tight corner. We have only twenty-five centimes between us, and I don't suppose the Jew will ever pay my two francs again. In any case his behaviour is becoming intolerable. Will you believe it, the other night he had the indecency to bring a woman in here, while I was there on the floor. The low animal! And I have a worse thing to tell you. The Jew intends clearing out of here. He owes a week's rent, and his idea is to avoid paying that and give me the slip at the same time. If the Jew shoots the moon I shall be left without a roof, and the *patron* will take my suitcase in lieu of rent, curse him! We have got to make a vigorous move.'

'All right. But what can we do? It seems to me that the only thing is to pawn our overcoats and get some food.'

'We'll do that, of course, but I must get my possessions out of this house first. To think of my photographs being seized! Well, my plan is ready. I'm going to forestall the Jew and shoot the moon myself. *Foutre le camp* – retreat, you understand. I think that is the correct move, eh?'

'But my dear Boris, how can you, in daytime? You're bound to be caught.'

'Ah well, it will need strategy, of course. Our *patron* is on the watch for people slipping out without paying their rent; he's been had that way before. He and his wife take it in turns all day to sit in the office – what misers, these Frenchmen! But I have thought of a way to do it, if you will help.'

I did not feel in a very helpful mood, but I asked Boris what his plan was. He explained it carefully.

'Now listen. We must start by pawning our overcoats. First go back to your room and fetch your overcoat, then come back here and fetch mine, and smuggle it out under cover of yours. Take them to the pawnshop in the Rue des Francs Bourgeois. You ought to get twenty francs for the two, with luck. Then go down to the Seine bank and fill your pockets with stones, and bring them back and put them in my suitcase. You see the idea? I shall wrap as many of my things as I can carry in a newspaper, and go down and ask the *patron* the way to the nearest laundry. I shall be very brazen and casual, you understand, and of course the *patron* will think the bundle is nothing but dirty linen. Or if he does suspect anything, he will do what he always does, the mean sneak; he will go up to my room and feel the weight of my suitcase. And when he feels the weight of stones he will think it is still full. Strategy, eh? Then afterwards I can come back and carry my other things out in my pockets.'

'But what about the suitcase?'

'Oh, that? We shall have to abandon it. The miserable thing only cost twenty francs. Besides, one always abandons something in a retreat. Look at Napoleon at the Beresina! He abandoned his whole army.'

Boris was so pleased with this scheme (he called it *une ruse de guerre*) that he almost forgot being hungry. Its main weakness – that he would have nowhere to sleep after shooting the moon – he ignored.

At first the *ruse de guerre* worked well. I went home and fetched my overcoat (that made already nine kilometres, on an empty belly) and smuggled Boris's coat out successfully. Then a hitch occured. The receiver at the pawnshop, a nasty sour-faced interfering little man – a typical French official – refused the coats on the ground that they were not wrapped up in anything. He said that they must be put either in a valise or a cardboard box. This spoiled everything, for we had no box of any kind, and with only twenty-five centimes between us we could not buy one.

I went back and told Boris the bad news. '*Merde!*' he said, 'that makes it awkward. Well, no matter, there is always a way. We'll put the overcoats in my suitcase.'

'But how are we to get the suitcase past the *patron*? He's sitting almost in the door of the office. It's impossible!'

'How easily you despair, *mon ami!* Where is that English obstinacy that I have read of? Courage! We'll manage it.'

Boris thought for a little while, and then produced another cunning plan. The essential difficulty was to hold the *patron*'s attention for perhaps five seconds, while we could slip past with the suitcase. But, as it happened, the *patron* had just one weak spot – that he was interested in *Le Sport*, and was ready to talk if you approached him on this subject. Boris read an article about bicycle races in an old copy of the *Petit Parisien*, and then, when we had reconnoitred the stairs, went down and managed to set the *patron* talking. Meanwhile I waited at the foot of the stairs, with the overcoats under one arm and the suitcase under the other. Boris was to give a cough when he thought the moment favourable. I waited trembling, for at any moment the *patron*'s wife might come out of the door opposite the office, and then the game was up. However, presently Boris coughed. I sneaked rapidly past the office and out into the street, rejoicing that my shoes did not creak. The plan might have failed if Boris had been thinner, for his big shoulders blocked the doorway of the office. His nerve was splendid, too; he went on laughing and talking in the most casual way, and so loud that he quite covered any noise I made. When I was well away he came and joined me round the corner, and we bolted.

And then, after all our trouble, the receiver at the pawnshop again refused the overcoats. He told me (one could see his French soul revelling in the pedantry of it) that I had not sufficient papers of identification; my *carte d'identité* was not enough, and I must show a passport or addressed envelopes. Boris had addressed envelopes by the score, but his *carte d'identité* was out of order (he never renewed it, so as to avoid the tax), so we could not pawn the overcoats in his name. All we could do was to trudge up to my room, get the necessary papers, and take the coats to the pawnshop in the Boulevard Port Royal.

I left Boris at my room and went down to the pawnshop. When I got there I found that it was shut and would not open till four in the afternoon. It was now about half-past one, and I had walked twelve kilometres and had had no food for sixty hours. Fate seemed to be playing a series of extraordinarily unamusing jokes.

Then the luck changed as though by a miracle. I was walking home through the Rue Broca, when suddenly, glittering on the cobbles, I saw a five-sou piece. I pounced on it, hurried home, got our other five-sou piece, and bought a pound of potatoes. There was only enough alcohol in the stove to parboil them, and we had no salt, but we wolfed them skins and all. After that we felt like new men, and sat playing chess till the pawnshop opened.

At four o'clock I went back to the pawnshop. I was not hopeful, for if I had only got seventy francs before, what could I expect for two shabby overcoats in a cardboard suitcase? Boris had said twenty francs, but I thought it would be ten francs, or even five. Worse yet, I might be refused altogether, like poor *Numéro 83* on the previous occasion. I sat on the front bench, so as not to see people laughing when the clerk said five francs.

At last the clerk called my number: '*Numéro 117!*'

'Yes,' I said, standing up

'Fifty francs?'

It was almost as great a shock as the seventy francs had been the time before. I believe now that the clerk had mixed my number up with someone else's, for one could not have sold the coats outright for fifty francs. I hurried home and walked into my room with my hands behind my back, saying nothing. Boris was playing with the chessboard. He looked up eagerly.

'What did you get?' he exclaimed. 'What, not twenty francs? Surely you got ten francs, anyway? *Nom de Dieu*, five francs – that is a bit too thick. *Mon ami, don't* say it was five francs. If you say it was five francs I shall really begin to think of suicide.'

I threw the fifty-franc note onto the table. Boris turned white as chalk, and then, springing up, seized my hand and gave it a grip that almost broke the bones. We ran out, bought bread and wine, a piece of meat and alcohol for the stove, and gorged.

After eating, Boris became more optimistic than I had ever known him. 'What did I tell you?' he said. 'The fortune of war! This morning with five sous, and now look at us. I have always said it, there is nothing easier to get than money. And that reminds me, I have a friend in the Rue Fondary whom we might go and see. He has cheated me of four thousand francs, the thief. He is the greatest thief alive when he is sober, but it is a curious thing, he is quite honest when he is drunk. I should think he would be drunk by six in the evening. Let's go and find him. Very likely he will pay up a hundred on account. *Merde!* He might pay two hundred. *Allons-y!*'

We went to the Rue Fondary and found the man, and he was drunk, but we did not get our hundred francs. As soon as he and Boris met there was a terrible altercation on the pavement. The other man declared that he did not owe Boris a penny, but that on the contrary Boris owed *him* four thousand francs, and both of them kept appealing to me for my opinion. I never understood the rights of the matter. The two argued and argued, first in the street, then in a *bistro*, then in a *prix fixe* restaurant where we went for dinner, then in another *bistro*. Finally, having called one another thieves for two hours, they went off together on a drinking bout that finished up the last sou of Boris's money.

Boris slept the night at the house of a cobbler, another Russian refugee, in the Commerce quarter. Meanwhile I had eight francs left, and plenty of cigarettes, and was stuffed to the eyes with food and drink. It was a marvellous change for the better after two bad days.

VIII

We had now twenty-eight francs in hand, and could start looking for work once more. Boris was still sleeping, on some mysterious terms, at the house of the cobbler, and he had managed to borrow another twenty francs from a Russian friend. He had friends, mostly ex-officers like himself, here and there all over Paris. Some were waiters or dishwashers, some drove taxis, a few lived on women, some had managed to bring money away from Russia and owned garages or dancing-halls. In general, the Russian refugees in Paris are hard-working people, and have put up with their bad luck far better than one can imagine Englishmen of the same class doing. There are exceptions, of course. Boris told me of an exiled Russian duke whom he had once met, who frequented expensive restaurants. The duke would find out if there was a Russian officer among the waiters, and, after he had dined, call him in a friendly way to his table.

'Ah,' the duke would say, 'so you are an old soldier, like myself? These are bad days, eh? Well, well, the Russian soldier fears nothing. And what was your regiment?'

'The so-and-so, sir,' the waiter would answer.

'A very gallant regiment! I inspected them in 1912. By the way, I have unfortunately left my notecase at home. A Russian officer will, I know, oblige me with three hundred francs.'

If the waiter had three hundred francs he would hand it over, and, of course, never see it again. The duke made quite a lot in this way. Probably the waiters did not mind being swindled. A duke is a duke, even in exile.

It was through one of these Russian refugees that Boris heard of something which seemed to promise money. Two days after we had pawned the overcoats, Boris said to me rather mysteriously:

'Tell me, *mon ami*, have you any political opinions?'

'No,' I said.

'Neither have I. Of course, one is always a patriot; but still — Did not Moses say something about spoiling the Egyptians? As an Englishman you will have read the Bible. What I mean is, would you object to earning money from Communists?'

'No, of course not.'

'Well, it appears that there is a Russian secret society in Paris who might do something for us. They are Communists; in fact they are agents for the Bolsheviks. They act as a friendly society, get in touch with exiled Russians, and try to get them to turn Bolshevik. My friend has joined their society, and he thinks they would help us if we went to them.'

'But what can they do for us? In any case they won't help me, as I'm not a Russian.'

'That is just the point. It seems that they are correspondents for a Moscow paper, and they want some articles on English politics. If we go to them at once they may commission you to write the articles.'

'Me? But I don't know anything about politics.'

'*Merde!* Neither do they. Who *does* know anything about politics? It's easy. All you have to do is to copy it out of the English papers. Isn't there a Paris *Daily Mail*? Copy it from that.'

'But the *Daily Mail* is a Conservative paper. They loathe the Communists.'

'Well, say the opposite of what the *Daily Mail* says, then you *can't* be wrong. We mustn't throw this chance away, *mon ami*. It might mean hundreds of francs.'

I did not at all like the idea, for the Paris police are very hard on Communists, especially if they are foreigners, and I was already under suspicion. Some months before, a detective had seen me come out of the office of a Communist weekly paper, and I had had a great deal of trouble with the police. If they caught me going to this secret society, it might mean deportation. However, the chance seemed too good to be missed. That afternoon Boris's friend, another waiter, came to take us to the rendezvous. I cannot remember the name of the street – it was a shabby street running south from the Seine bank, somewhere near the Chamber of Deputies. Boris's friend insisted on great caution. We loitered casually down the street, marked the doorway we were to enter – it was a laundry – and then strolled back again, keeping an eye on all the windows and cafés. If the place were known as a haunt of Communists it was probably watched, and we intended to go home if we saw anyone at all like a detective. I was frightened, but Boris enjoyed these conspiratorial proceedings, and quite forgot that he was about to trade with the slayers of his parents.

When we were certain that the coast was clear we dived quickly into the doorway. In the laundry was a Frenchwoman ironing clothes, who told us that 'the Russian gentlemen' lived up a staircase across the courtyard. We went up several flights of dark stairs and emerged onto a landing. A strong, surly-looking young man, with hair growing low on his head, was standing at the top of the stairs. As I came up he looked at me suspiciously, barred the way with his arm and said something in Russian.

'*Mot d'ordre!*' he said sharply when I did not answer.

I stopped, startled. I had not expected passwords.

'*Mot d'ordre!*' repeated the Russian.

Boris's friend, who was walking behind, now came forward and said something in Russian, either the password or an explanation. At this the surly young man seemed satisfied, and led us into a small shabby room with frosted windows. It was like a very poverty-stricken office, with propaganda posters in Russian lettering and a huge, crude picture of Lenin tacked on the walls. At the table sat an unshaven Russian in shirt sleeves, addressing newspaper wrappers from a pile in front of him. As I came in he spoke to me in French, with a bad accent.

'This is very careless!' he exclaimed fussily. 'Why have you come here without a parcel of washing?'

'Washing?'

'Everybody who comes here brings washing. It looks as though they were going to the laundry downstairs. Bring a good large bundle next time. We don't want the police on our tracks.'

This was even more conspiratorial than I had expected. Boris sat down in the only vacant chair, and there was a great deal of talking in Russian. Only the unshaven man talked; the surly one leaned against the wall with his eyes on me, as though he still suspected me. It was queer, standing in the little secret room with its revolutionary posters, listening to a conversation of which I did not understand a word. The Russians talked quickly and eagerly, with smiles and shrugs of the shoulders. I wondered what it was all about. They would be calling each other 'little father', I thought, and 'little dove', and 'Ivan Alexandrovitch', like the characters in Russian novels. And the talk would be of revolutions. The unshaven man would be saying firmly, 'We never argue. Controversy is a bourgeois pastime. Deeds are our arguments.' Then I gathered that it was not this exactly. Twenty francs was being demanded, for an entrance fee apparently, and Boris was promising to pay it (we had just seventeen francs in the world). Finally Boris produced our precious store of money and paid five francs on account.

At this the surly man looked less suspicious, and sat down on the edge of the table. The unshaven one began to question me in French, making notes on a slip of paper. Was I a Communist? he asked. By sympathy, I answered; I had never joined any organisation. Did I understand the political situation in England? Oh, of course, of course. I mentioned the names of various Ministers, and made some contemptuous remarks about the Labour Party. And what about *Le Sport*? Could I do articles on *Le Sport*? (Football and Socialism have some mysterious connection on the Continent.) Oh, of course, again. Both men nodded gravely. The unshaven one said:

'*Évidemment*, you have a thorough knowledge of conditions in England. Could you undertake to write a series of articles for a Moscow weekly paper? We will give you the particulars.'

'Certainly.'

'Then, comrade, you will hear from us by the first post tomorrow. Or possibly the second post. Our rate of pay is a hundred and fifty francs an article. Remember to bring a parcel of washing next time you come. *Au revoir*, comrade.'

We went downstairs, looked carefully out of the laundry to see that there was no one in the street, and slipped out. Boris was wild with joy. In a sort of sacrificial ecstasy he rushed into the nearest tobacconist's and spent fifty centimes on a cigar. He came out thumping his stick on the pavement and beaming.

'At last! At last! Now, *mon ami*, our fortune really *is* made. You took them in finely. Did you hear him call you comrade? A hundred and fifty francs an article – *Nom de Dieu*, what luck!'

Next morning when I heard the postman I rushed down to the *bistro* for my letter; to my disappointment, it had not come. I stayed at home for the second post; still no letter. When three days had gone by and I had not heard from the secret society, we gave up hope, deciding that they must have found somebody else to do their articles.

Ten days later we made another visit to the office of the secret society, taking care to bring a parcel that looked like washing. And the secret society had vanished! The woman in the laundry knew nothing – she simply said that '*ces messieurs*' had left some days ago, after trouble about the rent. What fools we looked, standing there with our parcel! But it was a consolation that we had paid only five francs instead of twenty.

And that was the last we ever heard of the secret society. Who or what they really were, nobody knew. Personally I do not think they had anything to do with the Communist Party; I think they were simply swindlers, who preyed upon Russian refugees by extracting entrance fees to an imaginary society. It was quite safe, and no doubt they are still doing it in some other city. They were clever fellows, and played their part admirably. Their office looked exactly as a secret Communist office should look, and as for that touch about bringing a parcel of washing, it was genius.

IX

For three more days we continued traipsing about looking for work, coming home for diminishing meals of soup and bread in my bedroom. There were now two gleams of hope. In the first place, Boris had heard of a possible job at the Hôtel X., near the Place de la Concorde, and in the second, the *patron* of the new restaurant in the Rue du Commerce had at last come back. We went down in the afternoon and saw him. On the way Boris talked of the vast fortunes we should make if we got this job, and of the importance of making a good impression on the *patron*.

'Appearance – appearance is everything, *mon ami*. Give me a new suit and I will borrow a thousand francs by dinner-time. What a pity I did not buy a collar when we had money. I turned my collar inside out this morning; but what is the use, one side is as dirty as the other. Do you think I look hungry, *mon ami*?'

'You look pale.'

'Curse it, what can one do on bread and potatoes? It is fatal to look hungry. It makes people want to kick you. Wait.'

He stopped at a jeweller's window and smacked his cheeks sharply to bring the blood into them. Then, before the flush had faded, we hurried into the restaurant and introduced ourselves to the *patron*.

The *patron* was a short, fattish, very dignified man with wavy grey hair, dressed in a smart double-breasted flannel suit and smelling of scent. Boris told me that he was an ex-colonel of the Russian Army. His wife was there too, a horrid fat Frenchwoman with a dead-white face and scarlet lips, reminding me of cold veal and tomatoes. The *patron* greeted Boris genially, and they talked together in Russian for a few minutes. I stood in the background, preparing to tell some big lies about my experience as a dishwasher.

Then the *patron* came over towards me. I shuffled uneasily, trying to look servile. Boris had rubbed it into me that a *plongeur* is a slave's slave, and I expected the *patron* to treat me like dirt. To my astonishment, he seized me warmly by the hand.

'So you are an Englishman!' he exclaimed. 'But how charming! I need not ask, then, whether you are a golfer?'

'*Mais certainement,*' I said, seeing that this was expected of me.

'All my life I have wanted to play golf. Will you, my dear *monsieur*, be so kind as to show me a few of the principal strokes?'

Apparently this was the Russian way of doing business. The *patron* listened attentively while I explained the difference between a driver and an iron, and then suddenly informed me that it was all *entendu;* Boris was to be *maître d'hôtel* when the restaurant opened, and I *plongeur*, with a chance of rising to lavatory attendant if trade was good. When would the restaurant open? I asked. 'Exactly a fortnight from today,' the *patron* answered grandly (he had a manner of waving his hand and flicking off his cigarette ash at the same time, which looked very grand), 'exactly a fortnight from today, in time for lunch.' Then, with obvious pride, he showed us over the restaurant.

It was a smallish place, consisting of a bar, a dining-room, and a kitchen no bigger than the average bathroom. The *patron* was decorating it in a trumpery 'picturesque' style (he called it '*normand*'; it was a matter of sham beams stuck on the plaster, and the like) and proposed to call it the Auberge de Jehan Cottard, to give a medieval effect. He had had a leaflet printed, full of lies about the historical associations of the quarter, and this leaflet actually claimed, among other things, that there had once been an inn on the site of the restaurant which was frequented by Charlemagne. The *patron* was very pleased with this touch. He was also having the bar decorated with indecent pictures by an artist from the Salon. Finally he gave us each an expensive cigarette, and after some more talk we went home.

I felt strongly that we should never get any good from this restaurant. The *patron* had looked to me like a cheat, and, what was worse, an incompetent cheat, and I had seen two unmistakable duns hanging about the back door. But Boris, seeing himself a *maître d'hôtel* once more, would not be discouraged.

'We've brought it off – only a fortnight to hold out. What is a fortnight? Food? *Je m'en fous.* To think that in only three weeks I shall have my mistress! Will she be dark or fair, I wonder? I don't mind, so long as she is not too thin.'

Two bad days followed. We had only sixty centimes left, and we spent it on half a pound of bread, with a piece of garlic to rub it with. The point of rubbing garlic on bread is that the taste lingers and gives one the illusion of having fed recently. We sat most of that day in the Jardin des Plantes. Boris had shots with stones at the tame pigeons, but always missed them, and after that we wrote dinner menus on the backs of envelopes. We were too hungry even to try and think of anything except food. I remember the dinner Boris finally selected for himself. It was: a dozen oysters, borscht soup (the red, sweet, beetroot soup with cream on top), crayfishes, a young chicken *en casserole*, beef with stewed plums, new potatoes, a salad, suet pudding and Roquefort cheese, with a litre of Burgundy and some old brandy. Boris had international tastes in food. Later on, when we were prosperous, I occasionally saw him eat meals almost as large without difficulty.

When our money came to an end I stopped looking for work, and was another day without food. I did not believe that the Auberge de Jehan Cottard was really going to open, and I could see no other prospect, but I was too lazy to do anything but lie in bed. Then the luck changed abruptly. At night, at about ten o'clock, I heard an eager shout from the street. I got up and went to the window. Boris was there, waving his stick and beaming. Before speaking he dragged a bent loaf from his pocket and threw it up to me.

'*Mon ami, mon cher ami*, we're saved! What do you think?'

'Surely you haven't got a job!'

'At the Hôtel X., near the Place de la Concorde – five hundred francs a month, and food. I have been working there today. Name of Jesus Christ, how I have eaten!'

After ten or twelve hours' work, and with his game leg, his first thought had been to walk three kilometres to my hotel and tell me the good news! What was more, he told me to meet him in the Tuileries the next day during his afternoon interval, in case he should be able to steal some food for me. At the appointed time I met Boris on a public bench. He undid his waistcoat and produced a large, crushed newspaper packet; in it were some minced veal, a wedge of Camembert cheese, bread and an éclair, all jumbled together.

'*Voilà!*' said Boris, 'that's all I could smuggle out for you. The door-keeper is a cunning swine.'

It is disagreeable to eat out of a newspaper on a public seat, especially in the Tuileries, which are generally full of pretty girls, but I was too hungry to care. While I ate, Boris explained that he was working in the *cafeterie* of the hotel – that is, in English, the stillroom. It appeared that the *cafeterie* was the very lowest post in the hotel, and a dreadful comedown for a waiter, but it would do until the Auberge de Jehan Cottard opened. Meanwhile I was to meet Boris every day in the Tuileries, and he would smuggle out as much food as he dared. For three days we continued with this arrangement, and I lived entirely on the stolen food. Then all our troubles came to an end, for one of the *plongeurs* left the Hôtel X., and on Boris's recommendation I was given a job there myself.

x

The Hôtel X. was a vast grandiose place with a classical façade, and at one side a little dark doorway like a rat-hole, which was the service entrance. I arrived at a quarter to seven in the morning. A stream of men with greasy trousers were hurrying in and being checked by a doorkeeper who sat in a tiny office. I waited, and presently the *chef du personnel*, a sort of assistant manager, arrived and began to question me. He was an Italian, with a round, pale face, haggard from overwork. He asked whether I was an experienced dishwasher, and I said that I was; he glanced at my hands and saw that I was lying, but on hearing that I was an Englishman he changed his tone and engaged me.

'We have been looking for someone to practise our English on,' he

said. 'Our clients are all Americans, and the only English we know is —'
He repeated something that little boys write on the walls in London. 'You
may be useful. Come downstairs.'

He led me down a winding staircase into a narrow passage, deep
underground, and so low that I had to stoop in places. It was stiflingly
hot and very dark, with only dim yellow bulbs several yards apart. There
seemed to be miles of dark labyrinthine passages – actually, I suppose, a
few hundred yards in all – that reminded one queerly of the lower decks
of a liner; there were the same heat and cramped space and warm reek of
food, and a humming, whirring noise (it came from the kitchen furnaces)
just like the whir of engines. We passed doorways which let out sometimes
a shouting of oaths, sometimes the red glare of a fire, once a shuddering
draught from an ice chamber. As we went along, something struck me
violently in the back. It was a hundred-pound block of ice, carried by a
blue-aproned porter. After him came a boy with a great slab of veal on
his shoulder, his cheek pressed into the damp, spongy flesh. They shoved
me aside with a cry of '*Range-toi, idiot!*' and rushed on. On the wall, under
one of the lights, someone had written in a very neat hand: 'Sooner will
you find a cloudless sky in winter, than a woman at the Hôtel X. who has
her maidenhead.' It seemed a queer sort of place.

One of the passages branched off into a laundry, where an old skull-face
woman gave me a blue apron and a pile of dishcloths. Then the *chef du
personnel* took me to a tiny underground den – a cellar below a cellar, as
it were – where there were a sink and some gas-ovens. It was too low for
me to stand quite upright, and the temperature was perhaps 110 degrees
Fahrenheit. The *chef du personnel* explained that my job was to fetch meals
for the higher hotel employees, who fed in a small dining-room above,
clean their room and wash their crockery. When he had gone, a waiter,
another Italian, thrust a fierce fuzzy head into the doorway and looked
down at me.

'English, eh?' he said. 'Well, I'm in charge here. If you work well' – he
made the motion of up-ending a bottle and sucked noisily. 'If you don't'
– he gave the doorpost several vigorous kicks. 'To me, twisting your neck
would be no more than spitting on the floor. And if there's any trouble,
they'll believe me, not you. So be careful.'

After this I set to work rather hurriedly. Except for about an hour, I was at work from seven in the morning till a quarter-past nine at night; first at washing crockery, then at scrubbing the tables and floors of the employees' dining-room, then at polishing glasses and knives, then at fetching meals, then at washing crockery again, then at fetching more meals and washing more crockery. It was easy work, and I got on well with it except when I went to the kitchen to fetch meals. The kitchen was like nothing I had ever seen or imagined – a stifling, low-ceilinged inferno of a cellar, red-lit from the fires, and deafening with oaths and the clanging of pots and pans. It was so hot that all the metal-work except the stoves had to be covered with cloth. In the middle were furnaces, where twelve cooks skipped to and fro, their faces dripping sweat in spite of their white caps. Round that were counters where a mob of waiters and *plongeurs* clamoured with trays. Scullions, naked to the waist, were stoking the fires and scouring huge copper saucepans with sand. Everyone seemed to be in a hurry and a rage. The head cook, a fine scarlet man with big moustachios, stood in the middle booming continuously, '*Ça marche, deux œufs brouillés! Ça marche, un Châteaubriand pommes sautées!*' except when he broke off to curse at a *plongeur*. There were three counters, and the first time I went to the kitchen I took my tray unknowingly to the wrong one. The head cook walked up to me, twisted his moustaches, and looked me up and down. Then he beckoned to the breakfast cook and pointed at me.

'Do you see *that*? That is the type of *plongeur* they send us nowadays. Where do you come from, idiot? From Charenton, I suppose?' (There is a large lunatic asylum at Charenton.)

'From England,' I said.

'I might have known it. Well, *mon cher monsieur l'Anglais*, may I inform you that you are the son of a whore? And now, *fous-moi le camp* to the other counter, where you belong.'

I got this kind of reception every time I went to the kitchen, for I always made some mistake; I was expected to know the work, and was cursed accordingly. From curiosity I counted the number of times I was called *maquereau* during the day, and it was thirty-nine.

At half-past four the Italian told me that I could stop working, but that it was not worth going out, as we began again at five. I went to the lavatory for a smoke; smoking was strictly forbidden, and Boris had warned me that the lavatory was the only safe place. After that I worked again till a quarter-past nine, when the waiter put his head into the doorway and told me to leave the rest of the crockery. To my astonishment, after calling me pig, mackerel, etc., all day, he had suddenly grown quite friendly. I realised that the curses I had met with were only a kind of probation.

'That'll do, *mon p'tit*,' said the waiter. '*Tu n'es pas débrouillard*, but you work all right. Come up and have your dinner. The hotel allows us two litres of wine each, and I've stolen another bottle. We'll have a fine booze.'

We had an excellent dinner from the leavings of the higher employees. The waiter, grown mellow, told me stories about his love-affairs, and about two men whom he had stabbed in Italy, and about how he had dodged his military service. He was a good fellow when one got to know him; he reminded me of Benvenuto Cellini, somehow. I was tired and drenched with sweat, but I felt a new man after a day's solid food. The work did not seem difficult, and I felt that this job would suit me. It was not certain, however, that it would continue, for I had been engaged as an 'extra' for the day only, at twenty-five francs. The sour-faced doorkeeper counted out the money, less fifty centimes which he said was for insurance (a lie, I discovered afterwards). Then he stepped out into the passage, made me take off my coat, and carefully prodded me all over, searching for stolen food. After this the *chef du personnel* appeared and spoke to me. Like the waiter, he had grown more genial on seeing that I was willing to work.

'We will give you a permanent job if you like,' he said. 'The head waiter says he would enjoy calling an Englishman names. Will you sign on for a month?'

Here was a job at last, and I was ready to jump at it. Then I remembered the Russian restaurant, due to open in a fortnight. It seemed hardly fair to promise working a month, and then leave in the middle. I said that I had other work in prospect – could I be engaged for a fortnight? But at that the *chef du personnel* shrugged his shoulders and said that the hotel only engaged men by the month. Evidently I had lost my chance of a job.

Boris, by arrangement, was waiting for me in the Arcade of the Rue de Rivoli. When I told him what had happened, he was furious. For the first time since I had known him he forgot his manners and called me a fool.

'Idiot! Species of idiot! What's the good of my finding you a job when you go and chuck it up the next moment? How could you be such a fool as to mention the other restaurant? You'd only to promise you would work for a month.'

'It seemed more honest to say I might have to leave,' I objected.

'Honest! Honest! Who ever heard of a *plongeur* being honest? *Mon ami*' – suddenly he seized my lapel and spoke very earnestly – '*mon ami*, you have worked here all day. You see what hotel work is like. Do you think a *plongeur* can afford a sense of honour?'

'No, perhaps not.'

'Well, then, go back quickly and tell the *chef du personnel* you are quite ready to work for a month. Say you will throw the other job over. Then, when our restaurant opens, we have only to walk out.'

'But what about my wages if I break my contract?'

Boris banged his stick on the pavement and cried out at such stupidity. 'Ask to be paid by the day, then you won't lose a sou. Do you suppose they would prosecute a *plongeur* for breaking his contract? A *plongeur* is too low to be prosecuted.'

I hurried back, found the *chef du personnel*, and told him that I would work for a month, whereat he signed me on. This was my first lesson in *plongeur* morality. Later I realised how foolish it had been to have any scruples, for the big hotels are quite merciless towards their employees. They engage or discharge men as the work demands, and they all sack ten per cent. or more of their staff when the season is over. Nor have they any difficulty in replacing a man who leaves at short notice, for Paris is thronged by hotel employees out of work.

XI

As it turned out, I did not break my contract, for it was six weeks before the Auberge de Jehan Cottard even showed signs of opening. In the meantime I worked at the Hôtel X., four days a week in the *cafeterie*, one day helping the waiter on the fourth floor, and one day replacing the woman who washed up for the dining-room. My day off, luckily, was Sunday, but sometimes another man was ill and I had to work that day as well. The hours were from seven in the morning till two in the afternoon, and from five in the evening till nine – eleven hours; but it was a fourteen-hour day when I washed up for the dining-room. By the ordinary standards of a Paris *plongeur*, these are exceptionally short hours. The only hardship of the life was the fearful heat and stuffiness of those labyrinthine cellars. Apart from this the hotel, which was large and well organised, was considered a comfortable one.

Our *cafeterie* was a murky cellar measuring twenty feet by seven by eight high, and so crowded with coffee-urns, breadcutters and the like that one could hardly move without banging against something. It was lighted by one dim electric bulb, and four or five gas-fires that sent out a fierce red breath. There was a thermometer there, and the temperature never fell below 110 degrees Fahrenheit – it neared 130 at some times of the day. At one end were five service lifts, and at the other an ice cupboard where we stored milk and butter. When you went into the ice cupboard you dropped a hundred degrees of temperature at a single step; it used to remind me of the hymn about Greenland's icy mountains and India's coral strand. Two men worked in the *cafeterie* besides Boris and myself. One was Mario, a huge, excitable Italian – he was like a city policeman with operatic gestures – and the other, a hairy, uncouth animal whom we called the Magyar; I think he was a Transylvanian, or something even more remote. Except the Magyar we were all big men, and at the rush hours we collided incessantly.

The work in the *cafeterie* was spasmodic. We were never idle, but the real work only came in bursts of two hours at a time – we called each burst '*un coup de feu*'. The first *coup de feu* came at eight, when the guests upstairs began to wake up and demand breakfast. At eight a sudden banging and yelling would break out all through the basement; bells rang on all sides, blue-aproned men rushed through the passages, our service lifts came down with a simultaneous crash, and the waiters on all five floors began shouting Italian oaths down the shafts. I don't remember all our duties, but they included making tea, coffee and chocolate, fetching meals from the kitchen, wines from the cellar, and fruit and so forth from the dining-room, slicing bread, making toast, rolling pats of butter, measuring jam, opening milk-cans, counting lumps of sugar, boiling eggs, cooking porridge, pounding ice, grinding coffee – all this for from a hundred to two hundred customers. The kitchen was thirty yards away, and the dining-room sixty or seventy yards. Everything we sent up in the service lifts had to be covered by a voucher, and the vouchers had to be carefully filed, and there was trouble if even a lump of sugar was lost. Besides this, we had to supply the staff with bread and coffee, and fetch the meals for the waiters upstairs. All in all, it was a complicated job.

I calculated that one had to walk and run about fifteen miles during the day, and yet the strain of the work was more mental than physical. Nothing could be easier, on the face of it, than this stupid scullion work, but it is astonishingly hard when one is in a hurry. One has to leap to and fro between a multitude of jobs – it is like sorting a pack of cards against the clock. You are, for example, making toast, when bang! down comes a service lift with an order for tea, rolls and three different kinds of jam, and simultaneously bang! down comes another demanding scrambled eggs, coffee and grapefruit; you run to the kitchen for the eggs and to the dining-room for the fruit, going like lightning so as to be back before your toast burns, and having to remember about the tea and coffee, besides half a dozen other orders that are still pending; and at the same time some waiter is following you and making trouble about a lost bottle of soda-water, and you are arguing with him. It needs more brains than one might think. Mario said, no doubt truly, that it took a year to make a reliable *cafetier*.

The time between eight and half-past ten was a sort of delirium. Sometimes we were going as though we had only five minutes to live; sometimes there were sudden lulls when the orders stopped and everything seemed quiet for a moment. Then we swept up the litter from the floor, threw down fresh sawdust, and swallowed gallipots of wine or coffee or water – anything, so long as it was wet. Very often we used to break off chunks of ice and suck them while we worked. The heat among the gas-fires was nauseating; we swallowed quarts of drink during the day, and after a few hours even our aprons were drenched with sweat. At times we were hopelessly behind with the work, and some of the customers would have gone without their breakfast, but Mario always pulled us through. He had worked fourteen years in the *cafeterie*, and he had the skill that never wastes a second between jobs. The Magyar was very stupid, and I was inexperienced, and Boris was inclined to shirk, partly because of his lame leg, partly because he was ashamed of working in the *cafeterie* after being a waiter; but Mario was wonderful. The way he would stretch his great arms right across the *cafeterie* to fill a coffee-pot with one hand and boil an egg with the other, at the same time watching toast and shouting directions to the Magyar, and between whiles singing snatches from *Rigoletto*, was beyond all praise. The *patron* knew his value, and he was paid a thousand francs a month, instead of five hundred like the rest of us.

The breakfast pandemonium stopped at half-past ten. Then we scrubbed the *cafeterie* tables, swept the floor and polished the brasswork, and, on good mornings, went one at a time to the lavatory for a smoke. This was our slack time – only relatively slack, however, for we had only ten minutes for lunch, and we never got through it uninterrupted. The customers' luncheon hour, between twelve and two, was another period of turmoil like the breakfast hour. Most of our work was fetching meals from the kitchen, which meant constant *engueulades* from the cooks. By this time the cooks had sweated in front of their furnaces for four or five hours, and their tempers were all warmed up.

At two we were suddenly free men. We threw off our aprons and put on our coats, hurried out of doors, and, when we had money, dived into the nearest *bistro*. It was strange, coming up into the street from those firelit cellars. The air seemed blindingly clear and cold, like arctic summer; and how sweet the petrol did smell, after the stenches of sweat and food! Sometimes we met some of our cooks and waiters in the *bistros*, and they were friendly and stood us drinks. Indoors we were their slaves, but it is an etiquette in hotel life that between hours everyone is equal, and the *engueulades* do not count.

At a quarter to five we went back to the hotel. Till half-past six there were no orders, and we used this time to polish silver, clean out the coffee-urns, and do other odd jobs. Then the grand turmoil of the day started – the dinner hour. I wish I could be Zola for a little while, just to describe that dinner hour. The essence of the situation was that a hundred or two hundred people were demanding individually different meals of five or six courses, and that fifty or sixty people had to cook and serve them and clean up the mess afterwards; anyone with experience of catering will know what that means. And at this time when the work was doubled, the whole staff were tired out, and a number of them were drunk. I could write pages about the scene without giving a true idea of it. The chargings to and fro in the narrow passages, the collisions, the yells, the struggling with crates and trays and blocks of ice, the heat, the darkness, the furious festering quarrels which there was no time to fight out – they pass description. Anyone coming into the basement for the first time would have thought himself in a den of maniacs. It was only later, when I understood the working of the hotel, that I saw order in all this chaos.

At half-past eight the work stopped very suddenly. We were not free till nine, but we used to throw ourselves full length on the floor, and lie there resting our legs, too lazy even to go to the ice cupboard for a drink. Sometimes the *chef du personnel* would come in with bottles of beer, for the hotel stood us extra beer when we had had a hard day. The food we were given was no more than eatable, but the *patron* was not mean about drink; he allowed us two litres of wine a day each, knowing that if a *plongeur* is not given two litres he will steal three. We had the heeltaps of bottles as well, so that we often drank too much – a good thing, for one seemed to work faster when partially drunk.

Four days of the week passed like this; of the other two working days, one was better and one worse. After a week of this life I felt in need of a holiday. It was Saturday night, so the people in our *bistro* were busy getting drunk, and with a free day ahead of me I was ready to join them. We all went to bed, drunk, at two in the morning, meaning to sleep till noon. At half-past five I was suddenly awakened. A night-watchman, sent from the hotel, was standing at my bedside. He stripped the clothes back and shook me roughly.

'Get up!' he said. '*Tu t'es bien saoulé la gueule, pas vrai?* Well, never mind that, the hotel's a man short. You've got to work today.'

'Why should I work?' I protested. 'This is my day off.'

'Day off, nothing! The work's got to be done. Get up!'

I got up and went out, feeling as though my back were broken and my skull filled with hot cinders. I did not think that I could possibly do a day's work. And yet, after only an hour in the basement, I found that I was perfectly well. It seemed that in the heat of those cellars, as in a Turkish bath, one could sweat out almost any quantity of drink. *Plongeurs* know this, and count on it. The power of swallowing quarts of wine, and then sweating it out before it can do much damage, is one of the compensations of their life.

XII

By far my best time at the hotel was when I went to help the waiter on the fourth floor. We worked in a small pantry which communicated with the *cafeterie* by service lifts. It was delightfully cool after the cellars, and the work was chiefly polishing silver and glasses, which is a humane job. Valenti, the waiter, was a decent sort, and treated me almost as an equal when we were alone, though he had to speak roughly when there was anyone else present, for it does not do for a waiter to be friendly with *plongeurs*. He used sometimes to tip me five francs when he had had a good day. He was a comely youth, aged twenty-four but looking eighteen, and, like most waiters, he carried himself well and knew how to wear his clothes. With his black tail-coat and white tie, fresh face and sleek brown hair, he looked just like an Eton boy; yet he had earned his living since he was twelve, and worked his way up literally from the gutter. Crossing the Italian frontier without a passport, and selling chestnuts from a barrow on the northern boulevards, and being given fifty days' imprisonment in London for working without a permit, and being made love to by a rich old woman in a hotel, who gave him a diamond ring and afterwards accused him of stealing it, were among his experiences. I used to enjoy talking to him, at slack times when we sat smoking down the lift shaft.

My bad day was when I washed up for the dining-room. I had not to wash the plates, which were done in the kitchen, but only the other crockery, silver, knives and glasses; yet, even so, it meant thirteen hours' work, and I used between thirty and forty dishcloths during the day. The antiquated methods used in France double the work of washing up. Plate-racks are unheard-of, and there are no soap-flakes, only the treacly soft soap, which refuses to lather in the hard Paris water. I worked in a dirty, crowded little den, a pantry and scullery combined, which gave straight on the dining-room. Besides washing up, I had to fetch the waiters' food and serve them at table; most of them were intolerably insolent, and I had to use my fists more than once to get common civility. The person who normally washed up was a woman, and they made her life a misery.

It was amusing to look round the filthy little scullery and think that only a double door was between us and the dining-room. There sat the customers in all their splendour – spotless table-cloths, bowls of flowers, mirrors and gilt cornices and painted cherubim; and here, just a few feet away, we in our disgusting filth. For it really was disgusting filth. There was no time to sweep the floor till evening, and we slithered about in a compound of soapy water, lettuce-leaves, torn paper and trampled food. A dozen waiters with their coats off, showing their sweaty armpits, sat at the table mixing salads and sticking their thumbs into the cream pots. The room had a dirty mixed smell of food and sweat. Everywhere in the cupboards, behind the piles of crockery, were squalid stores of food that the waiters had stolen. There were only two sinks, and no washing basin, and it was nothing unusual for a waiter to wash his face in the water in which clean crockery was rinsing. But the customers saw nothing of this. There were a coconut mat and a mirror outside the dining-room door, and the waiters used to preen themselves up and go in looking the picture of cleanliness.

It is an instructive sight to see a waiter going into a hotel dining-room. As he passes the door a sudden change comes over him. The set of his shoulders alters; all the dirt and hurry and irritation have dropped off in an instant. He glides over the carpet, with a solemn priest-like air. I remember our assistant *maître d'hôtel*, a fiery Italian, pausing at the dining-room door to address an apprentice who had broken a bottle of wine. Shaking his fist above his head he yelled (luckily the door was more or less soundproof):

'*Tu me fais chier.* Do you call yourself a waiter, you young bastard? You a waiter! You're not fit to scrub floors in the brothel your mother came from. *Maquereau!*'

Words failing him, he turned to the door; and as he opened it he farted loudly, a favourite Italian insult.

Then he entered the dining-room and sailed across it dish in hand, graceful as a swan. Ten seconds later he was bowing reverently to a customer. And you could not help thinking, as you saw him bow and smile, with that benign smile of the trained waiter, that the customer was put to shame by having such an aristocrat to serve him.

This washing up was a thoroughly odious job – not hard, but boring and silly beyond words. It is dreadful to think that some people spend whole decades at such occupations. The woman whom I replaced was quite sixty years old, and she stood at the sink thirteen hours a day, six days a week, the year round; she was, in addition, horribly bullied by the waiters. She gave out that she had once been an actress – actually, I imagine, a prostitute; most prostitutes end as charwomen. It was strange to see that in spite of her age and her life she still wore a bright blonde wig, and darkened her eyes and painted her face like a girl of twenty. So apparently even a seventy-eight-hour week can leave one with some vitality.

XIII

On my third day at the hotel the *chef du personnel*, who had generally spoken to me in quite a pleasant tone, called me up and said sharply:

'Here, you, shave that moustache off at once! *Nom de Dieu*, who ever heard of a *plongeur* with a moustache?'

I began to protest, but he cut me short. 'A *plongeur* with a moustache – nonsense! Take care I don't see you with it tomorrow.'

On the way home I asked Boris what this meant. He shrugged his shoulders. 'You must do what he says, *mon ami*. No one in a hotel wears a moustache, except the cooks. I should have thought you would have noticed it. Reason? There is no reason. It is the custom.'

I saw that it was an etiquette, like not wearing a white tie with a dinner-jacket, and shaved off my moustache. Afterwards I found out the explanation of the custom, which is this: waiters in good hotels do not wear moustaches, and to show their superiority they decree that *plongeurs* shall not wear them either; and the cooks wear their moustaches to show their contempt for the waiters.

This gives some idea of the elaborate caste system existing in a hotel. Our staff, amounting to about a hundred and ten, had their prestige graded as accurately as that of soldiers, and a cook or waiter was as much above a *plongeur* as a captain above a private. Highest of all came the manager, who could sack anybody, even the cooks. We never saw the *patron*, and all we knew of him was that his meals had to be prepared more carefully than those of the customers; all the discipline of the hotel depended on the manager. He was a conscientious man, and always on the lookout for slackness, but we were too clever for him. A system of service bells ran through the hotel, and the whole staff used these for signalling to one another. A long ring and a short ring, followed by two more long rings, meant that the manager was coming, and when we heard it we took care to look busy.

Below the manager came the *maître d'hôtel*. He did not serve at table, unless to a lord or someone of that kind, but directed the other waiters and helped with the catering. His tips, and his bonus from the champagne companies (it was two francs for each cork he returned to them), came to two hundred francs a day. He was in a position quite apart from the rest of the staff, and took his meals in a private room, with silver on the table and two apprentices in clean white jackets to serve him. A little below the head waiter came the head cook, drawing about five thousand francs a month; he dined in the kitchen, but at a separate table, and one of the apprentice cooks waited on him. Then came the *chef du personnel*; he drew only fifteen hundred francs a month, but he wore a black coat and did no manual work, and he could sack *plongeurs* and fine waiters. Then came the other cooks, drawing anything between three thousand and seven hundred and fifty francs a month; then the waiters, making about seventy francs a day in tips, besides a small retaining fee; then the laundresses and sewing-women; then the apprentice waiters, who received no tips, but were paid seven hundred and fifty francs a month; then the *plongeurs*, also at seven hundred and fifty francs; then the chambermaids, at five or six hundred francs a month; and lastly the *cafetiers*, at five hundred a month. We of the *cafeterie* were the very dregs of the hotel, despised and *tutoied* by everyone.

There were various others – the office employees, called generally couriers, the storekeeper, the cellarman, some porters and pages, the ice man, the bakers, the night-watchman, the doorkeeper. Different jobs were done by different races. The office employees and the cooks and sewing-women were French, the waiters Italians and Germans (there is hardly such a thing as a French waiter in Paris), the *plongeurs* of every race in Europe, besides Arabs and negroes. French was the lingua franca, even the Italians speaking it to one another.

All the departments had their special perquisites. In all Paris hotels it is the custom to sell the broken bread to bakers for eight sous a pound, and the kitchen scraps to pigkeepers for a trifle, and to divide the proceeds of this among the *plongeurs*. There was much pilfering, too. The waiters all stole food – in fact, I seldom saw a waiter trouble to eat the rations provided for him by the hotel – and the cooks did it on a larger scale in the kitchen, and we in the *cafeterie* swilled illicit tea and coffee. The cellarman stole brandy. By a rule of the hotel the waiters were not allowed to keep stores of spirits, but had to go to the cellarman for each drink as it was ordered. As the cellarman poured out the drinks he would set aside perhaps a teaspoonful from each glass, and he amassed quantities in this way. He would sell you the stolen brandy for five sous a swig if he thought he could trust you.

There were thieves among the staff, and if you left money in your coat pockets it was generally taken. The doorkeeper, who paid our wages and searched us for stolen food, was the greatest thief in the hotel. Out of my five hundred francs a month, this man actually managed to cheat me of a hundred and fourteen francs in six weeks. I had asked to be paid daily, so the doorkeeper paid me sixteen francs each evening, and, by not paying for Sundays (for which of course payment was due), pocketed sixty-four francs. Also, I sometimes worked on a Sunday, for which, though I did not know it, I was entitled to an extra twenty-five francs. The doorkeeper never paid this either, and so made away with another seventy-five francs. I only realised during my last week that I was being cheated, and, as I could prove nothing, only twenty-five francs were refunded. The doorkeeper played similar tricks on any employee who was fool enough to be taken in. He called himself a Greek, but in reality he was an Armenian. After knowing him I saw the force of the proverb 'Trust a snake before a Jew and a Jew before a Greek, but don't trust an Armenian.'

There were queer characters among the waiters. One was a gentleman – a youth who had been educated at a university, and had had a well-paid job in a business office. He had caught a venereal disease, lost his job, drifted, and now considered himself lucky to be a waiter. Many of the waiters had slipped into France without passports, and one or two of them were spies – it is a common profession for a spy to adopt. One day there was a fearful row in the waiters' dining-room between Morandi, a dangerous-looking man with eyes set too far apart, and another Italian. It appeared that Morandi had taken the other man's mistress. The other man, a weakling and obviously frightened of Morandi, was threatening vaguely.

Morandi jeered at him. 'Well, what are you going to do about it? I've slept with your girl, slept with her three times. It was fine. What can you do, eh?'

'I can denounce you to the secret police. You are an Italian spy.'

Morandi did not deny it. He simply produced a razor from his tail pocket and made two swift strokes in the air, as though slashing a man's cheeks open. Whereat the other waiter took it back.

The queerest type I ever saw in the hotel was an 'extra'. He had been engaged at twenty-five francs for the day to replace the Magyar, who was ill. He was a Serbian, a thick-set nimble fellow of about twenty-five, speaking six languages, including English. He seemed to know all about hotel work, and up till midday he worked like a slave. Then, as soon as it had struck twelve, he turned sulky, shirked his work, stole wine, and finally crowned all by loafing about openly with a pipe in his mouth. Smoking, of course, was forbidden under severe penalties. The manager himself heard of it and came down to interview the Serbian, fuming with rage.

'What the devil do you mean by smoking here?' he cried.

'What the devil do you mean by having a face like that?' answered the Serbian, calmly.

I cannot convey the blasphemy of such a remark. The head cook, if a *plongeur* had spoken to him like that, would have thrown a saucepan of hot soup in his face. The manager said instantly, 'You're sacked!' and at two o'clock the Serbian was given his twenty-five francs and duly sacked. Before he went out Boris asked him in Russian what game he was playing. He said the Serbian answered:

'Look here, *mon vieux*, they've got to pay me a day's wages if I work up to midday, haven't they? That's the law. And where's the sense of working after I get my wages? So I'll tell you what I do. I go to a hotel and get a job as an extra, and up to midday I work hard. Then, the moment it's struck twelve, I start raising such hell that they've no choice but to sack me. Neat, eh? Most days I'm sacked by half-past twelve; today it was two o'clock; but I don't care, I've saved four hours' work. The only trouble is, one can't do it at the same hotel twice.'

It appeared that he had played this game at half the hotels and restaurants in Paris. It is probably quite an easy game to play during the summer, though the hotels protect themselves against it as well as they can by means of a black list.

XIV

In a few days I had grasped the main principles on which the hotel was run. The thing that would astonish anyone coming for the first time into the service quarters of a hotel would be the fearful noise and disorder during the rush hours. It is something so different from the steady work in a shop or a factory that it looks at first sight like mere bad management. But it is really quite unavoidable, and for this reason. Hotel work is not particularly hard, but by its nature it comes in rushes and cannot be economised. You cannot, for instance, grill a steak two hours before it is wanted; you have to wait till the last moment, by which time a mass of other work has accumulated, and then do it all together, in frantic haste. The result is that at mealtimes everyone is doing two men's work, which is impossible without noise and quarrelling. Indeed the quarrels are a necessary part of the process, for the pace would never be kept up if everyone did not accuse everyone else of idling. It was for this reason that during the rush hours the whole staff raged and cursed like demons. At those times there was scarcely a verb in the hotel except *foutre*. A girl in the bakery, aged sixteen, used oaths that would have defeated a cabman. (Did not Hamlet say 'cursing like a scullion'? No doubt Shakespeare had watched scullions at work.) But we were not losing our heads and wasting time; we were just stimulating one another for the effort of packing four hours' work into two hours.

What keeps a hotel going is the fact that the employees take a genuine pride in their work, beastly and silly though it is. If a man idles, the others soon find him out, and conspire against him to get him sacked. Cooks, waiters and *plongeurs* differ greatly in outlook, but they are all alike in being proud of their efficiency.

Undoubtedly the most workmanlike class, and the least servile, are the cooks. They do not earn quite so much as waiters, but their prestige is higher and their employment steadier. The cook does not look upon himself as a servant, but as a skilled workman; he is generally called '*un ouvrier*', which a waiter never is. He knows his power – knows that he alone makes or mars a restaurant, and that if he is five minutes late everything is out of gear. He despises the whole non-cooking staff, and makes it a point of honour to insult everyone below the head waiter. And he takes a genuine artistic pride in his work, which demands very great skill. It is not the cooking that is so difficult, but the doing everything to time. Between breakfast and luncheon the head cook at the Hôtel X. would receive orders for several hundred dishes, all to be served at different times; he cooked few of them himself, but he gave instructions about all of them and inspected them before they were sent up. His memory was wonderful. The vouchers were pinned on a board, but the head cook seldom looked at them; everything was stored in his mind, and exactly to the minute, as each dish fell due, he would call out, '*Faites marcher une côtelette de veau*' (or whatever it was) unfailingly. He was an insufferable bully, but he was also an artist. It is for their punctuality, and not for any superiority in technique, that men cooks are preferred to women.

The waiter's outlook is quite different. He too is proud in a way of his skill, but his skill is chiefly in being servile. His work gives him the mentality, not of a workman, but of a snob. He lives perpetually in sight of rich people, stands at their tables, listens to their conversation, sucks up to them with smiles and discreet little jokes. He has the pleasure of spending money by proxy. Moreover, there is always the chance that he may become rich himself, for, though most waiters die poor, they have long runs of luck occasionally. At some cafés on the Grand Boulevard there is so much money to be made that the waiters actually pay the *patron* for their employment. The result is that between constantly seeing money, and hoping to get it, the waiter comes to identify himself to some extent with his employers. He will take pains to serve a meal in style, because he feels that he is participating in the meal himself.

I remember Valenti telling me of some banquet at Nice at which he had once served, and of how it cost two hundred thousand francs and was talked of for months afterwards. 'It was splendid, *mon p'tit, mais magnifique!* Jesus Christ! The champagne, the silver, the orchids – I have never seen anything like them, and I have seen some things. Ah, it was glorious!'

'But,' I said, 'you were only there to wait?'

'Oh, of course. But still, it was splendid.'

The moral is, never be sorry for a waiter. Sometimes when you sit in a restaurant, still stuffing yourself half an hour after closing time, you feel that the tired waiter at your side must surely be despising you. But he is not. He is not thinking as he looks at you, 'What an overfed lout'; he is thinking, 'One day, when I have saved enough money, I shall be able to imitate that man.' He is ministering to a kind of pleasure he thoroughly understands and admires. And that is why waiters are seldom Socialists, have no effective trade union, and will work twelve hours a day – they work fifteen hours, seven days a week, in many cafés. They are snobs, and they find the servile nature of their work rather congenial.

The *plongeurs*, again, have a different outlook. Theirs is a job which offers no prospects, is intensely exhausting, and at the same time has not a trace of skill or interest; the sort of job that would always be done by women if women were strong enough. All that is required of them is to be constantly on the run, and to put up with long hours and a stuffy atmosphere. They have no way of escaping from this life, for they cannot save a penny from their wages, and working from sixty to a hundred hours a week leaves them no time to train for anything else. The best they can hope is to find a slightly softer job as night-watchman or lavatory attendant.

And yet the *plongeurs*, low as they are, also have a kind of pride. It is the pride of the drudge – the man who is equal to no matter what quantity of work. At that level, the mere power to go on working like an ox is about the only virtue attainable. *Débrouillard* is what every *plongeur* wants to be called. A *débrouillard* is a man who, even when he is told to do the impossible, will *se débrouiller* – get it done somehow. One of the kitchen *plongeurs* at the Hôtel X., a German, was well known as a *débrouillard*. One night an English lord came to the hotel, and the waiters were in despair, for the lord had asked for peaches, and there were none in stock; it was late at night, and the shops would be shut. 'Leave it to me,' said the German. He went out, and in ten minutes he was back with four peaches. He had gone into a neighbouring restaurant and stolen them. That is what is meant by a *débrouillard*. The English lord paid for the peaches at twenty francs each.

Mario, who was in charge of the *cafeterie*, had the typical drudge mentality. All he thought of was getting through the '*boulot*', and he defied you to give him too much of it. Fourteen years underground had left him with about as much natural laziness as a piston rod. '*Faut être un dur*,' he used to say when anyone complained. You will often hear *plongeurs* boast, '*Je suis un dur*' – as though they were soldiers, not male charwomen.

Thus everyone in the hotel had his sense of honour, and when the press of work came we were all ready for a grand concerted effort to get through it. The constant war between the different departments also made for efficiency, for everyone clung to his own privileges and tried to stop the others idling and pilfering.

This is the good side of hotel work. In a hotel a huge and complicated machine is kept running by an inadequate staff, because every man has a well-defined job and does it scrupulously. But there is a weak point, and it is this – that the job the staff are doing is not necessarily what the customer pays for. The customer pays, as he sees it, for good service; the employee is paid, as he sees it, for the *boulot* – meaning, as a rule, an imitation of good service. The result is that, though hotels are miracles of punctuality, they are worse than the worst private houses in the things that matter.

Take cleanliness, for example. The dirt in the Hôtel X., as soon as one penetrated into the service quarters, was revolting. Our *cafeterie* had year-old filth in all the dark corners, and the bread-bin was infested with cockroaches. Once I suggested killing these beasts to Mario. 'Why kill the poor animals?' he said reproachfully. The others laughed when I wanted to wash my hands before touching the butter. Yet we were clean where we recognised cleanliness as part of the *boulot*. We scrubbed the tables and polished the brasswork regularly, because we had orders to do that; but we had no orders to be genuinely clean, and in any case we had no time for it. We were simply carrying out our duties; and as our first duty was punctuality, we saved time by being dirty.

In the kitchen the dirt was worse. It is not a figure of speech, it is a mere statement of fact to say that a French cook will spit in the soup – that is, if he is not going to drink it himself. He is an artist, but his art is not cleanliness. To a certain extent he is even dirty because he is an artist, for food, to look smart, needs dirty treatment. When a steak, for instance, is brought up for the head cook's inspection, he does not handle it with a fork. He picks it up in his fingers and slaps it down, runs his thumb round the dish and licks it to taste the gravy, runs it round and licks it again, then steps back and contemplates the piece of meat like an artist judging a picture, then presses it lovingly into place with his fat, pink fingers, every one of which he has licked a hundred times that morning. When he is satisfied, he takes a cloth and wipes his fingerprints from the dish, and hands it to the waiter. And the waiter, of course, dips *his* fingers into the gravy – his nasty, greasy fingers which he is for ever running through his brilliantined hair. Whenever one pays more than, say, ten francs for a dish of meat in Paris, one may be certain that it has been fingered in this manner. In very cheap restaurants it is different; there, the same trouble is not taken over the food, and it is just forked out of the pan and flung onto a plate, without handling. Roughly speaking, the more one pays for food, the more sweat and spittle one is obliged to eat with it.

Dirtiness is inherent in hotels and restaurants, because sound food is sacrificed to punctuality and smartness. The hotel employee is too busy getting food ready to remember that it is meant to be eaten. A meal is simply '*une commande*' to him, just as a man dying of cancer is simply 'a case' to the doctor. A customer orders, for example, a piece of toast. Somebody, pressed with work in a cellar deep underground, has to prepare it. How can he stop and say to himself, 'This toast is to be eaten – I must make it catable'? All he knows is that it must look right and must be ready in three minutes. Some large drops of sweat fall from his forehead onto the toast. Why should he worry? Presently the toast falls among the filthy sawdust on the floor. Why trouble to make a new piece? It is much quicker to wipe the sawdust off. On the way upstairs the toast falls again, butter side down. Another wipe is all it needs. And so with everything. The only food at the Hôtel X. which was ever prepared cleanly was the staff's, and the *patron*'s. The maxim, repeated by everyone, was: 'Look out for the *patron*, and as for the clients, *s'en fout pas mal!*' Everywhere in the service quarters dirt festered – a secret vein of dirt, running through the great garish hotel like the intestines through a man's body.

Apart from the dirt, the *patron* swindled the customers wholeheartedly. For the most part the materials of the food were very bad, though the cooks knew how to serve it up in style. The meat was at best ordinary, and as to the vegetables, no good housekeeper would have looked at them in the market. The cream, by a standing order, was diluted with milk. The tea and coffee were of inferior sorts, and the jam was synthetic stuff out of vast unlabelled tins. All the cheaper wines, according to Boris, were corked *vin ordinaire*. There was a rule that employees must pay for anything they spoiled, and in consequence damaged things were seldom thrown away. Once the waiter on the third floor dropped a roast chicken down the shaft of our service lift, where it fell into a litter of broken bread, torn paper and so forth at the bottom. We simply wiped it with a cloth and sent it up again. Upstairs there were dirty tales of once-used sheets not being washed, but simply damped, ironed and put back on the beds. The *patron* was as mean to us as to the customers. Throughout that vast hotel there was not, for instance, such a thing as a brush and pan; one had to manage with a broom and a piece of cardboard. And the staff lavatory was worthy of Central Asia, and there was no place to wash one's hands, except the sinks used for washing crockery.

In spite of all this the Hôtel X. was one of the dozen most expensive hotels in Paris, and the customers paid startling prices. The ordinary charge for a night's lodging, not including breakfast, was two hundred francs. All wine and tobacco were sold at exactly double shop prices, though of course the *patron* bought at the wholesale price. If a customer had a title, or was reputed to be a millionaire, all his charges went up automatically. One morning on the fourth floor an American who was on a diet wanted only salt and hot water for his breakfast. Valenti was furious. 'Jesus Christ!' he said, 'what about my ten per cent? Ten per cent of salt and water!' And he charged twenty-five francs for the breakfast. The customer paid without a murmur.

According to Boris, the same kind of thing went on in all Paris hotels, or at least in all the big, expensive ones. But I imagine that the customers at the Hôtel X. were especially easy to swindle, for they were mostly Americans, with a sprinkling of English – no French – and seemed to know nothing whatever about good food. They would stuff themselves with disgusting American 'cereals', and eat marmalade at tea, and drink vermouth after dinner, and order a *poulet à la reine* at a hundred francs and then souse it in Worcester sauce. One customer, from Pittsburg, dined every night in his bedroom on grape-nuts, scrambled eggs and cocoa. Perhaps it hardly matters whether such people are swindled or not.

XV

I heard queer tales in the hotel. There were tales of dope fiends, of old debauchees who frequented hotels in search of pretty page-boys, of thefts and blackmail. Mario told me of a hotel in which he had been, where a chambermaid stole a priceless diamond ring from an American lady. For days the staff were searched as they left work, and two detectives searched the hotel from top to bottom, but the ring was never found. The chambermaid had a lover in the bakery, and he had baked the ring into a roll, where it lay unsuspected until the search was over.

Once Valenti, at a slack time, told me a story about himself.

'You know, *mon p'tit*, this hotel life is all very well, but it's the devil when you're out of work. I expect you know what it is to go without eating, eh? *Forcément*, otherwise you wouldn't be scrubbing dishes. Well, I'm not a poor devil of a *plongeur*; I'm a waiter, and *I* went five days without eating, once. Five days without even a crust of bread – Jesus Christ!

'I tell you, those five days were the devil. The only good thing was, I had my rent paid in advance. I was living in a dirty, cheap little hotel in the Rue Sainte Éloïse up in the Latin quarter. It was called the Hôtel —, after some famous prostitute who was born in that quarter, I expect. I was starving, and there was nothing I could do; I couldn't even go to the cafés where the hotel proprietors come to engage waiters, because I hadn't the price of a drink. All I could do was to lie in bed getting weaker and weaker, and watching the bugs running about the ceiling. I don't want to go through that again, I can tell you.

'In the afternoon of the fifth day I went half mad; at least, that's how it seems to me now. There was an old faded print of a woman's head hanging on the wall of my room, and I took to wondering who it could be; and after about an hour I realised that it must be Sainte Éloïse, who was the patron saint of the quarter. I had never taken any notice of the thing before, but now, as I lay staring at it, a most extraordinary idea came into my head.

' "*Écoute, mon cher*," I said to myself, "you'll be starving to death if this goes on much longer. You've got to do something. Why not try a prayer to Sainte Éloïse? Go down on your knees and ask her to send you some money. After all, it can't do any harm. Try it!"

'Mad, eh? Still, a man will do anything when he's hungry. Besides, as I said, it couldn't do any harm. I got out of bed and began praying. I said:

' "Dear Sainte Éloïse, if you exist, please send me some money. I don't ask for much – just enough to buy some bread and a bottle of wine and get my strength back. Three or four francs would do. You don't know how grateful I'll be, Sainte Éloïse, if you help me this once. And be sure, if you send me anything, the first thing I'll do will be to go and burn a candle for you, at your church down the street. Amen."

'I put in that about the candle, because I had heard that saints like having candles burnt in their honour. I meant to keep my promise, of course. But I am an atheist and I didn't really believe that anything would come of it.

'Well, I got into bed again, and five minutes later there came a bang at the door. It was a girl called Maria, a big fat peasant girl who lived at our hotel. She was a very stupid girl, but a good sort, and I didn't much care for her to see me in the state I was in.

'She cried out at the sight of me. "*Nom de Dieu!*" she said, "what's the matter with you? What are you doing in bed at this time of day? *T'en as une mine!* You look more like a corpse than a man."

'Probably I did look a sight. I had been five days without food, most of the time in bed, and it was three days since I had had a wash or a shave. The room was a regular pigsty, too.

' "What's the matter?" said Maria again.

' "The matter!" I said; "Jesus Christ! I'm starving. I haven't eaten for five days. That's what's the matter."

'Maria was horrified. "Not eaten for five days?" she said. "But why? Haven't you any money, then?"

' "Money!" I said. "Do you suppose I should be starving if I had money? I've got just five sous in the world, and I've pawned everything. Look round the room and see if there's anything more I can sell or pawn. If you can find anything that will fetch fifty centimes, you're cleverer than I am."

'Maria began looking round the room. She poked here and there among a lot of rubbish that was lying about, and then suddenly she got quite excited. Her great thick mouth fell open with astonishment.

' "You idiot!" she cried out. "Imbecile! What's *this*, then?"

'I saw that she had picked up an empty oil *bidon* that had been lying in the corner. I had bought it weeks before, for an oil lamp I had before I sold my things.

' "That?" I said. "That's an oil *bidon*. What about it?"

' "Imbecile! Didn't you pay three francs fifty deposit on it?"

'Now, of course I had paid the three francs fifty. They always make you pay a deposit on the *bidon*, and you get it back when the *bidon* is returned. But I'd forgotten all about it.

' "Yes —" I began.

' "Idiot!" shouted Maria again. She got so excited that she began to dance about until I thought her sabots would go through the floor. "Idiot! *T'es louf! T'es louf!* What have you got to do but take it back to the shop and get your deposit back? Starving, with three francs fifty staring you in the face! Imbecile!"

'I can hardly believe now that in all those five days I had never once thought of taking the *bidon* back to the shop. As good as three francs fifty in hard cash, and it had never occurred to me! I sat up in bed. "Quick!" I shouted to Maria, "you take it for me. Take it to the grocer's at the corner – run like the devil. And bring back food!"

'Maria didn't need to be told. She grabbed the *bidon* and went clattering down the stairs like a herd of elephants, and in three minutes she was back with two pounds of bread under one arm and a half-litre bottle of wine under the other. I didn't stop to thank her; I just seized the bread and sank my teeth in it. Have you noticed how bread tastes when you have been hungry for a long time? Cold, wet, doughy – like putty almost. But, Jesus Christ, how good it was! As for the wine, I sucked it all down in one draught, and it seemed to go straight into my veins and flow round my body like new blood. Ah, that made a difference!

'I wolfed the whole two pounds of bread without stopping to take breath. Maria stood with her hands on her hips, watching me eat. "Well, you feel better, eh?" she said when I had finished.

' "Better!" I said. "I feel perfect! I'm not the same man as I was five minutes ago. There's only one thing in the world I need now – a cigarette."

'Maria put her hand in her apron pocket. "You can't have it," she said. "I've no money. This is all I had left out of your three francs fifty – seven sous. It's no good; the cheapest cigarettes are twelve sous a packet."

'"Then I can have them!" I said. "Jesus Christ, what a piece of luck! I've got five sous – it's just enough."

'Maria took the twelve sous and was starting out to the tobacconist's. And then something I had forgotten all this time came into my head. There was that cursed Sainte Éloïse! I had promised her a candle if she sent me money; and really, who could say that the prayer hadn't come true? "Three or four francs," I had said; and the next moment along came three francs fifty. There was no getting away from it. I should have to spend my twelve sous on a candle.

'I called Maria back. "It's no use," I said; "there is Sainte Éloïse – I have promised her a candle. The twelve sous will have to go on that. Silly, isn't it? I can't have my cigarettes after all."

'"Sainte Éloïse?" said Maria. "What about Sainte Éloïse?"

'"I prayed to her for money and promised her a candle," I said. "She answered the prayer – at any rate, the money turned up. I shall have to buy that candle. It's a nuisance, but it seems to me I must keep my promise."

'"But what put Sainte Éloïse into your head?" said Maria.

'"It was her picture," I said, and I explained the whole thing. "There she is, you see," I said, and I pointed to the picture on the wall.

'Maria looked at the picture, and then to my surprise she burst into shouts of laughter. She laughed more and more, stamping about the room and holding her fat sides as though they would burst. I thought she had gone mad. It was two minutes before she could speak.

'"Idiot!" she cried at last. "*T'es louf! T'es louf!* Do you mean to tell me you really knelt down and prayed to that picture? Who told you it was Sainte Éloïse?"

'"But I made sure it was Sainte Éloïse!" I said.

'"Imbecile! It isn't Sainte Éloïse at all. Who do you think it is?"

'"Who?" I said.

'"It is —, the woman this hotel is called after."

'I had been praying to —, the famous prostitute of the Empire . . .

'But, after all, I wasn't sorry. Maria and I had a good laugh, and then we talked it over, and we made out that I didn't owe Sainte Éloïse anything. Clearly it wasn't she who had answered the prayer, and there was no need to buy her a candle. So I had my packet of cigarettes after all.'

XVI

Time went on and the Auberge de Jehan Cottard showed no signs of opening. Boris and I went down there one day during our afternoon interval and found that none of the alterations had been done, except the indecent pictures, and there were three duns instead of two. The *patron* greeted us with his usual blandness, and the next instant turned to me (his prospective dishwasher) and borrowed five francs. After that I felt certain that the restaurant would never get beyond talk. The *patron*, however, again named the opening for 'exactly a fortnight from today', and introduced us to the woman who was to do the cooking, a Baltic Russian five feet tall and a yard across the hips. She told us that she had been a singer before she came down to cooking, and that she was very artistic and adored English literature, especially *La Case de l'Oncle Tom*.

In a fortnight I had got so used to the routine of a *plongeur*'s life that I could hardly imagine anything different. It was a life without much variation. At a quarter to six one woke with a sudden start, tumbled into grease-stiffened clothes, and hurried out with dirty face and protesting muscles. It was dawn, and the windows were dark except for the workmen's cafés. The sky was like a vast flat wall of cobalt, with roofs and spires of black paper pasted upon it. Drowsy men were sweeping the pavements with ten-foot besoms, and ragged families picking over the dustbins. Workmen, and girls with a piece of chocolate in one hand and a *croissant* in the other, were pouring into the Metro stations. Trams, filled with more workmen, boomed gloomily past. One hastened down to the station, fought for a place – one does literally have to fight on the Paris Metro at six in the morning – and stood jammed in the swaying mass of passengers, nose to nose with some hideous French face, breathing sour wine and garlic. And then one descended into the labyrinth of the hotel basement, and forgot daylight till two o'clock, when the sun was hot and the town black with people and cars.

After my first week at the hotel I always spent the afternoon interval in sleeping, or, when I had money, in a *bistro*. Except for a few ambitious waiters who went to English classes, the whole staff wasted their leisure in this way; one seemed too lazy after the morning's work to do anything better. Sometimes half a dozen *plongeurs* would make up a party and go to an abominable brothel in the Rue de Sieyès, where the charge was only five francs twenty-five centimes – tenpence half-penny. It was nick-named '*le prix fixe*', and they used to describe their experiences there as a great joke. It was a favourite rendezvous of hotel workers. The *plongeurs'* wages did not allow them to marry, and no doubt work in the basement does not encourage fastidious feelings.

For another four hours one was in the cellars, and then one emerged, sweating, into the cool street. It was lamplight – that strange purplish gleam of the Paris lamps – and beyond the river the Eiffel Tower flashed from top to bottom with zigzag skysigns, like enormous snakes of fire. Streams of cars glided silently to and fro, and women, exquisite-looking in the dim light, strolled up and down the arcade. Sometimes a woman would glance at Boris or me, and then, noticing our greasy clothes, look hastily away again. One fought another battle in the Metro and was home by ten. Generally from ten to midnight I went to a little *bistro* in our street, an underground place frequented by Arab navvies. It was a bad place for fights, and I sometimes saw bottles thrown, once with fearful effect, but as a rule the Arabs fought among themselves and let Christians alone. *Raki*, the Arab drink, was very cheap, and the *bistro* was open at all hours, for the Arabs – lucky men – had the power of working all day and drinking all night.

It was the typical life of a *plongeur*, and it did not seem a bad life at the time. I had no sensation of poverty, for even after paying my rent and setting aside enough for tobacco and journeys and my food on Sundays, I still had four francs a day for drinks, and four francs was wealth. There was – it is hard to express it – a sort of heavy contentment, the contentment a well-fed beast might feel, in a life which had become so simple. For nothing could be simpler than the life of a *plongeur*. He lives in a rhythm between work and sleep, without time to think, hardly conscious of the exterior world; his Paris has shrunk to the hotel, the Metro, a few *bistros* and his bed. If he goes afield, it is only a few streets away, on a trip with some servant-girl who sits on his knee swallowing oysters and beer. On his free day he lies in bed till noon, puts on a clean shirt, throws dice for drinks, and after lunch goes back to bed again. Nothing is quite real to him but the *boulot*, drinks and sleep; and of these sleep is the most important.

One night, in the small hours, there was a murder just beneath my window. I was woken by a fearful uproar, and, going to the window, saw a man lying flat on the stones below; I could see the murderers, three of them, flitting away at the end of the street. Some of us went down and found that the man was quite dead, his skull cracked with a piece of lead piping. I remember the colour of his blood, curiously purple, like wine; it was still on the cobbles when I came home that evening, and they said the schoolchildren had come from miles round to see it. But the thing that strikes me in looking back is that I was in bed and asleep within three minutes of the murder. So were most of the people in the street; we just made sure that the man was done for, and went straight back to bed. We were working people, and where was the sense of wasting sleep over a murder?

Work in the hotel taught me the true value of sleep, just as being hungry had taught me the true value of food. Sleep had ceased to be a mere physical necessity; it was something voluptuous, a debauch more than a relief. I had no more trouble with the bugs. Mario had told me of a sure remedy for them, namely pepper, strewed thick over the bedclothes. It made me sneeze, but the bugs all hated it, and emigrated to other rooms.

XVII

With thirty francs a week to spend on drinks I could take part in the social life of the quarter. We had some jolly evenings, on Saturdays, in the little *bistro* at the foot of the Hôtel des Trois Moineaux.

The brick-floored room, fifteen feet square, was packed with twenty people, and the air dim with smoke. The noise was deafening, for everyone was either talking at the top of his voice or singing. Sometimes it was just a confused din of voices; sometimes everyone would burst out together in the same song – the 'Marseillaise', or the 'Internationale', or 'Madelon', or 'Les Fraises et les Framboises'. Azaya, a great clumping peasant girl who worked fourteen hours a day in a glass factory, sang a song about '*Elle a per*du *son pantalon, tout en dan*sant *le Charleston*'. Her friend Marinette, a thin, dark Corsican girl of obstinate virtue, tied her knees together and danced the *danse du ventre*. The old Rougiers wandered in and out, cadging drinks and trying to tell a long, involved story about someone who had once cheated them over a bedstead. R., cadaverous and silent, sat in his corner quietly boozing. Charlie, drunk, half danced, half staggered to and fro with a glass of sham absinthe balanced in one fat hand, pinching the women's breasts and declaiming poetry. People played darts and diced for drinks. Manuel, a Spaniard, dragged the girls to the bar and shook the dice-box against their bellies, for luck. Madame F. stood at the bar rapidly pouring *chopines* of wine through the pewter funnel, with a wet dishcloth always handy, because every man in the room tried to make love to her. Two children, bastards of big Louis the bricklayer, sat in a corner sharing a glass of *sirop*. Everyone was very happy, overwhelmingly certain that the world was a good place and we a notable set of people.

For an hour the noise scarcely slackened. Then about midnight there was a piercing shout of '*Citoyens!*' and the sound of a chair falling over. A blond, red-faced workman had risen to his feet and was banging a bottle on the table. Everyone stopped singing; the word went round, 'Sh! Fureux is starting!' Fureux was a strange creature, a Limousin stonemason who worked steadily all the week and drank himself into a kind of paroxysm on Saturdays. He had lost his memory and could not remember anything before the war, and he would have gone to pieces through drink if Madame F. had not taken care of him. On Saturday evenings at about five o'clock she would say to someone, 'Catch Fureux before he spends his wages,' and when he had been caught she would take away his money, leaving him enough for one good drink. One week he escaped, and, rolling blind drunk in the Place Monge, was run over by a car and badly hurt.

The queer thing about Fureux was that, though he was a Communist when sober, he turned violently patriotic when drunk. He started the evening with good Communist principles, but after four or five litres he was a rampant Chauvinist, denouncing spies, challenging all foreigners to fight, and, if he was not prevented, throwing bottles. It was at this stage that he made his speech – for he made a patriotic speech every Saturday night. The speech was always the same, word for word. It ran:

'Citizens of the Republic, are there any Frenchmen here? If there are any Frenchmen here, I rise to remind them – to remind them in effect, of the glorious days of the war. When one looks back upon that time of comradeship and heroism – one looks back, in effect, upon that time of comradeship and heroism. When one remembers the heroes who are dead – one remembers, in effect, the heroes who are dead. Citizens of the Republic, I was wounded at Verdun —'

Here he partially undressed and showed the wound he had received at Verdun. There were shouts of applause. We thought nothing in the world could be funnier than this speech of Fureux's. He was a well-known spectacle in the quarter; people used to come in from other *bistros* to watch him when his fit started.

The word was passed round to bait Fureux. With a wink to the others someone called for silence, and asked him to sing the 'Marseillaise'. He sang it well, in a fine bass voice, with patriotic gurgling noises deep down in his chest when he came to *'Aux armes, citoyens! Forrmez vos bataillons!'*. Veritable tears rolled down his cheeks; he was too drunk to see that everyone was laughing at him. Then, before he had finished, two strong workmen seized him by either arm and held him down, while Azaya shouted, *'Vive l'Allemagne!'* just out of his reach. Fureux's face went purple at such infamy. Everyone in the *bistro* began shouting together, *'Vive l'Allemagne! À bas la France!'* while Fureux struggled to get at them. But suddenly he spoiled the fun. His face turned pale and doleful, his limbs went limp, and before anyone could stop him he was sick on the table. Then Madame F. hoisted him like a sack and carried him up to bed. In the morning he reappeared, quiet and civil, and bought a copy of *L'Humanité*.

The table was wiped with a cloth, Madame F. brought more litre bottles and loaves of bread, and we settled down to serious drinking. There were more songs. An itinerant singer came in with his banjo and performed for five-sou pieces. An Arab and a girl from the *bistro* down the street did a dance, the man wielding a painted wooden phallus the size of a rolling-pin. There were gaps in the noise now. People had begun to talk about their love-affairs, and the war, and the barbel fishing in the Seine, and the best way to *faire la révolution*, and to tell stories. Charlie, grown sober again, captured the conversation and talked about his soul for five minutes. The doors and windows were opened to cool the room. The street was emptying, and in the distance one could hear the lonely milk train thundering down the Boulevard St Michel. The air blew cold on our foreheads, and the coarse African wine still tasted good; we were still happy, but meditatively, with the shouting and hilarious mood finished.

By one o'clock we were not happy any longer. We felt the joy of the evening wearing thin, and called hastily for more bottles, but Madame F. was watering the wine now, and it did not taste the same. Men grew quarrelsome. The girls were violently kissed and hands thrust into their bosoms and they made off lest worse should happen. Big Louis, the bricklayer, was drunk, and crawled about the floor barking and pretending to be a dog. The others grew tired of him and kicked at him as he went past. People seized each other by the arm and began long rambling confessions, and were angry when these were not listened to. The crowd thinned. Manuel and another man, both gamblers, went across to the Arab *bistro*, where card-playing went on till daylight. Charlie suddenly borrowed thirty francs from Madame F. and disappeared, probably to a brothel. Men began to empty their glasses, call briefly, *''sieurs, dames!'* and go off to bed.

By half-past one the last drop of pleasure had evaporated, leaving nothing but headaches. We perceived that we were not splendid inhabitants of a splendid world, but a crew of underpaid workmen grown squalidly and dismally drunk. We went on swallowing the wine, but it was only from habit, and the stuff seemed suddenly nauseating. One's head had swollen up like a balloon, the floor rocked, one's tongue and lips were stained purple. At last it was no use keeping it up any longer. Several men went out into the yard behind the *bistro* and were sick. We crawled up to bed, tumbled down half dressed, and stayed there ten hours.

Most of my Saturday nights went in this way. On the whole, the two hours when one was perfectly and wildly happy seemed worth the subsequent headache. For many men in the quarter, unmarried and with no future to think of, the weekly drinking-bout was the one thing that made life worth living.

XVIII

Charlie told us a good story one Saturday night in the *bistro*. Try and picture him – drunk, but sober enough to talk consecutively. He bangs on the zinc bar and yells for silence:

'Silence, *messieurs et dames* – silence, I implore you! Listen to this story that I am about to tell you. A memorable story, an instructive story, one of the souvenirs of a refined and civilised life. Silence, *messieurs et dames!*

'It happened at a time when I was hard up. You know what that is like – how damnable, that a man of refinement should ever be in such a condition. My money had not come from home; I had pawned everything, and there was nothing open to me except to work, which is a thing I will not do. I was living with a girl at the time – Yvonne her name was – a great half-witted peasant girl like Azaya there, with yellow hair and fat legs. The two of us had eaten nothing in three days. *Mon Dieu*, what sufferings! The girl used to walk up and down the room with her hands on her belly, howling like a dog that she was dying of starvation. It was terrible.

'But to a man of intelligence nothing is impossible. I propounded to myself the question, "What is the easiest way to get money without working?" And immediately the answer came: "To get money easily one must be a woman. Has not every woman something to sell?" And then, as I lay reflecting upon the things I should do if I were a woman, an idea came into my head. I remembered the Government maternity hospitals – you know the Government maternity hospitals? They are places where women who are *enceinte* are given meals free and no questions are asked. It is done to encourage childbearing. Any woman can go there and demand a meal, and she is given it immediately.

' "*Mon Dieu!*" I thought, "if only I were a woman! I would eat at one of those places every day. Who can tell whether a woman is *enceinte* or not, without an examination?"

'I turned to Yvonne. "Stop that insufferable bawling," I said; "I have thought of a way to get food."

' "How?" said she.

' "It is simple," I said. "Go to the Government maternity hospital. Tell them you are *enceinte* and ask for food. They will give you a good meal and ask no questions."

'Yvonne was appalled. "*Mais, mon Dieu*," she cried, "I am not *enceinte*!"

' "Who cares?" I said. "That is easily remedied. What do you need except a cushion – two cushions if necessary? It is an inspiration from heaven, *ma chère*. Don't waste it."

'Well, in the end I persuaded her, and then we borrowed a cushion and I got her ready and took her to the maternity hospital. They received her with open arms. They gave her cabbage soup, a ragoût of beef, a purée of potatoes, bread and cheese and beer, and all kinds of advice about her baby. Yvonne gorged till she almost burst her skin, and managed to slip some of the bread and cheese into her pocket for me. I took her there every day until I had money again. My intelligence had saved us.

'Everything went well until a year later. I was with Yvonne again, and one day we were walking down the Boulevard Port Royal, near the barracks. Suddenly Yvonne's mouth fell open, and she began turning red and white, and red again.

'"*Mon Dieu!*" she cried, "look at that who is coming! It is the nurse who was in charge at the maternity hospital. I am ruined!"

'"Quick!" I said, "run!" But it was too late. The nurse had recognised Yvonne, and she came straight up to us, smiling. She was a big fat woman with a gold pince-nez and red cheeks like the cheeks of an apple. A motherly, interfering kind of woman.

'"I hope you are well, *ma petite*?" she said kindly. "And your baby, is he well too? Was it a boy, as you were hoping?"

'Yvonne had begun trembling so hard that I had to grip her arm. "No," she said at last.

'"Ah, then, *évidemment*, it was a girl?"

'Thereupon Yvonne, the idiot, lost her head completely. "No," she actually said again!

'The nurse was taken aback. "*Comment!*" she exclaimed, "neither a boy nor a girl! But how can that be?"

'Figure to yourselves, *messieurs et dames*, it was a dangerous moment. Yvonne had turned the colour of a beetroot and looked ready to burst into tears; another second and she would have confessed everything. Heaven knows what might have happened. But as for me, I had kept my head; I stepped in and saved the situation.

'"It was twins," I said calmly.

'"Twins!" exclaimed the nurse. And she was so pleased that she took Yvonne by the shoulders and embraced her on both cheeks, publicly.

'Yes, twins . . .'

XIX

One day, when we had been at the Hôtel X. five or six weeks, Boris disappeared without notice. In the evening I found him waiting for me in the Rue de Rivoli. He slapped me gaily on the shoulder.

'Free at last, *mon ami!* You can give notice in the morning. The Auberge opens tomorrow.'

'Tomorrow?'

'Well, possibly we shall need a day or two to arrange things. But, at any rate, no more *cafeterie! Nous voilà lancés, mon ami!* My tail coat is out of pawn already.'

His manner was so hearty that I felt sure there was something wrong, and I did not at all want to leave my safe and comfortable job at the hotel. However, I had promised Boris, so I gave notice, and the next morning at seven went down to the Auberge de Jehan Cottard. It was locked, and I went in search of Boris, who had once more bolted from his lodgings and taken a room in the Rue de la Croix Nivert. I found him asleep, together with a girl whom he had picked up the night before, and who he told me was 'of a very sympathetic temperament'. As to the restaurant, he said that it was all arranged; there were only a few little things to be seen to before we opened.

At ten I managed to get Boris out of bed, and we unlocked the restaurant. At a glance I saw what the 'few little things' amounted to; it was briefly this: that the alterations had not been touched since our last visit. The stoves for the kitchen had not arrived, the water and electricity had not been laid on, and there was all manner of painting, polishing and carpentering to be done. Nothing short of a miracle could open the restaurant within ten days, and by the look of things it might collapse without even opening. It was obvious what had happened. The *patron* was short of money, and he had engaged the staff (there were four of us) in order to use us instead of workmen. He would be getting our services almost free, for waiters are paid no wages, and, though he would have to pay me, he would not be feeding me till the restaurant opened. In effect, he had swindled us of several hundred francs by sending for us before the restaurant was open. We had thrown up a good job for nothing.

Boris, however, was full of hope. He had only one idea in his head, namely, that here at last was a chance of being a waiter and wearing a tail coat once more. For this he was quite willing to do ten days' work unpaid, with the chance of being left jobless in the end. 'Patience!' he kept saying. 'That will arrange itself. Wait till the restaurant opens, and we'll get it all back. Patience, *mon ami!*'

We needed patience, for days passed and the restaurant did not even progress towards opening. We cleaned out the cellars, fixed the shelves, distempered the walls, polished the woodwork, whitewashed the ceiling, stained the floor; but the main work, the plumbing and gasfitting and electricity, was still not done, because the *patron* could not pay the bills. Evidently he was almost penniless, for he refused the smallest charges, and he had a trick of swiftly disappearing when asked for money. His blend of shiftiness and aristocratic manners made him very hard to deal with. Melancholy duns came looking for him at all hours, and by instruction we always told them that he was at Fontainebleau, or Saint Cloud, or some other place that was safely distant. Meanwhile I was getting hungrier and hungrier. I had left the hotel with thirty francs, and I had to go back immediately to a diet of dry bread. Boris had managed in the beginning to extract an advance of sixty francs from the *patron*, but he had spent half of it in redeeming his waiter's clothes, and half on the girl of sympathetic temperament. He borrowed three francs a day from Jules, the second waiter, and spent it on bread. Some days we had not even money for tobacco.

Sometimes the cook came to see how things were getting on, and when she saw that the kitchen was still bare of pots and pans she usually wept. Jules, the second waiter, refused steadily to help with the work. He was a Magyar, a little dark, sharp-featured fellow in spectacles, and very talkative; he had been a medical student, but had abandoned his training for lack of money. He had a taste for talking while other people were working, and he told me all about himself and his ideas. It appeared that he was a Communist, and had various strange theories (he could prove to you by figures that it was wrong to work), and he was also, like most Magyars, passionately proud. Proud and lazy men do not make good waiters. It was Jules's dearest boast that once when a customer in a restaurant had insulted him, he had poured a plate of hot soup down the customer's neck, and then walked straight out without even waiting to be sacked.

As each day went by Jules grew more and more enraged at the trick the *patron* had played on us. He had a spluttering, oratorical way of talking. He used to walk up and down shaking his fist, and trying to incite me not to work:

'Put that brush down, you fool! You and I belong to proud races; we don't work for nothing, like these damned Russian serfs. I tell you, to be cheated like this is torture to me. There have been times in my life, when someone has cheated me even of five sous, when I have vomited – yes, vomited with rage.

'Besides, *mon vieux*, don't forget that I'm a Communist. *À bas les bourgeois!* Did any man alive ever see me working when I could avoid it? No. And not only I don't wear myself out working, like you other fools, but I steal, just to show my independence. Once I was in a restaurant where the *patron* thought he could treat me like a dog. Well, in revenge I found out a way to steal milk from the milk-cans and seal them up again so that no one should know. I tell you, I just swilled that milk down night and morning. Every day I drank four litres of milk, besides half a litre of cream. The *patron* was at his wits' end to know where the milk was going. It wasn't that I wanted milk, you understand, because I hate the stuff; it was principle, just principle.

'Well, after three days I began to get dreadful pains in my belly, and I went to the doctor. "What have you been eating?" he said. I said: "I drink four litres of milk a day, and half a litre of cream." "Four litres!" he said. "Then stop it at once. You'll burst if you go on." "What do I care?" I said. "With me principle is everything. I shall go on drinking that milk, even if I do burst."

'Well, the next day the *patron* caught me stealing milk. "You're sacked," he said; "you leave at the end of the week." "*Pardon, monsieur,*" I said, "I shall leave this morning." "No, you won't," he said, "I can't spare you till Saturday." "Very well, *mon patron,*" I thought to myself, "we'll see who gets tired of it first." And then I set to work to smash the crockery. I broke nine plates the first day and thirteen the second; after that the *patron* was glad to see the last of me.

'Ah, I'm not one of your Russian *moujiks* . . .'

Ten days passed. It was a bad time. I was absolutely at the end of my money, and my rent was several days overdue. We loafed about the dismal empty restaurant, too hungry even to get on with the work that remained.

Only Boris now believed that the restaurant would open. He had set his heart on being *maître d'hôtel*, and he invented a theory that the *patron*'s money was tied up in shares and he was waiting a favourable moment for selling. On the tenth day I had nothing to eat or smoke, and I told the *patron* that I could not continue working without an advance on my wages. As blandly as usual, the *patron* promised the advance, and then, according to his custom, vanished. I walked part of the way home, but I did not feel equal to a scene with Madame F. over the rent, so I passed the night on a bench on the boulevard. It was very uncomfortable – the arm of the seat cuts into your back – and much colder than I had expected. There was plenty of time, in the long boring hours between dawn and work, to think what a fool I had been to deliver myself into the hands of these Russians.

Then, in the morning, the luck changed. Evidently the *patron* had come to an understanding with his creditors, for he arrived with money in his pockets, set the alterations going, and gave me my advance. Boris and I bought macaroni and a piece of horse's liver, and had our first hot meal in ten days.

The workmen were brought in and the alterations made, hastily and with incredible shoddiness. The tables, for instance, were to be covered with baize, but when the *patron* found that baize was expensive he bought instead disused army blankets, smelling incorrigibly of sweat. The table-cloths (they were check, to go with the 'Norman' decorations) would cover them, of course. On the last night we were at work till two in the morning, getting things ready. The crockery did not arrive till eight, and, being new, had all to be washed. The cutlery did not arrive till the next morning, nor the linen either, so that we had to dry the crockery with a shirt of the *patron*'s and an old pillowslip belonging to the concierge. Boris and I did all the work. Jules was skulking, and the *patron* and his wife sat in the bar with a dun and some Russian friends, drinking success to the restaurant. The cook was in the kitchen with her head on the table, crying, because she was expected to cook for fifty people, and there were not pots and pans enough for ten. About midnight there was a fearful interview with some duns, who came intending to seize eight copper saucepans which the *patron* had obtained on credit. They were bought off with half a bottle of brandy.

Jules and I missed the last Metro home and had to sleep on the floor of the restaurant. The first thing we saw in the morning were two large rats sitting on the kitchen table, eating from a ham that stood there. It seemed a bad omen, and I was surer than ever that the Auberge de Jehan Cottard would turn out a failure.

XX

The *patron* had engaged me as kitchen *plongeur*; that is, my job was to wash up, keep the kitchen clean, prepare vegetables, make tea, coffee and sandwiches, do the simpler cooking, and run errands. The terms were, as usual, five hundred francs a month and food, but I had no free day and no fixed working hours. At the Hôtel X. I had seen catering at its best, with unlimited money and good organisation. Now, at the Auberge, I learned how things are done in a thoroughly bad restaurant. It is worth describing, for there are hundreds of similar restaurants in Paris, and every visitor feeds in one of them occasionally.

I should add, by the way, that the Auberge was not the ordinary cheap eating-house frequented by students and workmen. We did not provide an adequate meal at less than twenty-five francs, and we were picturesque and artistic, which sent up our social standing. There were the indecent pictures in the bar, and the Norman decorations – sham beams on the walls, electric lights done up as candlesticks, 'peasant' pottery, even a mounting-block at the door – and the *patron* and the head waiter were Russian officers, and many of the customers titled Russian refugees. In short, we were decidedly chic.

Nevertheless, the conditions behind the kitchen door were suitable for a pigsty. For this is what our service arrangements were like:

The kitchen measured fifteen feet long by eight broad, and half this space was taken up by the stoves and tables All the pots had to be kept on shelves out of reach, and there was only room for one dustbin. This dustbin used to be crammed full by midday, and the floor was normally an inch deep in a compost of trampled food.

For firing we had nothing but three gas-stoves, without ovens, and all joints had to be sent out to the bakery.

There was no larder. Our substitute for one was a half-roofed shed in the yard, with a tree growing in the middle of it. The meat, vegetables and so forth lay there on the bare earth, raided by rats and cats.

There was no hot water laid on. Water for washing up had to be heated in pans, and, as there was no room for these on the stoves when meals were cooking, most of the plates had to be washed in cold water. This, with soft soap and the hard Paris water, meant scraping the grease off with bits of newspaper.

We were so short of saucepans that I had to wash each one as soon as it was done with, instead of leaving them till the evening. This alone wasted probably an hour a day.

Owing to some scamping of expense in the installation, the electric light usually fused at eight in the evening. The *patron* would only allow us three candles in the kitchen, and the cook said three were unlucky, so we had only two.

Our coffee-grinder was borrowed from a *bistro* near by, and our dustbin and brooms from the concierge. After the first week a quantity of linen did not come back from the wash, as the bill was not paid. We were in trouble with the inspector of labour, who had discovered that the staff included no Frenchmen; he had several private interviews with the *patron*, who, I believe, was obliged to bribe him. The electric company was still dunning us, and when the duns found that we would buy them off with *apéritifs*, they came every morning. We were in debt at the grocery, and credit would have been stopped, only the grocer's wife (a moustachio'd woman of sixty) had taken a fancy to Jules, who was sent every morning to cajole her. Similarly I had to waste an hour every day haggling over vegetables in the Rue du Commerce, to save a few centimes.

These are the results of starting a restaurant on insufficient capital. And in these conditions the cook and I were expected to serve thirty or forty meals a day, and would later on be serving a hundred. From the first day it was too much for us. The cook's working hours were from eight in the morning till midnight, and mine from seven in the morning till half-past twelve the next morning – seventeen and a half hours, almost without a break. We never had time to sit down till five in the afternoon, and even then there was no seat except the top of the dustbin. Boris, who lived near by and had not to catch the last Metro home, worked from eight in the morning till two the next morning – eighteen hours a day, seven days a week. Such hours, though not usual, are nothing extraordinary in Paris.

Life settled at once into a routine that made the Hôtel X. seem like a holiday. Every morning at six I drove myself out of bed, did not shave, sometimes washed, hurried up to the Place d'Italie and fought for a place on the Metro. By seven I was in the desolation of the cold, filthy kitchen, with the potato skins and bones and fishtails littered on the floor, and a pile of plates, stuck together in their grease, waiting from overnight. I could not start on the plates yet, because the water was cold, and I had to fetch milk and make coffee, for the others arrived at eight and expected to find coffee ready. Also, there were always several copper saucepans to clean. Those copper saucepans are the bane of a *plongeur*'s life. They have to be scoured with sand and bunches of chain, ten minutes to each one, and then polished on the outside with Brasso. Fortunately the art of making them has been lost and they are gradually vanishing from French kitchens, though one can still buy them second-hand.

When I had begun on the plates the cook would take me away from the plates to begin skinning onions, and when I had begun on the onions the *patron* would arrive and send me out to buy cabbages. When I came back with the cabbages the *patron*'s wife would tell me to go to some shop half a mile away and buy a pot of rouge; by the time I came back there would be more vegetables waiting, and the plates were still not done. In this way our incompetence piled one job on another throughout the day, everything in arrears.

Till ten, things went comparatively easily, though we were working fast, and no one lost his temper. The cook would find time to talk about her artistic nature, and say did I not think Tolstoi was *épatant*, and sing in a fine soprano voice as she minced beef on the board. But at ten the waiters began clamouring for their lunch, which they had early, and at eleven the first customers would be arriving. Suddenly everything became hurry and bad temper. There was not the same furious rushing and yelling as at the Hôtel X., but an atmosphere of muddle, petty spite and exasperation. Discomfort was at the bottom of it. It was unbearably cramped in the kitchen, and dishes had to be put on the floor, and one had to be thinking constantly about not stepping on them. The cook's vast buttocks banged against me as she moved to and fro. A ceaseless, nagging chorus of orders streamed from her:

'Unspeakable idiot! How many times have I told you not to bleed the beetroots? Quick, let me get to the sink! Put those knives away; get on with the potatoes. What have you done with my strainer? Oh, leave those potatoes alone. Didn't I tell you to skim the *bouillon?* Take that can of water off the stove. Never mind the washing up, chop this celery. No, not like that, you fool, like this. There! Look at you letting those peas boil over! Now get to work and scale these herrings. Look, do you call this plate clean? Wipe it on your apron. Put that salad on the floor. That's right, put it where I'm bound to step in it! Look out, that pot's boiling over! Get me down that saucepan. No, the other one. Put this on the grill. Throw those potatoes away. Don't waste time, throw them on the floor. Tread them in. Now throw down some sawdust; this floor's like a skating-rink. Look, you fool, that steak's burning! *Mon Dieu*, why did they send me an idiot for a *plongeur?* Who are you talking to? Do you realise that my aunt was a Russian countess?' etc. etc. etc.

This went on till three o'clock without much variation, except that about eleven the cook usually had a *crise de nerfs* and a flood of tears. From three to five was a fairly slack time for the waiters, but the cook was still busy, and I was working my fastest, for there was a pile of dirty plates waiting, and it was a race to get them done, or partly done, before dinner began. The washing up was doubled by the primitive conditions – a cramped draining-board, tepid water, sodden cloths, and a sink that got blocked once in an hour. By five the cook and I were feeling unsteady on our feet, not having eaten or sat down since seven. We used to collapse, she on the dustbin and I on the floor, drink a bottle of beer, and apologise for some of the things we had said in the morning. Tea was what kept us going. We took care to have a pot always stewing, and drank pints during the day.

At half-past five the hurry and quarrelling began again, and now worse than before, because everyone was tired out. The cook had a *crise de nerfs* at six and another at nine; they came on so regularly that one could have told the time by them. She would flop down on the dustbin, begin weeping hysterically, and cry out that never, no, never had she thought to come to such a life as this; her nerves would not stand it; she had studied music at Vienna; she had a bedridden husband to support, etc. etc. At another time one would have been sorry for her, but, tired as we all were, her whimpering voice merely infuriated us. Jules used to stand in the doorway and mimic her weeping. The *patron*'s wife nagged, and

Boris and Jules quarrelled all day, because Jules shirked his work, and Boris, as head waiter, claimed the larger share of the tips. Only the second day after the restaurant opened, they came to blows in the kitchen over a two-franc tip, and the cook and I had to separate them. The only person who never forgot his manners was the *patron*. He kept the same hours as the rest of us, but he had no work to do, for it was his wife who really managed things. His sole job, besides ordering the supplies, was to stand in the bar smoking cigarettes and looking gentlemanly, and he did that to perfection.

The cook and I generally found time to eat our dinner between ten and eleven o'clock. At midnight the cook would steal a packet of food for her husband, stow it under her clothes, and make off, whimpering that these hours would kill her and she would give notice in the morning. Jules also left at midnight, usually after a dispute with Boris, who had to look after the bar till two. Between twelve and half-past I did what I could to finish the washing up. There was no time to attempt doing the work properly, and I used simply to rub the grease off the plates with table-napkins. As for the dirt on the floor, I let it lie, or swept the worst of it out of sight under the stoves.

At half-past twelve I would put on my coat and hurry out. The *patron*, bland as ever, would stop me as I went down the alley-way past the bar. '*Mais, mon cher monsieur*, how tired you look! Please do me the favour of accepting this glass of brandy.'

He would hand me the glass of brandy as courteously as though I had been a Russian duke instead of a *plongeur*. He treated all of us like this. It was our compensation for working seventeen hours a day.

As a rule the last Metro was almost empty – a great advantage, for one could sit down and sleep for a quarter of an hour. Generally I was in bed by half-past one. Sometimes I missed the train and had to sleep on the floor of the restaurant, but it hardly mattered, for I could have slept on cobblestones at that time.

XXI

This life went on for about a fortnight, with a slight increase of work as more customers came to the restaurant. I could have saved an hour a day by taking a room near the restaurant, but it seemed impossible to find time to change lodgings – or, for that matter, to get my hair cut, look at a newspaper, or even undress completely. After ten days I managed to find a free quarter of an hour, and wrote to my friend B. in London asking him if he could get me a job of some sort – anything, so long as it allowed more than five hours sleep. I was simply not equal to going on with a seventeen-hour day, though there are plenty of people who think nothing of it. When one is overworked, it is a good cure for self-pity to think of the thousands of people in Paris restaurants who work such hours, and will go on doing it, not for a few weeks, but for years. There was a girl in a *bistro* near my hotel who worked from seven in the morning till midnight for a whole year, only sitting down to her meals. I remember once asking her to come to a dance, and she laughed and said that she had not been further than the street corner for several months. She was consumptive, and died about the time I left Paris.

After only a week we were all neurasthenic with fatigue, except Jules, who skulked persistently. The quarrels, intermittent at first, had now become continuous. For hours one would keep up a drizzle of useless nagging, rising into storms of abuse every few minutes. 'Get me down that saucepan, idiot!' the cook would cry (she was not tall enough to reach the shelves where the saucepans were kept). 'Get it down yourself, you old whore,' I would answer. Such remarks seemed to be generated spontaneously from the air of the kitchen.

We quarrelled over things of inconceivable pettiness. The dustbin, for instance, was an unending source of quarrels – whether it should be put where I wanted it, which was in the cook's way, or where she wanted it, which was between me and the sink. Once she nagged and nagged until at last, in pure spite, I lifted the dustbin up and put it out in the middle of the floor, where she was bound to trip over it.

'Now, you cow,' I said, 'move it yourself.'

Poor old woman, it was too heavy for her to lift, and she sat down, put her head on the table and burst out crying. And I jeered at her. This is the kind of effect that fatigue has upon one's manners.

After a few days the cook had ceased talking about Tolstoi and her artistic nature, and she and I were not on speaking terms, except for the purposes of work, and Boris and Jules were not on speaking terms, and neither of them was on speaking terms with the cook. Even Boris and I were barely on speaking terms. We had agreed beforehand that the *engueulades* of working hours did not count between times; but we had called each other things too bad to be forgotten – and besides, there were no between times. Jules grew lazier and lazier, and he stole food constantly – from a sense of duty, he said. He called the rest of us *jaune* – blackleg – when we would not join with him in stealing. He had a curious, malignant spirit. He told me, as a matter of pride, that he had sometimes wrung a dirty dishcloth into a customer's soup before taking it in, just to be revenged upon a member of the bourgeoisie.

The kitchen grew dirtier and the rats bolder, though we trapped a few of them. Looking round that filthy room, with raw meat lying among the refuse on the floor, and cold, clotted saucepans sprawling everywhere, and the sink blocked and coated with grease, I used to wonder whether there could be a restaurant in the world as bad as ours. But the other three all said that they had been in dirtier places. Jules took a positive pleasure in seeing things dirty. In the afternoon, when he had not much to do, he used to stand in the kitchen doorway jeering at us for working too hard:

'Fool! Why do you wash that plate? Wipe it on your trousers. Who cares about the customers? *They* don't know what's going on. What is restaurant work? You are carving a chicken and it falls on the floor. You apologise, you bow, you go out; and in five minutes you come back by another door – with the same chicken. That is restaurant work,' etc.

And, strange to say, in spite of all this filth and incompetence, the Auberge de Jehan Cottard was actually a success. For the first few days all our customers were Russians, friends of the *patron*, and these were followed by Americans and other foreigners – no Frenchmen. Then one night there was tremendous excitement, because our first Frenchman had arrived. For a moment our quarrels were forgotten and we all united in the effort to serve a good dinner. Boris tiptoed into the kitchen, jerked his thumb over his shoulder and whispered conspiratorially:

'*Sh! Attention, un Français!*'

A moment later the *patron*'s wife came and whispered:

'*Attention, un Français!* See that he gets a double portion of all vegetables.'

While the Frenchman ate, the *patron*'s wife stood behind the grille of the kitchen door and watched the expression of his face. Next night the Frenchman came back with two other Frenchmen. This meant that we were earning a good name; the surest sign of a bad restaurant is to be frequented only by foreigners. Probably part of the reason for our success was that the *patron*, with the sole gleam of sense he had shown in fitting out the restaurant, had bought very sharp table-knives. Sharp knives, of course, are *the* secret of a successful restaurant. I am glad that this happened, for it destroyed one of my illusions, namely, the idea that Frenchmen know good food when they see it. Or perhaps we *were* a fairly good restaurant by Paris standards; in which case the bad ones must be past imagining.

In a very few days after I had written to B. he replied to say that there was a job he could get for me. It was to look after a congenital imbecile, which sounded a splendid rest cure after the Auberge de Jehan Cottard. I pictured myself loafing in the country lanes, knocking thistle-heads off with my stick, feeding on roast lamb and treacle tart, and sleeping ten hours a night in sheets smelling of lavender. B. sent me a fiver to pay my passage and get my clothes out of pawn, and as soon as the money arrived I gave one day's notice and left the restaurant. My leaving so suddenly embarrassed the *patron*, for as usual he was penniless, and he had to pay my wages thirty francs short. However, he stood me a glass of Courvoisier '48 brandy, and I think he felt that this made up the difference. They engaged a Czech, a thoroughly competent *plongeur*, in my place, and the poor old cook was sacked a few weeks later. Afterwards I heard that, with two first-rate people in the kitchen, the *plongeur*'s work had been cut down to fifteen hours a day. Below that no one could have cut it, short of modernising the kitchen.

XXII

For what they are worth I want to give my opinions about the life of a Paris *plongeur*. When one comes to think of it, it is strange that thousands of people in a great modern city should spend their waking hours swabbing dishes in hot dens underground. The question I am raising is why this life goes on – what purpose it serves, and who wants it to continue, and why. I am not taking the merely rebellious, *fainéant* attitude. I am trying to consider the social significance of a *plongeur*'s life.

I think one should start by saying that a *plongeur* is one of the slaves of the modern world. Not that there is any need to whine over him, for he is better off than many manual workers, but still, he is no freer than if he were bought and sold. His work is servile and without art; he is paid just enough to keep him alive; his only holiday is the sack. He is cut off from marriage, or, if he marries, his wife must work too. Except by a lucky chance, he has no escape from this life, save into prison. At this moment there are men with university degrees scrubbing dishes in Paris for ten or fifteen hours a day. One cannot say that it is mere idleness on their part, for an idle man cannot be a *plongeur*; they have simply been trapped by a routine which makes thought impossible. If *plongeurs* thought at all, they would long ago have formed a union and gone on strike for better treatment. But they do not think, because they have no leisure for it; their life has made slaves of them.

The question is, why does this slavery continue? People have a way of taking it for granted that all work is done for a sound purpose. They see somebody else doing a disagreeable job, and think that they have solved things by saying that the job is necessary. Coal-mining, for example, is hard work, but it is necessary – we must have coal. Working in the sewers is unpleasant, but somebody must work in the sewers. And similarly with a *plongeur*'s work. Some people must feed in restaurants, and so other people must swab dishes for eighty hours a week. It is the work of civilisation, therefore unquestionable. This point is worth considering.

Is a *plongeur*'s work really necessary to civilisation? We have a vague feeling that it must be 'honest' work, because it is hard and disagreeable, and we have made a sort of fetish of manual work. We see a man cutting down a tree, and we make sure that he is filling a social need, just because he uses his muscles; it does not occur to us that he may only be cutting down a beautiful tree to make room for a hideous statue. I believe it is the same with a *plongeur*. He earns his bread in the sweat of his brow, but it does not follow that he is doing anything useful; he may be only supplying a luxury which, very often, is not a luxury.

As an example of what I mean by luxuries which are not luxuries, take an extreme case, such as one hardly sees in Europe. Take an Indian rickshaw puller, or a gharry pony. In any Far Eastern town there are rickshaw pullers by the hundred, black wretches weighing eight stone, clad in loincloths. Some of them are diseased; some of them are fifty years old. For miles on end they trot in the sun or rain, head down, dragging at the shafts, with the sweat dripping from their grey moustaches. When they go too slowly the passenger calls them *bahinchut*.* They earn thirty or forty rupees a month, and cough their lungs out after a few years. The gharry ponies are gaunt, vicious things that have been sold cheap as having a few years' work left in them. Their master looks on the whip as a substitute for food. Their work expresses itself in a sort of equation – whip plus food equals energy; generally it is about sixty per cent whip and forty per cent food. Sometimes their necks are encircled by one vast sore, so that they drag all day on raw flesh. It is still possible to make them work, however; it is just a question of thrashing them so hard that the pain behind outweighs the pain in front. After a few years even the whip loses its virtue, and the pony goes to the knacker. These are instances of unnecessary work, for there is no real need for gharries and rickshaws; they only exist because Orientals consider it vulgar to walk. They are luxuries, and, as anyone who has ridden in them knows, very poor luxuries. They afford a small amount of convenience, which cannot possibly balance the suffering of the men and animals.

Similarly with the *plongeur*. He is a king compared with a rickshaw puller or a gharry pony, but his case is analogous. He is the slave of a hotel or a restaurant, and his slavery is more or less useless. For, after all, where is the *real* need of big hotels and smart restaurants? They are supposed to provide luxury, but in reality they provide only a cheap, shoddy imitation of it. Nearly everyone hates hotels. Some restaurants are better than others, but it is impossible to get as good a meal in a restaurant as one can get, for the same expense, in a private house. No doubt hotels and restaurants must exist, but there is no need that they should enslave hundreds of people. What makes the work in them is not the essentials; it is the shams that are supposed to represent luxury. Smartness, as it is called, means, in effect, merely that the staff work more and the customers pay more; no one benefits except the proprietor, who will presently buy himself a striped villa at Deauville. Essentially, a 'smart' hotel is a place where a hundred people toil like devils in order that two hundred may pay through the nose for things they do not really want. If the nonsense were cut out of hotels and restaurants, and the work done with simple

* See footnote p. 194.

efficiency, *plongeurs* might work six or eight hours a day instead of ten or fifteen.

Suppose it is granted that a *plongeur*'s work is more or less useless. Then the question follows, why does anyone want him to go on working? I am trying to go beyond the immediate economic cause, and to consider what pleasure it can give anyone to think of men swabbing dishes for life. For there is no doubt that people – comfortably situated people – do find a pleasure in such thoughts. A slave, Marcus Cato said, should be working when he is not sleeping. It does not matter whether his work is needed or not, he must work, because work in itself is good – for slaves, at least. This sentiment still survives, and it has piled up mountains of useless drudgery.

I believe that this instinct to perpetuate useless work is, at bottom, simply fear of the mob. The mob (the thought runs) are such low animals that they would be dangerous if they had leisure; it is safer to keep them too busy to think. A rich man who happens to be intellectually honest, if he is questioned about the improvement of working conditions, usually says something like this:

'We know that poverty is unpleasant; in fact, since it is so remote, we rather enjoy harrowing ourselves with the thought of its unpleasantness. But don't expect us to do anything about it. We are sorry for you lower classes, just as we are sorry for a cat with the mange, but we will fight like devils against any improvement of your condition. We feel that you are much safer as you are. The present state of affairs suits us, and we are not going to take the risk of setting you free, even by an extra hour a day. So, dear brothers, since evidently you must sweat to pay for our trips to Italy, sweat and be damned to you.'

This is particularly the attitude of intelligent, cultivated people; one can read the substance of it in a hundred essays. Very few cultivated people have less than (say) four hundred pounds a year, and naturally they side with the rich, because they imagine that any liberty conceded to the poor is a threat to their own liberty. Foreseeing some dismal Marxian Utopia as the alternative, the educated man prefers to keep things as they are. Possibly he does not like his fellow rich very much, but he supposes that even the vulgarest of them are less inimical to his pleasures, more his kind of people, than the poor, and that he had better stand by them. It is this fear of a supposedly dangerous mob that makes nearly all intelligent people conservative in their opinions.

Fear of the mob is a superstitious fear. It is based on the idea that there is some mysterious, fundamental difference between rich and poor, as though they were two different races, like negroes and white men. But in reality there is no such difference. The mass of the rich and the poor are differentiated by their incomes and nothing else, and the average million-aire is only the average dishwasher dressed in a new suit. Change places, and handy dandy, which is the justice, which is the thief? Everyone who has mixed on equal terms with the poor knows this quite well. But the trouble is that intelligent, cultivated people, the very people who might be expected to have liberal opinions, never do mix with the poor. For what do the majority of educated people know about poverty? In my copy of Villon's poems the editor has actually thought it necessary to explain the line '*Ne pain ne voyent qu'aux fenestres*' by a footnote; so remote is even hunger from the educated man's experience. From this ignorance a superstitious fear of the mob results quite naturally. The educated man pictures a horde of submen, wanting only a day's liberty to loot his house, burn his books, and set him to work minding a machine or sweeping out a lavatory. 'Anything,' he thinks, 'any injustice, sooner than let that mob loose.' He does not see that since there is no difference between the mass of rich and poor, there is no question of setting the mob loose. The mob is in fact loose now, and – in the shape of rich men – is using its power to set up enormous treadmills of boredom, such as 'smart' hotels.

To sum up. A *plongeur* is a slave, and a wasted slave, doing stupid and largely unnecessary work. He is kept at work, ultimately, because of a vague feeling that he would be dangerous if he had leisure. And educated people, who should be on his side, acquiesce in the process, because they know nothing about him and consequently are afraid of him. I say this of the *plongeur* because it is his case I have been considering; it would apply equally to numberless other types of worker. These are only my own ideas about the basic facts of a *plongeur*'s life, made without reference to immediate economic questions, and no doubt largely platitudes. I present them as a sample of the thoughts that are put into one's head by working in a hotel.

XXIII

As soon as I left the Auberge de Jehan Cottard I went to bed and slept the clock round, all but one hour. Then I washed my teeth for the first time in a fortnight, bathed and had my hair cut, and got my clothes out of pawn. I had two glorious days of loafing. I even went in my best suit to the Auberge, leant against the bar and spent five francs on a bottle of English beer. It is a curious sensation, being a customer where you have been a slave's slave. Boris was sorry that I had left the restaurant just at the moment when we were *lancés* and there was a chance of making money. I have heard from him since, and he tells me that he is making a hundred francs a day and has set up a girl who is *très serieuse* and never smells of garlic.

I spent a day wandering about our quarter, saying goodbye to everyone. It was on this day that Charlie told me about the death of old Roucolle the miser, who had once lived in the quarter. Very likely Charlie was lying as usual, but it was a good story.

Roucolle died, aged seventy-four, a year or two before I went to Paris, but the people in the quarter still talked of him while I was there. He never equalled Daniel Dancer* or anyone of that kind, but he was an interesting character. He went to Les Halles every morning to pick up damaged vegetables, and ate cat's meat, and wore newspaper instead of underclothes, and used the wainscoting of his room for firewood, and made himself a pair of trousers out of a sack – all this with half a million francs invested. I should like very much to have known him.

Like many misers, Roucolle came to a bad end through putting his money into a wildcat scheme. One day a Jew appeared in the quarter, an alert, businesslike young chap who had a first-rate plan for smuggling cocaine into England. It is easy enough, of course, to buy cocaine in Paris, and the smuggling would be quite simple in itself, only there is always some spy who betrays the plan to the customs or the police. It is said that this is often done by the very people who sell the cocaine, because the smuggling trade is in the hands of a large combine, who do not want competition. The Jew, however, swore that there was no danger. He knew

---

* *The French translation has this note (in French):* A famous English miser.

a way of getting cocaine direct from Vienna, not through the usual channels, and there would be no blackmail to pay. He had got into touch with Roucolle through a young Pole, a student at the Sorbonne, who was going to put four thousand francs into the scheme if Roucolle would put six thousand. For this they could buy ten pounds of cocaine, which would be worth a small fortune in England.

The Pole and the Jew had a tremendous struggle to get the money from between old Roucolle's claws. Six thousand francs was not much – he had more than that sewn into the mattress in his room – but it was agony for him to part with a sou. The Pole and the Jew were at him for weeks on end, explaining, bullying, coaxing, arguing, going down on their knees and imploring him to produce the money. The old man was half frantic between greed and fear. His bowels yearned at the thought of getting, perhaps, fifty thousand francs' profit, and yet he could not bring himself to risk the money. He used to sit in a corner with his head in his hands, groaning and sometimes yelling out in agony, and often he would kneel down (he was very pious) and pray for strength, but still he couldn't do it. But at last, more from exhaustion than anything else, he gave in quite suddenly; he slit open the mattress where his money was concealed and handed over six thousand francs to the Jew.

The Jew delivered the cocaine the same day, and promptly vanished. And meanwhile, as was not surprising after the fuss Roucolle had made, the affair had been noised all over the quarter. The very next morning the hotel was raided and searched by the police.

Roucolle and the Pole were in agonies. The police were downstairs, working their way up and searching every room in turn, and there was the great packet of cocaine on the table, with no place to hide it and no chance of escaping down the stairs. The Pole was for throwing the stuff out of the window, but Roucolle would not hear of it. Charlie told me that he had been present at the scene. He said that when they tried to take the packet from Roucolle he clasped it to his breast and struggled like a madman, although he was seventy-four years old. He was wild with fright, but he would go to prison rather than throw his money away.

At last, when the police were searching only one floor below, somebody had an idea. A man on Roucolle's floor had a dozen tins of face-powder which he was selling on commission; it was suggested that the cocaine could be put into the tins and passed off as face-powder. The powder was hastily thrown out of the window and the cocaine substituted, and the tins were put openly on Roucolle's table, as though there were nothing to conceal. A few minutes later the police came to search Roucolle's room. They tapped the walls and looked up the chimney and turned out the drawers and examined the floorboards, and then, just as they were about to give it up, having found nothing, the inspector noticed the tins on the table.

'*Tiens*,' he said, 'have a look at those tins. I hadn't noticed them. What's in them, eh?'

'Face-powder,' said the Pole as calmly as he could manage. But at the same instant Roucolle let out a loud groaning noise, from alarm, and the police became suspicious immediately. They opened one of the tins and tipped out the contents, and after smelling it, the inspector said that he believed it was cocaine. Roucolle and the Pole began swearing on the names of the saints that it was only face-powder; but it was no use, the more they protested the more suspicious the police became. The two men were arrested and led off to the police station, followed by half the quarter.

At the station, Roucolle and the Pole were interrogated by the Commissaire while a tin of the cocaine was sent away to be analysed. Charlie said that the scene Roucolle made was beyond description. He wept, prayed, made contradictory statements and denounced the Pole all at once, so loud that he could be heard half a street away. The policemen almost burst with laughing at him.

After an hour a policeman came back with the tin of cocaine and a note from the analyst. He was laughing.

'This is not cocaine, *monsieur*,' he said.

'What, not cocaine?' said the Commissaire. '*Mais, alors* – what is it, then?'

'It is face-powder.'

Roucolle and the Pole were released at once, entirely exonerated but very angry. The Jew had double-crossed them. Afterwards, when the excitement was over, it turned out that he had played the same trick on two other people in the quarter.

The Pole was glad enough to escape, even though he had lost his four thousand francs, but poor old Roucolle was utterly broken down. He took to his bed at once, and all that day and half the night they could hear him thrashing about, mumbling, and sometimes yelling out at the top of his voice:

'Six thousand francs! *Nom de Jésus Christ!* Six thousand francs!'

Three days later he had some kind of stroke, and in a fortnight he was dead – of a broken heart, Charlie said.

XXIV

I travelled to England third class via Dunkirk and Tilbury, which is the cheapest and not the worst way of crossing the Channel. You had to pay extra for a cabin, so I slept in the saloon, together with most of the third-class passengers. I find this entry in my diary for that day:

'Sleeping in the saloon, twenty-seven men, sixteen women. Of the women, not a single one has washed her face this morning. The men mostly went to the bathroom; the women merely produced vanity cases and covered the dirt with powder. Q. A secondary sexual difference?'

On the journey I fell in with a couple of Roumanians, mere children, who were going to England on their honeymoon trip. They asked innumerable questions about England, and I told them some startling lies. I was so pleased to be getting home, after being hard up for months in a foreign city, that England seemed to me a sort of Paradise. There are, indeed, many things in England that make you glad to get home; bathrooms, armchairs, mint sauce, new potatoes properly cooked, brown bread, marmalade, beer made with veritable hops – they are all splendid, if you can pay for them. England is a very good country when you are not poor; and, of course, with a tame imbecile to look after, I was not going to be poor. The thought of not being poor made me very patriotic. The more questions the Roumanians asked, the more I praised England: the climate, the scenery, the art, the literature, the laws – everything in England was perfect.

Was the architecture in England good? the Roumanians asked. 'Splendid!' I said. 'And you should just see the London statues! Paris is vulgar – half grandiosity and half slums. But London—'

Then the boat drew alongside Tilbury pier. The first building we saw on the waterside was one of those huge hotels, all stucco and pinnacles, which stare from the English coast like idiots staring over an asylum wall.

I saw the Roumanians, too polite to say anything, cocking their eyes at the hotel. 'Built by French architects,' I assured them; and even later, when the train was crawling into London through the eastern slums, I still kept it up about the beauties of English architecture. Nothing seemed too good to say about England, now that I was coming home and was not hard up any more.

I went to B.'s office, and his first words knocked everything to ruins. 'I'm sorry,' he said; 'your employers have gone abroad, patient and all. However, they'll be back in a month. I suppose you can hang on till then?'

I was outside in the street before it even occurred to me to borrow some more money. There was a month to wait, and I had exactly nineteen and sixpence in hand. The news had taken my breath away. For a long time I could not make up my mind what to do. I loafed the day in the streets, and at night, not having the slightest notion of how to get a cheap bed in London, I went to a 'family' hotel, where the charge was seven and sixpence. After paying the bill I had ten and twopence in hand.

By the morning I had made my plans. Sooner or later I should have to go to B. for more money, but it seemed hardly decent to do so yet, and in the meantime I must exist in some hole-and-corner way. Past experience set me against pawning my best suit. I would leave all my things at the station cloakroom, except my second-best suit, which I could exchange for some cheap clothes and perhaps a pound. If I was going to live a month on thirty shillings I must have bad clothes – indeed, the worse the better. Whether thirty shillings could be made to last a month I had no idea, not knowing London as I knew Paris. Perhaps I could beg, or sell bootlaces, and I remembered articles I had read in the Sunday papers about beggars who have two thousand pounds sewn into their trousers. It was, at any rate, notoriously impossible to starve in London, so there was nothing to be anxious about.

To sell my clothes I went down into Lambeth, where the people are poor and there are a lot of rag shops. At the first shop I tried the proprietor was polite but unhelpful; at the second he was rude; at the third he was stone deaf, or pretended to be so. The fourth shopman was a large blond young man, very pink all over, like a slice of ham. He looked at the clothes I was wearing and felt them disparagingly between thumb and finger.

'Poor stuff,' he said, 'very poor stuff, that is.' (It was quite a good suit.) 'What yer want for 'em?'

I explained that I wanted some older clothes and as much money as he could spare. He thought for a moment, then collected some dirty-looking rags and threw them onto the counter. 'What about the money?' I said, hoping for a pound. He pursed his lips, then produced *a shilling* and laid it beside the clothes. I did not argue – I was going to argue, but as I opened my mouth he reached out as though to take up the shilling again; I saw that I was helpless. He let me change in a small room behind the shop.

The clothes were a coat, once dark brown, a pair of black dungaree trousers, a scarf and a cloth cap; I had kept my own shirt, socks and boots, and I had a comb and razor in my pocket. It gives one a very strange feeling to be wearing such clothes. I had worn bad enough things before, but nothing at all like these; they were not merely dirty and shapeless, they had – how is one to express it? – a gracelessness, a patina of antique filth, quite different from mere shabbiness. They were the sort of clothes you see on a bootlace seller, or a tramp. An hour later, in Lambeth, I saw a hang-dog man, obviously a tramp, coming towards me, and when I looked again it was myself, reflected in a shop window. The dirt was plastering my face already. Dirt is a great respecter of persons; it lets you alone when you are well dressed, but as soon as your collar is gone it flies towards you from all directions.

I stayed in the streets till late at night, keeping on the move all the time. Dressed as I was, I was half afraid that the police might arrest me as a vagabond, and I dared not speak to anyone, imagining that they must notice a disparity between my accent and my clothes. (Later I discovered that this never happened.) My new clothes had put me instantly into a new world. Everyone's demeanour seemed to have changed abruptly. I helped a hawker pick up a barrow that he had upset. 'Thanks, mate,' he said with a grin. No one had called me mate before in my life – it was the clothes that had done it. For the first time I noticed, too, how the attitude of women varies with a man's clothes. When a badly dressed man passes them they shudder away from him with a quite frank movement of disgust, as though he were a dead cat. Clothes are powerful things. Dressed in a tramp's clothes it is very difficult, at any rate for the first day, not to feel that you are genuinely degraded. You might feel the same shame, irrational but very real, your first night in prison.

At about eleven I began looking for a bed. I had read about doss-houses (they are never called doss-houses, by the way), and I supposed that one could get a bed for fourpence or thereabouts. Seeing a man, a navvy or something of the kind, standing on the kerb in the Waterloo Road, I stopped and questioned him. I said that I was stony broke and wanted the cheapest bed I could get.

'Oh,' said he, 'you go to that 'ouse across the street there, with the sign "Good Beds for Single Men". That's a good kip [sleeping place], that is. I bin there myself on and off. You'll find it cheap *and* clean.'

It was a tall, battered-looking house, with dim lights in all the windows, some of which were patched with brown paper. I entered a stone passageway, and a little etiolated boy with sleepy eyes appeared from a door leading to a cellar. Murmurous sounds came from the cellar, and a wave of hot air and cheese. The boy yawned and held out his hand.

'Want a kip? That'll be a 'og, guv'nor.'

I paid the shilling, and the boy led me up a rickety unlighted staircase to a bedroom. It had a sweetish reek of paregoric and foul linen; the windows seemed to be tight shut, and the air was almost suffocating at first. There was a candle burning, and I saw that the room measured fifteen feet square by eight high, and had eight beds in it. Already six lodgers were in bed, queer lumpy shapes with all their own clothes, even their boots, piled on top of them. Someone was coughing in a loathsome manner in one corner.

When I got into the bed I found that it was as hard as a board, and as for the pillow, it was a mere hard cylinder like a block of wood. It was rather worse than sleeping on a table, because the bed was not six feet long, and very narrow, and the mattress was convex, so that one had to hold on to avoid falling out. The sheets stank so horribly of sweat that I could not bear them near my nose. Also, the bedclothes only consisted of the sheets and a cotton counterpane, so that though stuffy it was none too warm. Several noises recurred throughout the night. About once in an hour the man on my left – a sailor, I think – woke up, swore vilely, and lighted a cigarette. Another man, victim of bladder disease, got up and noisily used his chamber-pot half a dozen times during the night. The man in the corner had a coughing fit once in every twenty minutes, so regularly that one came to listen for it as one listens for the next yap when a dog is baying the moon. It was an unspeakably repellent sound; a foul bubbling and retching, as though the man's bowels were being churned up within him. Once when he struck a match I saw that he was a very old man, with a grey, sunken face like that of a corpse, and he was wearing his trousers wrapped round his head as a nightcap, a thing which for some reason disgusted me very much. Every time he coughed or the other man swore, a sleepy voice from one of the other beds cried out:

'Shut up! Oh, for Christ's—*sake* shut up!'

I had about an hour's sleep in all. In the morning I was woken by a dim impression of some large brown thing coming towards me. I opened my eyes and saw that it was one of the sailor's feet, sticking out of bed close to my face. It was dark brown, quite dark brown like an Indian's, with dirt. The walls were leprous, and the sheets, three weeks from the wash, were almost raw umber colour. I got up, dressed and went downstairs. In the cellar were a row of basins and two slippery roller towels. I had a piece of soap in my pocket, and I was going to wash, when I noticed that every basin was streaked with grime – solid, sticky filth as black as boot-blacking. I went out unwashed. Altogether, the lodging-house had not come up to its description as cheap *and* clean. It was however, as I found later, a fairly representative lodging-house.

I crossed the river and walked a long way eastward, finally going into a coffee-shop on Tower Hill. An ordinary London coffee-shop, like a thousand others, it seemed queer and foreign after Paris. It was a little stuffy room with the high-backed pews that were fashionable in the 'forties, the day's menu written on a mirror with a piece of soap, and a girl of fourteen handling the dishes. Navvies were eating out of newspaper parcels, and drinking tea in vast saucerless mugs like china tumblers. In a corner by himself a Jew, muzzle down in the plate, was guiltily wolfing bacon.

'Could I have some tea and bread and butter?' I said to the girl.

She stared. 'No butter, only marg.,' she said, surprised. And she repeated the order in the phrase that is to London what the eternal *coup de rouge* is to Paris: 'Large tea and two slices!'

On the wall beside my pew there was a notice saying 'Pocketing the sugar not allowed', and beneath it some poetic customer had written:

He that takes away the sugar,
Shall be called a dirty—

but someone else had been at pains to scratch out the last word. This was England. The tea-and-two-slices cost threepence halfpenny, leaving me with eight and two-pence.

XXV

The eight shillings lasted three days and four nights. After my bad experience in the Waterloo Road[1] I moved eastward, and spent the next night in a lodging-house in Pennyfields. This was a typical lodging-house, like scores of others in London. It had accommodation for between fifty and a hundred men, and was managed by a 'deputy' – a deputy for the owner, that is, for these lodging-houses are profitable concerns and are owned by rich men. We slept fifteen or twenty in a dormitory; the beds were again cold and hard, but the sheets were not more than a week from the wash, which was an improvement. The charge was ninepence or a shilling (in the shilling dormitory the beds were six feet apart instead of four) and the terms were cash down by seven in the evening or out you went.

Downstairs there was a kitchen common to all lodgers, with free firing and a supply of cooking-pots, tea-basins and toasting-forks. There were two great clinker fires, which were kept burning day and night the year through. The work of tending the fires, sweeping the kitchen and making the beds was done by the lodgers in rotation. One senior lodger, a fine Norman-looking stevedore named Steve, was known as 'head of the house', and was arbiter of disputes and unpaid chucker-out.

I liked the kitchen. It was a low-ceiled cellar deep underground, very hot and drowsy with coke fumes, and lighted only by the fires, which cast black velvet shadows in the corners. Ragged washing hung on strings from the ceiling. Red-lit men, stevedores mostly, moved about the fires with cooking-pots; some of them were quite naked, for they had been laundering and were waiting for their clothes to dry. At night there were

---

1. It is a curious but well-known fact that bugs are much commoner in south than north London. For some reason they have not yet crossed the river in any great numbers.

games of nap and draughts, and songs – 'I'm a chap what's done wrong by my parents' was a favourite, and so was another popular song about a shipwreck. Sometimes late at night men would come in with a pail of winkles they had bought cheap, and share them out. There was a general sharing of food, and it was taken for granted to feed men who were out of work. A little pale, wizened creature, obviously dying, referred to as 'pore Brown, bin under the doctor and cut open three times', was regularly fed by the others.

Two or three of the lodgers were old-age pensioners. Till meeting them I had never realised that there are people in England who live on nothing but the old-age pension of ten shillings a week. None of these old men had any other resource whatever. One of them was talkative, and I asked him how he managed to exist. He said:

'Well, there's ninepence a night for yer kip – that's five an' threepence a week. Then there's threepence on Saturdays for a shave – that's five an' six. Then say you 'as a 'aircut once a month for sixpence – that's another three'apence a week. So you 'as about four an' fourpence for food an' bacca.'

He could imagine no other expenses. His food was bread and margarine and tea – towards the end of the week dry bread and tea without milk – and perhaps he got his clothes from charity. He seemed contented, valuing his bed and the fire more than food. But, with an income of ten shillings a week, to spend money on a shave – it is awe-inspiring.

All day I loafed in the streets, east as far as Wapping, west as far as Whitechapel. It was queer after Paris; everything was so much cleaner and quieter and drearier. One missed the scream of the trams, and the noisy, festering life of the back streets, and the armed men clattering through the squares. The crowds were better dressed and the faces comelier and milder and more alike, without that fierce individuality and malice of the French. There was less drunkenness, and less dirt, and less quarrelling, and more idling. Knots of men stood at all the corners, slightly underfed, but kept going by the tea-and-two-slices which the Londoner swallows every two hours. One seemed to breathe a less feverish air than in Paris. It was the land of the tea urn and the Labour Exchange, as Paris is the land of the *bistro* and the sweatshop.

It was interesting to watch the crowds. The East London women are pretty (it is the mixture of blood, perhaps), and Limehouse was sprinkled with Orientals – Chinamen, Chittagonian lascars, Dravidians selling silk scarves, even a few Sikhs, come goodness knows how. Here and there were street meetings. In Whitechapel somebody called The Singing Evangel undertook to save you from hell for the charge of sixpence. In the East India Dock Road the Salvation Army were holding a service. They were singing 'Anybody here like sneaking Judas?' to the tune of 'What's to be done with a drunken sailor?'. On Tower Hill two Mormons were trying to address a meeting. Round their platform struggled a mob of men, shouting and interrupting. Someone was denouncing them for polygamists. A lame, bearded man, evidently an atheist, had heard the word God and was heckling angrily. There was a confused uproar of voices.

'My dear friends, if you would only let us finish what we were saying l   That's right, give 'em a say. Don't get on the argue!   No, no, you answer me. Can you *show* me God? You *show* 'im me, then I'll believe in 'im. – Oh, shut up, don't keep interrupting of 'em! – Interrupt yourself! F— polygamists! – Well, there's a lot to be said for polygamy. Take the f— women out of industry, anyway. – My dear friends, if you would just . . . – No, no, don't you slip out of it. 'Ave you *seen* God? 'Ave you *touched* 'im? 'Ave you shook *'ands* with 'im? – Oh, don't get on the argue, for Christ's sake don't get on the *argue*!' etc. etc. I listened for twenty minutes, anxious to learn something about Mormonism, but the meeting never got beyond shouts. It is the general fate of street meetings.

In Middlesex Street, among the crowds at the market, a draggled, down-at-heel woman was hauling a brat of five by the arm. She brandished a tin trumpet in its face. The brat was squalling.

'Enjoy yourself!' yelled the mother. 'What yer think I brought yer out 'ere for an' bought y'a trumpet an' all?. D'ya want to go across my knee? You little bastard, you *shall* enjoy yerself!'

Some drops of spittle fell from the trumpet. The mother and the child disappeared, both bawling. It was all very queer after Paris.

The last night that I was in the Pennyfields lodging-house there was a quarrel between two of the lodgers, a vile scene. One of the old-age pensioners, a man of about seventy, naked to the waist (he had been laundering), was violently abusing a short, thickset stevedore, who stood with his back to the fire. I could see the old man's face in the light of the fire, and he was almost crying with grief and rage. Evidently something very serious had happened.

The old-age pensioner: 'You —!'

The stevedore: 'Shut yer mouth, you ole —, afore I set about yer!'

The old-age pensioner: 'Jest you try it on, you —! I'm thirty year older'n you, but it wouldn't take much to make me give you one as'd knock you into a bucketful of piss!'

The stevedore: 'Ah, an' then p'raps I wouldn't smash you up after, you ole c—!'

Thus for five minutes. The lodgers sat round, unhappy, trying to disregard the quarrel. The stevedore looked sullen, but the old man was growing more and more furious. He kept making little rushes at the other, sticking out his face and screaming from a few inches distant like a cat on a wall, and spitting. He was trying to nerve himself to strike a blow, and not quite succeeding. Finally he burst out:

'A —, that's what you are, a — —! Take that in your dirty gob and suck it, you —! By —, I'll smash you afore I've done with you. A c—, that's what you are, a son of a — whore. Lick that, you —! That's what I think of you, you —, you —, you —, YOU BLACK BASTARD!'

Whereat he suddenly collapsed on a bench, took his face in his hands, and began crying. The other man, seeing that public feeling was against him, went out.

Afterwards I heard Steve explaining the cause of the quarrel. It appeared that it was all about a shilling's worth of food. In some way the old man had lost his store of bread and margarine, and so would have nothing to eat for the next three days, except what the others gave him in charity. The stevedore, who was in work and well fed, had taunted him; hence the quarrel.

When my money was down to one and fourpence I went for a night to a lodging-house in Bow, where the charge was only eightpence. One went down an area and through an alley-way into a deep, stifling cellar, ten feet square. Ten men, navvies mostly, were sitting in the fierce glare of the fire. It was midnight, but the deputy's son, a pale, sticky child of five, was there playing on the navvies' knees. An old Irishman was whistling to a blind bullfinch in a tiny cage. There were other songbirds there – tiny, faded things, that had lived all their lives underground. The lodgers habitually made water in the fire, to save going across a yard to the lavatory. As I sat at the table I felt something stir near my feet, and, looking down, saw a wave of black things moving slowly across the floor; they were black-beetles.

There were six beds in the dormitory, and the sheets, marked in huge letters 'Stolen from No. — Bow Road', smelt loathsome. In the next bed to me lay a very old man, a pavement artist, with some extraordinary curvature of the spine that made him stick right out of bed, with his back a foot or two from my face. It was bare, and marked with curious swirls of dirt, like a marble table-top. During the night a man came in drunk and was sick on the floor, close to my bed. There were bugs too – not so bad as in Paris, but enough to keep one awake. It was a filthy place. Yet the deputy and his wife were friendly people, and ready to make one a cup of tea at any hour of the day or night.

XXVI

In the morning, after paying for the usual tea-and-two-slices and buying half an ounce of tobacco, I had a half-penny left. I did not care to ask B. for more money yet, so there was nothing for it but to go to a casual ward. I had very little idea how to set about this, but I knew that there was a casual ward at Romton, so I walked out there, arriving at three or four in the afternoon. Leaning against the pigpens in Romton market-place was a wizened old Irishman, obviously a tramp. I went and leaned beside him, and presently offered him my tobacco-box. He opened the box and looked at the tobacco in astonishment:

'By God,' he said, 'dere's sixpennorth o' good baccy here! Where de hell d'you get hold o' dat? *You* ain't been on de road long.'

'What, don't you have tobacco on the road?' I said.

'Oh, we *has* it. Look.'

He produced a rusty tin which had once held Oxo Cubes. In it were twenty or thirty cigarette-ends, picked up from the pavement. The Irishman said that he rarely got any other tobacco; he added that, with care, one could collect two ounces of tobacco a day on the London pavements.

'D'you come out o' one o' de London spikes [casual wards], eh?' he asked me.

I said yes, thinking this would make him accept me as a fellow tramp, and asked him what the spike at Romton was like. He said:

'Well, 'tis a cocoa spike. Dere's tay spikes, and cocoa spikes, and skilly spikes. Dey don't give you skilly in Romton, t'ank God – leastways, dey didn't de last time I was here. I been up to York and round Wales since.'

'What is skilly?' I said.

'Skilly? A can o' hot water wid some bloody oatmeal at de bottom; dat's skilly. De skilly spikes is always de worst.'

We stayed talking for an hour or two. The Irishman was a friendly old man, but he smelt very unpleasant, which was not surprising when one learned how many diseases he suffered from. It appeared (he described his symptoms fully) that taking him from top to bottom he had the following things wrong with him: on his crown, which was bald, he had eczema; he was short-sighted, and had no glasses; he had chronic bronchitis; he had some undiagnosed pain in the back; he had dyspepsia; he had urethritis; he had varicose veins, bunions and flat feet. With this assemblage of diseases he had tramped the roads for fifteen years.

At about five the Irishman said, 'Could you do wid a cup o' tay? De spike don't open till six.'

'I should think I could.'

'Well, dere's a place here where dey gives you a free cup o' tay and a bun. *Good* tay it is. Dey makes you say a lot o' bloody prayers after; but hell! It all passes de time away. You come wid me.'

He led the way to a small tin-roofed shed in a side-street, rather like a village cricket pavilion. About twenty-five other tramps were waiting. A few of them were dirty old habitual vagabonds, the majority decent-looking lads from the north, probably miners or cotton operatives out of work. Presently the door opened and a lady in a blue silk dress, wearing gold spectacles and a crucifix, welcomed us in. Inside were thirty or forty hard chairs, a harmonium, and a very gory lithograph of the Crucifixion.

Uncomfortably we took off our caps and sat down. The lady handed out the tea, and while we ate and drank she moved to and fro, talking benignly. She talked upon religious subjects – about Jesus Christ always having a soft spot for poor rough men like us, and about how quickly the time passed when you were in church, and what a difference it made to a man on the road if he said his prayers regularly. We hated it. We sat against the wall fingering our caps (a tramp feels indecently exposed with his cap off), and turning pink and trying to mumble something when the lady addressed us. There was no doubt that she meant it all kindly. As she came up to one of the north country lads with the plate of buns, she said to him:

'And you, my boy, how long is it since you knelt down and spoke with your Father in Heaven?'

Poor lad, not a word could he utter; but his belly answered for him, with a disgraceful rumbling which it set up at sight of the food. Thereafter he was so overcome with shame that he could scarcely swallow his bun. Only one man managed to answer the lady in her style, and he was a spry, red-nosed fellow looking like a corporal who had lost his stripe for drunkenness. He could pronounce the words 'the dear Lord Jesus' with less shame than anyone I ever saw. No doubt he had learned the knack in prison.

Tea ended, and I saw the tramps looking furtively at one another. An unspoken thought was running from man to man – could we possibly make off before the prayers started? Someone stirred in his chair – not getting up actually, but with just a glance at the door, as though half suggesting the idea of departure. The lady quelled him with one look. She said in a more benign tone than ever:

'I don't think you need go *quite* yet. The casual ward doesn't open till six, and we have time to kneel down and say a few words to our Father first. I think we should all feel better after that, shouldn't we?'

The red-nosed man was very helpful, pulling the harmonium into place and handing out the prayer-books. His back was to the lady as he did this, and it was his idea of a joke to deal the books like a pack of cards, whispering to each man as he did so, 'There y'are, mate, there's a f— nap 'and for yer! Four aces and a king!' etc.

Bareheaded, we knelt down among the dirty teacups and began to mumble that we had left undone those things that we ought to have done, and done those things that we ought not to have done, and there was no health in us. The lady prayed very fervently, but her eyes roved over us all the time, making sure that we were attending. When she was not looking we grinned and winked at one another, and whispered bawdy jokes, just to show that we did not care; but it stuck in our throats a little.

No one except the red-nosed man was self-possessed enough to speak the responses above a whisper. We got on better with the singing, except that one old tramp knew no tune but 'Onward, Christian soldiers', and reverted to it sometimes, spoiling the harmony.

The prayers lasted half an hour, and then, after a handshake at the door, we made off. 'Well,' said somebody as soon as we were out of hearing, 'the trouble's over. I thought them f— prayers was never goin' to end.'

'You 'ad your bun,' said another; 'you got to pay for it.'

'Pray for it, you mean. Ah, you don't get give much for nothing. They can't even give you a twopenny cup of tea without you go down on your f— knees for it.'

There were murmurs of agreement. Evidently the tramps were not grateful for their free tea. And yet it was excellent tea, as different from coffee-shop tea as good Bordeaux is from the muck called colonial claret, and we were all glad of it. I am sure too that it was given in a good spirit, without any intention of humiliating us; so in fairness we ought to have been grateful – still, we were not.

XXVII

At about a quarter to six the Irishman led me to the spike. It was a grim, smoky yellow cube of brick, standing in a corner of the workhouse grounds. With its rows of tiny, barred windows, and a high wall and iron gates separating it from the road, it looked much like a prison. Already a long queue of ragged men had formed up, waiting for the gates to open. They were of all kinds and ages, the youngest a fresh-faced boy of sixteen, the oldest a doubled-up, toothless mummy of seventy-five. Some were hardened tramps, recognisable by their sticks and billies and dust-darkened faces; some were factory hands out of work, some agricultural labourers, one a clerk in collar and tie, two certainly imbeciles. Seen in the mass, lounging there, they were a disgusting sight; nothing villainous or dangerous, but a graceless, mangy crew, nearly all ragged and palpably underfed. They were friendly, however, and asked no questions. Many offered me tobacco – cigarette-ends, that is.

We leaned against the wall, smoking, and the tramps began to talk about the spikes they had been in recently. It appeared from what they said that all spikes are different, each with its peculiar merits and demerits, and it is important to know these when you are on the road. An old hand will tell you the peculiarities of every spike in England, as: at A you are allowed to smoke but there are bugs in the cells; at B the beds are comfortable but the porter is a bully; at C they let you out early in the morning but the tea is undrinkable; at D the officials steal your money if you have any – and so on interminably. There are regular beaten tracks where the spikes are within a day's march of one another. I was told that the Barnet–St Albans route is the best, and they warned me to steer clear of Billericay and Chelmsford, also Ide Hill in Kent. Chelsea was said to be the most luxurious spike in England; someone, praising it, said that the blankets there were more like prison than the spike. Tramps go far afield in summer, and in winter they circle as much as possible round the large towns, where it is warmer and there is more charity. But they have to keep moving, for you may not enter any one spike, or any two London spikes, more than once in a month, on pain of being confined for a week.

Some time after six the gates opened and we began to file in one at a time. In the yard was an office where an official entered in a ledger our names and trades and ages, also the places we were coming from and going to – this last is intended to keep a check on the movements of tramps. I gave my trade as 'painter'; I had painted water-colours – who has not? The official also asked us whether we had any money, and every man said no. It is against the law to enter the spike with more than eightpence, and any sum less than this one is supposed to hand over at the gate. But as a rule the tramps prefer to smuggle their money in, tying it tight in a piece of cloth so that it will not chink. Generally they put it in the bag of tea and sugar that every tramp carries, or among their 'papers'. The 'papers' are considered sacred and are never searched.

After registering at the office we were led into the spike by an official known as the Tramp Major (his job is to supervise casuals, and he is generally a workhouse pauper) and a great bawling ruffian of a porter in a blue uniform, who treated us like cattle. The spike consisted simply of a bathroom and lavatory, and, for the rest, long double rows of stone cells, perhaps a hundred cells in all. It was a bare, gloomy place of stone and whitewash, unwillingly clean, with a smell which, somehow, I had foreseen from its appearance; a smell of soft soap, Jeyes' fluid and latrines – a cold, discouraging, prisonish smell.

The porter herded us all into the passage, and then told us to come into the bathroom six at a time, to be searched before bathing. The search was for money and tobacco, Romton being one of those spikes where you can smoke once you have smuggled your tobacco in, but it will be confiscated if it is found on you. The old hands had told us that the porter never searched below the knee, so before going in we had all hidden our tobacco in the ankles of our boots. Afterwards, while undressing, we slipped it into our coats, which we were allowed to keep, to serve as pillows.

The scene in the bathroom was extraordinarily repulsive. Fifty dirty, stark-naked men elbowing each other in a room twenty feet square, with only two bath-tubs and two slimy roller towels between them all. I shall never forget the reek of dirty feet. Less than half the tramps actually bathed (I heard them saying that hot water is 'weakening' to the system), but they all washed their faces and feet, and the horrid greasy little clouts known as toerags which they bind round their toes. Fresh water was only allowed for men who were having a complete bath, so many men had to bathe in water where others had washed their feet. The porter shoved us to and fro, giving the rough side of his tongue when anyone wasted time. When my turn came for the bath, I asked if I might swill out the tub, which was streaked with dirt, before using it. He answered simply, 'Shut yer f— mouth and get on with yer bath!' That set the social tone of the place, and I did not speak again.

When we had finished bathing, the porter tied our clothes in bundles and gave us workhouse shirts – grey cotton things of doubtful cleanliness, like abbreviated nightgowns. We were sent along to the cells at once, and presently the porter and the Tramp Major brought our supper across from the workhouse. Each man's ration was a half-pound wedge of bread smeared with margarine, and a pint of bitter sugarless cocoa in a tin billy. Sitting on the floor, we wolfed this in five minutes, and at about seven o'clock the cell doors were locked on the outside, to remain locked till eight in the morning.

Each man was allowed to sleep with his mate, the cells being intended to hold two men apiece. I had no mate, and was put in with another solitary man, a thin scrubby-faced fellow with a slight squint. The cell measured eight feet by five by eight high, was made of stone, and had a tiny barred window high up in the wall and a spy-hole in the door, just like a cell in a prison. In it were six blankets, a chamberpot, a hot water pipe, and nothing else whatever. I looked round the cell with a vague feeling that there was something missing. Then, with a shock of surprise, I realised what it was, and exclaimed:

'But I say, damn it, where are the beds?'

'*Beds?*' said the other man, surprised. 'There aren't no beds! What yer expect? This is one of them spikes where you sleeps on the floor. Christ! Ain't you got used to that yet?'

It appeared that no beds was quite a normal condition in the spike. We rolled up our coats and put them against the hot-water pipe, and made ourselves as comfortable as we could. It grew foully stuffy, but it was not warm enough to allow of our putting all the blankets underneath, so that we could only use one to soften the floor. We lay a foot apart, breathing into one another's face, with our naked limbs constantly touching, and rolling against one another whenever we fell asleep. One fidgeted from side to side, but it did not do much good; whichever way one turned there would be first a dull numb feeling, then a sharp ache as the hardness of the floor wore through the blanket. One could sleep, but not for more than ten minutes on end.

About midnight the other man began making homosexual attempts upon me – a nasty experience in a locked, pitch-dark cell. He was a feeble creature and I could manage him easily, but of course it was impossible to go to sleep again. For the rest of the night we stayed awake, smoking and talking. The man told me the story of his life – he was a fitter, out of work for three years. He said that his wife had promptly deserted him when he lost his job, and he had been so long away from women that he had almost forgotten what they were like. Homosexuality is general among tramps of long standing, he said.

At eight the porter came along the passage unlocking the doors and shouting 'All out!'. The doors opened, letting out a stale, fetid stink. At once the passage was full of squalid, grey-shirted figures, each chamber-pot in hand, scrambling for the bathroom. It appeared that in the morning only one tub of water was allowed for the lot of us, and when I arrived twenty tramps had already washed their faces; I took one glance at the black scum floating on the water, and went unwashed. After this we were given a breakfast identical with the previous night's supper, our clothes were returned to us, and we were ordered out into the yard to work. The work was peeling potatoes for the paupers' dinner, but it was a mere formality, to keep us occupied until the doctor came to inspect us. Most of the tramps frankly idled. The doctor turned up at about ten o'clock and we were told to go back to our cells, strip and wait in the passage for the inspection.

Naked and shivering, we lined up in the passage. You cannot conceive what ruinous, degenerate curs we looked, standing there in the merciless morning light. A tramp's clothes are bad, but they conceal far worse things; to see him as he really is, unmitigated, you must see him naked. Flat feet, pot bellies, hollow chests, sagging muscles – every kind of physical rottenness was there. Nearly everyone was under-nourished, and some clearly diseased; two men were wearing trusses, and as for the old mummy-like creature of seventy-five, one wondered how he could possibly make his daily march. Looking at our faces, unshaven and creased from the sleepless night, you would have thought that all of us were recovering from a week on the drink.

The inspection was designed merely to detect smallpox, and took no notice of our general condition. A young medical student, smoking a cigarette, walked rapidly along the line glancing us up and down, and not inquiring whether any man was well or ill. When my cell companion stripped I saw that his chest was covered with a red rash, and, having spent the night a few inches away from him, I fell into a panic about smallpox. The doctor, however, examined the rash and said that it was due merely to under-nourishment.

After the inspection we dressed and were sent into the yard, where the porter called our names over, gave us back any possessions we had left at the office, and distributed meal tickets. These were worth sixpence each, and were directed to coffee-shops on the route we had named the night before. It was interesting to see that quite a number of the tramps could not read, and had to apply to myself and other 'scholards' to decipher their tickets.

The gates were opened, and we dispersed immediately. How sweet the air does smell – even the air of a back-street in the suburbs – after the shut-in, subfaecal stench of the spike! I had a mate now, for while we were peeling potatoes I had made friends with an Irish tramp named

Paddy Jaques, a melancholy, pale man who seemed clean and decent. He was going to Edbury spike, and suggested that we should go together. We set out, getting there at three in the afternoon. It was a twelve-mile walk, but we made it fourteen by getting lost among the desolate north London slums. Our meal tickets were directed to a coffee-shop in Ilford. When we got there, the little chit of a serving-maid, having seen our tickets and grasped that we were tramps, tossed her head in contempt and for a long time would not serve us. Finally she slapped on the table two 'large teas' and four slices of bread and dripping – that is, eightpennyworth of food. It appeared that the shop habitually cheated the tramps of twopence or so on each ticket; having tickets instead of money, the tramps could not protest or go elsewhere.

XXVIII

Paddy was my mate for about the next fortnight, and, as he was the first tramp I had known at all well, I want to give an account of him. I believe that he was a typical tramp and there are tens of thousands in England like him.

He was a tallish man aged about thirty-five, with fair hair going grizzled and watery blue eyes. His features were good, but his cheeks had lanked and had that greyish, dirty-in-the-grain look that comes of a bread and margarine diet. He was dressed, rather better than most tramps, in a tweed shooting-jacket and a pair of very old evening trousers with the braid still on them. Evidently the braid figured in his mind as a lingering scrap of respectability, and he took care to sew it on again when it came loose. He was careful of his appearance altogether, and carried a razor and bootbrush that he would not sell, though he had sold his 'papers' and even his pocket-knife long since. Nevertheless, one would have known him for a tramp a hundred yards away. There was something in his drifting style of walk, and the way he had of hunching his shoulders forward, essentially abject. Seeing him walk, you felt instinctively that he would sooner take a blow than give one.

He had been brought up in Ireland, served two years in the war, and then worked in a metal polish factory, where he had lost his job two years earlier. He was horribly ashamed of being a tramp, but he had picked up all a tramp's ways. He browsed the pavements unceasingly, never missing a cigarette-end, or even an empty cigarette packet, as he used the tissue paper for rolling cigarettes. On our way into Edbury he saw a newspaper parcel on the pavement, pounced on it, and found that it contained two mutton sandwiches, rather frayed at the edges; these he insisted on my sharing. He never passed an automatic machine without giving a tug at the handle, for he said that sometimes they are out of order and will eject pennies if you tug at them. He had no stomach for crime, however. When we were in the outskirts of Romton, Paddy noticed a bottle of milk on a doorstep, evidently left there by mistake. He stopped, eyeing the bottle hungrily.

'Christ!' he said, 'dere's good food goin' to waste. Somebody could knock dat bottle off, eh? Knock it off easy.'

I saw that he was thinking of 'knocking it off' himself. He looked up and down the street; it was a quiet residential street and there was nobody in sight. Paddy's sickly, chap-fallen face yearned over the milk. Then he turned away, saying gloomily:

'Best leave it. It don't do a man no good to steal. T'ank God, I ain't never stolen nothin' yet.'

It was funk, bred of hunger, that kept him virtuous. With only two or three sound meals in his belly, he would have found courage to steal the milk.

He had two subjects of conversation, the shame and come-down of being a tramp, and the best way of getting a free meal. As we drifted through the streets he would keep up a monologue in this style, in a whimpering, self-pitying Irish voice:

'It's hell bein' on de road, eh? It breaks yer heart goin' into dem bloody spikes. But what's a man to do else, eh? I ain't had a good meat meal for above two months, an' me boots is getting bad, an' – Christ! How'd it be if we was to try for a cup o' tay at one o' dem convents on de way to Edbury? Most times dey're good for a cup o' tay. Ah, what'd a man do widout religion, eh? I've took cups o' tay from de convents, an' de Baptists, an' de Church of England, an' all sorts. I'm a Catholic meself. Dat's to say, I ain't been to confession for above seventeen year, but still I got me religious feelin's, y'understand. An' dem convents is always good for a cup o' tay . . .' etc. etc. He would keep this up all day, almost without stopping.

His ignorance was limitless and appalling. He once asked me, for instance, whether Napoleon lived before Jesus Christ or after. Another time, when I was looking into a bookshop window, he grew very perturbed because one of the books was called *Of the Imitation of Christ*. He took this for blasphemy. 'What de hell do dey want to go imitatin' of *Him* for?' he demanded angrily. He could read, but he had a kind of loathing for books. On our way from Romton to Edbury I went into a public library, and, though Paddy did not want to read, I suggested that he should come in and rest his legs. But he preferred to wait on the pavement. 'No,' he said, 'de sight of all dat bloody print makes me sick.'

Like most tramps, he was passionately mean about matches. He had a box of matches when I met him, but I never saw him strike one, and he used to lecture me for extravagance when I struck mine. His method was to cadge a light from strangers, sometimes going without a smoke for half an hour rather than strike a match.

Self-pity was the clue to his character. The thought of his bad luck never seemed to leave him for an instant. He would break long silences to exclaim, apropos of nothing, 'It's hell when yer clo'es begin to go up de spout, eh?' or 'Dat tay in de spike ain't tay, it's piss', as though there were nothing else in the world to think about. And he had a low, worm-like envy of anyone who was better off – not of the rich, for they were beyond his social horizon, but of men in work. He pined for work as an artist pines to be famous. If he saw an old man working he would say bitterly, 'Look at dat old — keepin' able-bodied men out o' work'; or if it was a boy, 'It's dem young devils what's takin' de bread out of our mouths.' And all foreigners to him were 'dem bloody dagoes' – for, according to his theory, foreigners were responsible for unemployment.

He looked at women with a mixture of longing and hatred. Young, pretty women were too much above him to enter into his ideas, but his mouth watered at prostitutes. A couple of scarlet-lipped old creatures would go past; Paddy's face would flush pale pink, and he would turn and stare hungrily after the women. 'Tarts!' he would murmur, like a boy at a sweet-shop window. He told me once that he had not had to do with a woman for two years – since he had lost his job, that is – and he had forgotten that one could aim higher than prostitutes. He had the regular character of a tramp – abject, envious, a jackal's character.

Nevertheless he was a good fellow, generous by nature and capable of sharing his last crust with a friend; indeed he did literally share his last crust with me more than once. He was probably capable of work too, if he had been well fed for a few months. But two years of bread and margarine had lowered his standards hopelessly. He had lived on this filthy imitation of food till his whole mind and body were compounded of inferior stuff. It was malnutrition and not any native vice that had destroyed his manhood.

XXIX

On the way to Edbury I told Paddy that I had a friend from whom I could be sure of getting money, and suggested going straight into London rather than face another night in the spike. But Paddy had not been in Edbury spike recently, and, tramp-like, he would not waste a night's free lodging. We arranged to go into London the next morning. I had only a halfpenny, but Paddy had two shillings, which would get us a bed each and a few cups of tea.

The Edbury spike did not differ much from the one at Romton. The worst feature was that all tobacco was confiscated at the gate, and we were warned that any man caught smoking would be turned out at once. Under the Vagrancy Act tramps can be prosecuted for smoking in the spike – in fact, they can be prosecuted for almost anything; but the authorities generally save the trouble of a prosecution by turning disobedient men out of doors. There was no work to do, and the cells were fairly comfortable. We slept two in a cell, 'one up, one down' – that is, one on a wooden shelf and one on the floor, with straw palliasses and plenty of blankets, dirty but not verminous. The food was the same as at Romton, except that we had tea instead of cocoa. One could get extra tea in the morning, as the Tramp Major was selling it at a halfpenny a mug, illicitly no doubt. We were each given a hunk of bread and cheese to take away for our midday meal.

When we got into London we had eight hours to kill before the lodging-houses opened. It is curious how one does not notice things. I had been in London innumerable times, and yet till that day I had never noticed one of the worst things about London – the fact that it costs money even to sit down. In Paris, if you had no money and could not find a public bench, you would sit on the pavement. Heaven knows what sitting on the pavement would lead to in London – prison, probably. By

four we had stood five hours, and our feet seemed red hot from the
hardness of the stones. We were hungry, having eaten our ration as soon
as we left the spike, and I was out of tobacco – it mattered less to Paddy,
who picked up cigarette ends. We tried two churches and found them
locked. Then we tried a public library, but there were no seats in it. As a
last hope Paddy suggested trying a Rowton House; by the rules they
would not let us in before seven, but we might slip in unnoticed. We
walked up to the magnificent doorway (the Rowton Houses really are
magnificent) and very casually, trying to look like regular lodgers, began
to stroll in. Instantly a man lounging in the doorway, a sharp-faced fellow,
evidently in some position of authority, barred the way.

'You men sleep 'ere last night?'

'No.'

'Then f— off.'

We obeyed, and stood two more hours on the street corner. It was
unpleasant, but it taught me not to use the expression 'street corner loafer',
so I gained something from it.

At six we went to a Salvation Army shelter. We could not book beds
till eight and it was not certain that there would be any vacant, but an
official, who called us 'Brother', let us in on condition that we paid for
two cups of tea. The main hall of the shelter was a great whitewashed
barn of a place, oppressively clean and bare, with no fires. Two hundred
decentish, rather subdued-looking people were sitting packed on long
wooden benches. One or two officers in uniform prowled up and down.
On the wall were pictures of General Booth, and notices prohibiting
cooking, drinking, spitting, swearing, quarrelling and gambling. As a
specimen of these notices, here is one that I copied word for word:

> Any man found gambling or playing cards will be expelled and will not
> be admitted under any circumstances.
>
> A reward will be given for information leading to the discovery of such
> persons.
>
> The officers in charge appeal to all lodgers to assist them in keeping this
> hostel free from the DETESTABLE EVIL OF GAMBLING.

'Gambling or playing cards' is a delightful phrase.

To my eye these Salvation Army shelters, though clean, are far drearier than the worst of the common lodging-houses. There is such a hopelessness about some of the people there – decent, broken-down types who have pawned their collars but are still trying for office jobs. Coming to a Salvation Army shelter, where it is at least clean, is their last clutch at respectability. At the next table to me were two foreigners, dressed in rags but manifestly gentlemen. They were playing chess verbally, not even writing down the moves. One of them was blind, and I heard them say that they had been saving up for a long time to buy a board, price half a crown, but could never manage it. Here and there were clerks out of work, pallid and moody. Among a group of them a tall, thin, deadly pale young man was talking excitedly. He thumped his fist on the table and boasted in a strange, feverish style. When the officers were out of hearing he broke out into startling blasphemies:

'I tell you what, boys, I'm going to get that job tomorrow. I'm not one of your bloody down-on-the-knee brigade; I can look after myself. Look at that — notice there! "The Lord will provide!" A bloody lot He's ever provided me with. You don't catch me trusting to the — Lord. You leave it to me, boys. *I'm going to get that job,*' etc. etc.

I watched him, struck by the wild, agitated way in which he talked; he seemed hysterical, or perhaps a little drunk. An hour later I went into a small room, apart from the main hall, which was intended for reading. It had no books or papers in it, so few of the lodgers went there. As I opened the door I saw the young clerk in there all alone; he was on his knees, *praying*. Before I shut the door again I had time to see his face, and it looked agonised. Quite suddenly I realised, from the expression of his face, that he was starving.

The charge for beds was eightpence each. Paddy and I had fivepence left, and we spent it at the 'bar', where food was cheap, though not so cheap as in some common lodging-houses. The tea appeared to be made with tea *dust*, which I fancy had been given to the Salvation Army in charity, though they sold it at three-halfpence a cup. It was foul stuff. At ten o'clock an officer marched round the hall blowing a whistle. Immediately everyone stood up.

'What's this for?' I said to Paddy, astonished.

'Dat means you has to go off to bed. An' you has to look sharp about it, too.'

Obediently as sheep, the whole two hundred men trooped off to bed, under the command of the officers.

The dormitory was a great attic like a barrack room, with sixty or seventy beds in it. They were clean and tolerably comfortable, but very narrow and very close together, so that one breathed straight into one's neighbour's face. Two officers slept in the room, to see that there was no smoking and no talking after lights-out. Paddy and I had scarcely a wink of sleep, for there was a man near us who had some nervous trouble, shell-shock perhaps, which made him cry out 'Pip!' at irregular intervals. It was a loud, startling noise, something like the toot of a small motor-horn. You never knew when it was coming, and it was a sure preventer of sleep. It appeared that Pip, as the others called him, slept regularly in the shelter, and he must have kept ten or twenty people awake every night. He was an example of the kind of thing that prevents one from ever getting enough sleep when men are herded as they are in these lodging-houses.

At seven another whistle blew, and the officers went round shaking those who did not get up at once. Since then I have slept in a number of Salvation Army shelters, and found that, though the different houses vary a little, this semi-military discipline is the same in all of them. They are certainly cheap, but they are too like workhouses for my taste. In some of them there is even a compulsory religious service once or twice a week, which the lodgers must attend or leave the house. The fact is that the Salvation Army are so in the habit of thinking themselves a charitable body that they cannot even run a lodging-house without making it stink of charity.

At ten I went to B.'s office and asked him to lend me a pound. He gave me two pounds and told me to come again when necessary, so that Paddy and I were free of money troubles for a week at least. We loitered the day in Trafalgar Square, looking for a friend of Paddy's who never turned up, and at night went to a lodging-house in a back alley near the Strand. The charge was elevenpence, but it was a dark, evil-smelling place, and a notorious haunt of the 'nancy boys'. Downstairs, in the murky kitchen, three ambiguous-looking youths in smartish blue suits were sitting on a bench apart, ignored by the other lodgers. I suppose they were 'nancy boys'. They looked the same type as the apache boys one sees in Paris, except that they wore no side-whiskers. In front of the fire a fully-dressed man and a stark-naked man were bargaining. They were newspaper sellers. The dressed man was selling his clothes to the naked man. He said:

"'Ere y'are, the best rig-out you ever 'ad. A tosheroon [half a crown] for the coat, two 'ogs for the trousers, one and a tanner for the boots, and a 'og for the cap and scarf. That's seven bob.'

'You got a 'ope! I'll give yer one and a tanner for the coat, a 'og for the trousers, and two 'ogs for the rest. That's four and a tanner.'

'Take the 'ole lot for five and a tanner, chum.'

'Right y'are, off with 'em. I got to get out to sell my late edition.'

The clothed man stripped, and in three minutes their positions were reversed; the naked man dressed, and the other kilted with a sheet of the *Daily Mail*.

The dormitory was dark and close, with fifteen beds in it. There was a horrible hot reek of urine, so beastly that at first one tried to breathe in small shallow puffs, not filling one's lungs to the bottom. As I lay down in bed a man loomed out of the darkness, leant over me and began babbling in an educated, half-drunken voice:

'An old public school boy, what? [He had heard me say something to Paddy.] Don't meet many of the old school here. I am an old Etonian. You know – twenty years hence this weather and all that.' He began to quaver out the Eton boating-song, not untunefully:

> *Jolly boating weather,*
> *And a hay harvest —*

'Stop that — noise!' shouted several lodgers.

'Low types,' said the old Etonian, 'very low types. Funny sort of place for you and me, eh? Do you know what my friends say to me? They say, "M——, you are past redemption." Quite true, I *am* past redemption. I've come down in the world; not like these ——s here, who couldn't come down if they tried. We chaps who have come down ought to hang together a bit. Youth will be still in our faces – you know. May I offer you a drink?'

He produced a bottle of cherry brandy, and at the same moment lost his balance and fell heavily across my legs. Paddy, who was undressing, pulled him upright.

'Get back to yer bed, you silly ole c——!'

The old Etonian walked unsteadily to his bed and crawled under the sheets with all his clothes on, even his boots. Several times in the night I heard him murmuring, 'M——, you are past redemption,' as though the phrase appealed to him. In the morning he was lying asleep fully dressed, with the bottle clasped in his arms. He was a man of about fifty, with a refined, worn face, and, curiously enough, quite fashionably dressed. It was queer to see his good patent-leather shoes sticking out of that filthy bed. It occurred to me, too, that the cherry brandy must have cost the equivalent of a fortnight's lodging, so he could not have been seriously hard up. Perhaps he frequented common lodging-houses in search of the 'nancy boys'.

The beds were not more than two feet apart. About midnight I woke up to find that the man next to me was trying to steal the money from beneath my pillow. He was pretending to be asleep while he did it, sliding his hand under the pillow as gently as a rat. In the morning I saw that he was a hunchback, with long, apelike arms. I told Paddy about the attempted theft. He laughed and said:

'Christ! You got to get used to dat. Dese lodgin'-houses is full o' thieves. In some houses dere's nothin' safe but to sleep wid all yer clo'es on. I seen 'em steal a wooden leg off of a cripple before now. Once I see a man – fourteen stone man he was – come into a lodgin'-house wid four pound ten. He puts it under his mattress. "Now," he says, "any——dat touches dat money does it over my body," he says. But dey done him all de same. In de mornin' he woke up on de floor. Four fellers had took his mattress by de corners an' lifted him off as light as a feather. He never saw his four pound ten again.'

XXX

The next morning we began looking once more for Paddy's friend, who was called Bozo, and was a screever – that is, a pavement artist. Addresses did not exist in Paddy's world, but he had a vague idea that Bozo might be found in Lambeth, and in the end we ran across him on the Embankment, where he had established himself not far from Waterloo Bridge. He was kneeling on the pavement with a box of chalks, copying a sketch of Winston Churchill from a penny note-book. The likeness was not at all bad. Bozo was a small, dark, hook-nosed man, with curly hair growing low on his head. His right leg was dreadfully deformed, the foot being twisted heel forward in a way horrible to see. From his appearance one could have taken him for a Jew, but he used to deny this vigorously. He spoke of his hook-nose as 'Roman', and was proud of his resemblance to some Roman Emperor – it was Vespasian, I think.

Bozo had a strange way of talking, Cockneyfied and yet very lucid and expressive. It was as though he had read good books but had never troubled to correct his grammar. For a while Paddy and I stayed on the Embankment, talking, and Bozo gave us an account of the screeving trade. I repeat what he said more or less in his own words:

'I'm what they call a serious screever. I don't draw in blackboard chalks like these others, I use proper colours the same as what painters use; bloody expensive they are, especially the reds. I use five bobs' worth of colours in a long day, and never less than two bobs' worth.[1] Cartoons is my line – you know, politics and cricket and that. Look here' – he showed me his note-book – 'here's likenesses of all the political blokes, what I've copied from the papers. I have a different cartoon every day. For instance, when the Budget was on I had one of Winston trying to push an elephant marked "Debt", and underneath I wrote, "Will he budge it?" See? You can have cartoons about any of the parties, but you mustn't put anything in favour of Socialism, because the police won't stand it. Once I did a cartoon of a boa constrictor marked Capital swallowing a rabbit marked Labour. The copper came along and saw it, and he says, "You rub that out, and look sharp about it," he says. I had to rub it out. The copper's got the right to move you on for loitering, and it's no good giving them a back answer.'

I asked Bozo what one could earn at screeving. He said:

'This time of year, when it don't rain, I take about three quid between Friday and Sunday – people get their wages Fridays, you see. I can't work when it rains; the colours get washed off straight away. Take the year round, I make about a pound a week, because you can't do much in the winter. Boat Race day, and Cup Final day, I've took as much as four pounds. But you have to *cut* it out of them, you know; you don't take a

---

1. Pavement artists buy their colours in the form of powder, and work them into cakes with condensed milk.

bob if you just sit and look at them. A halfpenny's the usual drop [gift], and you don't get even that unless you give them a bit of backchat. Once they've answered you they feel ashamed not to give you a drop. The best thing's to keep changing your picture, because when they see you drawing they'll stop and watch you. The trouble is, the beggars scatter as soon as you turn round with the hat. You really want a nobber [assistant] at this game. You keep at work and get a crowd watching you, and the nobber comes casual-like round the back of them. They don't know he's the nobber. Then suddenly he pulls his cap off, and you got them between two fires like. You'll never get a drop off real toffs. It's shabby sort of blokes you get most off, and foreigners. I've had even sixpences off Japs, and blackies, and that. They're not so bloody mean as what an Englishman is. Another thing to remember is to keep your money covered up, except perhaps a penny in the hat. People won't give you anything if they see you got a bob or two already.'

Bozo had the deepest contempt for the other screevers on the Embankment. He called them 'the salmon platers'. At that time there was a screever almost every twenty-five yards along the Embankment – twenty-five yards being the recognised minimum between pitches. Bozo contemptuously pointed out an old white-bearded screever fifty yards away.

'You see that silly old fool? He's bin doing the same picture every day for ten years. "A faithful friend" he calls it. It's of a dog pulling a child out of the water. The silly old bastard can't draw any better than a child of ten. He's learned just that one picture by rule of thumb, like you learn to put a puzzle together. There's a lot of that sort about here. They come pinching my ideas sometimes; but I don't care; the silly —s can't think of anything for themselves, so I'm always ahead of them. The whole thing with cartoons is being up to date. Once a child got its head stuck in the railings of Chelsea Bridge. Well, I heard about it, and my cartoon was on the pavement before they'd got the child's head out of the railings. Prompt, I am.'

Bozo seemed an interesting man, and I was anxious to see more of him. That evening I went down to the Embankment to meet him, as he had arranged to take Paddy and myself to a lodging-house south of the river. Bozo washed his pictures off the pavement and counted his takings – it was about sixteen shillings, of which he said twelve or thirteen would be profit. We walked down into Lambeth. Bozo limped slowly, with a queer crab-like gait, half sideways, dragging his smashed foot behind him. He carried a stick in each hand and slung his box of colours over his shoulder. As we were crossing the bridge he stopped in one of the alcoves to rest. He fell silent for a minute or two, and to my surprise I saw that he was looking at the stars. He touched my arm and pointed to the sky with his stick.

'Say, will you look at Aldebaran! Look at the colour. Like a — great blood orange!'

From the way he spoke he might have been an art critic in a picture gallery. I was astonished. I confessed that I did not know which Aldebaran was – indeed, I had never even noticed that the stars were of different colours. Bozo began to give me some elementary hints on astronomy, pointing out the chief constellations. He seemed concerned at my ignorance. I said to him, surprised:

'You seem to know a lot about stars.'

'Not a great lot. I know a bit, though. I got two letters from the Astronomer Royal thanking me for writing about meteors. Now and again I go out at night and watch for meteors. The stars are a free show; it don't cost anything to use your eyes.'

'What a good idea! I should never have thought of it.'

'Well, you got to take an interest in something. It don't follow that because a man's on the road he can't think of anything but tea-and-two-slices.'

'But isn't it very hard to take an interest in things – things like stars – living this life?'

'Screeving, you mean? Not necessarily. It don't need turn you into a bloody rabbit – that is, not if you set your mind to it.'

'It seems to have that effect on most people.'

'Of course. Look at Paddy – a tea-swilling old moocher, only fit to scrounge for fag-ends. That's the way most of them go. I despise them. But you don't *need* get like that. If you've got any education, it don't matter to you if you're on the road for the rest of your life.'

'Well, I've found just the contrary,' I said. 'It seems to me that when you take a man's money away he's fit for nothing from that moment.'

'No, not necessarily. If you set yourself to it, you can live the same life, rich or poor. You can still keep on with your books and your ideas. You just got to say to yourself, "I'm a free man in *here*"' – he tapped his forehead – 'and you're all right.'

Bozo talked further in the same strain, and I listened with attention. He seemed a very unusual screever, and he was, moreover, the first person I had heard maintain that poverty did not matter. I saw a good deal of him during the next few days, for several times it rained and he could not work. He told me the history of his life, and it was a curious one.

The son of a bankrupt bookseller, he had gone to work as a house-painter at eighteen, and then served three years in France and India during the war. After the war he had found a house-painting job in Paris, and had stayed there several years. France suited him better than England (he despised the English), and he had been doing well in Paris, saving money, and engaged to a French girl. One day the girl was crushed to death under the wheels of an omnibus. Bozo went on the drink for a week, and then returned to work, rather shaky; the same morning he fell from a stage on which he was working, forty feet onto the pavement, and smashed his right foot to pulp. For some reason he received only sixty pounds compensation. He returned to England, spent his money in looking for jobs, tried hawking books in Middlesex Street market, then tried selling toys from a tray, and finally settled down as a screever. He had lived hand to mouth ever since, half starved throughout the winter, and often sleeping in the spike or on the Embankment. When I knew him he owned nothing but the clothes he stood up in, and his drawing materials and a few books. The clothes were the usual beggar's rags, but he wore a collar and tie, of which he was rather proud. The collar, a year or more old, was constantly 'going' round the neck, and Bozo used to patch it with bits cut from the tail of his shirt so that the shirt had scarcely any tail left. His damaged leg was getting worse and would probably have to be amputated, and his knees, from kneeling on the stones, had pads of skin on them as thick as boot-soles. There was, clearly, no future for him but beggary and a death in the workhouse.

With all this, he had neither fear, nor regret, nor shame, nor self-pity. He had faced his position, and made a philosophy for himself. Being a beggar, he said, was not his fault, and he refused either to have any compunction about it or to let it trouble him. He was the enemy of society, and quite ready to take to crime if he saw a good opportunity. He refused on principle to be thrifty. In the summer he saved nothing, spending his surplus earnings on drink, as he did not care about women. If he was penniless when winter came on, then society must look after him. He was ready to extract every penny he could from charity, provided that he was not expected to say thank you for it. He avoided religious charities, however, for he said that it stuck in his throat to sing hymns for buns. He had various other points of honour; for instance, it was his boast that never in his life, even when starving, had he picked up a cigarette end. He considered himself in a class above the ordinary run of beggars, who, he said, were an abject lot, without even the decency to be ungrateful.

He spoke French passably, and had read some of Zola's novels, all Shakespeare's plays, *Gulliver's Travels*, and a number of essays. He could describe his adventures in words that one remembered. For instance, speaking of funerals, he said to me:

'Have you ever seen a corpse burned? I have, in India. They put the old chap on the fire, and the next moment I almost jumped out of my skin, because he'd started kicking. It was only his muscles contracting in the heat – still, it give me a turn. Well, he wriggled about for a bit like a kipper on hot coals, and then his belly blew up and went off with a bang you could have heard fifty yards away. It fair put me against cremation.'

Or, again, apropos of his accident:

'The doctor says to me, "You fell on one foot, my man. And bloody lucky for you you didn't fall on both feet," he says. "Because if you had of fallen on both feet you'd have shut up like a bloody concertina, and your thigh bones'd be sticking out of your ears!" '

Clearly the phrase was not the doctor's but Bozo's own. He had a gift for phrases. He had managed to keep his brain intact and alert, and so nothing could make him succumb to poverty. He might be ragged and cold, or even starving, but so long as he could read, think and watch for meteors, he was, as he said, free in his own mind.

He was an embittered atheist (the sort of atheist who does not so much disbelieve in God as personally dislike Him), and took a sort of pleasure in thinking that human affairs would never improve. Sometimes, he said, when sleeping on the Embankment, it had consoled him to look up at Mars or Jupiter and think that there were probably Embankment sleepers there. He had a curious theory about this. Life on earth, he said, is harsh because the planet is poor in the necessities of existence. Mars, with its cold climate and scanty water, must be far poorer, and life correspondingly harsher. Whereas on earth you are merely imprisoned for stealing sixpence, on Mars you are probably boiled alive. This thought cheered Bozo, I do not know why. He was a very exceptional man.

XXXI

The charge at Bozo's lodging-house was ninepence a night. It was a large, crowded place, with accommodation for five hundred men, and a well-known rendezvous of tramps, beggars and petty criminals. All races, even black and white, mixed in it on terms of equality. There were Indians there, and when I spoke to one of them in bad Urdu he addressed me as 'tum'* – a thing to make one shudder, if it had been in India. We had got below the range of colour prejudice. One had glimpses of curious lives. Old 'Grandpa', a tramp of seventy who made his living, or a great part of it, by collecting cigarette ends and selling the tobacco at threepence an ounce. 'The Doctor' – he was a real doctor, who had been struck off the register for some offence, and besides selling newspapers gave medical advice at a few pence a time. A little Chittagonian lascar, barefoot and starving, who had deserted his ship and wandered for days through London, so vague and helpless that he did not even know the name of the city he was in – he thought it was Liverpool, until I told him. A begging-letter writer, a friend of Bozo's, who wrote pathetic appeals for aid to pay for his wife's funeral, and, when a letter had taken effect, blew himself out with huge solitary gorges of bread and margarine. He was a nasty, hyena-like creature. I talked to him and found that, like most swindlers, he believed a great part of his own lies. The lodging-house was an Alsatia† for types like these.

---

* *The French translation has this note (in French)*: In Hindustani, there are two pronouns for the second person singular. One, *ap*, is the more respectful and corresponds to our [= *French*] polite use of *vous*. The other, *tum*, is used only between very close friends or by a superior to an inferior; it is the equivalent of our *tu*. An Englishman in India would not tolerate being called 'tum' by a native.

† *The French translation has this note (in French)*: A name once given to the district of Whitefriars, which was, in the seventeenth century, a regular refuge for all kinds of wrongdoers by virtue of a right of sanctuary which was finally abolished in 1697.

While I was with Bozo he taught me something about the technique of London begging. There is more in it than one might suppose. Beggars vary greatly, and there is a sharp social line between those who merely cadge and those who attempt to give some value for money. The amounts that one can earn by the different 'gags' also vary. The stories in the Sunday papers about beggars who die with two thousand pounds sewn into their trousers are, of course, lies; but the better-class beggars do have runs of luck, when they earn a living wage for weeks at a time. The most prosperous beggars are street acrobats and street photographers. On a good pitch – a theatre queue, for instance – a street acrobat will often earn five pounds a week. Street photographers can earn about the same, but they are dependent on fine weather. They have a cunning dodge to stimulate trade. When they see a likely victim approaching, one of them runs behind the camera and pretends to take a photograph. Then, as the victim reaches them, they exclaim:

'There y'are, sir, took yer photo lovely. That'll be a bob.'

'But I never asked you to take it,' protests the victim.

'What, you didn't want it took? Why, we thought you signalled with your 'and. Well, there's a plate wasted! That's cost us sixpence, that 'as.'

At this the victim usually takes pity and says he will have the photo after all. The photographers examine the plate and say that it is spoiled, and that they will take a fresh one free of charge. Of course, they have not really taken the first photo; and so, if the victim refuses, they waste nothing.

Organ-grinders, like acrobats, are considered artists rather than beggars. An organ-grinder named Shorty, a friend of Bozo's, told me all about his trade. He and his mate 'worked' the coffee-shops and public-houses round Whitechapel and the Commercial Road. It is a mistake to think that organ-grinders earn their living in the street; nine-tenths of their money is taken in coffee-shops and pubs – only the cheap pubs, for they are not allowed into the good-class ones. Shorty's procedure was to stop outside a pub and play one tune, after which his mate, who had a wooden leg and could excite compassion, went in and passed round the hat. It was a point of honour with Shorty always to play another tune after receiving the 'drop' – an encore, as it were; the idea being that he was a genuine entertainer and not merely paid to go away. He and his mate took two or three pounds a week between them, but, as they had to pay fifteen shillings a week for the hire of the organ, they only averaged a pound a week each. They were on the streets from eight in the morning till ten at night, and later on Saturdays.

Screevers can sometimes be called artists, sometimes not. Bozo introduced me to one who was a 'real' artist – that is, he had studied art in Paris and submitted pictures to the Salon in his day. His line was copies of Old Masters, which he did marvellously, considering that he was drawing on stone. He told me how he began as a screever.

'My wife and kids were starving. I was walking home late at night, with a lot of drawings I'd been taking round the dealers, and wondering how the devil to raise a bob or two. Then, in the Strand, I saw a fellow kneeling on the pavement drawing, and people giving him pennies. As I came past he got up and went into a pub. "Damn it," I thought, "if he can make money at that, so can I." So on the impulse I knelt down and began drawing with his chalks. Heaven knows how I came to do it; I must have been light-headed with hunger. The curious thing was that I'd never used pastels before; I had to learn the technique as I went along. Well, people began to stop and say that my drawing wasn't bad, and they gave me ninepence between them. At this moment the other fellow came out of the pub. "What in — are you doing on my pitch?" he said. I explained that I was hungry and had to earn something. "Oh," said he, "come and have a pint with me." So I had a pint, and since that day I've been a screever. I make a pound a week. You can't keep six kids on a pound a week, but luckily my wife earns a bit taking in sewing.

'The worst thing in this life is the cold, and the next worst is the interference you have to put up with. At first, not knowing any better, I used sometimes to copy a nude on the pavement. The first I did was outside St Martin's-in-the-Fields church. A fellow in black – I suppose he was a churchwarden or something – came out in a tearing rage. "Do you think we can have that obscenity outside God's holy house?" he cried. So I had to wash it out. It was a copy of Botticelli's Venus. Another time I copied the same picture on the Embankment. A policeman passing looked at it, and then, without a word, walked onto it and rubbed it out with his great flat feet.'

Bozo told the same tale of police interference. At the time when I was with him there had been a case of 'immoral conduct' in Hyde Park, in which the police had behaved rather badly. Bozo produced a cartoon of Hyde Park with policemen concealed in the trees, and the legend, 'Puzzle, find the policemen.' I pointed out to him how much more telling it would be to put, 'Puzzle, find the immoral conduct,' but Bozo would not hear of it. He said that any policeman who saw it would move him on, and he would lose his pitch for good.

Below screevers come the people who sing hymns, or sell matches, or bootlaces, or envelopes containing a few grains of lavender – called, euphemistically, perfume. All these people are frankly beggars, exploiting an appearance of misery, and none of them takes on an average more than half a crown a day. The reason why they have to pretend to sell matches and so forth instead of begging outright is that this is demanded by the absurd English law about begging. As the law now stands, if you approach a stranger and ask him for twopence, he can call a policeman and get you seven days for begging. But if you make the air hideous by droning 'Nearer, my God, to Thee', or scrawl some chalk daubs on the pavement, or stand about with a tray of matches – in short, if you make a nuisance of yourself – you are held to be following a legitimate trade and not begging. Match-selling and street-singing are simply legalised crimes. Not profitable crimes, however; there is not a singer or match-seller in London who can be sure of £50 a year – a poor return for standing eighty-four hours a week on the kerb, with the cars grazing your backside.

It is worth saying something about the social position of beggars, for when one has consorted with them, and found that they are ordinary human beings, one cannot help being struck by the curious attitude that society takes towards them. People seem to feel that there is some essential difference between beggars and ordinary 'working' men. They are a race apart – outcasts, like criminals and prostitutes. Working men 'work', beggars do not 'work'; they are parasites, worthless in their very nature. It is taken for granted that a beggar does not 'earn' his living, as a bricklayer or a literary critic 'earns' his. He is a mere social excrescence, tolerated because we live in a humane age, but essentially despicable.

Yet if one looks closely one sees that there is no *essential* difference between a beggar's livelihood and that of numberless respectable people. Beggars do not work, it is said; but, then, what is *work*? A navvy works by swinging a pick. An accountant works by adding up figures. A beggar works by standing out of doors in all weathers and getting varicose veins, chronic bronchitis, etc. It is a trade like any other; quite useless, of course – but, then, many reputable trades are quite useless. And as a social type a beggar compares well with scores of others. He is honest compared with the sellers of most patent medicines, high-minded compared with a Sunday newspaper proprietor, amiable compared with a hire-purchase tout – in short, a parasite, but a fairly harmless parasite. He seldom extracts more than a bare living from the community, and, what should justify him according to our ethical ideas, he pays for it over and over in suffering. I do not think there is anything about a beggar that sets him in a different class from other people, or gives most modern men the right to despise him.

Then the question arises, Why are beggars despised? – for they are despised, universally. I believe it is for the simple reason that they fail to earn a decent living. In practice nobody cares whether work is useful or useless, productive or parasitic; the sole thing demanded is that it shall be profitable. In all the modern talk about energy, efficiency, social service and the rest of it, what meaning is there except 'Get money, get it legally, and get a lot of it'? Money has become the grand test of virtue. By this test beggars fail, and for this they are despised. If one could earn even ten pounds a week at begging, it would become a respectable profession immediately. A beggar, looked at realistically, is simply a businessman, getting his living, like other business men, in the way that comes to hand. He has not, more than most modern people, sold his honour; he has merely made the mistake of choosing a trade at which it is impossible to grow rich.

XXXII

I want to put in some notes, as short as possible, on London slang and swearing. These (omitting the ones that everyone knows) are some of the cant words now used in London:

A gagger – a beggar or street performer of any kind. A moocher – one who begs outright, without pretence of doing a trade. A nobber – one who collects pennies for a beggar. A chanter – a street singer. A clodhopper – a street dancer. A mugfaker – a street photographer. A glimmer – one who watches vacant motor-cars. A gee (or jee – it is pronounced jee) – the accomplice of a cheapjack, who stimulates trade by pretending to buy something. A split – a detective. A flattie – a policeman. A didecai – a gypsy. A toby – a tramp.

A drop – money given to a beggar. Funkum – lavender or other perfume sold in envelopes. A boozer – a public-house. A slang – a hawker's licence. A kip – a place to sleep in, or a night's lodging. Smoke – London. A judy – a woman. The spike – the casual ward. The lump – the casual ward. A tosheroon – a half-crown. A deaner – a shilling. A hog – a shilling. A sprowsie – a sixpence. Clods – coppers. A drum – a billy can. Shackles – soup. A chat – a louse. Hard-up – tobacco made from cigarette ends. A stick or cane – a burglar's jemmy. A peter – a safe. A bly – a burglar's oxy-acetylene blowlamp.

To bawl – to suck or swallow. To knock off – to steal. To skipper – to sleep in the open.

About half of these words are in the larger dictionaries. It is interesting to guess at the derivation of some of them, though one or two – for instance, 'funkum' and 'tosheroon' – are beyond guessing. 'Deaner' presumably comes from 'denier'. 'Glimmer' (with the verb 'to glim') may have something to do with the old word 'glim', meaning a light, or another old word 'glim', meaning a glimpse; but it is an instance of the formation of new words, for in its present sense it can hardly be older than motor-cars. 'Gee' is a curious word; conceivably it has arisen out of 'gee', meaning horse, in the sense of stalking horse. The derivation of 'screever' is mysterious. It must come ultimately from *scribo*, but there has been no similar word in English for the past hundred and fifty years; nor can it have come directly from French, for pavement artists are unknown in France. 'Judy' and 'bawl' are East End words, not found west of Tower Bridge. 'Smoke' is a word used only by tramps. 'Kip' is Danish. Till quite recently the word 'doss' was used in this sense, but it is now quite obsolete.

London slang and dialect seem to change very rapidly. The old London accent described by Dickens and Surtees, with v for w and w for v and so forth, has now vanished utterly. The Cockney accent as we know it seems to have come up in the 'forties (it is first mentioned in an American book, Herman Melville's *White-Jacket*), and Cockney is already changing; there are few people now who say 'fice' for 'face', 'nawce' for 'nice' and so forth as consistently as they did twenty years ago. The slang changes together with the accent. Twenty-five or thirty years ago, for instance, the 'rhyming slang' was all the rage in London. In the 'rhyming slang' everything was named by something rhyming with it – a 'hit or miss' for a kiss, 'plates of meat' for feet, etc. It was so common that it was even reproduced in novels; now it is almost extinct.[1] Perhaps all the words I have mentioned above will have vanished in another twenty years.

The swear words also change – or, at any rate, they are subject to fashions. For example, twenty years ago the London working classes habitually used the word 'bloody'. Now they have abandoned it utterly, though novelists still represent them as using it. No born Londoner (it is different with people of Scotch or Irish origin) now says 'bloody', unless he is a man of some education. The word has, in fact, moved up in the social scale and ceased to be a swear word for the purposes of the working classes. The current London adjective, now tacked onto every noun, is 'fucking'. No doubt in time 'fucking', like 'bloody', will find its way into the drawing-room and be replaced by some other word.

The whole business of swearing, especially English swearing, is mysterious. Of its very nature swearing is as irrational as magic – indeed, it is a species of magic. But there is also a paradox about it, namely this: Our intention in swearing is to shock and wound, which we do by mentioning something that should be kept secret – usually something to do with the sexual functions. But the strange thing is that when a word is well established as a swear word, it seems to lose its original meaning; that is, it loses the thing that made it into a swear word. A word becomes an oath because it means a certain thing, and, because it has become an oath, it ceases to mean that thing. For example, 'fuck'. The Londoners do not now use, or very seldom use, this word in its original meaning; it is on their lips from morning till night, but it is a mere expletive and means nothing. Similarly with 'bugger', which is rapidly losing its original sense. One can think of similar instances in French – for example, '*foutre*', which is now a quite meaningless expletive. The word '*bougre*', also, is still used occasionally in Paris, but the people who use it, or most of them, have no

1. It survives in certain abbreviations, such as 'Use your twopenny' for 'Use your head'. 'Twopenny' is arrived at like this: head – loaf of bread – twopenny loaf – twopenny.

idea of what it once meant. The rule seems to be that words accepted as swear words have some magical character, which sets them apart and makes them useless for ordinary conversation.

Words used as insults seem to be governed by the same paradox as swear words. A word becomes an insult, one would suppose, because it means something bad; but in practice its insult-value has little to do with its actual meaning. For example, the most bitter insult one can offer to a Londoner is 'bastard' – which, taken for what it means, is hardly an insult at all. And the worst insult to a woman, either in London or Paris, is 'cow'; a name which might even be a compliment, for cows are among the most likeable of animals. Evidently a word is an insult simply because it is meant as an insult, without reference to its dictionary meaning; words, especially swear words, being what public opinion chooses to make them. In this connection it is interesting to see how a swear word can change character by crossing a frontier. In England you can print *'Je m'en fous'* without protest from anybody. In France you have to print it *'Je m'en f...'* Or, as another example, take the word 'barnshoot' – a corruption of the Hindustani word *bahinchut*.* A vile and unforgiveable insult in India, this word is a piece of gentle badinage in England. I have even seen it in a school text-book; it was in one of Aristophanes' plays, and the annotator suggested it as a rendering of some gibberish spoken by a Persian ambassador. Presumably the annotator knew what *bahinchut* meant. But, because it was a foreign word, it had lost its magical swear-word quality and could be printed.

One other thing is noticeable about swearing in London, and that is that the men do not usually swear in front of the women. In Paris it is quite different. A Parisian workman may prefer to suppress an oath in front of a woman, but he is not at all scrupulous about it, and the women themselves swear freely. The Londoners are more polite, or more squeamish, in this matter.

These are a few notes that I have set down more or less at random. It

---

* *The French translation has this note (in French):* A word for which there is no precise equivalent in French. In Hindustani, *bahin* means 'sister' and *chut* 'the sexual organ'. To call someone *bahinchut* is to remind him gratuitously that you are on the most intimate terms with his sister. *Barnshoot* is the same word corrupted by the English soldiers who brought it back to England; it has completely lost its original meaning.

is a pity that someone capable of dealing with the subject does not keep a year-book of London slang and swearing, registering the changes accurately. It might throw useful light upon the formation, development and obsolescence of words.

XXXIII

The two pounds that B. had given me lasted about ten days. That it lasted so long was due to Paddy, who had learned parsimony on the road and considered even one sound meal a day a wild extravagance. Food, to him, had come to mean simply bread and margarine – the eternal tea-and-two-slices, which will cheat hunger for an hour or two. He taught me how to live, food, bed, tobacco and all, at the rate of half a crown a day. And he managed to earn a few extra shillings by 'glimming' in the evenings. It was a precarious job, because illegal, but it brought in a little and eked out our money.

One morning we tried for a job as sandwich men. We went at five to an alley-way behind some offices, but there was already a queue of thirty or forty men waiting, and after two hours we were told that there was no work for us. We had not missed much, for sandwich men have an unenviable job. They are paid about three shillings a day for ten hours' work – it is hard work, especially in windy weather, and there is no skulking, for an inspector comes round frequently to see that the men are on their beats. To add to their troubles, they are only engaged by the day, or sometimes for three days, never weekly, so that they have to wait hours for their job every morning. The number of unemployed men who are ready to do the work makes them powerless to fight for better treatment. The job all sandwich men covet is distributing handbills, which is paid for at the same rate. When you see a man distributing handbills you can do him a good turn by taking one, for he goes off duty when he has distributed all his bills.

Meanwhile we went on with the lodging-house life – a squalid, eventless life of crushing boredom. For days together there was nothing to do but sit in the underground kitchen, reading yesterday's newspaper, or, when one could get hold of it, a back number of the *Union Jack*. It rained a great deal at this time, and everyone who came in steamed, so that the kitchen stank horribly. One's only excitement was the periodical tea-and-two-slices. I do not know how many men are living this life in London – it must be thousands at the least. As to Paddy, it was actually the best life he had known for two years past. His interludes from tramping, the times when he had somehow laid hands on a few shillings, had all been like this; the tramping itself had been slightly worse. Listening to his whimpering voice – he was always whimpering when he was not eating – one realised what torture unemployment must be to him. People are wrong when they think that an unemployed man only worries about losing his wages; on the contrary, an illiterate man, with the work habit in his bones, needs work even more than he needs money. An educated man can put up with enforced idleness, which is one of the worst evils of poverty. But a man like Paddy, with no means of filling up time, is as miserable out of work as a dog on the chain. That is why it is such nonsense to pretend that those who have 'come down in the world' are to be pitied above all others. The man who really merits pity is the man who has been down from the start, and faces poverty with a blank, resourceless mind.

It was a dull time, and little of it stays in my mind, except for talks with Bozo. Once the lodging-house was invaded by a slumming-party. Paddy and I had been out, and, coming back in the afternoon, we heard sounds of music downstairs. We went down, to find three gentlepeople, sleekly dressed, holding a religious service in our kitchen. They were a grave and reverend seignior in a frock coat, a lady sitting at a portable harmonium, and a chinless youth toying with a crucifix. It appeared that they had marched in and started to hold the service, without any kind of invitation whatever.

It was a pleasure to see how the lodgers met this intrusion. They did not offer the smallest rudeness to the slummers; they just ignored them. By common consent everyone in the kitchen – a hundred men, perhaps – behaved as though the slummers had not existed. There they stood patiently singing and exhorting, and no more notice was taken of them than if they had been earwigs. The gentleman in the frock coat preached a sermon, but not a word of it was audible; it was drowned in the usual din of songs, oaths and the clattering of pans. Men sat at their meals and card games three feet away from the harmonium, peaceably ignoring it. Presently the slummers gave it up and cleared out, not insulted in any way, but merely disregarded. No doubt they consoled themselves by thinking how brave they had been, 'freely venturing into the lowest dens', etc. etc.

Bozo said that these people came to the lodging-house several times a month. They had influence with the police, and the 'deputy' could not exclude them. It is curious how people take it for granted that they have a right to preach at you and pray over you as soon as your income falls below a certain level.

After nine days B.'s two pounds was reduced to one and ninepence. Paddy and I set aside eighteenpence for our beds, and spent threepence on the usual tea-and-two-slices, which we shared – an appetiser rather than a meal. By the afternoon we were damnably hungry and Paddy remembered a church near King's Cross Station where a free tea was given once a week to tramps. This was the day, and we decided to go there. Bozo, though it was rainy weather and he was almost penniless, would not come, saying that churches were not his style.

Outside the church quite a hundred men were waiting, dirty types who had gathered from far and wide at the news of a free tea, like kites round a dead buffalo. Presently the doors opened and a clergyman and some girls shepherded us into a gallery at the top of the church. It was an evangelical church, gaunt and wilfully ugly, with texts about blood and fire blazoned on the walls, and a hymn-book containing twelve hundred and fifty-one hymns; reading some of the hymns, I concluded that the book would do as it stood for an anthology of bad verse. There was to be a service after the tea, and the regular congregation were sitting in the well of the church below. It was a weekday, and there were only a few dozen of them, mostly stringy old women who reminded one of boiling-fowls. We ranged ourselves in the gallery pews and were given our tea; it was a one-pound jam-jar of tea each, with six slices of bread and margarine. As soon as tea was over, a dozen tramps who had stationed themselves near the door bolted to avoid the service; the rest stayed, less from gratitude than lacking the cheek to go.

The organ let out a few preliminary hoots and the service began. And instantly, as though at a signal, the tramps began to misbehave in the most outrageous way. One would not have thought such scenes possible in a church. All round the gallery men lolled in their pews, laughed,

chattered, leaned over and flicked pellets of bread among the congregation; I had to restrain the man next to me, more or less by force, from
lighting a cigarette. The tramps treated the service as a purely comic
spectacle. It was, indeed, a sufficiently ludicrous service – the kind where
there are sudden yells of 'Hallelujah!' and endless extempore prayers –
but their behaviour passed all bounds. There was one old fellow in the
congregation – Brother Bootle or some such name – who was often called
on to lead us in prayer, and whenever he stood up the tramps would begin
stamping as though in a theatre; they said that on a previous occasion he
had kept up an extempore prayer for twenty-five minutes, until the
minister had interrupted him. Once when Brother Bootle stood up a
tramp called out, 'Two to one 'e don't beat seven minutes!' so loud that
the whole church must hear. It was not long before we were making far
more noise than the minister. Sometimes somebody below would send up
an indignant 'Hush!' but it made no impression. We had set ourselves to
guy the service, and there was no stopping us.

It was a queer, rather disgusting scene. Below were the handful of
simple, well-meaning people, trying hard to worship; and above were the
hundred men whom they had fed, deliberately making worship impossible.
A ring of dirty, hairy faces grinned down from the gallery, openly jeering.
What could a few women and old men do against a hundred hostile tramps?
They were afraid of us, and we were frankly bullying them. It was our
revenge upon them for having humiliated us by feeding us.

The minister was a brave man. He thundered steadily through a long
sermon on Joshua, and managed almost to ignore the sniggers and
chattering from above. But in the end, perhaps goaded beyond endurance,
he announced loudly:

'I shall address the last five minutes of my sermon to the *unsaved* sinners!'

Having said which, he turned his face to the gallery and kept it so for
five minutes, lest there should be any doubt about who were saved and
who unsaved. But much we cared! Even while the minister was threatening
hell fire, we were rolling cigarettes, and at the last amen we clattered
down the stairs with a yell, many agreeing to come back for another free
tea next week.

The scene had interested me. It was so different from the ordinary
demeanour of tramps – from the abject worm-like gratitude with which

they normally accept charity. The explanation, of course, was that we out-numbered the congregation and so were not afraid of them. A man receiving charity practically always hates his benefactor – it is a fixed characteristic of human nature; and, when he has fifty or a hundred others to back him, he will show it.

In the evening, after the free tea, Paddy unexpectedly earned another eighteenpence at 'glimming'. It was exactly enough for another night's lodging, and we put it aside and went hungry till nine the next evening. Bozo, who might have given us some food, was away all day. The pavements were wet, and he had gone to the Elephant and Castle, where he knew of a pitch under shelter. Luckily I still had some tobacco, so that the day might have been worse.

At half-past eight Paddy took me to the Embankment, where a clergyman was known to distribute meal tickets once a week. Under Charing Cross Bridge fifty men were waiting, mirrored in the shivering puddles. Some of them were truly appalling specimens – they were Embankment sleepers, and the Embankment dredges up worse types than the spike. One of them, I remember, was dressed in an overcoat without buttons, laced up with rope, a pair of ragged trousers, and boots exposing his toes – not a rag else. He was bearded like a fakir, and he had managed to streak his chest and shoulders with some horrible black filth resembling train oil. What one could see of his face under the dirt and hair was bleached white as paper by some malignant disease. I heard him speak, and he had a goodish accent, as of a clerk or shopwalker.

Presently the clergyman appeared and the men ranged themselves in a queue in the order in which they had arrived. The clergyman was a nice, chubby, youngish man, and, curiously enough, very like Charlie, my friend in Paris. He was shy and embarrassed, and did not speak except for a brief good evening; he simply hurried down the line of men, thrusting a ticket upon each, and not waiting to be thanked. The consequence was that, for once, there was genuine gratitude, and everyone said that the clergyman was a — good feller. Someone (in his hearing, I believe) called out: 'Well, *he'll* never be a f— bishop!' – this, of course, intended as a warm compliment.

The tickets were worth sixpence each, and were directed to an eating-house not far away. When we got there we found that the proprietor, knowing that the tramps could not go elsewhere, was cheating by only giving four penny-worth of food for each ticket. Paddy and I pooled our tickets, and received food which we could have got for sevenpence or eightpence at most coffee-shops. The clergyman had distributed well over a pound in tickets, so that the proprietor was evidently swindling the tramps to the tune of seven shillings or more a week. This kind of victimisation is a regular part of a tramp's life, and it will go on as long as people continue to give meal tickets instead of money.

Paddy and I went back to the lodging-house and, still hungry, loafed in the kitchen, making the warmth of the fire a substitute for food. At half-past ten Bozo arrived, tired out and haggard, for his mangled leg made walking an agony. He had not earned a penny at screeving, all the pitches under shelter being taken, and for several hours he had begged outright, with one eye on the policemen. He had amassed eightpence – a penny short of his kip. It was long past the hour for paying, and he had only managed to slip indoors when the deputy was not looking; at any moment he might be caught and turned out, to sleep on the Embankment. Bozo took the things out of his pockets and looked them over, debating what to sell. He decided on his razor, took it round the kitchen, and in a few minutes he had sold it for threepence – enough to pay his kip, buy a basin of tea, and leave a halfpenny over.

Bozo got his basin of tea and sat down by the fire to dry his clothes. As he drank the tea I saw that he was laughing to himself, as though at some good joke. Surprised, I asked him what he had to laugh at.

'It's bloody funny!' he said. 'It's funny enough for *Punch*. What do you think I been and done?'

'What?'

'Sold my razor without having a shave first! Of all the — fools!'

He had not eaten since the morning, had walked several miles with a twisted leg, his clothes were drenched, and he had a halfpenny between himself and starvation. With all this, he could laugh over the loss of his razor. One could not help admiring him.

XXXIV

The next morning, our money being at an end, Paddy and I set out for the spike. We went southward by the Old Kent Road, making for Cromley; we could not go to a London spike, for Paddy had been in one recently and did not care to risk going again. It was a sixteen-mile walk over asphalt, blistering to the heels, and we were acutely hungry. Paddy browsed the pavement, laying up a store of cigarette ends against his time in the spike. In the end his perseverance was rewarded, for he picked up a penny. We bought a large piece of stale bread, and devoured it as we walked.

When we got to Cromley, it was too early to go to the spike, and we walked several miles further, to a plantation beside a meadow, where one could sit down. It was a regular caravanserai of tramps – one could tell it by the worn grass and the sodden newspaper and rusty cans that they had left behind. Other tramps were arriving by ones and twos. It was jolly autumn weather. Near by, a deep bed of tansies was growing; it seems to me that even now I can smell the sharp reek of those tansies, warring with the reek of tramps. In the meadow two carthorse colts, raw sienna colour with white manes and tails, were nibbling at a gate. We sprawled about on the ground, sweaty and exhausted. Someone managed to find dry sticks and get a fire going, and we all had milkless tea out of a tin 'drum' which was passed round.

Some of the tramps began telling stories. One of them, Bill, was an interesting type, a genuine sturdy beggar of the old breed, strong as Hercules and a frank foe of work. He boasted that with his great strength he could get a navvying job any time he liked, but as soon as he drew his first week's wages he went on a terrific drunk and was sacked. Between whiles he 'mooched', chiefly from shopkeepers. He talked like this:

'I ain't goin' far in — Kent. Kent's a tight county, Kent is. There's too many bin moochin' about 'ere. The — bakers get so as they'll throw their bread away sooner'n give it you. Now Oxford, that's the place for moochin', Oxford is. When I was in Oxford I mooched bread, and I mooched bacon, and I mooched beef, and every night I mooched tanners for my kip off of the students. The last night I was twopence short of my kip, so I goes up to a parson and mooches 'im for threepence. He give me threepence, and the next moment he turns round and gives me in charge for beggin'. "You bin beggin'," the copper says. "No I ain't," I says, "I was askin' the gentlemen the time," I says. The copper starts feelin' inside my coat, and he pulls out a pound of meat and two loaves of bread. "Well, what's all this, then?" he says. "You better come 'long to the station," he says. The beak give me seven days. I don't mooch from no more — parsons. But Christ! what do I care for a lay-up of seven days?' etc. etc.

It seemed that his whole life was this – a round of mooching, drunks and lay-ups. He laughed as he talked of it, taking it all for a tremendous joke. He looked as though he made a poor thing out of begging, for he wore only a corduroy suit, scarf and cap – no socks or linen. Still, he was fat and jolly, and he even smelt of beer, a most unusual smell in a tramp nowadays.

Two of the tramps had been in Cromley spike recently, and they told a ghost story connected with it. Years earlier, they said, there had been a suicide there. A tramp had managed to smuggle a razor into his cell, and there cut his throat. In the morning, when the Tramp Major came round, the body was jammed against the door, and to open it they had to break the dead man's arm. In revenge for this, the dead man haunted his cell, and anyone who slept there was certain to die within the year; there were copious instances, of course. If a cell door stuck when you tried to open it, you should avoid that cell like the plague, for it was the haunted one.

Two tramps, ex-sailors, told another grisly story. A man (they swore they had known him) had planned to stow away on a boat bound for Chile. It was laden with manufactured goods packed in big wooden crates, and with the help of a docker the stowaway had managed to hide himself in one of these. But the docker had made a mistake about the order in which the crates were to be loaded. The crane gripped the stowaway, swung him aloft, and deposited him – at the very bottom of the hold, beneath hundreds of crates. No one discovered what had happened until the end of the voyage, when they found the stowaway rotting, dead of suffocation.

Another tramp told the story of Gilderoy, the Scottish robber. Gilderoy was the man who was condemned to be hanged, escaped, captured the judge who had sentenced him, and (splendid fellow!) hanged him. The tramps liked the story, of course, but the interesting thing was to see that they had got it all wrong. Their version was that Gilderoy escaped to America, whereas in reality he was recaptured and put to death. The story had been amended, no doubt deliberately; just as children amend the stories of Samson and Robin Hood, giving them happy endings which are quite imaginary.

This set the tramps talking about history, and a very old man declared that the 'one bite law' was a survival from days when the nobles hunted men instead of deer. Some of the others laughed at him, but he had the idea firm in his head. He had heard, too, of the Corn Laws, and the *jus primae noctis* (he believed it had really existed); also of the Great Rebellion, which he thought was a rebellion of poor against rich – perhaps he had got it mixed up with the peasant rebellions. I doubt whether the old man could read, and certainly he was not repeating newspaper articles. His scraps of history had been passed from generation to generation of tramps, perhaps for centuries in some cases. It was oral tradition lingering on, like a faint echo from the Middle Ages.

Paddy and I went to the spike at six in the evening, getting out at ten in the morning. It was much like Romton and Edbury, and we saw nothing of the ghost. Among the casuals were two young men named William and Fred, ex-fishermen from Norfolk, a lively pair and fond of singing. They had a song called 'Unhappy Bella' that is worth writing down. I heard them sing it half a dozen times during the next two days, and I managed to get it by heart, except a line or two which I have guessed. It ran:

> *Bella was young and Bella was fair*
> *With bright blue eyes and golden hair,*
> *O unhappy Bella!*
> *Her step was light and her heart was gay,*
> *But she had no sense, and one fine day*
> *She got herself put in the family way*
> *By a wicked, heartless, cruel deceiver.*
>
> *Poor Bella was young, she didn't believe*
> *That the world is hard and men deceive,*
> *O unhappy Bella!*
> *She said, 'My man will do what's just,*

He'll marry me now, because he must';
Her heart was full of loving trust
In a wicked, heartless, cruel deceiver.

She went to his house; that dirty skunk
Had packed his bags and done a bunk,
O unhappy Bella!
Her landlady said, 'Get out, you whore,
I won't have your sort a-darkening my door.'
Poor Bella was put to affliction sore
By a wicked, heartless, cruel deceiver.

All night she tramped the cruel snows,
What she must have suffered nobody knows,
O unhappy Bella!
And when the morning dawned so red,
Alas, alas, poor Bella was dead,
Sent so young to her lonely bed
By a wicked, heartless, cruel deceiver.

So thus, you see, do what you will,
The fruits of sin are suffering still,
O unhappy Bella!
As into the grave they laid her low,
The men said, 'Alas, but life is so,'
But the women chanted, sweet and low,
'It's all the men, the dirty bastards!'

Written by a woman, perhaps.

William and Fred, the singers of this song, were thorough scallywags, the sort of men who get tramps a bad name. They happened to know that the Tramp Major at Cromley had a stock of old clothes, which were to be given at need to casuals. Before going in William and Fred took off their boots, ripped the seams and cut pieces off the soles, more or less ruining them. Then they applied for two pairs of boots, and the Tramp Major, seeing how bad their boots were, gave them two almost new pairs. William and Fred were scarcely outside the spike in the morning before they had sold these boots for one and ninepence. It seemed to them quite worth while, for one and ninepence, to make their own boots practically unwearable.

Leaving the spike, we all started southward, a long slouching procession, for Lower Binfield and Ide Hill. On the way there was a fight between two of the tramps. They had quarrelled overnight (there was some silly *casus belli* about one saying to the other, 'Bullshit', which was taken for Bolshevik – a deadly insult), and they fought it out in a field. A dozen of us stayed to watch them. The scene sticks in my mind for one thing – the man who was beaten going down, and his cap falling off and showing that his hair was quite white. After that some of us intervened and stopped the fight. Paddy had meanwhile been making inquiries, and found that the real cause of the quarrel was, as usual, a few pennyworth of food.

We got to Lower Binfield quite early, and Paddy filled in the time by asking for work at back doors. At one house he was given some boxes to chop up for firewood, and, saying he had a mate outside, he brought me in and we did the work together. When it was done the householder told the maid to take us out a cup of tea. I remember the terrified way in which she brought it out, and then, losing her courage, set the cups down on the path and bolted back to the house, shutting herself in the kitchen. So dreadful is the name of 'tramp'. They paid us sixpence each, and we bought a threepenny loaf and half an ounce of tobacco, leaving fivepence.

Paddy thought it wiser to bury our fivepence, for the Tramp Major at Lower Binfield was renowned as a tyrant and might refuse to admit us if we had any money at all. It is quite a common practice of tramps to bury their money. If they intend to smuggle at all a large sum into the spike they generally sew it into their clothes, which may mean prison if they are caught, of course. Paddy and Bozo used to tell a good story about this. An Irishman (Bozo said it was an Irishman; Paddy said an Englishman), not a tramp, and in possession of thirty pounds, was stranded in a small village where he could not get a bed. He consulted a tramp, who advised him to go to the workhouse. It is quite a regular proceeding, if one cannot get a bed elsewhere, to get one at the workhouse, paying a reasonable sum for it. The Irishman, however, thought he would be clever and get a bed for nothing, so he presented himself at the workhouse as an ordinary casual. He had sewn the thirty pounds into his clothes. Meanwhile the tramp who had advised him had seen his chance, and that night he privately asked the Tramp Major for permission to leave the spike early in the morning, as he had to see about a job. At six in the morning he was released, and went out – in the Irishman's clothes. The Irishman complained of the theft, and was given thirty days for going into a casual ward under false pretences.

XXXV

Arrived at Lower Binfield, we sprawled for a long time on the green, watched by cottagers from their front gates. A clergyman and his daughter came and stared silently at us for a while, as though we had been aquarium fishes, and then went away again. There were several dozen of us waiting. William and Fred were there, still singing, and the men who had fought, and Bill the moocher. He had been mooching from bakers, and had quantities of stale bread tucked away between his coat and his bare body. He shared it out, and we were all glad of it. There was a woman among us, the first woman tramp I had ever seen. She was a fattish, battered, very dirty woman of sixty, in a long, trailing black skirt. She put on great airs of dignity, and if anyone sat down near her she sniffed and moved further off.

'Where you bound for, missis?' one of the tramps called to her.

The woman sniffed and looked into the distance.

'Come on, missis,' he said, 'cheer up. Be chummy. We're all in the same boat 'ere.'

'Thank you,' said the woman bitterly, 'when I want to get mixed up with a set of *tramps*, I'll let you know.'

I enjoyed the way she said *tramps*. It seemed to show you in a flash the whole of her soul; a small, blinkered, feminine soul, that had learned absolutely nothing from years on the road. She was, no doubt, a respectable widow woman, become a tramp through some grotesque accident.

The spike opened at six. This was Saturday, and we were to be confined over the week-end, which is the usual practice; why, I do not know, unless it is from a vague feeling that Sunday merits something disagreeable. When we registered I gave my trade as 'journalist'. It was truer than 'painter', for I had sometimes earned money from newspaper articles, but it was a silly thing to say, being bound to lead to questions. As soon as we were inside the spike and had been lined up for the search, the Tramp Major called my name. He was a stiff, soldierly man of forty, not looking the bully he had been represented, but with an old soldier's gruffness. He said sharply:

'Which of you is Blank?' (I forget what name I had given.)

'Me, sir.'

'So you are a journalist?'

'Yes, sir,' I said, quaking. A few questions would betray the fact that I had been lying, which might mean prison. But the Tramp Major only looked me up and down and said:

'Then you are a gentleman?'

'I suppose so.'

He gave me another long look. 'Well, that's bloody bad luck, guv'nor,' he said; 'bloody bad luck that is.' And thereafter he treated me with unfair favouritism, and even with a kind of deference. He did not search me, and in the bathroom he actually gave me a clean towel to myself – an unheard-of luxury. So powerful is the word 'gentleman' in an old soldier's ear.

By seven we had wolfed our bread and tea and were in our cells. We slept one in a cell, and there were bedsteads and straw palliasses, so that one ought to have had a good night's sleep. But no spike is perfect, and the peculiar shortcoming at Lower Binfield was the cold. The hot pipes were not working, and the two blankets we had been given were thin cotton things and almost useless. It was only autumn, but the cold was bitter. One spent the long twelve-hour night in turning from side to side, falling asleep for a few minutes and waking up shivering. We could not smoke, for our tobacco, which we had managed to smuggle in, was in our clothes and we should not get these back till the morning. All down the passage one could hear groaning noises, and sometimes a shouted oath. No one, I imagine, got more than an hour or two of sleep.

In the morning, after breakfast and the doctor's inspection, the Tramp Major herded us all into the dining-room and locked the door upon us. It was a limewashed, stone-floored room, unutterably dreary, with its furniture of deal boards and benches, and its prison smell. The barred windows were too high to look out of, and there were no ornaments save a clock and a copy of the workhouse rules. Packed elbow to elbow on the benches, we were bored already, though it was barely eight in the morning. There was nothing to do, nothing to talk about, not even room to move. The sole consolation was that one could smoke, for smoking was connived at so long as one was not caught in the act. Scotty, a little hairy tramp with a bastard accent sired by Cockney out of Glasgow, was tobaccoless, his tin of cigarette ends having fallen out of his boot during the search and been impounded. I stood him the makings of a cigarette. We smoked furtively, thrusting our cigarettes into our pockets, like schoolboys, when we heard the Tramp Major coming.

Most of the tramps spent ten continuous hours in this comfortless, soulless room. Heaven knows how they put up with it. I was luckier than the others, for at ten o'clock the Tramp Major told off a few men for odd jobs, and he picked me out to help in the workhouse kitchen, the most coveted job of all. This, like the clean towel, was a charm worked by the word 'gentleman'.

There was no work to do in the kitchen, and I sneaked off into a small shed used for storing potatoes, where some workhouse paupers were skulking to avoid the Sunday morning service. There were comfortable packing-cases to sit on, and some back numbers of the *Family Herald*, and even a copy of *Raffles* from the workhouse library. The paupers talked interestingly about workhouse life. They told me, among other things, that the thing really hated in the workhouse, as a stigma of charity, is the uniform; if the men could wear their own clothes, or even their own caps and scarves, they would not mind being paupers. I had my dinner from the workhouse table, and it was a meal fit for a boa-constrictor – the largest meal I had eaten since my first day at the Hôtel X. The paupers said that they habitually gorged to the bursting-point on Sunday and were underfed the rest of the week. After dinner the cook set me to do the washing up, and told me to throw away the food that remained. The wastage was astonishing and, in the circumstances, appalling. Half-eaten joints of meat, and bucketfuls of broken bread and vegetables, were pitched away like so much rubbish and then defiled with tea-leaves. I filled five dustbins to overflowing with quite eatable food. And while I did so fifty tramps were sitting in the spike with their bellies half filled by the spike dinner of bread and cheese, and perhaps two cold boiled potatoes each in honour of Sunday. According to the paupers, the food was thrown away from deliberate policy, rather than that it should be given to the tramps.

At three I went back to the spike. The tramps had been sitting there since eight, with hardly room to move an elbow, and they were now half mad with boredom. Even smoking was at an end, for a tramp's tobacco is picked-up cigarette ends, and he starves if he is more than a few hours away from the pavement. Most of the men were too bored even to talk; they just sat packed on the benches, staring at nothing, their scrubby faces split in two by enormous yawns. The room stank of *ennui*.

Paddy, his backside aching from the hard bench, was in a whimpering mood, and to pass the time away I talked with a rather superior tramp, a young carpenter who wore a collar and tie and was on the road, he said, for lack of a set of tools. He kept a little aloof from the other tramps, and held himself more like a free man than a casual. He had literary tastes, too, and carried a copy of *Quentin Durward* in his pocket. He told me that he never went into a spike unless driven there by hunger, sleeping under hedges and behind ricks in preference. Along the south coast he had begged by day and slept in bathing-huts for weeks at a time.

We talked of life on the road. He criticised the system that makes a tramp spend fourteen hours a day in the spike, and the other ten in walking and dodging the police. He spoke of his own case – six months at the public charge for want of a few pounds' worth of tools. It was idiotic, he said.

Then I told him about the wastage of food in the workhouse kitchen, and what I thought of it. And at that he changed his tone instantly. I saw that I had awakened the pew-renter who sleeps in every English workman. Though he had been famished along with the others, he at once saw reasons why the food should have been thrown away rather than given to the tramps. He admonished me quite severely.

'They have to do it,' he said. 'If they made these places too comfortable, you'd have all the scum of the country flocking into them. It's only the bad food as keeps all that scum away. These here tramps are too lazy to work, that's all that's wrong with them. You don't want to go encouraging of them. They're scum.'

I produced arguments to prove him wrong, but he would not listen. He kept repeating:

'You don't want to have any pity on these here tramps – scum, they are. You don't want to judge them by the same standards as men like you and me. They're scum, just scum.'

It was interesting to see the subtle way in which he disassociated himself from 'these here tramps'. He had been on the road six months, but in the sight of God, he seemed to imply, he was not a tramp. I imagine there are quite a lot of tramps who thank God they are not tramps. They are like the trippers who say such cutting things about trippers.

Three hours dragged by. At six supper arrived, and turned out to be quite uneatable; the bread, tough enough in the morning (it had been cut into slices on Saturday night), was now as hard as ship's biscuit. Luckily it was spread with dripping, and we scraped the dripping off and ate that alone, which was better than nothing. At a quarter-past six we were sent to bed. New tramps were arriving, and in order not to mix the tramps of different days (for fear of infectious diseases) the new men were put in the cells and we in dormitories. Our dormitory was a barnlike room with thirty beds close together, and a tub to serve as a common chamber-pot. It stank abominably, and the older men coughed and got up all night. But being so many together kept the room warm, and we had some sleep.

We dispersed at ten in the morning, after a fresh medical inspection, with a hunk of bread and cheese for our midday dinner. William and Fred, strong in the possession of a shilling, impaled their bread on the spike railings – as a protest, they said. This was the second spike in Kent that they had made too hot to hold them, and they thought it a great joke. They were cheerful souls, for tramps. The imbecile (there is an imbecile in every collection of tramps) said that he was too tired to walk and clung to the railings, until the Tramp Major had to dislodge him and start him with a kick. Paddy and I turned north, for London. Most of the others were going on to Ide Hill, said to be about the worst spike in England.[1]

Once again it was jolly autumn weather, and the road was quiet, with few cars passing. The air was like sweet-briar after the spike's mingled stenches of sweat, soap and drains. We two seemed the only tramps on the road. Then I heard a hurried step behind us, and someone calling. It was little Scotty, the Glasgow tramp, who had run after us panting. He

---

1. I have been in it since, and it is not so bad.

produced a rusty tin from his pocket. He wore a friendly smile, like someone repaying an obligation.

'Here y'are, mate,' he said cordially. 'I owe you some fag-ends. You stood me a smoke yesterday. The Tramp Major give me back my box of fag-ends when we come out this morning. One good turn deserves another – here y'are.'

And he put four sodden, debauched, loathly cigarette-ends into my hand.

XXXVI

I want to set down some general remarks about tramps. When one comes to think of it, tramps are a queer product and worth thinking over. It is queer that a tribe of men, tens of thousands in number, should be marching up and down England like so many Wandering Jews. But though the case obviously wants considering, one cannot even start to consider it until one has got rid of certain prejudices. These prejudices are rooted in the idea that every tramp, *ipso facto*, is a blackguard. In childhood we have been taught that tramps are blackguards, and consequently there exists in our minds a sort of ideal or typical tramp – a repulsive, rather dangerous creature, who would die rather than work or wash, and wants nothing but to beg, drink and rob hen-houses. This tramp-monster is no truer to life than the sinister Chinaman of the magazine stories, but he is very hard to get rid of. The very word 'tramp' evokes his image. And the belief in him obscures the real questions of vagrancy.

To take a fundamental question about vagrancy: Why do tramps exist at all? It is a curious thing, but very few people know what makes a tramp take to the road. And, because of the belief in the tramp-monster, the most fantastic reasons are suggested. It is said, for instance, that tramps tramp to avoid work, to beg more easily, to seek opportunities for crime, even – least probable of reasons – because they like tramping. I have even read in a book of criminology that the tramp is an atavism, a throw-back to the nomadic stage of humanity. And meanwhile the quite obvious cause of vagrancy is staring one in the face. Of course a tramp is not a nomadic atavism – one might as well say that a commercial traveller is an atavism. A tramp tramps, not because he likes it, but for the same reason as a car keeps to the left; because there happens to be a law compelling him to do so. A destitute man, if he is not supported by the parish, can only get relief at the casual wards, and as each casual ward will only admit him for one night, he is automatically kept moving. He is a vagrant because, in the state of the law, it is that or starve. But people have been brought up to believe in the tramp-monster, and so they prefer to think that there must be some more or less villainous motive for tramping.

As a matter of fact, very little of the tramp-monster will survive inquiry. Take the generally accepted idea that tramps are dangerous characters. Quite apart from experience, one can say *a priori* that very few tramps are dangerous, because if they were dangerous they would be treated accordingly. A casual ward will often admit a hundred tramps in one night, and these are handled by a staff of at most three porters. A hundred ruffians could not be controlled by three unarmed men. Indeed, when one sees how tramps let themselves be bullied by the workhouse officials, it is obvious that they are the most docile, broken-spirited creatures imaginable. Or take the idea that all tramps are drunkards – an idea ridiculous on the face of it. No doubt many tramps would drink if they got the chance, but in the nature of things they cannot get the chance. At this moment a pale watery stuff called beer is sevenpence a pint in England. To be drunk on it would cost at least half a crown, and a man who can command half a crown at all often is not a tramp. The idea that tramps are impudent social parasites ('sturdy beggars') is not absolutely unfounded, but it is only true in a few per cent of the cases. Deliberate, cynical parasitism, such as one reads of in Jack London's books on American tramping, is not in the English character. The English are a conscience-ridden race, with a strong sense of the sinfulness of poverty. One cannot imagine the average Englishman deliberately turning parasite, and this national character does not necessarily change because a man is thrown out of work. Indeed, if one remembers that a tramp is only an Englishman out of work, forced by law to live as a vagabond, then the tramp-monster vanishes. I am not saying, of course, that most tramps are ideal characters; I am only saying that they are ordinary human beings, and that if they are worse than other people it is the result and not the cause of their way of life.

It follows that the 'Serve them damned well right' attitude that is normally taken towards tramps is no fairer than it would be towards cripples or invalids. When one has realised that, one begins to put oneself in a tramp's place and understand what his life is like. It is an extraordinarily futile, acutely unpleasant life. I have described the casual ward – the routine of a tramp's day – but there are three especial evils that need insisting upon. The first is hunger, which is the almost general fate of tramps. The casual ward gives them a ration which is probably not even meant to be sufficient, and anything beyond this must be got by begging – that is, by breaking the law. The result is that nearly every tramp is rotted by malnutrition; for proof of which one need only look at the men lining up outside any casual ward. The second great evil of a tramp's life – it seems much smaller at first sight, but it is a good second – is that he is entirely cut off from contact with women. This point needs elaborating.

Tramps are cut off from women, in the first place, because there are very few women at their level of society. One might imagine that among destitute people the sexes would be as equally balanced as elsewhere. But it is not so; in fact, one can almost say that below a certain level society is entirely male. The following figures, published by the LCC from a night census taken on February 13th, 1931, will show the relative numbers of destitute men and destitute women:

Spending the night in the streets, 60 men, 18 women.[1]
In shelters and homes not licensed as common lodging-houses, 1,057 men, 137 women.
In the crypt of St Martin's-in-the-Fields Church, 88 men, 12 women.
In LCC casual wards and hostels, 674 men, 15 women.

It will be seen from these figures that at the charity-level men outnumber women by something like ten to one. The cause is presumably that unemployment affects women less than men; also that any presentable woman can, in the last resort, attach herself to some man. The result, for a tramp, is that he is condemned to perpetual celibacy. For of course it goes without saying that if a tramp finds no women at his own level, those above – even a very little above – are as far out of his reach as the moon. The reasons are not worth discussing, but there is no doubt that

1. This must be an underestimate. Still, the proportions probably hold good.

women never, or hardly ever, condescend to men who are much poorer than themselves. A tramp, therefore, is a celibate from the moment when he takes to the road. He is absolutely without hope of getting a wife, a mistress, or any kind of woman except – very rarely, when he can raise a few shillings – a prostitute.

It is obvious what the results of this must be: homosexuality, for instance, and occasional rape cases. But deeper than these there is the degradation worked in a man who knows that he is not even considered fit for marriage. The sexual impulse, not to put it any higher, is a fundamental impulse, and starvation of it can be almost as demoralising as physical hunger. The evil of poverty is not so much that it makes a man suffer as that it rots him physically and spiritually. And there can be no doubt that sexual starvation contributes to this rotting process. Cut off from the whole race of women, a tramp feels himself degraded to the rank of a cripple or a lunatic. No humiliation could do more damage to a man's self-respect.

The other great evil of a tramp's life is enforced idleness. By our vagrancy laws things are so arranged that when he is not walking the road he is sitting in a cell; or, in the intervals, lying on the ground waiting for the casual ward to open. It is obvious that this is a dismal, demoralising way of life, especially for an uneducated man.

Besides these one could enumerate scores of minor evils – to name only one, discomfort, which is inseparable from life on the road; it is worth remembering that the average tramp has no clothes but what he stands up in, wears boots that are ill-fitting, and does not sit in a chair for months together. But the important point is that a tramp's sufferings are entirely useless. He lives a fantastically disagreeable life, and lives it to no purpose whatever. One could not, in fact, invent a more futile routine than walking from prison to prison, spending perhaps eighteen hours a day in the cell and on the road. There must be at the least several tens of thousands of tramps in England. Each day they expend innumerable foot-pounds of energy – enough to plough thousands of acres, build miles of road, put up dozens of houses – in mere, useless walking. Each day they waste between them possibly ten years of time in staring at cell walls. They cost the country at least a pound a week a man, and give nothing in return for it. They go round and round, on an endless boring game of general post, which is of no use, and is not even meant to be of any use to any person whatever. The law keeps this process going, and we have got so accustomed to it that we are not surprised. But it is very silly.

Granting the futility of a tramp's life, the question is whether anything could be done to improve it. Obviously it would be possible, for instance, to make the casual wards a little more habitable, and this is actually being done in some cases. During the last year some of the casual wards have been improved – beyond recognition, if the accounts are true – and there is talk of doing the same to all of them. But this does not go to the heart of the problem. The problem is how to turn the tramp from a bored, half-alive vagrant into a self-respecting human being. A mere increase of comfort cannot do this. Even if the casual wards became positively luxurious (they never will),[2] a tramp's life would still be wasted. He would still be a pauper, cut off from marriage and home life, and a dead loss to the community. What is needed is to depauperise him, and this can only be done by finding him work – not work for the sake of working, but work of which he can enjoy the benefit. At present, in the great majority of casual wards, tramps do no work whatever. At one time they were made to break stones for their food, but this was stopped when they had broken enough stone for years ahead and put the stone-breakers out of work. Nowadays they are kept idle, because there is seemingly nothing for them to do. Yet there is a fairly obvious way of making them useful, namely this: Each workhouse could run a small farm, or at least a kitchen garden, and every able-bodied tramp who presented himself could be made to do a sound day's work. The produce of the farm or garden could be used for feeding the tramps, and at the worst it would be better than the filthy diet of bread and margarine and tea. Of course, the casual wards could never be quite self-supporting, but they could go a long way towards it, and the rates would probably benefit in the long run. It must be remembered that under the present system tramps are as dead a loss to the country as they could possibly be, for they not only do no work, but they live on a diet that is bound to undermine their health; the system, therefore, loses lives as well as money. A scheme which fed them decently,

2. In fairness it must be added that a few of the casual wards have been improved recently, at least from the point of view of sleeping accommodation. But most of them are the same as ever, and there has been no real improvement in the food.

and made them produce at least a part of their own food, would be worth trying.

It may be objected that a farm or even a garden could not be run with casual labour. But there is no real reason why tramps should only stay a day at each casual ward; they might stay a month or even a year, if there were work for them to do. The constant circulation of tramps is something quite artificial. At present a tramp is an expense to the rates, and the object of each workhouse is therefore to push him on to the next; hence the rule that he can stay only one night. If he returns within a month he is penalised by being confined for a week, and, as this is much the same as being in prison, naturally he keeps moving. But if he represented labour to the workhouse, and the workhouse represented sound food to him, it would be another matter. The workhouses would develop into partially self-supporting institutions, and the tramps, settling down here or there according as they were needed, would cease to be tramps. They would be doing something comparatively useful, getting decent food, and living a settled life. By degrees, if the scheme worked well, they might even cease to be regarded as paupers, and be able to marry and take a respectable place in society.

This is only a rough idea, and there are some obvious objections to it. Nevertheless, it does suggest a way of improving the status of tramps without piling new burdens on the rates. And the solution must, in any case, be something of this kind. For the question is, what to do with men who are underfed and idle; and the answer – to make them grow their own food – imposes itself automatically.

XXXVII

A word about the sleeping accommodation open to a homeless person in London. At present it is impossible to get a *bed* in any non-charitable institution in London for less than sevenpence a night. If you cannot afford sevenpence for a bed, you must put up with one of the following substitutes:

1. The Embankment. Here is the account that Paddy gave me of sleeping on the Embankment:

'De whole t'ing wid de Embankment is gettin' to sleep early. You got to be on your bench by eight o'clock, because dere ain't too many benches and sometimes dey're all taken. And you got to try to get to sleep at once. 'Tis too cold to sleep much after twelve o'clock, an' de police turns you off at four in de mornin'. It ain't easy to sleep, dough, wid dem bloody trams flyin' past your head all de time, an' dem sky-signs across de river flickin' on an' off in your eyes. De cold's cruel. Dem as sleeps dere generally wraps demselves up in newspaper, but it don't do much good. You'd be bloody lucky if you got t'ree hours' sleep.'

I have slept on the Embankment and found that it corresponded to Paddy's description. It is, however, much better than not sleeping at all, which is the alternative if you spend the night in the streets, elsewhere than on the Embankment. According to the law in London, you may sit down for the night, but the police must move you on if they see you asleep; the Embankment and one or two odd corners (there is one behind the Lyceum Theatre) are special exceptions. This law is evidently a piece of wilful offensiveness. Its object, so it is said, is to prevent people from dying of exposure; but clearly if a man has no home and is going to die of exposure, die he will, asleep or awake. In Paris there is no such law. There, people sleep by the score under the Seine bridges, and in doorways, and on benches in the squares, and round the ventilating shafts of the Metro, and even inside the Metro stations. It does no apparent harm. No one will spend a night in the street if he can possibly help it, and if he is going to stay out of doors he might as well be allowed to sleep, if he can.

2. The Twopenny Hangover. This comes a little higher than the Embankment. At the Twopenny Hangover, the lodgers sit in a row on a bench; there is a rope in front of them, and they lean on this as though leaning over a fence. A man, humorously called the valet, cuts the rope at five in the morning. I have never been there myself, but Bozo had been there often. I asked him whether anyone could possibly sleep in such an attitude, and he said that it was more comfortable than it sounded – at any rate, better than the bare floor. There are similar shelters in Paris, but the charge there is only twenty-five centimes (a halfpenny) instead of twopence.

3. The Coffin, at fourpence a night. At the Coffin you sleep in a wooden box, with a tarpaulin for covering. It is cold, and the worst thing about it are the bugs, which, being enclosed in a box, you cannot escape.

Above this come the common lodging-houses, with charges varying between sevenpence and one and a penny a night. The best are the Rowton Houses, where the charge is a shilling, for which you get a cubicle to yourself, and the use of excellent bathrooms. You can also pay half a crown for a 'special', which is practically hotel accommodation. The Rowton Houses are splendid buildings, and the only objection to them is the strict discipline, with rules against cooking, card-playing, etc. Perhaps the best advertisement for the Rowton Houses is the fact that they are always full to overflowing. The Bruce Houses, at one and a penny, are also excellent.

Next best, in point of cleanliness, are the Salvation Army hostels, at sevenpence or eightpence. They vary (I have been in one or two that were as dirty as ordinary common lodging-houses), but most of them are clean, and they have good bathrooms; you have to pay extra for a bath, however. You can get a cubicle for a shilling. In the eightpenny dormitories the beds are comfortable, but there are so many of them (as a rule at least forty to a room), and so close together, that it is impossible to get a quiet night. The numerous restrictions stink of prison and charity. The Salvation Army hostels would only appeal to people who put cleanliness before anything else.

Beyond this there are the ordinary common lodging-houses. Whether you pay sevenpence or a shilling, they are all stuffy and noisy, and the beds are uniformly dirty and uncomfortable. What redeems them are their *laissez-faire* atmosphere and the warm home-like kitchens where one can lounge at all hours of the day or night. They are squalid dens, but some kind of social life is possible in them. The women's lodging-houses are said to be generally worse than the men's, and there are very few houses with accommodation for married couples. In fact, it is nothing out of the common for a homeless man to sleep in one lodging-house and his wife in another.

At this moment at least fifteen thousand people in London are living in common lodging-houses. For an unattached man earning two pounds a week, or less, a lodging-house is a great convenience. He could hardly get a furnished room so cheaply, and the lodging-house gives him free firing, a bathroom of sorts, and plenty of society. As for the dirt, it is a minor evil. The really bad fault of lodging-houses is that they are places in which one pays to sleep, and in which sound sleep is impossible. All one gets for one's money is a bed measuring five feet six by two feet six, with a hard convex mattress and a pillow like a block of wood, covered by one cotton counterpane and two grey, stinking sheets. In winter there are blankets, but never enough. And this bed is in a room where there are never less than five, and sometimes fifty or sixty beds, a yard or two apart. Of course, no one can sleep soundly in such circumstances. The only other places where people are herded like this are barracks and hospitals. In the public wards of a hospital no one even hopes to sleep well. In barracks the soldiers are crowded, but they have good beds, and they are healthy; in a common lodging-house nearly all the lodgers have chronic coughs, and a large number have bladder diseases which make them get up at all hours of the night. The result is a perpetual racket, making sleep impossible. So far as my observation goes, no one in a lodging-house sleeps more than five hours a night – a damnable swindle when one has paid sevenpence or more.

Here legislation could accomplish something. At present there is all manner of legislation by the LCC about lodging-houses, but it is not done in the interests of the lodgers. The LCC only exert themselves to forbid drinking, gambling, fighting, etc. etc. There is no law to say that the beds in a lodging-house must be comfortable. This would be quite an easy thing to enforce – much easier, for instance, than restrictions upon gambling. The lodging-house keepers should be compelled to provide adequate bedclothes and better mattresses, and above all to divide their dormitories into cubicles. It does not matter how small a cubicle is, the important thing is that a man should be alone when he sleeps. These few changes, strictly enforced, would make an enormous difference. It is not impossible to make a lodging-house reasonably comfortable at the usual rates of payment. In the Croydon municipal lodging-house, where the charge is only ninepence, there are cubicles, good beds, chairs (a very rare luxury in lodging-houses), and kitchens above ground instead of in a cellar. There is no reason why every ninepenny lodging-house should not come up to this standard.

Of course, the owners of lodging-houses would be opposed *en bloc* to any improvement, for their present business is an immensely profitable one. The average house takes five or ten pounds a night, with no bad debts (credit being strictly forbidden), and except for rent the expenses are small. Any improvement would mean less crowding, and hence less profit. Still, the excellent municipal lodging-house at Croydon shows how well one *can* be served for ninepence. A few well-directed laws could make these conditions general. If the authorities are going to concern themselves with lodging-houses at all, they ought to start by making them more comfortable, not by silly restrictions that would never be tolerated in a hotel.

XXXVIII

After we left the spike at Lower Binfield, Paddy and I earned half a crown at weeding and sweeping in somebody's garden, stayed the night at Cromley, and walked back to London. I parted from Paddy a day or two later. B. lent me a final two pounds, and, as I had only another eight days to hold out, that was the end of my troubles. My tame imbecile turned out worse than I had expected, but not bad enough to make me wish myself back in the spike or the Auberge de Jehan Cottard.

Paddy set out for Portsmouth, where he had a friend who might conceivably find work for him, and I have never seen him since. A short time ago I was told that he had been run over and killed, but perhaps my informant was mixing him up with someone else. I had news of Bozo only three days ago. He is in Wandsworth – fourteen days, for begging. I do not suppose prison worries him very much.

My story ends here. It is a fairly trivial story, and I can only hope that it has been interesting in the same way as a travel diary is interesting. I can at least say, Here is the world that awaits you if you are ever penniless. Some day I want to explore that world more thoroughly. I should like to know people like Mario and Paddy and Bill the moocher, not from casual encounters, but intimately; I should like to understand what really goes on in the souls of *plongeurs* and tramps and Embankment sleepers. At present I do not feel that I have seen more than the fringe of poverty.

Still, I can point to one or two things I have definitely learned by being hard up. I shall never again think that all tramps are drunken scoundrels, nor expect a beggar to be grateful when I give him a penny, nor be surprised if men out of work lack energy, nor subscribe to the Salvation Army, nor pawn my clothes, nor refuse a handbill, nor enjoy a meal at a smart restaurant. That is a beginning.

THE END

Introduction to the French Edition of Down and Out in Paris and London
15 October 1934

The original English text of this introduction has not survived. The date is that given by Orwell at the end of the introduction. The translation from the French was made by Shirley Jones, with revisions by Sonia Orwell.

My kind translators have asked me to write a short preface for the French edition of this book. As probably many of my French readers will wonder what chain of events brought me to Paris at the time when the incidents described in this book took place, I think it would be best to begin by giving them a few biographical details.

I was born in 1903. In 1922 I went to Burma where I joined the Indian Imperial Police. It was a job for which I was totally unsuited: so, at the beginning of 1928, while on leave in England, I gave in my resignation in the hopes of being able to earn my living by writing. I did just about as well at it as do most young people who take up a literary career – that is to say, not at all. My literary efforts in the first year barely brought me in twenty pounds.

In the spring of 1928 I set off for Paris so as to live cheaply while writing two novels[1] – which I regret to say were never published – and also to learn French. One of my Parisian friends found me a room in a cheap hotel in a working-class district which I have described briefly in the first chapter of this book, and which any sharp-witted Parisian will doubtless recognise. During the summer of 1929 I had written my two novels, which the publishers left on my hands, to find myself almost penniless and in urgent need of work. At that time it was not illegal – or at any rate not seriously illegal – for foreigners living in France to take jobs and it seemed more natural to me to stay in the city I was in, rather than return to England where, at that time, there were about two and a half million unemployed. So I stayed on in Paris and the events which I describe in this book took place towards the end of the autumn of 1929.

As for the truth of my story, I think I can say that I have exaggerated nothing except in so far as all writers exaggerate by selecting. I did not feel I had to describe events in the exact order in which they happened, but everything I have described did take place at one time or another. At the same time I have refrained, as far as possible, from drawing individual portraits of particular people. All the characters I have described in both parts of the book are intended more as representative types of the Parisian or Londoner of the class to which they belong than as individuals.

I should also add that this book makes no claims to giving a complete picture of life in Paris or London but only to portray one particular aspect. As almost without exception all the scenes and incidents in which I was involved have something repugnant about them it might seem that, without wishing to do so, I have given the impression that I think Paris and London are unpleasant cities. This was never my intention and if, at first sight, the reader should get this impression this is simply because the subject-matter of my book is essentially unattractive: my theme is poverty. When you haven't a penny in your pocket you are forced to see any city or country in its least favourable light and all human beings, or nearly all, appear to you either as fellow sufferers or as enemies. I want to emphasise this point particularly for my French readers because I would be distressed if they thought I have the least animosity towards a city of which I have very happy memories.

At the beginning of this preface I promised to give the reader some biographical details. So, for those it might interest, I will just add that after leaving Paris towards the end of 1929 I earned my living largely by teaching and in a small way by writing. Since the publication in England of *Down and Out in Paris and London* – the book here translated – I have written two novels, the second of which I have, indeed, just completed.[2] The first of these is due to be published in a day or two by a New York publishing house.[3]

George Orwell

1. The manuscript of neither novel survives. Writing to Michael Meyer on 12 March 1949, Orwell said, 'I simply destroyed my first novel after unsuccessfully submitting it to one publisher, for which I'm rather sorry now.'

2. *A Clergyman's Daughter.*

3. *Burmese Days*, published by Harper & Brothers, 25 October 1934.

[159, 160]

To the Editor, The Times
11 February 1933

On 31 January 1933, The Times *published the following letter from M. Umberto (printed as 'Humbert') Possenti of the Hotel Splendide, 105 Piccadilly, London, W1:*

Sir, – I do not want to push myself forward, but I feel that, as no one else in my profession has come out to defend the good name of French restaurateurs and hotelkeepers, I have no choice but to do so. In your Literary Supplement *of January 12 your reviewer, dealing with a recently published book of reminiscences, says that the author 'found work as a washer-up in a famous restaurant, gaining there experiences which, he alleges, have made him vow never to eat a meal in a Parisian restaurant as long as he lives'. Other papers have quoted the disgusting passage to which your reviewer refers, and in this way the author's allegations have secured a large publicity. In effect he claims to have proved by his experience that the kitchens of Parisian restaurants are filthy. That kitchen which he specially describes is said to be that of 'one of the dozen most expensive hotels in Paris'; and it is further said to be 'near the Place de la Concorde' . . . The ordinary charge for a night's lodging, not including breakfast, was 200 francs.'*

Now, one of my French confrères *ought to have dealt with this nonsense, but, as no one else has done so and as the allegations are by implication against all other luxury hotels and restaurants in Paris, and, since Paris may now be said to be the nursery of hotel management, against those of London, I am moved, as a restaurateur and hôtelier of 40 years' experience, to deny in the most emphatic manner possible the truth of what the author says. Such a disgusting state of things as he describes is in such places inconceivable. The kitchens of large and 'smart' restaurants have to be clean; the work has to be done in a cleanly and orderly manner or it would not get done at all. Such kitchens, I assert, are cleaner than those of most private houses; they have to be. Moreover, it has long been the custom to allow the curious customer to see over the restaurant's kitchen. Speaking generally, the customer has only to ask the director of any restaurant of the first class to be allowed to see how the work is done and someone is at once detailed to show him round immediately – mind, no previous notice is demanded. To permit the book's statements to appear unchallenged would mean that infinite harm would be done to the London and Paris restaurant trade. By the way, I do not wish to be* méchant *but in your issue of January 17 I saw with amusement that M. François de la Rochefoucauld, writing in 1784, says in a private letter that in English kitchens 'the dirt is indescribable'. That was 150 years ago; his experience could not have been great; and he was not attacking institutions in which hundreds of thousands of English pounds are invested.*

Sir, –

I have read a letter in your columns from M. Humbert Possenti attacking the truthfulness of my book *Down and Out in London and Paris*°, which was reviewed in your *Literary Supplement* of 12 January. Referring to alleged dirtiness in the service quarters of a Paris hotel M. Possenti says:

I am moved, as a *restaurateur* and *hôtelier* of 40 years' experience, to deny in the most emphatic manner possible the truth of what the author says. Such a disgusting state of things as he describes is in such places inconceivable. The kitchens of large and 'smart' restaurants have to be clean: the work has to be done in an orderly and cleanly manner or it would not get done at all. Such kitchens, I assert, are cleaner than those of most private houses, &c.

M. Possenti seems not to realise that these remarks are quite beside the point. The passages objected to in my book did not refer to Paris hotels in general, but to one particular hotel. And as M. Possenti does not know which hotel this was he has no means of testing the truth of my statements. So I am afraid that, in spite of his 40 years' experience, my evidence in this case is worth more than his.

M. Possenti adds that hotel kitchens could not be seriously dirty, because 'speaking generally' it is usual to allow inspection by customers. I do not know how 'general' this practice is, but I do know that in our hotel there were places which no customer could possibly have been allowed to see with any hope of retaining his custom. M. Possenti also misquotes me by saying that I had 'vowed never to eat a meal in a Parisian restaurant as long as I lived'. I said nothing of the kind. What I did say was that I should never again enjoy a meal in a 'smart' restaurant – *i.e.* a restaurant in which the food, in order to make it sufficiently elegant in appearance, has to be mauled about by sweaty hands.

By the way, M. Possenti seems to think that I have some patriotic animus against French restaurants as opposed to English ones. Far from it. I wrote about a Paris hotel and restaurant because it was of those that I had direct experience. I had no wish whatever to suggest that in this matter of kitchen dirtiness the French are worse than any other nation.

Yours faithfully,
'George Orwell'

On 17 February 1933, The Times *published a letter from St Clair Thomson of 64 Wimpole St, London, W1, in which he said, 'hotelkeepers and restaurateurs would inspire still more confidence if they had a very visible notice inviting clients to inspect the kitchens at any hour, unannounced'. M. Possenti of the Hotel Splendide, Piccadilly, London, in a reply published on 21 February 1933, said that his kitchen would 'without notice, be open to the inspection of those who lunch and dine here – not too many at a time, of course, or the cooks will not be able to get on with their work!'.*

The Splendide is no longer a hotel; for a time it housed the Arts Council of Great Britain. It is not known in which Paris hotel Orwell worked. The Georges V has been suggested; and also the Hôtel Lotti, to which Ashenden is summoned in chapter 7 of Somerset Maugham's Ashenden *(1928), a book Orwell recommended to Brenda Salkeld in a list of 'Best Books' he made for her (see X/166). It is also mentioned in chapter 2 of Evelyn Waugh's* Vile Bodies *(1930). The dates are possibly significant, but the implications can be taken in contrary ways defying positive identification. Sam White (1911–88), the* Evening Standard's *Paris correspondent for many years, reported in the issue for 16 June 1967 a conversation he had had with Sonia Orwell in which two other hotels were suggested: the Ritz and the Crillon. Following that conversation, he said, 'It is now clear . . . that the hotel concerned was the Crillon.' Recent holiday guides give all these hotels the highest recommendations.*

[182]

'A dressed man and a naked man'
The Adelphi, *October 1933*[1]

A dressed man and a naked man
Stood by the kip-house fire,
Watching the sooty cooking-pots
That bubble on the wire;

And bidding tanners up and down,
Bargaining for a deal,
Naked skin for empty skin,
Clothes against a meal.

'Ten bob it is,' the dressed man said,
'These boots cost near a pound,
This coat's a blanket of itself
When you kip on the frosty ground.'

'One dollar,' said the naked man,
'And that's a hog too dear;
I've seen a man strip off his shirt
For a fag and a pot of beer.'

'Eight and a tanner,' the dressed man said,
'And my life-work is yours,
All I've earned at the end of a life
Knocking at farmers' doors;

Turnips, apples, hops and peas,
And the spike when times are slack,
Fifty years I've tobied it
For these clothes upon my back.'

'Take seven,' said the naked man,
'It's cold and the spikes are shut;
Better be naked here in kip
Than dressed in Lambeth Cut.'

'One tanner more,' the dressed man said,
'One tanner says the word,
Off comes my coat of ratcatcher
And my breeches of velvet cord;

Now pull my shirt over my head,
I'm naked sole to crown,
And that's the end of fifty years
Tobying up and down.'

A minute and they had changed about,
And each had his desire;
A dressed man and a naked man
Stood by the kip-house fire.   Eric Blair

1. See pp. 179–80, above.

---

[240]

Review of Caliban Shrieks *by Jack Hilton*
The Adelphi, *March 1935*

This witty and unusual book may be described as an autobiography without narrative. Mr. Hilton[1] lets us know, briefly and in passing, that he is a cotton operative who has been in and out of work for years past, that he served in France during the latter part of the War, and that he has also been on the road, been in prison, etc., etc.; but he wastes little time in explanations and none in description. In effect his book is a series of comments on life as it appears when one's income is two pounds a week or less. Here, for instance, is Mr. Hilton's account of his own marriage:

Despite the obvious recognition of marriage's disabilities, the bally thing took place. With it came, not the entrancing mysteries of the bedroom, nor the passionate soul-stirring emotion of two sugar-candied Darby and Joans, but the practical resolve that, come what may, be the furnisher's dues met or no, the rent paid or spent, we – the wife and I – would commemorate our marriage by having, every Sunday morn, ham and eggs for breakfast. So it was we got one over on the poet with his madness of love, the little dove birds, etc.

There are obvious disadvantages in this manner of writing – in particular, it assumes a width of experience which many readers would not possess. On the other hand, the book has a quality which the objective, descriptive kind of book almost invariably misses. It deals with its subject *from the inside*, and consequently it gives one, instead of a catalogue of facts relating to poverty, a vivid notion of what it *feels* like to be poor. All the time that one reads one seems to hear Mr. Hilton's voice, and what is more, one seems to hear the voices of the innumerable industrial workers whom he typifies. The humorous courage, the fearful realism and the utter imperviousness to middle-class ideals, which characterise the best type of industrial worker, are all implicit in Mr. Hilton's way of talking. This is one of those books that succeed in conveying a frame of mind, and that takes more doing than the mere telling of a story.

Books like this, which come from genuine workers and present a genuinely working-class outlook, are exceedingly rare and correspondingly important. They are the voices of a normally silent multitude. All over England, in every industrial town, there are men by scores of thousands whose attitude to life, if only they could express it, would be very much what Mr. Hilton's is. If all of them could get their thoughts on to paper they would change the whole consciousness of our race. Some of them try to do so, of course; but in almost every case, inevitably, what a mess they make of it! I knew a tramp once who was writing his autobiography. He was quite young, but he had had a most interesting life which included, among other things, a jail-escape in America, and he could talk about it entrancingly. But as soon as he took a pen in his hand he became not only boring beyond measure but utterly unintelligible. His prose style was modelled upon *Peg's Paper* ('With a wild cry I sank in a stricken heap', etc.), and his ineptitude with words was so great that after wading through two pages of laboured description you could not even be certain what he was attempting to describe. Looking back upon that autobiography, and a number of similar documents that I have seen, I realise what a considerable literary gift must have gone to the making of Mr. Hilton's book.

As to the sociological information that Mr. Hilton provides, I have only one fault to find. He has evidently not been in the Casual Ward since the years just after the War, and he seems to have been taken in by the lie, widely published during the last few years, to the effect that casual paupers are now given a 'warm meal' at mid-day. I could a tale unfold about those 'warm meals'. Otherwise, all his facts are entirely accurate so far as I am able to judge, and his remarks on prison life, delivered with an extraordinary absence of malice, are some of the most interesting that I have read.[2]

1. John (Jack) Hilton (1900–1983) was born to a general labourer and his wife in Oldham, Lancashire. He published a number of books (see also review of *English Ways*, below), and contributed, as did Orwell, to *The Adelphi*, 1934–9. He and Orwell met several times in 1945. See Clive Fleay, ' "Voices in the Gallery". George Orwell, and Jack Hilton', *Middlesex Polytechnic History Journal*, 2 (Spring 1985), 55–81.

2. This is the first review to be signed 'George Orwell'.

[261]

'St Andrew's Day, 1935'
The Adelphi, *November 1935*[1]

Sharply the menacing wind sweeps over
The bending poplars, newly bare,
And the dark ribbons of the chimneys
Veer downward; flicked by whips of air,

Torn posters flutter; coldly sound
The boom of trams and the rattling of hooves,
And the clerks who hurry to the station
Look, shuddering, over the Eastern rooves,

Thinking, each one, 'Here comes the winter!
Please God I keep my job this year!'
And bleakly, as the cold strikes through
Their entrails like an icy spear,

They think of rent, rates, season tickets,
Insurance, coal, the skivvy's wages,
Boots, schoolbills, and the next instalment
Upon the two twin beds from Drage's.[2]

For if in careless summer days
In groves of Ashtaroth³ we whored,
Repentant now, when winds blow cold,
We kneel before our rightful lord;

The lord of all, the money-god,
Who owns us, blood and hand and brain,
Who gives the roof that stops the wind,
And, giving, takes away again;

Who marks with jealous, watchful care
Our thoughts, our dreams, our secret ways,
Who picks our words and cuts our clothes
And maps the pattern of our days;

Who chills our anger, curbs our hope,
And buys our lives and pays with toys,
Who claims as tribute broken faith,
Accepted insults, muted joys;

Who binds with chains the poet's wit,
The navvy's strength, the soldier's pride,
And lays the sleek, estranging shield
Between the lover and his bride.

1. In a letter to Brenda Salkeld in January, Orwell said he had written a poem that was to be part of his new novel, *Keep the Aspidistra Flying* (1936). It was first printed in *The Adelphi* under a title not used in the novel. The choice of title may have been an afterthought (possibly not Orwell's) and suggested by the issue in which the poem appeared. Differences between the poem in *The Adelphi* (and here) and at the end of Section VII of *Keep the Aspidistra Flying* are (*Adelphi* first):

       line   8: Eastern] eastern   25: marks] spies
              15: schoolbills,] school-bills   25: care] care,
              22: owns us,] rules us   27: clothes] clothes,

2. Drage's was a chain of furniture stores.

3. Ashtoroth (or Ashtoreth) was the Canaanite and Phoenician goddess of fertility and reproduction. Her Greek name was Astarte and she was often equated with the moon goddess. See Milton, *Ode on the Nativity*, 'Moonëd Ashtaroth, / Heaven's queen and mother both'. The prophet Jeremiah rebukes the Israelites for offering incense to the pagan 'queen of heaven' (Jeremiah 44:17–19).

[488]

Extract *from* Orwell's Morocco Diary

Orwell suffered a tubercular lesion in one lung on 8 March 1938. He was
a patient at Preston Hall sanatorium at Aylesford, Kent, from 15 March to
1 September 1938. It was thought, erroneously as it proved, that Orwell's
health might improve if he spent the winter in North Africa. An anonymous
gift of £300 from the novelist L. H. Myers (which Orwell accepted as a
loan and later repaid) enabled Orwell and his wife, Eileen, to travel to
Marrakesh. While there he wrote Coming Up for Air *(1939) and, as*
usual, kept a diary. This extract from his diary, written on 27 September
1938, describes some of the poverty he found in Marrakesh. See Crick, 368–
70, 419–20; Shelden, 316–19, 324–5; and A Literary Life, *111–12, 129.*
Orwell used the spelling 'Marrakech'.

'POVERTY IN MARRAKECH'

There is no doubt that poverty in the town itself is very severe by European
standards. People sleep in the streets by hundreds and thousands, and
beggars, especially children, swarm everywhere. It is noticeable that this
is so not only in quarters normally frequented by tourists, but also in the
purely native quarters, where any European is promptly followed by a
retinue of children. Most beggars are quite satisfied with a sou (twenty
sous equal a penny halfpenny). Two illustrative incidents: I asked a boy
of about 10 to call a cab for me, and when he returned with the cab gave
him 50 centimes (three farthings, but by local standards an overpayment).
Meanwhile about a dozen other boys had collected, and when they saw
me take a handful of small change out of my pocket they flung themselves
on it with such violence as to draw blood from my hand. When I had
managed to extricate myself and give the boy his 50 centimes a number
of others flung themselves on him, forced his hand open and robbed him
of the money. Another day I was feeding the gazelles in the public gardens
with bread when an Arab employee of the local authorities who was
doing navvy work nearby came up to me and asked for a piece of the
bread. I gave it him and he pocketed it gratefully. The only doubt raised

in one's mind about all this is that in certain quarters the population, at any rate the younger ones, have been hopelessly debauched by tourism and led to think of Europeans as immensely rich and easily swindled. Numbers of young men make a living ostensibly as guides and interpreters, actually by a species of blackmail.

When one works out the earnings of the various kinds of petty craftsmen and pieceworkers here, carpenters, metal-workers, porters etc., it generally comes to about 1d or 2d an hour. As a result many products are very cheap, but certain staple ones are not, eg. bread, which is eaten by all Arabs when they can get it, is very expensive. ¾lb of inferior white bread (the European bread is dearer) costs 1 franc or 1½d. It is habitually sold in half cakes. The lowest sum on which an Arab, living in the streets with no home, can exist is said to be 2 francs a day. The poorer French residents regard 10 francs or even 8 francs a day as a suitable wage for an Arab servant (out of this wage he has to provide his own food).*

The poverty in the Jewish quarter is worse, or at any rate more obtrusive than in the Arab quarters. Apart from the main streets, which are themselves very narrow, the alleys where the people live are 6 feet or less across and most of the houses have no windows at all. Overcrowding evidently goes on to an unbelievable extent and the stench is utterly insupportable, people in the narrowest alleys habitually urinating in the street and against the wall. Nevertheless it is evident that there are often quite rich people living among this general filth. There are about 10,000† Jews in the town. They do most of the metal work and much of the woodwork. Among them are a few who are extremely wealthy. The Arabs are said to feel much more hostility towards the Jews than towards the Europeans. The Jews are noticeably more dirty in their clothes and bodies than the Arabs. Impossible to say to what extent they are orthodox, but all evidently observe the Jewish festivals and almost all, at any rate of those over 30, wear the Jewish costume (black robe and skull-cap). In spite of poverty, begging in the Jewish quarters [is] not worse than in the Arab quarters.

---

* *Female servants receive 3–5 Fr. a day* [Orwell's note].
† *13000* [Orwell's note].

[508]

Review of Gypsies *by Martin Block; translated by Barbara Kuczynski and Duncan Taylor*
The Adelphi, *December 1938*

M. Martin Block's book deals mainly with the gypsies of south-eastern Europe, who are far more numerous and evidently live at a much more primitive level than those of England. They use tents, oxen and pack animals rather than horses and caravans, never sit on chairs, are dirty beyond belief, speak Romany among themselves and follow hereditary trades such as locksmithing, bear-leading and the making of wooden spoons and basins. Rather unfortunately M. Block does not include a chapter on the Romany language, but much of the information he has compiled is profoundly interesting, and his photographs, unlike the 'illustrations' in the majority of books, do really illustrate. It is a pity that, so far as I know, no one has produced an equally detailed and up-to-date book on the gypsies of England.

As a matter of fact, the existence of this primitive nomadic people, with strongly marked racial characteristics, in a crowded country like England is a very curious thing. Why do they continue being gypsies? According to all precedent they ought long ago to have been seduced by the delights of civilisation. In England the 'true' gypsies probably own rather more property and live at a slightly higher level than the average farm labourer, but they can only follow their distinctive way of life by constantly breaking the law. One is obliged to conclude that they do it because they like it. A gypsy makes part of his living by begging, and consequently, when he thinks he can get anything out of you, he is offensively servile, pours out gross flatteries and exploits his picturesqueness and even his bad English. But if you happen to meet gypsies on equal terms – or, at any rate, when they have nothing to gain by flattering you – you get a totally different impression. So far from being envious of the industrial civilisation which they see about them, they are merely contemptuous of it. They despise the 'gorgios' for their physical softness, their bad sexual morals and, above all, their lack of liberty. To serve in the army, for instance, seems to them merely a despicable slavery. They have preserved most of the mental characteristics of a nomadic people, including a complete lack of interest in the future and the past. Hence the curious fact that though they first appeared in Europe as late as the fifteenth century, no one knows for certain where they came from. Perhaps it is not fanciful to say that the gypsy is, in the West, the nearest existing approach to the Noble Savage. And considering their admirable physique, their strict morals – strict according to their own peculiar code, that is – and their love of liberty, one must admit that they have a strain of nobility.

They also appear to be fairly successful in surviving. M. Block estimates that the number of gypsies in the world, if one includes the gypsy tribes of India, is about five millions, and that in Europe alone, counting only 'true' gypsies, *i.e.*, those who are wholly or partly of gypsy blood, the number would be from one to one-and-a-half million. There are supposed to be 18,000 in Great Britain and 100,000 in the U.S.A. Considering that any nomadic population is necessarily small, these are respectable numbers.

Will they survive? M. Block's book seems to have been originally published in 1937, but unfortunately it says nothing about the effect on the gypsies of the recent political changes in Europe. There seem to be very few gypsies in Germany proper, but there is a considerable number in Austria and also in Russia. What is Hitler doing about the gypsies? Or Stalin? It seems almost impossible that the totalitarian régimes will fail to persecute these people on the pretext of civilising them. In the past they have survived countless attempts to stamp them out. 'There is no country in western or central Europe,' says M. Block, 'which has not tried to get rid of gypsies by means of cruelty and persecution. None, however, has succeeded.' But the terrifying thing about modern methods of persecution is that we cannot be sure, as yet, that they will not succeed. The Inquisition failed, but there is no certainty that the 'liquidation' of Jews and Trotskyists will fail. It may be that the wretched gypsies, like the Jews, are already serving as a *corpus vile*,[1] and it is only because they do not have friends who own newspapers that we hear nothing about it. Perhaps the concentration camps are already crowded with them. If so, let us hope that they survive it.[2] No civilised person would wish for an instant to imitate the gypsies' habits, but that is not the same as saying that one would like to see them disappear. Existing in the teeth of a civilisation which disapproves of them, they are a heartening reminder of the largeness of the earth and the power of human obstinacy.

1. Worthless body, appropriate for experimentation.
2. Several hundred thousand gypsies were killed in the concentration camps.

---

[568]

'Democracy in the British Army'

Left Forum, *September 1939*

When the Duke of Wellington described the British Army as 'the scum of the earth, enlisted for drink', he was probably speaking no more than the truth. But what is significant is that his opinion would have been echoed by any non-military Englishman for nearly a hundred years subsequently.

The French Revolution and the new conception of 'national' war changed the character of most Continental armies, but England was in the exceptional position of being immune from invasion and of being governed during most of the nineteenth century by non-military bourgeoisie. Consequently its army remained, as before, a small professional force more or less cut off from the rest of the nation. The war-scare of the sixties produced the Volunteers, later to develop into the Territorials, but it was not till a few years before the Great War that there was serious talk of universal service. Until the late nineteenth century the total number of white troops, even in war-time, never reached a quarter of a million men, and it is probable that every great British land battle between Blenheim and Loos[1] was fought mainly by foreign soldiers.

In the nineteenth century the British common soldier was usually a farm labourer or slum proletarian who had been driven into the army by brute starvation. He enlisted for a period of at least seven years – sometimes as much as twenty-one years – and he was inured to a barrack life of endless drilling, rigid and stupid discipline, and degrading physical punishments. It was virtually impossible for him to marry, and even after the extension of the franchise he lacked the right to vote. In Indian garrison towns he could kick the 'niggers' with impunity, but at home he was hated or looked down upon by the ordinary population, except in wartime, when for brief periods he was discovered to be a hero. Obviously such a man had severed his links with his own class. He was essentially a mercenary, and his self-respect depended on his conception of himself not as a worker or a citizen but simply as a fighting animal.

Since the war the conditions of army life have improved and the conception of discipline has grown more intelligent, but the British Army has retained its special characteristics – small size, voluntary enlistment, long service and emphasis on regimental loyalty. Every regiment has its own name (not merely a number, as in most armies), its history and relics, its special customs, traditions, etc., etc., thanks to which the whole army is honeycombed with snobberies which are almost unbelievable unless one has seen them at close quarters. Between the officers of a 'smart' regiment and those of an ordinary infantry regiment, or still more a regiment of the Indian Army, there is a degree of jealousy almost amounting to a class difference. And there is no question that the long-term private soldier often identifies with his own regiment almost as closely as the officer does. The effect is to make the narrow 'non-political' outlook of the mercenary come more easily to him. In addition, the fact that the British Army is rather heavily officered probably diminishes class friction and thus makes the lower ranks less accessible to 'subversive' ideas.

But the thing which above all else forces a reactionary viewpoint on the common soldier is his service in overseas garrisons. An infantry regiment is usually quartered abroad for eighteen years consecutively, moving from place to place every four or five years, so that many soldiers serve their entire term in India, Africa, China, etc. They are only there to hold down a hostile population and the fact is brought home to them in unmistakable ways. Relations with the 'natives' are almost invariably bad, and the soldiers – not so much the officers as the men – are the obvious targets for anti-British feeling. Naturally they retaliate, and as a rule they develop an attitude towards the 'niggers' which is far more brutal than that of the officials or business men. In Burma I was constantly struck by the fact that the common soldiers were the best-hated section of the white community, and, judged simply by their behaviour, they certainly deserved to be. Even as near home as Gibraltar they walk the streets with a swaggering air which is directed at the Spanish 'natives'. And in practice some such attitude is absolutely necessary; you could not hold down a subject empire with troops infected by notions of class-solidarity. Most of the dirty work of the French empire, for instance, is done not by French conscripts but by illiterate negroes and by the Foreign Legion, a corps of pure mercenaries.

To sum up: in spite of the technical advances which do not allow the professional officer to be quite such an idiot as he used to be, and in spite of the fact that the common soldier is now treated a little more like a human being, the British Army remains essentially the same machine as it was fifty years ago. A little while back any Socialists would have admitted this without argument. But we happen to be at a moment when the rise of Hitler has scared the official leaders of the Left into an attitude not far removed from jingoism. Large numbers of Left-wing publicists are almost openly agitating for war. Without discussing this subject at length, it can be pointed out that a Left-wing party which, within a capitalist society, becomes a war party, has already thrown up the sponge, because it is demanding a policy which can only be carried out by its opponents. The Labour leaders are intermittently aware of this – witness their shufflings on the subject of conscription. Hence, in among the cries of 'Firm front!', 'British prestige!' etc., there mingles a quite contradictory line of talk. It is to the effect that 'this time' things are going to be 'different'. Militarisation is not going to mean militarisation. Colonel Blimp[2] is no longer Colonel Blimp. And in the more soft-boiled Left-wing papers a phrase is bandied to and fro – 'democratising the army'. It is worth considering what it implies.

'Democratising' an army, if it means anything, means doing away with the predominance of a single class and introducing a less mechanical form of discipline. In the British Army this would mean an entire reconstruction which would rob the army of efficiency for five or ten years. Such a process is only doubtfully possible while the British Empire exists, and quite unthinkable while the simultaneous aim is to 'stop Hitler'. What will actually happen during the next couple of years, war or no war, is that the armed forces will be greatly expanded, but the new units will take their colour from the existing professional army. As in the Great War, it will be the same army, only bigger. Poorer sections of the middle-class will be drawn on for the supply of officers, but the professional military caste will retain its grip. As for the new Militias, it is probably quite a mistake to imagine that they are the nucleus of a 'democratic army' in which all classes will start from scratch. It is fairly safe to prophesy that even if there is no class-favouritism (as there will be, presumably), Militiamen of bourgeois origin will tend to be promoted first. Hore-Belisha[3] and others have already hinted as much in a number of speeches. A fact not always appreciated by Socialists is that in England the whole of the bourgeoisie is to some extent militarised. Nearly every boy who has been to a public school has passed through the O.T.C.[4] (theoretically voluntary but in practice compulsory), and though this training is done between the ages of 13 and 18, it ought not to be despised. In effect the Militiaman with an O.T.C. training behind him will start with several months' advantage of the others. In any case the Military Training Act is only an experiment, aimed partly at impressing opinion abroad and partly at accustoming the English people to the idea of conscription. Once the novelty has worn off some method will be devised of keeping proletarians out of positions of command.

It is probable that the nature of modern war has made 'democratic army' a contradiction in terms. The French Army, for instance, based on universal service, is hardly more democratic than the British. It is just as much dominated by the professional officer and the long-service N.C.O., and the French officer is probably rather more 'Prussian' in outlook than his British equivalent. The Spanish Government militias during the first six months of war – the first year, in Catalonia – were a genuinely democratic army, but they were also a very primitive type of army, capable only of defensive actions. In that particular case a defensive strategy, coupled with propaganda, would probably have had a better chance of victory than the methods casually adopted. But if you want military efficiency in the ordinary sense, there is no escaping from the professional soldier, and so long as the professional soldier is in control he will see to it that the army is not democratised. And what is true within the armed forces is true of the nation as a whole; every increase in the strength of the military machine means more power for the forces of reaction. It is possible that some of our Left-wing jingoes are acting with their eyes open. If they are, they must be aware that the *News Chronicle* version of 'defence of democracy' leads directly *away* from democracy, even in the narrow nineteenth-century sense of political liberty, independence of the trade unions and freedom of speech and the press.

1. The English and their allies under the Duke of Marlborough defeated the French and Bavarians under Marshal Tallard and the Elector of Bavaria at the Battle of Blenheim, 13 August 1704. The Battle of Loos was fought between British and German forces in September

1915. The death toll exceeded in intensity that of any previous battle. Among those killed was Rudyard Kipling's son, John, whose body was recovered only very recently. The British used gas for the first time and one battalion was famously 'led in its assault by men dribbling a football across No-Man's Land' (Martin Gilbert, *First World War* (1994), 197–200).

2. In the First World War, a Blimp was a captive observation balloon. The name was adopted by the cartoonist David Low for over-large, choleric, bumbling, very traditional, senior army officers resistant to change. The character is featured (not unsympathetically) in Michael Powell and Emeric Pressburger's fine film, *The Life and Death of Colonel Blimp* (1943).

3. Leslie Hore-Belisha (1893–1957), politician, barrister, journalist and Liberal Party MP, 1923–45. He organized the support of the National Liberal Party for the National Government led by Ramsay MacDonald (Labour) and Stanley Baldwin (Conservative) in August 1931. He was Minister of Transport, 1934–7, and is remembered for the pedestrian-crossing sign then introduced, 'The Belisha Beacon'. In 1937 Neville Chamberlain appointed him Minister of War, charged with modernizing the armed forces.

4. The Officers' Training Corps. Cadet corps were not restricted to public schools; there were also some associated with regular regiments (some going back before the establishment of the OTC).

---

[598]

'Boys' Weeklies'

Horizon, *11 March 1940*

You never walk far through any poor quarter in any big town without coming upon a small newsagent's shop. The general appearance of these shops is always very much the same: a few posters for the *Daily Mail* and the *News of the World* outside, a poky little window with sweet-bottles and packets of Players, and a dark interior smelling of liquorice allsorts and festooned from floor to ceiling with vilely printed twopenny papers, most of them with lurid cover-illustrations in three colours.

Except for the daily and evening papers, the stock of these shops hardly overlaps at all with that of the big newsagents. Their main selling line is the twopenny weekly, and the number and variety of these are almost unbelievable. Every hobby and pastime – cage-birds, fretwork, carpentering, bees, carrier-pigeons, home conjuring, philately, chess – has at least one paper devoted to it, and generally several. Gardening and livestock-keeping must have at least a score between them. Then there are the sporting papers, the radio papers, the children's comics, the various snippet papers such as *Tit-bits*, the large range of papers devoted to the movies and all more or less exploiting women's legs, the various trade papers, the women's story-papers (the *Oracle, Secrets, Peg's Paper*, etc. etc.), the needlework papers – these so numerous that a display of them alone will often fill an entire window – and in addition the long series of 'Yank Mags' (*Fight Stories, Action Stories, Western Short Stories*, etc.), which are imported shop-soiled from America and sold at twopence halfpenny or threepence. And the periodical proper shades off into the fourpenny novelette, the *Aldine Boxing Novels*, the *Boys' Friend Library*, the *Schoolgirls' Own Library* and many others.

Probably the contents of these shops is the best available indication of what the mass of the English people really feels and thinks. Certainly nothing half so revealing exists in documentary form. Best-seller novels, for instance, tell one a great deal, but the novel is aimed almost exclusively at people above the £4-a-week level. The movies are probably a very unsafe guide to popular taste, because the film industry is virtually a monopoly, which means that it is not obliged to study its public at all closely. The same applies to some extent to the daily papers, and most of all to the radio. But it does not apply to the weekly paper with a smallish circulation and specialised subject-matter. Papers like the *Exchange and Mart*, for instance, or *Cage Birds*, or the *Oracle*,[1] or *Prediction*, or the *Matrimonial Times*, only exist because there is a definite demand for them, and they reflect the minds of their readers as a great national daily with a circulation of millions cannot possibly do.

Here I am only dealing with a single series of papers, the boys' twopenny weeklies, often inaccurately described as 'penny dreadfuls'. Falling strictly within this class there are at present ten papers, the *Gem, Magnet, Modern Boy, Triumph* and *Champion*, all owned by the Amalgamated Press, and the *Wizard, Rover, Skipper, Hotspur* and *Adventure*, all owned by D. C. Thomson & Co.[2] What the circulations of these papers are, I do not know. The editors and proprietors refuse to name any figures, and in any case the circulation of a paper carrying serial stories is bound to fluctuate widely. But there is no question that the combined public of the ten papers is a very large one. They are on sale in every town in England, and nearly every boy who reads at all goes through a phase of reading one or more of them. The *Gem* and *Magnet*, which are much the oldest of these papers, are of rather different type from the rest, and they have evidently lost some of their popularity during the past few years. A good many boys now regard them as old fashioned and 'slow'. Nevertheless I want to discuss them first, because they are more interesting psychologically than the others, and also because the mere survival of such papers into the nineteen-thirties is a rather startling phenomenon.

The *Gem* and *Magnet* are sister-papers (characters out of one paper frequently appear in the other), and were both started more than thirty years ago. At that time, together with *Chums* and the old *B.O.P.*,[3] they were the leading papers for boys, and they remained dominant till quite recently. Each of them carries every week a fifteen- or twenty-thousand-word school story, complete in itself, but usually more or less connected with the story of the week before. The *Gem* in addition to its school story carries one or more adventure serials. Otherwise the two papers are so much alike that they can be treated as one, though the *Magnet* has always been the better known of the two, probably because it possesses a really first-rate character in the fat boy, Billy Bunter.

The stories are stories of what purports to be public-school-life, and the schools (Greyfriars in the *Magnet* and St. Jim's in the *Gem*) are represented as ancient and fashionable foundations of the type of Eton or Winchester. All the leading characters are fourth-form boys aged fourteen or fifteen, older or younger boys only appearing in very minor parts. Like Sexton Blake and Nelson Lee, these boys continue week after week and year after year, never growing any older. Very occasionally a new boy arrives or a minor character drops out, but in at any rate the last twenty-five years the personnel has barely altered. All the principal characters in both papers – Bob Cherry, Tom Merry, Harry Wharton, Johnny Bull, Billy Bunter and the rest of them – were at Greyfriars or St. Jim's long before the Great War, exactly the same age as at present, having much the same kind of adventures and talking almost exactly the same dialect. And not only the characters but the whole atmosphere of both *Gem* and *Magnet* has been preserved unchanged, partly by means of very elaborate stylisation. The stories in the *Magnet* are signed 'Frank Richards' and those in the *Gem*, 'Martin Clifford' but a series lasting thirty years could hardly be the work of the same person every week.*4 Consequently they have to be written in a style that is easily imitated – an extraordinary, artificial, repetitive style, quite different from anything else now existing in English literature. A couple of extracts will do as illustrations. Here is one from the *Magnet*:

> Groan!
>
> 'Shut up, Bunter!'
>
> Groan!
>
> Shutting up was not really in Billy Bunter's line. He seldom shut up, though often requested to do so. On the present awful occasion the fat Owl of Greyfriars was less inclined than ever to shut up. And he did not shut up! He groaned, and groaned, and went on groaning.
>
> Even groaning did not fully express Bunter's feelings. His feelings, in fact, were inexpressible.
>
> There were six of them in the soup! Only one of the six uttered sounds of woe and lamentation. But that one, William George Bunter, uttered enough for the whole party and a little over.
>
> Harry Wharton & Co. stood in a wrathy and worried group. They were landed and stranded, diddled, dished and done! etc. etc. etc.

Here is one from the *Gem*:

> 'Oh cwumbs!'
>
> 'Oh gum!'
>
> 'Oooogh!'
>
> 'Urrggh!'
>
> Arthur Augustus sat up dizzily. He grabbed his handkerchief and pressed it to his damaged nose. Tom Merry sat up, gasping for breath. They looked at one another.
>
> 'Bai Jove! This is a go, deah boy!' gurgled Arthur Augustus. 'I have been thwown into quite a fluttah! Oogh! The wottahs! The wuffians! The feahful outsidahs! Wow!' etc. etc. etc.

---

* In a footnote dated 1945, added to *Critical Essays*, Orwell wrote: 'This is quite incorrect. These stories have been written throughout the whole period by "Frank Richards" and "Martin Clifford", who are one and the same person! See articles in *Horizon*, May 1940 [599] and *Summer Pie*, summer 1944.'

Both of these extracts are entirely typical; you would find something like them in almost every chapter of every number, today or twenty-five years ago. The first thing that anyone would notice is the extraordinary amount of tautology (the first of these two passages contains a hundred and twenty-five words and could be compressed into about thirty), seemingly designed to spin out the story, but actually playing its part in creating the atmosphere. For the same reason various facetious expressions are repeated over and over again; 'wrathy', for instance, is a great favourite, and so is 'diddled, dished and done'. 'Oooogh!', 'Grooo!' and 'Yaroo!' (stylised cries of pain) recur constantly, and so does 'Ha! ha! ha!', always given a line to itself, so that sometimes a quarter of a column or thereabouts consists of 'Ha! ha! ha!'. The slang ('Go and eat coke!', 'What the thump!', 'You frabjous ass!', etc. etc.) has never been altered, so that the boys are now using slang which is at least thirty years out of date. In addition, the various nicknames are rubbed in on every possible occasion. Every few lines we are reminded that Harry Wharton & Co. are 'the Famous Five', Bunter is always 'the fat Owl' or 'the Owl of the Remove', Vernon-Smith is always 'the Bounder of Greyfriars', Gussy (the Honourable Arthur Augustus D'Arcy) is always 'the swell of St. Jim's', and so on and so forth. There is a constant, untiring effort to keep the atmosphere intact and to make sure that every new reader learns immediately who is who. The result has been to make Greyfriars and St. Jim's into an extraordinary little world of their own, a world which cannot be taken seriously by anyone over fifteen, but which at any rate is not easily forgotten. By a debasement of the Dickens technique a series of stereotyped 'characters' has been built up, in several cases very successfully. Billy Bunter, for instance, must be one of the best-known figures in English fiction; for the mere number of people who know him he ranks with Sexton Blake, Tarzan, Sherlock Holmes and a handful of characters in Dickens.

Needless to say, these stories are fantastically unlike life at a real public school. They run in cycles of rather differing types, but in general they are the clean-fun, knockabout type of story, with interest centring round horseplay, practical jokes, ragging masters, fights, canings, football, cricket and food. A constantly recurring story is one in which a boy is accused of some misdeed committed by another and is too much of a sportsman to reveal the truth. The 'good' boys are 'good' in the clean-living Englishman tradition – they keep in hard training, wash behind their ears, never hit below the belt, etc. etc. – and by way of contrast there is a series of 'bad' boys, Racke, Crooke, Loder and others, whose badness consists in betting, smoking cigarettes and frequenting public-houses. All these boys are constantly on the verge of expulsion, but as it would mean a change of personnel if any boy were actually expelled, no one is ever caught out in any really serious offence. Stealing, for instance, barely enters as a motif. Sex is completely taboo, especially in the form in which it actually arises at public schools. Occasionally girls enter into the stories, and very rarely there is something approaching a mild flirtation, but it is always entirely in the spirit of clean fun. A boy and a girl enjoy going for bicycle rides together – that is all it ever amounts to. Kissing, for instance, would be regarded as 'soppy'. Even the bad boys are presumed to be completely sexless. When the *Gem* and *Magnet* were started, it is probable that there was a deliberate intention to get away from the guilty sex-ridden atmosphere that pervaded so much of the earlier literature for boys. In the 'nineties the *Boy's Own Paper*, for instance, used to have its correspondence columns full of terrifying warnings against masturbation, and books like *St. Winifred's* and *Tom Brown's Schooldays* were heavy with homosexual feeling, though no doubt the authors were not fully aware of it. In the *Gem* and *Magnet* sex simply does not exist as a problem. Religion is also taboo; in the whole thirty years' issue of the two papers the word 'God' probably does not occur, except in 'God save the King'. On the other hand, there has always been a very strong 'temperance' strain. Drinking and, by association, smoking are regarded as rather disgraceful even in an adult ('shady' is the usual word), but at the same time as something irresistibly fascinating, a sort of substitute for sex. In their moral atmosphere the *Gem* and *Magnet* have a great deal in common with the Boy Scout movement, which started at about the same time.

All literature of this kind is partly plagiarism. Sexton Blake, for instance, started off quite frankly as an imitation of Sherlock Holmes, and still resembles him fairly strongly; he has hawklike features, lives in Baker Street, smokes enormously and puts on a dressing-gown when he wants to think. The *Gem* and *Magnet* probably owe something to the school story writers who were flourishing when they began, Gunby Hadath,

Desmond Coke[5] and the rest, but they owe more to nineteenth-century models. In so far as Greyfriars and St. Jim's are like real schools at all, they are much more like Tom Brown's Rugby than a modern public school. Neither school has an O.T.C., for instance, games are not compulsory, and the boys are even allowed to wear what clothes they like. But without doubt the main origin of these papers is *Stalky & Co.*[6] This book has had an immense influence on boys' literature, and it is one of those books which have a sort of traditional reputation among people who have never even seen a copy of it. More than once in boys' weekly papers I have come across a reference to *Stalky & Co.* in which the word was spelt 'Storky'. Even the name of the chief comic among the Greyfriars masters, Mr. Prout, is taken from *Stalky & Co.*, and so is much of the slang; 'jape', 'merry', 'giddy', 'bizney' (business), 'frabjous', 'don't' for 'doesn't' – all of them out of date even when *Gem* and *Magnet* started. There are also traces of earlier origins. The name 'Greyfriars' is probably taken from Thackeray, and Gosling, the school porter in the *Magnet*, talks in an imitation of Dickens's dialect.

With all this, the supposed 'glamour' of public-school life is played for all it is worth. There is all the usual paraphernalia – lock-up, roll-call, house matches, fagging, prefects, cosy teas round the study fire, etc. etc. – and constant reference to the 'old school', the 'old grey stones' (both schools were founded in the early sixteenth century), the 'team spirit' of the 'Greyfriars men'. As for the snob-appeal, it is completely shameless. Each school has a titled boy or two whose titles are constantly thrust in the reader's face; other boys have the names of well-known aristocratic families, Talbot, Manners, Lowther. We are for ever being reminded that Gussy is the Honourable Arthur A. D'Arcy, son of Lord Eastwood, that Jack Blake is heir to 'broad acres', that Hurree Jamset Ram Singh (nicknamed Inky) is the Nabob of Bhanipur, that Vernon-Smith's father is a millionaire. Till recently the illustrations in both papers always depicted the boys in clothes imitated from those of Eton; in the last few years Greyfriars has changed over to blazers and flannel trousers, but St. Jim's still sticks to the Eton jacket, and Gussy sticks to his top-hat. In the school magazine which appears every week as part of the *Magnet*, Harry Wharton writes an article discussing the pocket-money received by the 'fellows in the Remove',[7] and reveals that some of them get as much as five pounds a week! This kind of thing is a perfectly deliberate incitement to wealth-fantasy. And here it is worth noticing a rather curious fact, and that is that the school story is a thing peculiar to England. So far as I know, there are extremely few school stories in foreign languages. The reason, obviously, is that in England education is mainly a matter of status. The most definite dividing-line between the petite-bourgeoisie and the working class is that the former pay for their education, and within the bourgeoisie there is another unbridgeable gulf between the 'public' school and the 'private' school. It is quite clear that there are tens and scores of thousands of people to whom every detail of life at a 'posh' public school is wildly thrilling and romantic. They happen to be outside that mystic world of quadrangles and house-colours, but they yearn after it, day-dream about it, live mentally in it for hours at a stretch. The question is, Who are these people? Who reads the *Gem* and *Magnet*?

Obviously one can never be quite certain about this kind of thing. All I can say from my own observation is this. Boys who are likely to go to public schools themselves generally read the *Gem* and *Magnet*, but they nearly always stop reading them when they are about twelve; they may continue for another year from force of habit, but by that time they have ceased to take them seriously. On the other hand, the boys at very cheap private schools, the schools that are designed for people who can't afford a public school but consider the Council schools 'common', continue reading the *Gem* and *Magnet* for several years longer. A few years ago I was a teacher at two of these schools myself. I found that not only did virtually all the boys read the *Gem* and *Magnet*, but that they were still taking them fairly seriously when they were fifteen or even sixteen. These boys were the sons of shopkeepers, office employees and small business and professional men, and obviously it is this class that the *Gem* and *Magnet* are aimed at. But they are certainly read by working-class boys as well. They are generally on sale in the poorest quarters of big towns, and I have known them to be read by boys whom one might expect to be completely immune from public-school 'glamour'. I have seen a young coalminer, for instance, a lad who had already worked a year or two underground, eagerly reading the *Gem*. Recently I offered a batch of English papers to some British legionaries of the French Foreign Legion in North Africa; they picked out the *Gem* and *Magnet* first. Both papers are much read by girls,* and the Pen Pals department of the *Gem* shows that it is read in every corner of the British Empire, by Australians, Canadians, Palestine Jews, Malays, Arabs, Straits Chinese, etc. etc. The editors evidently expect their readers to be aged round about fourteen, and the advertisements (milk chocolate, postage stamps, water pistols, blushing cured, home conjuring tricks, itching powder, the Phine Phun Ring which runs a needle into your friend's hand, etc. etc.) indicate roughly the same age; there are also the Admiralty advertisements, however, which call for youths between seventeen and twenty-two. And there is no question that these papers are also read by adults. It is quite common for people to write to the editor and say that they have read every number of the *Gem* or *Magnet* for the past thirty years. Here, for instance, is a letter from a lady in Salisbury:

> I can say of your splendid yarns of Harry Wharton & Co., of Greyfriars, that they never fail to reach a high standard. Without doubt they are the finest stories of their type on the market to-day, which is saying a good deal. They seem to bring you face to face with Nature. I have taken the *Magnet* from the start, and have followed the adventures of Harry Wharton & Co. with rapt interest. I have no sons, but two daughters, and there's always a rush to be the first to read the grand old paper. My husband, too, was a staunch reader of the *Magnet* until he was suddenly taken away from us.

It is well worth getting hold of some copies of the *Gem* and *Magnet*, especially the *Gem*, simply to have a look at the correspondence columns. What is truly startling is the intense interest with which the pettiest details of life at Greyfriars and St. Jim's are followed up. Here, for instance, are a few of the questions sent in by readers:

'What age is Dick Roylance?' 'How old is St. Jim's?' 'Can you give me a list of the Shell and their studies?' 'How much did D'Arcy's monocle cost?' 'How is it fellows like Crooke are in the Shell and decent fellows like yourself are only in the Fourth?' 'What are the Form captain's three chief duties?' 'Who is the chemistry master at St. Jim's?' (From a girl) 'Where is St. Jim's situated? *Could* you tell me

---

* There are several corresponding girls' papers. The *Schoolgirl* is a companion-paper to the *Magnet* and has stories by 'Hilda Richards'.[8] The characters are interchangeable to some extent. Bessie Bunter, Billy Bunter's sister, figures in the *Schoolgirl* [Orwell's footnote].

how to get there, as I would love to see the building? Are you boys just "phoneys", as I think you are?'

It is clear that many of the boys and girls who write these letters are living a complete fantasy-life. Sometimes a boy will write, for instance, giving his age, height, weight, chest and bicep° measurements and asking which member of the Shell or Fourth Form he most exactly resembles. The demand for a list of the studies on the Shell passage, with an exact account of who lives in each, is a very common one. The editors, of course, do everything in their power to keep up the illusion. In the *Gem* Jack Blake is supposed to write the answers to correspondents, and in the *Magnet* a couple of pages is always given up to the school magazine (the *Greyfriars Herald*, edited by Harry Wharton), and there is another page in which one or other character is written up each week. The stories run in cycles, two or three characters being kept in the foreground for several weeks at a time. First there will be a series of rollicking adventure stories, featuring the Famous Five and Billy Bunter; then a run of stories turning on mistaken identity, with Wibley (the make-up wizard) in the star part; then a run of more serious stories in which Vernon-Smith is trembling on the verge of expulsion. And here one comes upon the real secret of the *Gem* and *Magnet* and the probable reason why they continue to be read in spite of their obvious out-of-dateness.

It is that the characters are so carefully graded as to give almost every type of reader a character he can identify himself with. Most boys' papers aim at doing this, hence the boy-assistant (Sexton Blake's Tinker, Nelson Lee's Nipper, etc.) who usually accompanies the explorer, detective or what-not on his adventures. But in these cases there is only one boy, and usually it is much the same type of boy. In the *Gem* and *Magnet* there is a model for very nearly everybody. There is the normal, athletic, high-spirited boy (Tom Merry, Jack Blake, Frank Nugent), a slightly rowdier version of this type (Bob Cherry), a more aristocratic version (Talbot, Manners), a quieter, more serious version (Harry Wharton), and a stolid, 'bulldog' version (Johnny Bull). Then there is the reckless, dare-devil type of boy (Vernon-Smith), the definitely 'clever', studious boy (Mark Linley, Dick Penfold), and the eccentric boy who is not good at games but possesses some special talent (Skinner, Wibley). And there is the scholarship-boy (Tom Redwing), an important figure in this class of story because he makes it possible for boys from very poor homes to project themselves into the public-school atmosphere. In addition there are Australian, Irish, Welsh, Manx, Yorkshire and Lancashire boys to play upon local patriotism. But the subtlety of characterisation goes deeper than this. If one studies the correspondence columns one sees that there is probably *no* character in the *Gem* and *Magnet* whom some or other reader does not identify with, except the out-and-out comics, Coker, Billy Bunter, Fisher T. Fish (the money-grubbing American boy) and, of course, the masters. Bunter, though in his origin he probably owed something to the fat boy in *Pickwick*, is a real creation. His tight trousers against which boots and canes are constantly thudding, his astuteness in search of food, his postal order which never turns up, have made him famous wherever the Union Jack waves. But he is not a subject for daydreams. On the other hand, another seeming figure of fun, Gussy (the Honourable Arthur A. D'Arcy, 'the swell of St. Jim's'), is evidently much admired. Like everything else in the *Gem* and *Magnet*, Gussy is at least thirty years out of date. He is the 'knut' of the early twentieth century or even the 'masher' of the 'nineties ('Bai Jove, deah boy!' and 'Weally, I shall be obliged to give you a feahful thwashin'!'), the monocled idiot who made good on the fields of Mons and Le Cateau.[9] And his evident popularity goes to show how deep the snob-appeal of this type is. English people are extremely fond of the titled ass (cf. Lord Peter Wimsey) who always turns up trumps in the moment of emergency. Here is a letter from one of Gussy's girl admirers:

I think you're too hard on Gussy. I wonder he's still in existence, the way you treat him. He's my hero. Did you know I write lyrics? How's this – to the tune of 'Goody Goody'?

> Gonna get my gas-mask, join the A. R. P.[10]
> 'Cos I'm wise to all those bombs you drop on me.
>> Gonna dig myself a trench
>> Inside the garden fence;
>> Gonna seal my windows up with tin
>> So that the tear gas can't get in;
> Gonna park my cannon right outside the kerb
> With a note to Adolf Hitler: 'Don't disturb!'

> And if I never fall in Nazi hands
> That's soon enough for me –
> Gonna get my gas-mask, join the A. R. P.

P.S. – Do you get on well with girls?

I quote this in full because (dated April 1939) it is interesting as being probably the earliest mention of Hitler in the *Gem*. In the *Gem* there is also a heroic fat boy, Fatty Wynn, as a set-off against Bunter. Vernon-Smith, 'the Bounder of the Remove', a Byronic character, always on the verge of the sack, is another great favourite. And even some of the cads probably have their following. Loder, for instance, 'the rotter of the Sixth', is a cad, but he is also a highbrow and given to saying sarcastic things about football and the team spirit. The boys of the Remove only think him all the more of a cad for this, but a certain type of boy would probably identify with him. Even Racke, Crooke and Co. are probably admired by small boys who think it diabolically wicked to smoke cigarettes. (A frequent question in the correspondence column: 'What brand of cigarettes does Racke smoke?')

Naturally the politics of the *Gem* and *Magnet* are Conservative, but in a completely pre-1914 style, with no Fascist tinge. In reality their basic political assumptions are two: nothing ever changes, and foreigners are funny. In the *Gem* of 1939 Frenchmen are still Froggies and Italians are still Dagoes. Mossoo, the French master at Greyfriars, is the usual comic-paper Frog, with pointed beard, pegtop trousers, etc. Inky, the Indian boy, though a rajah, and therefore possessing snob-appeal, is also the comic babu of the *Punch* tradition. (' "The rowfulness is not the proper caper, my esteemed Bob," said Inky. "Let dogs delight in the barkfulness and bitefulness, but the soft answer is the cracked pitcher that goes longest to a bird in the bush, as the English proverb remarks." ') Fisher T. Fish is the old-style stage Yankee (' "Waal, I guess" ', etc.) dating from a period of Anglo-American jealousy. Wun Lung, the Chinese boy (he has rather faded out of late, no doubt because some of the *Magnet*'s readers are Straits Chinese), is the nineteenth-century pantomime Chinaman, with saucer-shaped hat, pigtail and pidgin-English. The assumption all along is not only that foreigners are comics who are put there for us to laugh at, but that they can be classified in much the same way as insects. That is why in all boys' papers, not only the *Gem* and *Magnet*, a Chinese[11] is invariably portrayed with a pigtail. It is the thing you recognise him by, like the Frenchman's beard or the Italian's barrel-organ. In papers of this kind it occasionally happens that when the setting of a story is in a foreign country some attempt is made to describe the natives as individual human beings, but as a rule it is assumed that foreigners of any one race are all alike and will conform more or less exactly to the following patterns:[12]

FRENCHMAN: Excitable. Wears beard, gesticulates wildly.
SPANIARD, MEXICAN, etc.: Sinister, treacherous.
ARAB, AFGHAN, etc.: Sinister, treacherous.
CHINESE: Sinister, treacherous. Wears pigtail.
ITALIAN: Excitable. Grinds barrel-organ or carries stiletto.
SWEDE, DANE, etc.: Kind hearted, stupid.
NEGRO: Comic, very faithful.

The working classes only enter into the *Gem* and *Magnet* as comics or semi-villains (race-course touts, etc.). As for class-friction, trade unionism, strikes, slumps, unemployment, Fascism and civil war – not a mention. Somewhere or other in the thirty years' issue of the two papers you might perhaps find the word 'Socialism', but you would have to look a long time for it. If the Russian Revolution is anywhere referred to, it will be indirectly, in the word 'Bolshy' (meaning a person of violent disagreeable habits). Hitler and the Nazis are just beginning to make their appearance, in the sort of reference I quoted above. The war-crisis of September 1938 made just enough impression to produce a story in which Mr. Vernon-Smith, the Bounder's millionaire father, cashed in on the general panic by buying up country houses in order to sell them to 'crisis scuttlers'. But that is probably as near to noticing the European situation as the *Gem* and *Magnet* will come, until the war actually starts.* That does not mean that these papers are unpatriotic – quite the contrary! Throughout the Great War the *Gem* and *Magnet* were perhaps the most consistently and cheerfully patriotic papers in England. Almost every week the boys caught a spy or pushed a conchy into the army, and during the rationing period

---

* This was written some months before the outbreak of war. Up to the end of September 1939 no mention of the war has appeared in either paper [Orwell's footnote].

'EAT LESS BREAD' was printed in large type on every page.[13] But their patriotism has nothing whatever to do with power-politics or 'ideological' warfare. It is more akin to family loyalty, and actually it gives one a valuable clue to the attitude of ordinary people, especially the huge untouched block of the middle class and the better-off working class. These people are patriotic to the middle of their bones, but they do not feel that what happens in foreign countries is any of their business. When England is in danger they rally to its defence as a matter of course, but in between-times they are not interested. After all, England is always in the right and England always wins, so why worry? It is an attitude that has been shaken during the past twenty years, but not so deeply as is sometimes supposed. Failure to understand it is one of the reasons why leftwing political parties are seldom able to produce an acceptable foreign policy.

The mental world of the *Gem* and *Magnet*, therefore, is something like this:

The year is 1910 – or 1940, but it is all the same. You are at Greyfriars, a rosy-cheeked boy of fourteen in posh tailor-made clothes, sitting down to tea in your study on the Remove passage after an exciting game of football which was won by an odd goal in the last half-minute. There is a cosy fire in the study, and outside the wind is whistling. The ivy clusters thickly round the old grey stones. The King is on his throne and the pound is worth a pound. Over in Europe the comic foreigners are jabbering and gesticulating, but the grim grey battleships of the British Fleet are steaming up the Channel and at the outposts of Empire the monocled Englishmen are holding the niggers at bay. Lord Mauleverer has just got another fiver and we are all settling down to a tremendous tea of sausages, sardines, crumpets, potted meat, jam and doughnuts. After tea we shall sit round the study fire having a good laugh at Billy Bunter and discussing the team for next week's match against Rookwood. Everything is safe, solid and unquestionable. Everything will be the same for ever and ever. That approximately is the atmosphere.

But now turn from the *Gem* and *Magnet* to the more up-to-date papers which have appeared since the Great War. The truly significant thing is that they have more points of resemblance to the *Gem* and *Magnet* than points of difference. But it is better to consider the differences first.

There are eight of these newer papers, the *Modern Boy*, *Triumph*,

Champion, Wizard, Rover, Skipper, Hotspur and *Adventure*. All of these have appeared since the Great War, but except for the *Modern Boy* none of them is less than five years old. Two papers which ought also to be mentioned briefly here, though they are not strictly in the same class as the rest, are the *Detective Weekly* and the *Thriller*, both owned by the Amalgamated Press. The *Detective Weekly* has taken over Sexton Blake. Both of these papers admit a certain amount of sex-interest into their stories, and though certainly read by boys, they are not aimed at them exclusively. All the others are boys' papers pure and simple, and they are sufficiently alike to be considered together.

There does not seem to be any notable difference between Thomson's publications and those of the Amalgamated Press.

As soon as one looks at these papers one sees their technical superiority to the *Gem* and *Magnet*. To begin with, they have the great advantage of not being written entirely by one person. Instead of one long complete story, a number of the *Wizard* or *Hotspur* consists of half a dozen or more serials, none of which goes on for ever. Consequently there is far more variety and far less padding, and none of the tiresome stylisation and facetiousness of the *Gem* and *Magnet*. Look at these two extracts, for example:

Billy Bunter groaned.

A quarter of an hour had elapsed out of the two hours that Bunter was booked for extra French.

In a quarter of an hour there were only fifteen minutes! But every one of those minutes seemed inordinately long to Bunter. They seemed to crawl by like tired snails.

Looking at the clock in Class-room No. 10 the fat Owl could hardly believe that only fifteen minutes had passed. It seemed more like fifteen hours, if not fifteen days!

Other fellows were in extra French as well as Bunter. They did not matter. Bunter did! (*Magnet*).

After a terrible climb, hacking out handholds in the smooth ice every step of the way up, Sergeant Lionheart Logan of the Mounties was now clinging like a human fly to the face of an icy cliff, as smooth and treacherous as a giant pane of glass.

An Arctic blizzard, in all its fury, was buffeting his body, driving the blinding snow into his face, seeking to tear his fingers loose from their handholds and dash him to death on the jagged boulders which lay at the foot of the cliff a hundred feet below.

Crouching among those boulders were eleven villainous trappers who had done their best to shoot down Lionheart and his companion, Constable Jim Rogers – until the blizzard had blotted the two Mounties out of sight from below (*Wizard*).

The second extract gets you some distance with the story, the first takes a hundred words to tell you that Bunter is in the detention class. Moreover, by not concentrating on school stories (in point of numbers the school story slightly predominates in all these papers, except the *Thriller* and *Detective Weekly*), the *Wizard, Hotspur*, etc., have far greater opportunities for sensationalism. Merely looking at the cover illustrations of the papers which I have on the table in front of me, here are some of the things I see. On one a cowboy is clinging by his toes to the wing of an aeroplane in mid-air and shooting down another aeroplane with his revolver. On another a Chinese is swimming for his life down a sewer with a swarm of ravenous-looking rats swimming after him. On another an engineer is lighting a stick of dynamite while a steel robot feels for him with its claws. On another a man in airman's costume is fighting barehanded against a rat somewhat larger than a donkey. On another a nearly naked man of terrific muscular development had just seized a lion by the tail and flung it thirty yards over the wall of an arena, with the words, 'Take back your blooming lion!' Clearly no school story can compete with this kind of thing. From time to time the school buildings may catch fire or the French master may turn out to be the head of an international anarchist gang, but in a general way the interest must centre round cricket, school rivalries, practical jokes, etc. There is not much room for bombs, death-rays, sub-machine guns, aeroplanes, mustangs, octopuses, grizzly bears or gangsters.

Examination of a large number of these papers shows that, putting aside school stories, the favourite subjects are Wild West, Frozen North, Foreign Legion, crime (always from the detective's angle), the Great War (Air Force or Secret Service, not the infantry), the Tarzan motif in varying forms, professional football, tropical exploration, historical romance

(Robin Hood, Cavaliers and Roundheads, etc.) and scientific invention. The Wild West still leads, at any rate as a setting, though the Red Indian seems to be fading out. The one theme that is really new is the scientific one. Death-rays, Martians, invisible men, robots, helicopters and inter-planetary rockets figure largely; here and there there are even far-off rumours of psychotherapy and ductless-glands. Whereas the *Gem* and *Magnet* derive from Dickens and Kipling, the *Wizard, Champion, Modern Boy*, etc., owe a great deal to H. G. Wells, who, rather than Jules Verne, is the father of 'Scientifiction'. Naturally it is the magical, Martian aspect of science that is most exploited, but one or two papers include serious articles on scientific subjects, besides quantities of informative snippets. (Examples: 'A Kauri tree in Queensland, Australia, is over 12,000 years old'; 'Nearly 50,000 thunderstorms occur every day'; 'Helium gas costs £1 per 1000 cubic feet'; 'There are over 500 varieties of spiders in Great Britain'; 'London firemen use 14,000,000 gallons of water annually', etc. etc.) There is a marked advance in intellectual curiosity and, on the whole, in the demand made on the reader's attention. In practice the *Gem* and *Magnet* and the post-war papers are read by much the same public, but the mental age aimed at seems to have risen by a year or two years – an improvement probably corresponding to the improvement in elementary education since 1909.

The other thing that has emerged in the post-war boys' papers, though not to anything like the extent one would expect, is bully-worship and the cult of violence.

If one compares the *Gem* and *Magnet* with a genuinely modern paper, the thing that immediately strikes one is the absence of the leader-principle. There is no central dominating character; instead there are fifteen or twenty characters, all more or less on an equality, with whom readers of different types can identify. In the more modern papers this is not usually the case. Instead of identifying with a schoolboy of more or less his own age, the reader of the *Skipper, Hotspur*, etc., is led to identify with a G-man, with a Foreign Legionary, with some variant of Tarzan, with an air ace, a master spy, an explorer, a pugilist – at any rate with some single all-powerful character who dominates everyone about him and whose usual method of solving any problem is a sock on the jaw. This character is intended as a superman, and as physical strength is the form of power that boys can best understand, he is usually a sort of human gorilla; in the Tarzan type of story he is sometimes actually a giant, eight or ten feet high. At the same time the scenes of violence in nearly all these stories are remarkably harmless and unconvincing. There is a great difference in tone between even the most bloodthirsty English paper and the threepenny Yank Mags, *Fight Stories, Action Stories*, etc. (not strictly boys' papers, but largely read by boys). In the Yank Mags you get real blood-lust, really gory descriptions of the all-in, jump-on-his-testicles style of fighting, written in a jargon that has been perfected by people who brood endlessly on violence. A paper like *Fight Stories*, for instance, would have very little appeal except to sadists and masochists. You can see the comparative gentleness of the English civilisation by the amateurish way in which prize-fighting is always described in the boys' weeklies. There is no specialised vocabulary. Look at these four extracts, two English, two American:

When the gong sounded, both men were breathing heavily, and each had great red marks on his chest. Bill's chin was bleeding, and Ben had a cut over his right eye.

Into their corners they sank, but when the gong clanged again they were up swiftly, and they went like tigers at each other (*Rover*).

He walked in stolidly and smashed a clublike right to my face. Blood spattered and I went back on my heels, but surged in and ripped my right under the heart. Another right smashed full on Sven's already battered mouth, and, spitting out the fragments of a tooth, he crashed a flailing left to my body (*Fight Stories*).

It was amazing to watch the Black Panther at work. His muscles rippled and slid under his dark skin. There was all the power and grace of a giant cat in his swift and terrible onslaught.

He volleyed blows with a bewildering speed for so huge a fellow. In a moment Ben was simply blocking with his gloves as well as he could. Ben was really a past-master of defence. He had many fine victories behind him. But the Negro's rights and lefts crashed through openings that hardly any other fighter could have found (*Wizard*).

Haymakers which packed the bludgeoning weight of forest monarchs crashing down under the ax hurled into the bodies of the two heavies as they swapped punches (*Fight Stories*).

Notice how much more knowledgeable the American extracts sound. They are written for devotees of the prize-ring, the others are not. Also, it ought to be emphasised that on its level the moral code of the English boys' papers is a decent one. Crime and dishonesty are never held up to admiration, there is none of the cynicism and corruption of the American gangster story. The huge sale of the Yank Mags in England shows that there is a demand for that kind of thing, but very few English writers seem able to produce it. When hatred of Hitler became a major emotion in America, it was interesting to see how promptly 'anti-Fascism' was adapted to pornographic purposes by the editors of the Yank Mags. One magazine which I have in front of me is given up to a long, complete story, 'When Hell Came to America', in which the agents of a 'blood-maddened European dictator' are trying to conquer the U.S.A. with death-rays and invisible aeroplanes. There is the frankest appeal to sadism, scenes in which the Nazis tie bombs to women's backs and fling them off heights to watch them blown to pieces in mid-air, others in which they tie naked girls together by their hair and prod them with knives to make them dance, etc. etc. The editor comments solemnly on all this, and uses it as a plea for tightening up restrictions against immigrants. On another page of the same paper: 'LIVES OF THE HOTCHA CHORUS GIRLS. Reveals all the intimate secrets and fascinating pastimes of the famous Broadway Hotcha girls. NOTHING IS OMITTED. Price 10C.' 'HOW TO LOVE. 10C.' 'FRENCH PHOTO RING. 25C.' 'NAUGHTY NUDIES TRANSFERS. From the outside of the glass you see a beautiful girl, innocently dressed. Turn it around and look through the glass and oh! what a difference! Set of 3 transfers 25c.', etc. etc. etc. There is nothing at all like this in any English paper likely to be read by boys. But the process of Americanisation is going on all the same. The American ideal, the 'he-man', the 'tough guy', the gorilla who puts everything right by socking everybody else on the jaw, now figures in probably a majority of boys' papers. In one serial now running in the *Skipper* he is always portrayed, ominously enough, swinging a rubber truncheon.

The development of the *Wizard, Hotspur*, etc., as against the earlier boys' papers, boils down to this: better technique, more scientific interest, more bloodshed, more leader-worship. But, after all, it is the *lack* of development that is the really striking thing.

To begin with, there is no political development whatever. The world of the *Skipper* and the *Champion* is still the pre-1914 world of the *Magnet* and the *Gem*. The Wild West story, for instance, with its cattle-rustlers, lynch-law and other paraphernalia belonging to the 'eighties, is a curiously archaic thing. It is worth noticing that in papers of this type it is always taken for granted that adventures only happen at the ends of the earth, in tropical forests, in Arctic wastes, in African deserts, on Western prairies, in Chinese opium dens – everywhere, in fact, except the places where things really *do* happen. That is a belief dating from thirty or forty years ago, when the new continents were in process of being opened up. Nowadays, of course, if you really want adventure, the place to look for it is in Europe. But apart from the picturesque side of the Great War, contemporary history is carefully excluded. And except that Americans are now admired instead of being laughed at, foreigners are exactly the same figures of fun that they always were. If a Chinese character appears, he is still the sinister pig-tailed opium-smuggler of Sax Rohmer; no indication that things have been happening in China since 1912 – no indication that a war is going on there, for instance. If a Spaniard appears, he is still a 'dago' or 'greaser' who rolls cigarettes and stabs people in the back; no indication that things have been happening in Spain. Hitler and the Nazis have not yet appeared, or are barely making their appearance. There will be plenty about them in a little while, but it will be from a strictly patriotic angle (Britain *versus* Germany), with the real meaning of the struggle kept out of sight as much as possible. As for the Russian Revolution, it is extremely difficult to find any reference to it in any of these papers. When Russia is mentioned at all it is usually in an information snippet (example: 'There are 29,000 centenarians in the U.S.S.R.'), and any reference to the Revolution is indirect and twenty years out of date. In one story in the *Rover*, for instance, somebody has a tame bear, and as it is a Russian bear, it is nicknamed Trotsky – obviously an echo of the 1917–23 period and not of recent controversies. The clock has stopped at 1910. Britannia rules the waves, and no one has heard of slumps, booms, unemployment, dictatorships, purges or concentration camps.

And in social outlook there is hardly any advance. The snobbishness is somewhat less open than in the *Gem* and *Magnet* – that is the most one can possibly say. To begin with, the school story, always partly dependent on snob-appeal, is by no means eliminated. Every number of a boys' paper includes at least one school story, these stories slightly outnumbering the Wild Westerns. The very elaborate fantasy-life of the *Gem* and *Magnet* is not imitated and there is more emphasis on extraneous adventure, but the social atmosphere (old grey stones) is much the same. When a new school is introduced at the beginning of a story we are often told in just those words that 'it was a very posh school'. From time to time a story appears which is ostensibly directed *against* snobbery. The scholarship-boy (cf. Tom Redwing in the *Magnet*) makes fairly frequent appearances, and what is essentially the same theme is sometimes presented in this form: there is great rivalry between two schools, one of which considers itself more 'posh' than the other, and there are fights, practical jokes, football matches, etc., always ending in the discomfiture of the snobs. If one glances very superficially at some of these stories it is possible to imagine that a democratic spirit has crept into the boys' weeklies, but when one looks more closely one sees that they merely reflect the bitter jealousies that exist within the white-collar class. Their real function is to allow the boy who goes to a cheap private school (*not* a Council school) to feel that his school is just as 'posh' in the sight of God as Winchester or Eton. The sentiment of school loyalty ('We're better than the fellows down the road'), a thing almost unknown to the real working class, is still kept up. As these stories are written by many different hands, they do, of course, vary a good deal in tone. Some are reasonably free from snobbishness, in others money and pedigree are exploited even more shamelessly than in the *Gem* and *Magnet*. In one that I came across an actual *majority* of the boys mentioned were titled.

Where working-class characters appear, it is usually either as comics (jokes about tramps, convicts, etc.), or as prize-fighters, acrobats, cowboys, professional footballers and Foreign Legionaries – in other words, as adventurers. There is no facing of the facts about working-class life, or, indeed, about *working* life of any description. Very occasionally one may come across a realistic description of, say, work in a coal-mine, but in all probability it will only be there as the background of some lurid adventure. In any case the central character is not likely to be a coal-miner. Nearly all the time the boy who reads these papers – in nine cases out of ten a boy who is going to spend his life working in a shop, in a factory or in some subordinate job in an office – is led to identify with people in positions of command, above all with people who are never troubled by shortage of money. The Lord Peter Wimsey figure, the seeming idiot who drawls and wears a monocle but is always to the fore in moments of danger, turns up over and over again. (This character is a great favourite in Secret Service stories.) And, as usual, the heroic characters all have to talk B.B.C.; they may talk Scottish or Irish or American, but no one in a star part is ever permitted to drop an aitch. Here it is worth comparing the social atmosphere of the boys' weeklies with that of the women's weeklies, the *Oracle*, the *Family Star*, *Peg's Paper*, etc.

The women's papers are aimed at an older public and are read for the most part by girls who are working for a living. Consequently they are on the surface much more realistic. It is taken for granted, for example, that nearly everyone has to live in a big town and work at a more or less dull job. Sex, so far from being taboo, is *the* subject. The short, complete stories, the special feature of these papers, are generally of the 'came the dawn' type: the heroine narrowly escapes losing her 'boy' to a designing rival, or the 'boy' loses his job and has to postpone marriage, but presently gets a better job. The changeling-fantasy (a girl brought up in a poor home is 'really' the child of rich parents) is another favourite. Where sensationalism comes in, usually in the serials, it arises out of the more domestic type of crime, such as bigamy, forgery or sometimes murder; no Martians, death-rays or international anarchist gangs. These papers are at any rate aiming at credibility, and they have a link with real life in their correspondence columns, where genuine problems are being discussed. Ruby M. Ayres's[14] column of advice in the *Oracle*, for instance, is extremely sensible and well written. And yet the world of the *Oracle* and *Peg's Paper* is a pure fantasy-world. It is the same fantasy all the time: pretending to be richer than you are. The chief impression that one carries away from almost every story in these papers is of a frightful, overwhelming 'refinement'. Ostensibly the characters are working-class people, but their habits, the interiors of their houses, their clothes, their outlook and, above all, their speech are entirely middle class. They are all living at several pounds a week above their income. And needless to say, that is just the impression that is intended. The idea is to give the bored factory-girl or worn-out mother of five a dream-life in which she pictures herself – not actually as a duchess (that convention has gone out) but as, say, the wife of a bank-manager. Not only is a five-to-six-pound-a-week standard of life set up as the ideal, but it is tacitly assumed that that is how working-class people really *do* live. The major facts are simply not faced. It is admitted, for instance, that people sometimes lose their jobs; but then the dark clouds roll away and they get better jobs instead. No mention of unemployment as something permanent and inevitable, no mention of the dole, no mention of trade unionism. No suggestion anywhere that there can be anything wrong with the system *as a system*; there are only individual misfortunes, which are generally due to somebody's wickedness and can in any case be put right in the last chapter. Always the dark clouds roll away, the kind employer raises Alfred's wages, and there are jobs for everybody except the drunks. It is still the world of the *Wizard* and the *Gem*, except that there are orange-blossoms instead of machine-guns.

The outlook inculcated by all these papers is that of a rather exceptionally stupid member of the Navy League[15] in the year 1910. Yes, it may be said, but what does it matter? And in any case, what else do you expect?

Of course no one in his senses would want to turn the so-called penny dreadful into a realistic novel or a Socialist tract. An adventure story must of its nature be more or less remote from real life. But, as I have tried to make clear, the unreality of the *Wizard* and the *Gem* is not so artless as it looks. These papers exist because of a specialised demand, because boys at certain ages find it necessary to read about Martians, death-rays, grizzly bears and gangsters. They get what they are looking for, but they get it wrapped up in the illusions which their future employers think suitable for them. To what extent people draw their ideas from fiction is disputable. Personally I believe that most people are influenced far more than they would care to admit by novels, serial stories, films and so forth, and that from this point of view the worst books are often the most important, because they are usually the ones that are read earliest in life. It is probable that many people who would consider themselves extremely sophisticated and 'advanced' are actually carrying through life an imaginative background which they acquired in childhood from (for instance) Sapper and Ian Hay.[16] If that is so, the boys' twopenny weeklies are of the deepest importance. Here is the stuff that is read somewhere between the ages of twelve and eighteen by a very large proportion, perhaps an actual majority, of English boys, including many who will never read anything else except newspapers; and along with it they are absorbing a set of beliefs which would be regarded as hopelessly out of date in the Central Office of the Conservative Party. All the better because it is done indirectly, there is being pumped into them the conviction that the major problems of our time do not exist, that there is nothing wrong with *laissez-faire* capitalism, that foreigners are unimportant comics and that the British Empire is a sort of charity-concern which will last for ever. Considering who owns these papers, it is difficult to believe that this is unintentional. Of the twelve papers I have been discussing (*i.e.* twelve including the *Thriller* and *Detective Weekly*), seven are the property of the Amalgamated Press, which is one of the biggest press-combines in the world and controls more than a hundred different papers. The *Gem* and *Magnet*, therefore, are closely linked up with the *Daily Telegraph* and the *Financial Times*. This in itself would be enough to rouse certain suspicions, even if it were not obvious that the stories in the boys' weeklies are politically vetted. So it appears that if you feel the need of a fantasy-life in which you travel to Mars and fight lions bare-handed (and what boy doesn't?), you can only have it by delivering yourself over, mentally, to people like Lord Camrose.[17] For there is no competition. Throughout the whole of this run of papers the differences are negligible, and on this level no others exist. This raises the question, why is there no such thing as a left-wing boys' paper?

At first glance such an idea merely makes one slightly sick. It is so horribly easy to imagine what a left-wing boys' paper would be like, if it existed. I remember in 1920 or 1921 some optimistic person handing round Communist tracts among a crowd of public-school boys. The tract I received was of the question-and-answer kind:

Q. 'Can a Boy Communist be a Boy Scout, Comrade?'

A. 'No, Comrade.'

Q. 'Why, Comrade?'

A. 'Because, Comrade, a Boy Scout must salute the Union Jack, which is the symbol of tyranny and oppression.' Etc. etc.

Now, suppose that at this moment somebody started a left-wing paper deliberately aimed at boys of twelve or fourteen. I do not suggest that the whole of its contents would be exactly like the tract I have quoted above, but does anyone doubt that they would be *something* like it? Inevitably such a paper would either consist of dreary uplift or it would be under Communist influence and given over to adulation of Soviet Russia; in either case no normal boy would ever look at it. Highbrow literature apart, the whole of the existing left-wing Press, in so far as it is at all vigorously 'left', is one long tract. The one Socialist paper in England which could live a week on its merits *as a paper* is the *Daily Herald*: and how much Socialism is there in the *Daily Herald*? At this moment, therefore, a paper with a 'left' slant and at the same time likely to have an appeal to ordinary boys in their teens is something almost beyond hoping for.

But it does not follow that it is impossible. There is no clear reason why every adventure story should necessarily be mixed up with snob-bishness and gutter patriotism. For, after all, the stories in the *Hotspur* and the *Modern Boy* are not Conservative tracts; they are merely adventure stories with a Conservative bias. It is fairly easy to imagine the process being reversed. It is possible, for instance, to imagine a paper as thrilling and lively as the *Hotspur*, but with subject-matter and 'ideology' a little more up to date. It is even possible (though this raises other difficulties) to imagine a women's paper at the same literary level as the *Oracle*, dealing in approximately the same kind of story, but taking rather more account of the realities of working-class life. Such things have been done before, though not in England. In the last years of the Spanish monarchy there was a large output in Spain of left-wing novelettes, some of them evidently of Anarchist origin. Unfortunately at the time when they were appearing I did not see their social significance, and I lost the collection of them that I had, but no doubt copies would still be procurable. In get-up and style of story they were very similar to the English fourpenny novelette, except that their inspiration was 'left'. If, for instance, a story described police pursuing Anarchists through the mountains, it would be from the point of view of the Anarchists and not of the police. An example nearer to hand is the Soviet film *Chapaiev*,[18] which has been shown a number of times in London. Technically, by the standards of the time when it was made, *Chapaiev* is a first-rate film, but mentally, in spite of the unfamiliar Russian background, it is not so very remote from Hollywood. The one thing that lifts it out of the ordinary is the remarkable performance by the actor who takes the part of the White officer (the fat one) – a performance which looks very like an inspired piece of gagging. Otherwise the atmosphere is familiar. All the usual paraphernalia is there – heroic fight against odds, escape at the last moment, shots of galloping horses, love interest, comic relief. The film is in fact a fairly ordinary one, except that its tendency is 'left'. In a Hollywood film of the Russian Civil War the Whites would probably be angels and the Reds demons. In the Russian version the Reds are angels and the Whites demons. That also is a lie, but, taking the long view, it is a less pernicious lie than the other.

Here several difficult problems present themselves. Their general nature is obvious enough, and I do not want to discuss them. I am merely pointing to the fact that, in England, popular imaginative literature is a field that left-wing thought has never begun to enter. *All* fiction from the novels in the mushroom libraries[19] downwards is censored in the interests of the ruling class. And boys' fiction above all, the blood-and-thunder stuff which nearly every boy devours at some time or other, is sodden in the worst illusions of 1910. The fact is only unimportant if one believes that what is read in childhood leaves no impression behind. Lord Camrose and his colleagues evidently believe nothing of the kind, and, after all, Lord Camrose ought to know.

> *Shortly after 'Boy's Weeklies' appeared in* Horizon, *its editor, Cyril Connolly (a friend of Orwell's from their time at St Cyprian's Preparatory School, Eastbourne, and at Eton) was amazed to receive a letter from 'Frank Richards', the author of the stories in* Magnet *and* Gem. *He was clearly very much alive. He asked for space to reply to 'the charges' made against him. His reply appeared in* Horizon *for May 1940 and was reprinted in* CEJL *and in* CW *(XII/599). Before he had seen it, Orwell expressed his apprehension as to what 'Richards' would say, in a letter to Geoffrey Gorer of 3 April 1940 (XII/607). The reply was much discussed and enjoyed in literary circles in London, and, indeed, by Orwell himself. 'Richards' responded to a number of Orwell's individual charges: plagiarism; the accusation that he was snobbish; patriotism ('an affronting word to Mr Orwell'); that foreigners are funny ('foreigners are funny'); that the working-classes enter only as comics and semi-villains ('This is sheer perversity on Mr Orwell's part'); the absence of any reference to strikes, slumps and unemployment; and especially that he was believed to be out of date. He*

responded ironically to Orwell's finding it 'difficult to believe that a series running for thirty years can possibly have been written by one and the same person. In the presence of such authority, I speak with diffidence: and can only say that, to the best of my knowledge and belief, I am only one person, and have never been two or three' (CEJL, 81). After rebutting Orwell's indictment, he wittily expected a telegram 'worded like that of the invader of Scinde', referring to Sir Charles Napier's victory at Hyderabad in the Province of Scinde, India, in 1843, which consisted of the single word Peccavi (I have sinned/Scinde). It is now believed that a schoolgirl, Catherine Winkworth, made this pun, not Napier; it was published in Punch, 18 May 1844.

The real name of Frank Richards was Charles Hamilton (1876–1961). He certainly wrote most of the stories, and those under other pseudonyms (see n. 4, below), but he did not write them all. Despite Hamilton's protestations, Orwell was correct in claiming that Hamilton's style was easily imitated. (Hamilton argued that he 'could hardly count the number of authors who have striven to imitate Frank Richards, not one of whom has been successful'.) Hamilton was 'a great traveller and an inveterate gambler'. He would disappear without notice to leave others to write his 20,000-word stories overnight. One of those who wrote over a hundred Greyfriars' stories was George Richard Samways, who died aged 101 on 8 August 1996. Samways never received credit and got only half Hamilton's fee. Hamilton later 'expressed only contempt' for those who had to help him out in this way. (See Samways's obituaries in the Independent (by Jack Adrian), 24 August 1996, and Daily Telegraph, 26 August 1996.)

Denise Ruthers, who had contributed to Lucky Star, Golden Star, Silver Star, Peg's Paper, Glamour, Flame, Secrets, Oracle, Miracle, and others, and had worked on some of these journals, wrote to Horizon on 6 March 1940 commenting on aspects of Orwell's article. She said she knew, from experience, that correspondence columns were 'sometimes, though not always, as much fiction as the rest of the periodical . . . Perhaps it is [Ruby M. Ayres's] secretary who has written them, or . . . an overworked member of the editorial staff.' She pointed out: 'One of the first rules of all these periodicals is that the detail should be realistic. This is essential to carry the ultimate escapism . . . The ideal of most of these stories is not an income worthy of a bank manager's wife, but a life that is "good". A life without *crooks and dishonesty and trickery – and illness . . . A life with an upright kind husband, however poor . . . The stories are conditioned to show that the meagre life is not so bad.'* She noted that Oracle-*type stories, for working-class girls, nearly always had provincial settings – she had never seen the London Underground mentioned – whereas in middle-class periodicals the setting was London and cosmopolitan, with 'romance on the Tube and adventures in aeroplanes'.* She agreed with Orwell that a left-wing Oracle *could and 'should be imagined, and created'.* Orwell annotated her letter, *'See also letter printed in* New Leader *(book of press-cuttings).'* Denise Ruthers's letter was with Orwell's papers at his death; the book of press cuttings has not survived. The article that prompted the letter can be traced. New Leader, *25 April 1940,* reviewed Orwell's article, concentrating on *'Boys' Weeklies',* under the title *'Billy Bunter or The Skipper as Britain's Dr. Goebbels?'.* George W. Woodman replied on 9 May: *'Writer of "Penny Dreadfuls" Disagrees.'* He and his brother had written boys' stories (*'Boys' Books',* he called them) for five years. They were different from those in Magnet *and* Gem: *'The D. C. Thomson crowd are very astute, and played up to their "poor-boy" readers for all they were worth. Almost every story was about some poor youngster who defied authority and beat his "superiors" and "betters". "Colonel Blimps" were always getting thrown into duck ponds. One tough-guy hero leads the privates of a regiment in revolt against their officers – and so on. My brother wrote a very popular serial about a "Peacemaker" – a semi-humorous character who defied dictators, governments and intriguers and stopped a war every week! I wrote one story with Sexton Blake in the lead about Spain before the Civil War, in which Tinker threw in his lot with the anarchists and ousted the dictator – fictitious of course! – of the Asturias. I noticed from Readers' letters that it went down well. (It might amuse you to know that the editor at that time was a member of the Communist Party!) There was nothing "honest" of course in this semi-revolutionary line. The publishing houses were merely playing to the gallery since the gallery contained the most people, but it proved at least where the feelings of thousands of boy readers lay.'* He had later written stories for girls. These were *'ten thousand times more snobbish'* than were those for boys: *'I know Newnes and the A. P. girls' publications pretty well, and any story which does not have the heroine marrying the young works' manager is doomed. They are all Cinderella plots, and the "advice" articles and "Replies to Readers" are appalling in their snobbery. They don't "play down" to their readers, they "play up" to them. Girls who will never have the chance of getting farther than Southend or Blackpool are told in detail what to wear on their summer cruise to the Mediterranean!' The only thing that kept him writing such stuff was the thought that otherwise he would be 'out in the gutter'. See also pp. 350–52, below.*

1. *Oracle* was founded in 1933. It was said in the 1945 *Writers' and Artists' Year Book* to be aimed at 'women readers of the working class'.

2. *Gem* (1907–39; when incorporated in *Triumph*), *Magnet* (1908–40; when incorporated in *Knock-Out*) and *Champion* (1922–55) were the most successful of the Amalgamated Press weeklies mentioned by Orwell. Four of the D. C. Thomson weeklies outlived Orwell: *Adventure* (1921–61); *Rover* (1922–61); *Wizard* (1922–   ) and *Hotspur* (1933–59). *Skipper* (1930–41) fell victim to wartime paper rationing. See E. S. Turner, *Boys Will Be Boys* (1948; revd edn, 1957) and W. G. O. Lofts and D. J. Adley, *Old Boys' Books: A Complete Catalogue* (1970). *Modern Boy* (mentioned later) was published from 1928 to 1939.

3. *Boy's Own Paper* (not *Boys'*, as sometimes printed), founded in 1879 by the Religious Tract Society, was a weekly to 1912, then monthly. It outlived Orwell. *Chums*, founded in 1892, was published by Cassell as a rival to *Boy's Own Paper*.

4. In fact, the stories were *not* all the work of 'Frank Richards' (Charles Hamilton). He is credited with 1,380 of the 1,683 stories in *Magnet*; there were some twenty-five substitute writers. Nevertheless, he wrote some 5,000 stories, 'created' more than a hundred schools, used two dozen pen-names (including Hilda Richards, for girls-school stories, and Martin Clifford). He probably published some 100 million words. See W. G. O. Lofts and D. J. Adley, *The Men Behind Boys' Fiction* (1970), and afterword, above.

5. John Edward Gunby Hadath (*c.* 1880–1954), author of *Schoolboy Grit* (1913), *Carey of Cobhouse* (1928) and other school stories. See Orwell's review of his *From Pillar to Post*, 7 December 1940, XII/718. Desmond Francis Talbot Coke (1879–1931), author of *The House Prefect* (1908) and other books for children.

6. Orwell had 'books' for 'papers' in *Horizon*. He may have been confused by the publication history of *Stalky & Co*. The first collection of Kipling's Stalky stories was published in book form in 1899, but its nine stories had earlier appeared in magazines.

7. Shell and Remove were school classes intermediate between numbered forms in some (mainly public) schools, often between fifth and sixth forms. The terms go back to the eighteenth century, Shell deriving from the shape of the room used for this purpose at Westminster School.

8. Another pen-name for Charles Hamilton; see n. 4, above.

9. Mons, in Belgium, marked the limit of a British advance in August 1914. The German army under von Kluck was badly mauled, but success was short lived. In what became a famous fighting retreat, the British II Corps held the Germans at the costly battle of Le Cateau.

10. Air Raid Precautions.

11. Orwell originally wrote 'Chinaman' for 'Chinese'. He discussed making such changes to avoid giving racial offence in his *Tribune* column, 'As I Please', 2, on 10 December 1943 (XVI/ *2391*). For example, that 'Moslem' should be used instead of 'Mahomedan', and 'Negro' (then commonly used) should always have a capital 'N'.

12. Orwell may have been prompted here by Tolstoy's national stereotypes in *War and Peace*, Book IX, ch. X. Both describe Italians as excitable. He refers to this novel in his essay on Dickens (XII/53).

13. The EAT LESS BREAD campaign was also prevalent in another area of popular culture: the music hall. The slogan provided a refrain for Ernie Mayne's lugubrious, somewhat apatriotic song, 'All for the Sake of England', during World War I.

14. Ruby M. Ayres (1883–1955) was a prolific and popular romantic novelist and short-story writer, many of whose novels were made into films. Despite writing in this vein, she gave down-to-earth advice in her column in *Oracle*, the more convincing, perhaps, because her stories were so widely read.

15. The Navy League was founded in 1895 to foster national interest in the Royal Navy. Orwell was a member when he was seven years old.

16. Sapper was Herman Cyril McNeile (1888–1937), adventure-story writer and creator of the popular hero Bulldog Drummond. Ian Hay (John Hay Beith; 1876–1952) was a Scottish author and dramatist. His *The First Hundred Thousand* gave a propagandist account of Kitchener's First Army in France at the beginning of World War I and was widely read. He followed this with *Carrying On – After the First Hundred Thousand* (1917) and *The Last Million* (1919), on the US army in France at the end of that war.

17. William Ewart Berry (1879–1954; Baron Camrose, 1929; Viscount, 1941) began his working life as a reporter and rose to control (with his brother, Lord Kemsley) a newspaper and periodical empire that included the *Sunday Times, Daily Telegraph, Financial Times*, twenty-two provincial newspapers and some seventy periodicals, including *Women's Journal* and *Boxing*. He was Controller of Press Relations at the Ministry of Information for a short time in 1939.

18. *Chapaiev* (1935) was directed by the Vassiliev Brothers. In 1944 Roger Manvell wrote, 'This film . . . was notable for developing, with sound, the personality of a character. It had star-value without a star . . . It was bright and fresh and clean and realistic. It threw aside the cobwebs of the silent days and solved the problem of how to make a good story about a great Soviet hero in a realistic but not pedestrian manner' (*Film* (1944), 51).

19. Mushroom libraries sprang up overnight and rapidly died away as do mushrooms. They were usually found in poor parts of towns. They stocked the cheapest kinds of fiction and it usually cost two (old) pence a week to borrow a book. In *Keep the Aspidistra Flying*, Stephen Comstock, when destitute, works in Mr Cheeseman's twopenny library in Lambeth (pp. 224–8).

[604]

'Notes on the Way'
Time and Tide, *30 March 1940*

When the other day I read Dr Ley's[1] statement that 'inferior races, such as Poles and Jews' do not need so much to eat as Germans, I was suddenly reminded of the first sight I saw when I set foot on the soil of Asia – or rather, just before setting foot there.

The liner I was travelling in was docking at Colombo, and the usual swarm of coolies had come aboard to deal with the luggage. Some policemen, including a white sergeant, were superintending them. One of the coolies had got hold of a long tin uniform-case and was carrying it so clumsily as to endanger people's heads. Someone cursed at him for his carelessness. The police sergeant looked round, saw what the man was doing, and caught him a terrific kick on the bottom that sent him staggering across the deck. Several passengers, including women, murmured their approval.

Now transfer this scene to Paddington Station or Liverpool Docks. It simply could not happen. An English luggage-porter who was kicked would hit back, or at least there would be a chance of his doing so. The policeman would not kick him on such small provocation, and certainly not in front of witnesses. Above all, the onlookers would be disgusted. The most selfish millionaire in England, if he saw a fellow-Englishman kicked in that manner, would feel at least a momentary resentment. And yet here were ordinary, decent, middling people, people with incomes of about £500 a year, watching the scene with no emotion whatever except a mild approval. They were white, and the coolie was black. In other words he was sub-human, a different kind of animal.

That was nearly twenty years ago. Are things of this kind still happening in India? I should say that they probably are, but that they are happening less and less frequently. On the other hand it is tolerably certain that at this moment a German somewhere or other is kicking a Pole. It is quite certain that a German somewhere or other is kicking a Jew. And it is also certain (*vide* the German newspapers) that German farmers are being sentenced to terms of imprisonment for showing 'culpable kindness' to the Polish prisoners working for them. For the sinister development of the past twenty years has been the spread of racialism to the soil of Europe itself.

Racialism is not merely an aberration of crazy professors, and it has nothing to do with nationalism. Nationalism is probably desirable, up to a point; at any rate it is unavoidable. Peoples with a well-developed national culture don't like being governed by foreigners, and the history of countries like Ireland and Poland is very largely the history of this fact. As for the theory that 'the proletarian has no country', it always turns out to be nonsense in practice. We have just had another demonstration of this in Finland.

But racialism is something totally different. It is the invention not of conquered nations but of conquering nations. It is a way of pushing exploitation beyond the point that is normally possible, by pretending that the exploited *are not human beings*.

Nearly all aristocracies having real power have depended on a difference of race, Norman rules over Saxon, German over Slav, Englishman over Irishman, white man over black man, and so on and so forth. There are traces of the Norman predominance in our own language to this day. And it is much easier for the aristocrat to be ruthless if he imagines that the serf is different from himself in blood and bone. Hence the tendency to exaggerate race-differences, the current rubbish about shapes of skulls, colour of eyes, blood-counts, etc., etc. In Burma I have listened to racial theories which were less brutal than Hitler's theories about the Jews, but certainly not less idiotic.

The English in India have built up a whole mythology turning upon the supposed differences between their own bodies and those of orientals. I have often heard it asserted, for instance, that no white man can sit on his heels in the same attitude as an oriental – the attitude, incidentally, in which coal-miners sit when they eat their dinners in the pit.

People of mixed blood, even when they are completely white, are supposed to be detectable by mysterious peculiarities in their fingernails. As for the various superstitions centring round sunstroke, they ought to have been monographed long ago. And there is no question that this kind of nonsense has made it easier for us to squeeze the juice out of India. We could not, at this date, treat English industrial workers quite as Indian industrial workers are treated; not merely because they wouldn't tolerate it, but because, beyond a certain point, *we* wouldn't tolerate it. I doubt whether anyone in England now thinks it right for children of six to work in factories. But there are plenty of businessmen in India who would welcome child-labour if the law allowed it.

If I thought that a victory in the present war would mean nothing beyond a new lease of life for British imperialism, I should be inclined to side with Russia and Germany. And I am aware that some of our rulers intend no more than that. They imagine that if they can win the war (or perhaps call it off and turn Germany against Russia), they will be able to enjoy another twenty years of colonial exploitation. But I believe there is a good chance that things will not work out like that. To begin with, the world-struggle is no longer between Socialism and capitalism. In so far as Socialism means no more than centralized ownership and planned production, all the industralized countries will be 'Socialist' before long. The real issue is between democratic Socialism and some form of rational-ized caste-society. The former is much likelier to prevail if the western countries, where democratic ideas are deeply ingrained in the common people, are not deprived of all influence.

Socialism in the narrow economic sense has nothing to do with liberty, equality or common decency of any description. There is no reason, for instance, why a State should not be internally Socialist and externally imperialist. Technically it would be possible to 'Socialize' England tomorrow and still continue to exploit India and the crown colonies for the benefit of the home population. Germany, almost without doubt, is moving rapidly towards Socialism; and yet side by side with this development there goes a perfectly clear, open determination to turn the subject peoples into a reserve of slave labour. It is quite practicable, so long as the myth of 'inferior races' is believed in. Jews and Poles aren't human beings; therefore why not rob them? Hitler is only the ghost of our own past rising against us. He stands for the extension and perpetuation of our own methods, just at the moment when we are beginning to be ashamed of them.

Our real relationship with India has not altered much since the Mutiny of 1857, but our feelings about it have altered enormously in the last twenty years, and therein there is a gleam of hope. If we had to win India once again, as it was won in the eighteenth and nineteenth centuries, we should find ourselves unable to do it. Not because the military task would be harder – it would be far easier – but because the necessary supply of ruffians would not be forthcoming.

The men who conquered India for us, the Puritan adventurers with their Bibles and their swords – men who could blow hundreds of 'natives' from the mouths of guns and describe the scene in their memoirs with the greatest realism and with no more compunction than one would feel for killing a chicken – they are simply a vanished race. The outlook even of ordinary Anglo-Indians has been deeply infected by Left-wing opinion at home. Gone are the days – which were only the day before yesterday – when you sent your disobedient servant along to the jail with a note saying 'Please give the bearer fifteen lashes'. Somehow we don't believe in our divine mission quite as we used to. When the time comes to pay our debts we shall undoubtedly wriggle, but I think there is just a chance that we shall pay up.

When war has once started there is no such thing as neutrality. All activities are war activities. Whether you want to or not, you are obliged to help either your own side or the enemy. The Pacifists, Communists, Fascists, etc., are at this moment helping Hitler. They have a perfect right to do so, provided they believe that Hitler's cause is the better and are willing to take the consequences. If I side with Britain and France, it is because I would sooner side with the older imperialisms – decadent, as Hitler quite rightly calls them – than with the new ones which are completely sure of themselves and therefore completely merciless. Only, for Heaven's sake let us not pretend that we go into this war with clean hands. It is only while we cling to the consciousness that our hands are *not* clean that we retain the right to defend ourselves.

A second instalment of 'Notes on the Way' was published on 6 April 1940.
It discusses some implications of Malcolm Muggeridge's The Thirties,
Hilaire Belloc's The Servile State *and Aldous Huxley's* Brave New
World. *See* XII/124–7.

1. Dr Robert Ley (1890–1945) was a pilot in the German air force who was shot down in 1917 and made a prisoner of war. He worked as a chemist until 1922, when he was dismissed for drunkenness. He became a leader of the German Labour Front from 1933 to 1945. From 1938 he diverted money from the Volkswagen car project to his own pocket. He committed suicide while awaiting trial for war crimes at Nuremberg.

[609]

To Humphry House
11 April 1940

The Stores, Wallington, Nr. Baldock, Herts

Dear Mr House,[1]

Many thanks for your letter. I was glad to hear from you. With ref. to the manifesto, I haven't a copy of it by me, but as to the specific point you raise, about 'the churches', I should say that it is a good rule of thumb never to mention religion if you can possibly avoid it. I don't know how many practising religious believers there are in England, but it couldn't conceivably be more than 10 million (probably more like 6 million), and even among those there is an active minority which will be offended by the suggestion that the churches don't put their professions into practice. In any case the churches no longer have any hold on the working class, except perhaps for the Catholic Irish labourers. On the other hand you can always appeal to common decency, which the vast majority of people believe in without the need to tie it up with any transcendental belief. As to the 'white-man-coloured-man' business, I can't give an opinion.

As to the manifesto in general. If I had been drawing it up I would of course have put it quite differently. Whether that kind of thing can ever have a wide appeal, except when something has happened which brings the issue into the ordinary person's mind, I am not sure. The very fact that this manifesto of 'common men' has to be drawn up by a baronet M.P. and handed out to fifty persons to sign on the dotted line, instead of coming spontaneously from the people themselves, carries its own suggestion. I was willing to give what little help I could, because I was in general agreement, ie. I think it is vitally necessary to do something towards equalising incomes, abolishing class privilege and setting free the subject peoples. Not to put it on any wider ground, I don't believe the war can otherwise be won, if it goes to full lengths, and one simply can't see the present or any probable future government doing anything of the kind unless they are bullied into it. But had the manifesto been anything like Acland's book, *Unser Kampf*,[2] I would have had nothing to do with it. The actual effect of a book like that, whatever the intention might be, is simply to spread defeatism. One has got to remember that most people see things in very simple terms and that the urgent question of the moment is 'Do we fight Hitler or do we surrender?' Ninety-nine people of a hundred would conclude from reading *Unser Kampf* that we ought to surrender as quickly and ignominiously as possible. Acland seems to me an almost complete ass, though of course well-meaning enough. All through the pre-war years, when it was just conceivably possible to avert war by reviving the international Socialist movement, he tied himself up with the warmongering Popular Front gang, and now that war has started, under the influence of the same people, he suddenly discovers that Hitler is no worse than we are and in fact rather better. He allows himself to become the tool of hired liars like Pritt[3] and is apparently not capable of seeing that Nazi propaganda in this country has to pose as Russian propaganda. However, in the manifesto he steered clear of that kind of thing, so I was willing to associate myself with it, because I do agree about the absolute necessity of moving towards equality. But I would have worded the manifesto more strongly and emphasised both ends of the programme (defeat Hitler – equalise incomes) more plainly.

As to Dickens. You evidently know much more about him than I do. I have never really 'studied' him, merely read and enjoyed him, and I dare say there are works of his I have never read. The point you took up, about Dickens not writing about work, was one I did not express very well. What I should have said was that when Dickens gives a detailed description of someone working, it is always someone seen from the outside and usually a burlesque (like Wemmick or Venus). I avoided following this up because it would have led me into a discussion of the burlesque in English novels which would have strayed too far afield. As to D.'s 'discontent', I think I stick to it that some such quality is necessary, and I think the disappearance of it in the modern intelligentsia is a very sinister thing. Dickens, of course, had the most childish views on politics etc., but I think that because his *moral* sense was sound he would have been able to find his bearings in any political or economic milieu. So I think would most Victorians. The thing that frightens me about the modern intelligentsia is their inability to see that human society must be based on common decency, whatever the political and economic forms may be. To revert to Acland and his *Unser Kampf,* he is apparently incapable of seeing that there is something wrong with the present Russian régime. Private property has been abolished, therefore (so he argues) everything *must* be more or less all right. This seems to me to indicate the lack of a moral nose. Dickens, without the slightest understanding of Socialism etc., would have seen at a glance that there is something wrong with a régime that needs a pyramid of corpses every few years. It is as Nietzsche[4] said about Christianity (I'm quoting from memory), if you are all right inside you don't have to be *told* that it is putrid. You can smell it – it stinks. All people who are morally sound have known since about 1931 that the Russian régime stinks. Part of the trouble, as I pointed out in my book, is that the English intelligentsia have been so conditioned that they simply cannot imagine what a totalitarian government is like. They have also become infected with the inherently mechanistic Marxist notion that if you make the necessary technical advance the moral advance will follow of itself. I have never accepted this. I don't believe that capitalism, as against feudalism, improved the actual quality of human life, and I don't believe that Socialism *in itself* need work any real improvement either. Hitler is perhaps a large-scale demonstration of this. I believe that these economic advances merely provide the opportunity for a step forward which, as yet, hasn't happened. A year ago I was in the Atlas mountains, and looking at the Berber villagers there, it struck me that we were, perhaps, 1000 years ahead of these people, but no *better* than they, perhaps on balance rather worse. We are physically inferior to them, for instance, and manifestly less happy. All we have done is to advance to a point at which we *could* make a real improvement in human life, but we shan't do it without the recognition that common decency is necessary. My chief hope for the future is that the common people have never parted company with their moral code. I have never met a genuine working man who accepted Marxism, for instance. I have never had the slightest fear of a dictatorship of the proletariat, if it could happen, and certain things I saw in the Spanish war confirmed me in this. But I admit to having a perfect horror of a dictatorship of theorists, as in Russia and Germany.

I would like to meet some time. I am rather tied down here, as, apart from other things, I am trying to join a Government training centre and they may possibly call me up some time soon. Thank you for writing.

Yours sincerely
George Orwell

1. Humphry House (1908–55) was a Fellow of Wadham College, Oxford. His works include an edition of the *Notebooks and Papers of Gerard Manley Hopkins*, *The Dickens World* and three essays in *Ideas and Beliefs of the Victorians*.

2. Sir Richard Acland (1906–90; Bt.) had become a Liberal MP in 1935. From 1936 he was active in the campaign for a popular front. At the outbreak of war he announced his conversion to socialism, or, as he preferred to call it, 'Common Ownership'. In February 1940 he published *Unser Kampf*, one of the most successful of the Penguin Specials, and asked readers for their support. On 12 March 1940, about 150 of them attended a meeting he convened in the House of Commons and agreed on the draft of 'The Manifesto of the Common Man'. From 1942 he represented the Common Wealth Party in Parliament, and was a Labour MP, 1947–55, but was later expelled from the party. He then was a Senior Lecturer at St Luke's College of Education, Exeter, 1959–74. See Orwell's profile of him, XV/*2095*. The family home, Killerton, near Exeter, built in 1778, was given, with its beautiful garden and woodlands, to the nation by Sir Richard at the end of the war.

3. D. N. Pritt (1887–1972) was a well-known barrister and fervent supporter of left-wing causes and the Soviet Union and a Labour MP, 1935–40. After his expulsion from the party for policy disagreements, he was an Independent Socialist MP until 1950. He wrote *Light on Moscow* (1939) and in 1940 published four books, including *Must the War Spread?* Orwell included Pritt in his private list of crypto-communists and fellow-travellers (see XX/ *3732*, *3590A* and *3590B*). He wrote this comment against Pritt's name: 'Almost certainly underground member [of Communist Party]. Said to handle more money than is accounted for by his job. Good M.P. (i.e. locally). Very able & courageous.'

4. Friedrich Wilhelm Nietzsche (1844–1900), German philosopher and critic. For a time he was a close friend of Wagner's and dedicated *The Birth of Tragedy from the Spirit of Music* (1872) to him, but their ways parted. He was devoutly religious as a child but later rejected Christianity and developed the theory of the Superman (in *Thus Spake Zarathustra*, 1883–5) and the Will to Power (influenced by the earlier German philosopher, Arthur Schopenhauer, 1788–1860). He influenced the existentialist movement and the Nazis.

[647]

Review of English Ways *by Jack Hilton; with an introduction by J. Middleton Murry and photographs by J. Dixon Scott*[1]

The Adelphi, *July 1940*

Jack Hilton's book, which is the story of a tramp half across England and back, with his wife and himself pushing their tent and other belongings in a perambulator, has for its 'title-quote' a couplet from Crabbe[2] or some kindred author. A better one would have been:

For he might have been a Roos-i-an,
A French or Turk or Proos-i-an,
Or perhaps Eyetal-i-an:
But in spite of all temptat-i-ons
To belong to other nat-i-ons
He remains an Englishman.
He remains an Englishman.[3]

And how much an Englishman! Like a prize Sealyham terrier or Leghorn cock, he has all the 'points' developed to the verge of caricature. Lytton Strachey, in his essay on Stendhal, remarked that people who have the national characteristics in an exaggerated form are not always approved of by their own countrymen. He instanced Shelley and Nelson, and if he had been writing a little later he would probably have added D. H. Lawrence. It is rather the same with Jack Hilton, whose vagabondish, almost anti-social attitude to life is only the native English anarchism pushed a little beyond the normal.

Once or twice in this book he refers to himself as a 'lumpenproletarian'. He is not actually that, but he does belong to the poorer working class, the people who make up the bulk of the English population and whom in the normal way we never hear about. Reading Jack Hilton's book, one realises how unsatisfactory these people are from the point of view of all the Nosey Parkers who are constantly trying to elevate them. They are, for instance, completely irreligious. In the Catholic ages they were probably not so, but since then the Church has lost all hold on them, except for a sort of blackmail-hold in the rural districts, and the sects never made much headway. Then again, though deeply moral, they are not puritanical. Their chosen pleasures are exactly the ones that the religious and the secular reformer unite in disapproving. Gambling, for example. Jack Hilton is evidently an inveterate gambler, in a small way. The high spot of his journey is a visit to the Derby, and Ascot week runs it a good second. He belongs to, or at least he understands, the crowds who fill the cheap seats at Lord's, line the streets at royal weddings, and swell the profits of the football pools. At the Derby he is not above waiting outside the Royal enclosure to see the King arrive, and feeling a pang of disappointment because it is only a motor car that he comes in and not a coach and six. Although with part of his mind he can see through it and despise it, he enjoys a bit of glitter and swagger, and does not object to ladies in £50 dresses and gentlemen in grey top-hats and spongebag trousers. One feels instinctively that his favourite kings would be Charles II and Edward VII.

But from the point of view of the doctrinaire socialist such a man is equally hopeless. Of course Jack Hilton is 'left', as any thinking person below the £10 a week level must be, but the orthodoxy which even the mildest socialist would demand is impossible to him. He is pragmatical, a hater of theory, deeply infected with the English tradition of patching up and 'making do', and, above all, he is not unhappy. Necessarily one makes men into socialists by making them discontented, and in a fairly prosperous capitalist society that is not so easy. Moreover in modern England the conditions of class war do not exist. One sees this fact everywhere in Jack Hilton's work. He is troubled by the itch of class-difference, mildly dislikes the bourgeoisie, but he would not massacre them even if he could, and looking round him in contemporary society he observes almost as much good as evil. When he sees a filthy slum he denounces it as it ought to be denounced; but on the other hand when he sees a good piece of slum-clearance (probably done by a Conservative corporation) he praises it almost as fervently. For 'we must praise where there is cause as well as grouse when we find things awful' – very shocking, of course, but it probably gives one a truer idea of what the proletariat really do think than one can get from the Marxist textbooks, and it gives one a hint of what a proletarian revolution might be like, if such a thing could happen.

Our civilisation has put itself on record very elaborately in the years between the two world wars. If the British Museum library survives the bombings and heresy-hunts of the next twenty years, the people of 2000 A.D. will know us a great deal better than we know our ancestors. This book, in which life is seen mainly from the under side, is a valuable addition to contemporary history. It is more than I have indicated, because it happens to be the book of an individualist, a man who likes the country better than the town, does not object to solitude, has an eye for trees and flowers and prefers craftsmanship to mass production. But chiefly it is valuable for its glimpses of English working-class life in the late capitalist age, of the England of totes, dog-races, football pools, Woolworth's, the pictures, Gracie Fields, Wall's ice cream, potato crisps, celanese stockings, dart-boards, pin-tables, cigarettes, cups of tea, and Saturday evenings in the four ale bar. Lord knows how much of this civilisation, founded upon foreign investments and neglected agriculture, can survive, but it was a good civilisation while it lasted, and the people who grow up in it will carry some of their gentleness and decency into the iron ages that are coming.

1. For Jack Hilton, see n. 1 to review of *Caliban Shrieks*, above. John Middleton Murry (1889–1957) founded *The (New) Adelphi* in June 1923. He was its nominal editor for fourteen years but was associated with it throughout its life (to 1955). Much of Orwell's early work was published in *The Adelphi*. Murry was, successively, a fervent disciple of D. H. Lawrence, an unorthodox Marxist, a pacifist and an advocate of life back-to-the-land. Despite his pacifism, with which Orwell disagreed, both men remained on good terms.

2. George Crabbe (1754–1832). His poetry often depicts with ironic humour the life of ordinary people, e.g., 'Our farmers round, well pleased with constant gain,/Like other farmers, flourish and complain' (*The Parish Register*)

3. From *HMS Pinafore* by Gilbert and Sullivan.

---

[648]

Review of What Do Boys and Girls Read? by A.J. Jenkinson
Life and Letters, *July 1940*

This book, compiled mostly from questionnaires directed to teachers and pupils at Secondary and Elementary Schools, is a useful sociological fragment, a sort of detailed footnote to the researches of the Mass Observers.[1]

Mr. Jenkinson's main object was to decide whether the teaching of English literature, as now practised, is of any value and has any real relationship to the development of the child. He concludes that to drive a child of fourteen through Addison's Essays[2] is useless if not positively harmful, and that the less literature is taught as an examinable 'subject' the better. But incidentally his researches have brought out a number of interesting points. One is the sharp difference between children in the Secondary Schools and those of the same age in the 'Senior' Schools (higher forms of Elementary Schools). The former have been picked out by the scholarship system and belong to a more intellectual and more slowly-maturing type. The Secondary schoolgirl of fourteen is still a child, but a child with fairly good literary taste. The Elementary schoolgirl of the same age is for most purposes an under-developed adult; she is already reading sensational erotic novelettes side by side with 'comics' of the most infantile kind. Another point is the phase of philistinism that most children seem to go through between the ages of twelve and fourteen. And another is the importance of the 'blood' (or 'penny dreadful') in the development of the child. It seems that nearly all English-teachers now recognize this. Attempts to suppress the reading of 'bloods' have ceased, and some teachers even state that they make use of them in their English lessons.

But the most striking point of all is the improvement in literacy and intelligence that is unquestionably taking place. Mr. Jenkinson, starting out with very high standards, seems rather to underrate this. He gives detailed lists of the books taken out of school libraries, and though, of course, there is an immense consumption of trash, the fact remains that the children of both sexes do voluntarily read great numbers of 'good' books in their spare time. Dickens (especially *David Copperfield*), Defoe and Stevenson are steady favourites, and Wells, Kipling, Blackmore, Tom Hughes, Conan Doyle and G. K. Chesterton all appear in the lists. Poetry is less well-represented, the favourite poems usually being patriotic battle-pieces, but Shakespeare seems to be fairly extensively read. Considering that the children under examination are aged 12–15 and belong to the poorest class in the community, these results are extremely encouraging. It also appears that nearly all children now read the newspapers, and read the news as well as the comic columns, etc. It is unfortunate that the favourite paper should in most cases be the *Daily Mail*, but a child's choice of papers is governed by that of its parents. Except for the *Herald*, no left-wing paper appears to have any footing among school-children.

Students of social change should lay by this book. It casts a lot of light on the direction in which society is moving, and, were they capable of using it, could give valuable hints to the left-wing propagandists who at present totally fail to reach the mass of the population.[3]

1. Mass Observation was described by one of its founders, Tom Harrisson, as 'the science of ourselves'. The Movement, initiated in 1937, organized detailed observation of the masses. It depended upon large numbers of amateur 'observers' in order to compile and publish accurate accounts of the state of contemporary Britain. Its first and most famous report was

May the Twelfth (1937), the day George VI was crowned king. This was republished in 1987 by Faber & Faber. It was prepared by more than two hundred observers and edited by Humphrey Jennings (1907–50), later a distinguished documentary film-maker, and Charles Madge (1912–96), poet and later professor of sociology. Observers did not hesitate to disguise themselves or even pretend to be drunk in order to make their observations unnoticed. Mass Observations Diaries were still being compiled in 1981.

2. Joseph Addison (1672–1719), poet, dramatist and essayist. He wrote a large number of essays for the *Tatler, Spectator* and *Guardian*. Collections of his essays were frequently given to schoolboys to study in the first half of the twentieth century. His eleven essays on 'The Pleasure of the Imagination' (*Spectator*, Nos. 411–21, 1712) are important for their exploration of aesthetic issues of the day

3. Also reviewed, anonymously (as was then commonplace), by Orwell in the BBC publication, *The Listener*, 8 August 1940 (see XII/664).

---

[688]

Review of Barbarians and Philistines: Democracy and the Public Schools *by* T. C. Worsley[1]
Time and Tide, *14 September 1940*

The title of this book is not intended as a denunciation. It refers to the distinction drawn by Matthew Arnold between the 'barbarian' spirit of the old landed aristocracy and the 'Philistine' spirit of the monied bourgeoisie who progressively overwhelmed them from 1830 onwards.[2] The majority of our public schools were founded in the mid-nineteenth century, and the ones that already existed were altered out of recognition at about the same date. The new class who were coming into power naturally wanted a more civilized type of school than the Rugby described by Tom Hughes, and through the efforts of Dr Arnold and other reformers they got it. But the aristocracy had by no means disappeared, they intermarried with the bourgeoisie and deeply influenced their view of life, and the new schools were modified in consequence. The 'barbarous' element persisted in the hatred of intellectuality and the worship of games, which Arnold had certainly not foreseen or intended. And the fact that the British Empire needed administrators, less adventurous and more reliable than the men who had conquered it, set the public schools to turning out the brave, stupid, fairly decent mediocrities who are still their typical products today. Indeed the system has not altered markedly since the 'eighties of the last century.

Mr Worsley, writing from the angle of a Left Wing intellectual, is naturally hostile to the public schools, but it is doubtful whether his criticisms are altogether relevant. Broadly speaking, his charge is that the public schools are 'not democratic'. This is unquestionably true. The atmosphere of nearly all these schools is deeply reactionary. Ninety-nine public-school boys out of a hundred, if they had votes, would vote Tory. But that is not the same as saying – and this is what Mr Worsley suggests – that the public schools produce types favourable to Fascism. On the contrary, one of the striking things about the British ruling class has been their complete failure to understand Fascism, either to combat it or to imitate it, and the old-fashioned Toryism that is absorbed in the public schools is partly responsible for this. Again, when he says that the public schools breed an undemocratic mentality, he appears to mean that they do not turn out boys who can accommodate themselves to a world of equal suffrage, free speech, intellectual tolerance and international co-operation. This would be a valid criticism if any such world lay ahead of us. But unfortunately that version of democracy is even more a lost cause than feudalism. What is ahead of us is not an age of reason but an age of bombing planes, and the sort of 'democrat' that Mr Worsley seems to postulate would be even worse off in it than the average public-school boy, who has at any rate not been brought up as a pacifist or a believer in the League of Nations.[3] The brutal side of public-school life, which intellectuals always deprecate, is not a bad training for the real world. The trouble is that in every other way these schools have remained in the nineteenth century, breeding-grounds of a privileged class which could not bring itself up to date without losing its self-confidence in the process.

Merely to make fun of the public schools, *more* Beachcomber,[4] would hardly be worth while. It is too easy, and besides, it is flogging a dead horse, or a dying one, for all but three or four schools will be killed financially by the present war. Mr Worsley has some fun with Newbolt's celebrated *Vitäi Lampada*[5] but he makes constructive suggestions as well. Much in the public-school system, he thinks, is well suited to boys of sixteen or under. Up to that age boys profit by an atmosphere of gang-loyalty, games-worship and homosexuality, and it is in the last two years of school that the harm is done to them. What he advocates is a system of junior universities at which the type of boy who is still teachable at sixteen can continue his education in a comparatively adult atmosphere. This war, however it ends, will leave us with big educational problems, and when the public schools have finally vanished we shall see virtues in them that are now hidden from us. But it is too early to say so, and Mr Worsley's attack on an obsolete system, if not always quite fair, will do more good than harm.

1. T.C. Worsely was also the author of the Searchlight Book, *The End of the 'Old School Tie'*, for which Orwell wrote a Foreword in May 1941: see above.

2. See his *Culture and Anarchy* (1869), ch. 3; and specifically, 'Thus we have got three distinct terms, *Barbarians, Philistines, Populace*, to denote roughly the three great classes into which our society is divided' (ed. J. Dover Wilson (1932; 1960), 105). Contrast Disraeli's 'Two Nations' in his novel, *Sybil* (1845) – see n. 3 to Foreword to *The End of the Old School Tie*, above.

3. The League of Nations was inaugurated at the Paris Peace Conference, 1919, and was a precursor to the United Nations. Although initiated by President Woodrow Wilson (1856–1924), the United States refused to join, thus vitiating much of its power.

4. 'Beachcomber' was the pseudonym for a rather jokey column in the *Daily Express*. It was started by D. B. Wyndham Lewis (1891–1969) and run from 1924 by J. B. Morton (1893–1979), a fellow Roman Catholic. It was, for Orwell, a *bête noire*.

5. Sir Henry John Newbolt (1862–1938) was a writer of much patriotic verse ('Admirals All', 'Drake's Drum') that schoolboys often had to learn by heart in the first half of the twentieth century. His 'Vitäi Lampada' (originally given incorrectly in this review as 'Lampada Vitäi') includes the famous stanza beginning 'There's a breathless hush in the Close tonight' and concludes with a schoolboy rallying the troops with the cricket captain's adjuration, 'Play up! play up! and play the game!' (formerly inscribed on a plaque outside Lord's Cricket Ground). Orwell compares this poem and John Cornford's 'Before the Storming of Huesca' in 'My Country Right or Left', reprinted in this series in *Orwell's England*.

---

[715]

'The Proletarian Writer'

'The Writer in the Witness-Box', discussion between George Orwell and Desmond Hawkins, broadcast 6 December 1940; published in The Listener, *19 December 1940*

HAWKINS:[1] I have always doubted if there is such a thing as proletarian literature – or ever could be. The first question is what people mean by it. What do *you* mean by it? You would expect it to mean literature written specifically for the proletariat, and read by them, but does it?

ORWELL: No, obviously not. In that case the most definitely proletarian literature would be some of our morning papers. But you can see by the existence of publications like *New Writing*, or the Unity Theatre,[2] for instance, that the term has a sort of meaning, though unfortunately there are several different ideas mixed up in it. What people mean by it, roughly speaking, is a literature in which the viewpoint of the working class, which is supposed to be completely different from that of the richer classes, gets a hearing. And that, of course, has got mixed up with Socialist propaganda. I don't think the people who throw this expression about mean literature written *by* proletarians. W. H. Davies[3] was a proletarian, but he would not be called a proletarian writer. Paul Potts[4] would be called a proletarian writer, but he is not a proletarian. The reason why I am doubtful of the whole conception is that I don't believe the proletariat can create an independent literature while they are not the dominant class. I believe that their literature is and must be bourgeois literature with a slightly different slant. After all, so much that is supposed to be new is simply the old standing on its head. The poems that were written about the Spanish Civil War, for instance, were simply a deflated version of the stuff that Rupert Brooke and Co. were writing in 1914.

HAWKINS: Still, I think one must admit that the cult of proletarian literature – whether the theory is right or not – has had some effect. Look at writers like James Hanley,[5] for instance, or Jack Hilton, or Jack Common.[6] They have something new to say – something at any rate that could not quite be said by anyone who had had the ordinary middle-class upbringing. Of course there was a tremendous amount of cant about proletarian literature in the years after the Slump, when Bloomsbury went all Marxist, and Communism became fashionable. But the thing had really started earlier. I should say it started just before the last war, when Ford Madox Ford, the editor of the *English Review*, met D. H. Lawrence and saw in him the portent of a new class finding expression in literature. Lawrence's *Sons and Lovers* really did break new ground. It recorded a kind of experience that simply had not got into print before. And yet it was an experience that had been shared by millions of people. The question is why it had never been recorded earlier. Why would you say there had been no books like *Sons and Lovers* before that time?

ORWELL: I think it is simply a matter of education. After all, though

Lawrence was the son of a coalminer he had had an education that was not very different from that of the middle class. He was a university graduate, remember. Before a certain date – roughly speaking, before the 'nineties, when the Education Act[7] began to take effect – very few genuine proletarians could write: that is, write with enough facility to produce a book or a story. On the other hand the professional writers knew nothing about proletarian life. One feels this even with a really radical writer like Dickens. Dickens does not write about the working class; he does not know enough about them. He is *for* the working class, but he feels himself completely different from them – far more different than the average middle-class person would feel nowadays.

HAWKINS: Then, after all, the appearance of the proletariat as a class capable of producing books means a fresh development of literature, completely new subject-matter, and a new slant on life?

ORWELL: Yes, except in so far as the experience of all classes in society tends to become more and more alike. I maintain that the class distinctions in a country like England are now so unreal that they cannot last much longer. Fifty years ago or even twenty years ago a factory worker and a small professional man, for instance, were very different kinds of creature. Nowadays they are very much alike, though they may not realise it. They see the same films and listen to the same radio programmes, and they wear very similar clothes and live in very similar houses. What used to be called a proletarian – what Marx would have meant by a proletarian – only exists now in the heavy industries and on the land. All the same, there's no doubt that it was a big step forward when the *facts* of working-class life were first got on to paper. I think it has done something to push fiction back towards realities and away from the over-civilised stuff that Galsworthy and so forth used to write. I think possibly the first book that did this was *The Ragged-Trousered Philanthropists*,[8] which has always seemed to me a wonderful book, although it is very clumsily written. It recorded things that were everyday experience but which simply had not been noticed before – just as, so it is said, no one before A.D. 1800 ever noticed that the sea was blue. And Jack London[9] was another pioneer in the same line.

HAWKINS: And how about language and technique? Cyril Connolly, you may remember, said last week that the great innovations in literature have been made in technique rather than in content. As an example, he said that there is nothing new in Joyce except his technique. But surely these revolutionary proletarians have not shown much interest in technique? Some of them seem to be little different in manner from the pious moralising lady novelists of the last century. Their revolt is entirely in content, in theme – is that so?

ORWELL: I think in the main that's true. It's a fact that written English is much more colloquial now than it was twenty years ago, and that's all to the good. But we've borrowed much more from America than from the speech of the English working class. As for technique, one of the things that strikes one about the proletarian writers, or the people who are called proletarian writers, is how conservative they are. We might make an exception of Lionel Britton's *Hunger and Love*.[10] But if you look through a volume of *New Writing* or the *Left Review* you won't find many experiments.

HAWKINS: Then we come back to this: that what is called proletarian literature stands or falls by its subject-matter. The mystique behind these writers, I suppose, is the class war, the hope of a better future, the struggle of the working class against miserable living conditions.

ORWELL: Yes, proletarian literature is mainly a literature of revolt. It can't help being so.

HAWKINS: And my quarrel with it has always been that it is too much dominated by political considerations. I believe politicians and artists do not go well together. The goal of a politician is always limited, partial, short-term, over-simplified. It has to be, to have any hope of realisation. As a principle of action, it cannot afford to consider its own imperfections and the possible virtues of its opponents. It cannot afford to dwell on the pathos and the tragedy of all human endeavour. In short, it must exclude the very things that are valuable in art. Would you agree therefore that when proletarian literature becomes literature it ceases to be proletarian – in the political sense? Or that when it becomes propaganda it ceases to be literature?

ORWELL: I think that's putting it too crudely. I have always maintained that every artist is a propagandist. I don't mean a political propagandist. If he has any honesty or talent at all he cannot be that. Most political propaganda is a matter of telling lies, not only about the facts but about your own feelings. But every artist is a propagandist in the sense that he is trying, directly or indirectly, to impose a vision of life that seems to him desirable. I think we are broadly agreed about the vision of life that proletarian literature is trying to impose. As you said just now, the mystique behind it is the class war. That is something real; at any rate, it is something that is believed in. People will die for it as well as write about it. Quite a lot of people died for it in Spain. My point about proletarian literature is that though it has been important and useful so far as it went, it isn't likely to be permanent or to be the beginning of a new age in literature. It is founded on the revolt against capitalism, and capitalism is disappearing. In a Socialist State, a lot of our left-wing writers – people like Edward Upward, Christopher Caudwell, Alec Brown, Arthur Calder-Marshall and all the rest of them[11] – who have specialised in attacking the society they live in, would have nothing to attack. Just to revert for a moment to a book I mentioned above, Lionel Britton's *Hunger and Love*. This was an outstanding book and I think in a way it is representative of proletarian literature. Well, what is it about? It is about a young proletarian who wishes he wasn't a proletarian. It simply goes on and on about the intolerable conditions of working-class life, the fact that the roof leaks and the sink smells and all the rest of it. Now, you couldn't found a literature on the fact that the sink smells. As a convention it isn't likely to last so long as the siege of Troy. And behind this book, and lots of others like it, you can see what is really the history of a proletarian writer nowadays. Through some accident – very often it is simply due to having a long period on the dole – a young man of the working class gets a chance to educate himself. Then he starts writing books, and naturally he makes use of his early experiences, his sufferings under poverty, his revolt against the existing system, and so forth. But he isn't really creating an independent literature. He writes in the bourgeois manner, in the middle-class dialect. He is simply the black sheep of the bourgeois family, using the old methods for slightly different purposes. Don't mistake me. I'm not saying that he can't be as good a writer as anyone else; but if he is, it won't be because he is a working man but because he is a talented person who has learnt to write well. So long as the bourgeoisie are the dominant class, literature must be bourgeois. But I don't believe that they will be dominant much longer, or any other class either. I believe we are passing into a classless period, and what we call proletarian literature is one of the signs of the change. But I don't deny for an instant the good that it has done – the vitalising effect of getting working-class experience and working-class values on to paper.

HAWKINS: And, of course, as a positive gain, it has left behind quite a lot of good books?

ORWELL: Oh yes, lots. Jack London's book *The Road,* Jack Hilton's *Caliban Shrieks,* Jim Phelan's prison books. George Garratt's sea stories. Private Richards' *Old-Soldier Sahib,* James Hanley's *Grey Children* – to name just a few.

HAWKINS: All this time we have said nothing about the literature that the proletariat does read – not so much the daily papers, but the weeklies, the twopennies.

ORWELL: Yes, I should say that the small weekly press is much more representative. Papers like *Home Chat* or the *Exchange and Mart,* and *Cage Birds,* for instance.

HAWKINS: And the literature that really comes out of the people themselves – we have said nothing about that. Take for instance, the camp fire ballads of the men who built the Canadian Pacific Railway; the sea shanties; negro poems like 'Stagolee';[12] and the old street broadsheets – especially the ones about executions, the sort of thing that must have inspired Kipling's 'Danny Deever'. And epitaphs, limericks, advertisement jingles – sticking simply to poetry, those are the special literature of the proletariat, aren't they?

ORWELL: Yes, and don't forget the jokes on the comic coloured postcards, especially Donald McGill's.[13] I'm particularly attached to those. And above all the songs that the soldiers made up and sang for themselves in the last war. And the Army songs for bugle calls and military marches – those are the real popular poetry of our time, like the ballads in the Middle Ages. It's a pity they are always unprintable.[14]

HAWKINS: Yes, but I'm afraid now we are drifting into folk literature, and it seems to me that we must keep the two things distinct. From what you say I imagine that this word 'proletarian' is going to be quite meaningless if you detach it from revolutionary politics.

ORWELL: Yes, the term 'proletariat' is a political term belonging solely to the industrial age.

HAWKINS: Well, I think we are completely in agreement that the theory of a separate proletarian literature just doesn't work. For all its apparent difference it comes within the framework of what you call bourgeois writing.

ORWELL: By 'bourgeois' and 'bourgeoisie' I don't mean merely the people who buy and sell things. I mean the whole dominant culture of our time.

HAWKINS: If we agree about that, we have still got to assess the contribution that these so-called proletarian writers have made. Because it *is* a contribution and it would be absurd to pass that over in disposing of the theory.

ORWELL: I think they have made two kinds of contribution. One is that they have to some extent provided new subject-matter, which has also led other writers who are not of the working class to look at things which were under their noses, but not noticed, before. The other is that they have introduced a note of what you might call crudeness and vitality. They have been a sort of voice in the gallery, preventing people from becoming too toney and too civilised.

HAWKINS: And then there's another contribution, which you yourself mentioned earlier, and that is language. T. S. Eliot stressed the importance of constantly drawing newly-minted words into the language, and in recent years it is pre-eminently from the working class that new words and phrases have come. It may be from the film or the street or through any channel, but the proletarian writer deserves credit for giving modern English much of its raciness and colour.

ORWELL: Well, of course, the question is whether it has got much colour! But the thing you can say for the typical prose of the last ten years is that it has not got many frills or unnecessary adjectives. It's plain. It is rather questionable whether the sort of prose that has developed in this way is suitable for expressing very subtle thoughts, but it is excellent for describing action, and it is a good antidote to the over-refined type of prose which used to be fashionable – very good in its way, of course, but tending to emasculate the language altogether.

HAWKINS: Well, to conclude – it looks as if the slogan of Proletarian Literature has made a nice rallying point for some work that was well worth having and it has been a focus for working-class writers, whether they were revolutionary or not, either in technique or in politics or in subject. But the phrase itself as a critical term is virtually useless.

ORWELL: It has had a certain use as a label for a rather heterogeneous literature belonging to a transition period, but I do agree with you that for there to be what could really be called a proletarian literature the proletariat would have to be the dominant class.

HAWKINS: Yes, and in assuming that it would certainly have to change its character. And that still leaves open the question we have only just touched on – how far can politics be introduced into art without spoiling the art?

1. Desmond Hawkins (1908–1999; OBE, 1963), novelist, literary critic and broadcaster, did much freelance work with the BBC's Indian Service during the war. For broadcasting convenience, parts of the discussion were spoken by a participant whether or not he had generated the ideas initially.

2. The Unity Theatre Club specialized in left-wing productions. These had included *Waiting for Lefty* by Clifford Odets; *Busmen* (1938), a 'Living Newspaper' (a form first developed in the United States), on the London bus strike of that year, initially scripted by John Allen, written in association with a taxi-driver, Herbert Hodge, and Montagu Slater, a leading left-wing writer; and Sean O'Casey's communist play, *The Star Turns Red* (1940). Its satirical pantomime, *Babes in the Wood* (1938–9), had 162 performances.

3. William Henry Davies (1871–1940), prolific poet and author of *Autobiography of a Super-Tramp* (1907). He was the son of a poor Welsh innkeeper and lived as a tramp in the USA (where he lost a leg boarding a freight train) and England. He was eventually granted a Civil List pension.

4. Paul Potts (Hugh Patrick Howard; 1911–90), Canadian poet, who became a friend of Orwell's and visited him at Barnhill, Jura (where Orwell wrote *Nineteen Eighty-Four*). His *A Poet's Testament* was published in 1940. In his *Dante Called You Beatrice* (1960) he has a chapter on Orwell, 'Don Quixote on a Bicycle' (partially reprinted in *Orwell Remembered*, 248–60), in which he recalls Orwell with affection, saying, 'The happiest years of my life were those during which I was a friend of his.'

5. James Hanley (1901–85), novelist. His first novel, *Boy* (1931), told of the death of a boy at sea and was banned. He will be best remembered for his tetralogy, *The Furys* (1934), *The Secret Journey* (1936), *Our Time is Gone* (1940) and *Winter Song* (1950), and for the sombre *Say Nothing* (1962). Orwell reviewed his *Broken Water* (1937; XI/*406*) and *Grey Children* (1937; XI/*409*; see *Orwell's England* in this series).

6. For Jack Hilton, see n. 1 to Orwell's review of his *Caliban Shrieks*, above, and for his review of *English Ways*, see above. Jack Common (1903–68) worked in a solicitor's office, a shoe shop and as a mechanic. He was co-editor of *The Adelphi*, 1935–6. Crick calls him 'one of the few authentic English proletarian writers' and describes his first meeting with Orwell (204). He and Orwell remained friends despite a certain tension between them. Orwell reviewed his *Freedom of the Streets* (1938; XI/*453*), described by Crick as 'straight-talking or garrulous polemic' (354). Common also published *Kiddar's Luck* (1951) and *The Ampersand* (1954).

7. The Elementary Education Act of 1870 provided for a universal basic education.

8. *The Ragged-Trousered Philanthropists* by Robert Tressell is reviewed below, pp. 392–4.

9. Jack London (1876–1916), American novelist whom Orwell admired greatly. His *People of the Abyss* (1903), an account of the poverty in London's East End, was influential on him. Orwell gave two broadcasts for the BBC about Jack London (see XV/*1916* and XVII/*2761*) and wrote an introduction to London's *Love of Life and Other Stories* (XVII/*2781*).

10. Lionel Britton's *Hunger and Love* was reviewed by Orwell in 1931, see above.

11. Edward Upward (1903–), a Communist author of the thirties who left the Party in the forties because it was no longer sufficiently Marxist–Leninist. His major work is his trilogy, *The Spiral Ascent* (1977), of which the first novel, *In the Thirties* (1962), is the most impressive. In 'Inside the Whale' (XII/*600*), Orwell condemns Upward for stating in 'Sketch of a Marxist Interpretation of Literature' (*The Mind in Chains*, ed. C. Day Lewis, 1937): 'Literary criticism which aims at being Marxist must . . . proclaim that no book written *at the present time* can be "good" unless it is written from a Marxist or near-Marxist viewpoint.' Christopher Caudwell (Christopher St John Sprigg; 1907–37), Marxist critic, poet and novelist. He was killed in the Spanish Civil War. Alec Brown, a novelist whom Orwell described as 'an orthodox Communist' (X/*477*). Orwell described his *Daughters of Albion* (1937) as 'a huge wad of mediocre stuff' in his review of *The Novel Today* by Philip Henderson (X/*342*) and, more succinctly, wrote in his diary for 23 March 1936, 'I have glanced at Brown's novel. It is b—s' (X/*467*; Orwell does not spell out the word in full). Brown also wrote *The Fate of the Middle Classes*, which Orwell reviewed shortly after the diary entry (X/*307*). Arthur Calder-Marshall (1908–92), prolific author of novels, short stories, and non-fiction. He worked for the British Petroleum Warfare Department in 1941 and then for the Ministry of Information Films Division, 1942–5, writing many scripts for documentary films.

12. Stagolee (or Stackolee, or Stagger Lee, some of the many variants) was a legendary giant of Negro folklore, although as Edward Cray, editor of *The Erotic Muse* (1969), notes in his introduction, it has 'passed from Negro provenience to general currency' (xxxii). He prints the music and seventeen stanzas, with a short introduction, on pages 45–7. Stagolee has made a compact with the Devil and, in exchange, has been given a magic Stetson hat. When it is stolen, Stagolee kills the thief. He is arrested and his girl – 'None of that low-down trash' – hustles for him to raise bail money. However, he is executed in the electric chair and left his girl 'Havin' the electric chair blues . . . for Stagolee'.

13. See 'The Art Of Donald McGill', n. 3, below.

14. But see *Songs and Slang of the British Soldier, 1914–1918*, edited by John Brophy and Eric Partridge (1930; revised edition, also 1930). This includes words to bugle calls, chants and sayings (often with the 'unprintable' represented by dashes).

[725]

*'The Home Guard and You: George Orwell puts a personal
question to "make-believe democrats" – and real ones'*
Tribune, 20 December 1940

Conversation with an I.L.P.[1] member:

'Are you a pacifist?'

'No, certainly not. I would fight in any war for the establishment of
Socialism, or the defence of genuine democracy.'

'You don't think the present war is a war of that kind?'

'No.'

'Don't you think it is capable of being turned into that kind of war?'

'It might, but not till the workers are in control. The workers must
have the weapons in their own hands.'

'Well, then, why not join the Home Guard? They'll give you plenty of
weapons.'

'The Home Guard! But that's just a Fascist organisation.'

'I don't think it is. But if so, why not join it and try to make it less so?'

It was no use, of course. The argument went on for a long time, but
one never gets much further with people of that kind. Living almost
entirely in a world of make-believe, they are unable to see that merely
saying 'We demand a democratic People's Army' (or words to that effect)
does not put weapons into the workers' hands.

'Unless the workers control the armed forces, the armed forces will
control the workers' is a slogan that has been bandied to and fro these
twenty years, and it is perfectly true. Yet how many of the people who
utter it have ever tried to acquire any military knowledge themselves?
How many of those who talk glibly of barricades know how to build a
barricade, let alone deal with a stoppage in a machine-gun? And in
general, what use are revolutionary slogans without either weapons or a
knowledge of how to use them?

In reality the Home Guard is far from being 'Fascist'. At this moment
it is a politically neutral organisation which is capable of developing in
several quite different ways; and which direction it takes will depend
ultimately on who belongs to it. But before emphasising this point it is

worth recalling how the Home Guard came into being, and the peculiar history it has had since.

Seven months ago, at the most desperate moment of the war, when Belgium and Holland had been over-run, France was collapsing and the general public expected England to be invaded immediately, Anthony Eden appealed over the wireless for Local Defence Volunteers. I did not hear his speech, but I am told that it was not a particularly inspiring one. He got a quarter of a million volunteers in the first twenty-four hours and another million in the subsequent months. One has only to compare these figures with, say, the number of votes obtained by 'Stop the War' candidates at by-elections, to see what the common people of this island feel about Nazism.

But there were other features about the formation of the Home Guard that were less admirable. After the applicants had sent in their names, a skeleton organisation was formed in which, so far as it could be managed, all commands down to Section Leader (corresponding to sergeant) were given to people from the middle and upper classes. When the volunteers were called up it was to find already in being a corps of officers who had been chosen by no sort of democratic process and who were largely dug-out Blimps of sixty-years-old or more.

Since then two currents of thought have been clearly visible in the Home Guard. One school (for a long while it centred round the Osterley Park training school, run by Tom Wintringham and other veterans of the Spanish Civil War) wants to turn it into a democratic guerrilla force, like a more orderly version of the early Spanish Government militias. The other school aims at producing a force as similar to the regular army as can be managed with unpaid volunteers. During the summer months, when invasion seemed imminent, the first school had the better of it, but more recently the Blimp mentality has made a big come-back; elderly colonels, who had never again expected to have a squad of men to play with, are having the time of their lives, and there is an insistence on parade-ground 'smartness' which would hardly have been tolerated at the time when the first volunteers presented themselves.

At such a moment of transition, need I point out the decisive difference that could be made if Left-wingers in appreciable numbers would join the

Home Guard? The London area, in particular, is very short of men, owing to the calling-up of the younger members, and most London districts are looking for recruits. The Labour Party missed a big opportunity by not urging its members to join the Home Guard at the beginning, but now the opportunity is repeating itself.

For the first time in British history the chance exists for Socialists to have a certain amount of influence in the armed forces of the country. The Home Guard is trembling in the balance, uncertain whether it wants to become a real People's Army or a not-very-good imitation of the pre-war Territorials. Though neither of them may formulate their thoughts very clearly, most of the rank and file want it to become the former and most of the higher command want it to become the latter. At such a time a shove in the right direction might work wonders. And in the nature of things, that shove can only come from below – by people who know what they want, and what kind of war we are fighting, actually entering the ranks and diffusing political consciousness among their comrades.

Let no one mistake me. I am not suggesting that it is the duty of Socialists to enter the Home Guard with the idea of making trouble or spreading subversive opinions. That would be both treacherous and ineffective. Any Socialist who obtains influence in the Home Guard will do it by being as good a soldier as possible, by being conspicuously obedient, efficient, and self-sacrificing. But the influence of even a few thousand men who were known to be good comrades *and* to hold Left-wing views could be enormous. At this moment there is not, even in the narrowest and most old-fashioned sense of the word, anything unpatriotic in preaching Socialism.

We are in a strange period of history in which a revolutionary has to be a patriot and a patriot has to be a revolutionary.

We know, even if the Blimps don't, that without a radical change in our social system the war cannot be won. It is our duty to pass that knowledge on to all who are potentially on our side, which means the vast majority of the nation. In the case of the Home Guard – a million men, ninety-nine hundredths of them profoundly anti-Fascist in sentiment, but politically undirected – the opportunity is so obvious that it is amazing that it has not been grasped earlier.

One ought not to underrate the importance of the Home Guard, present or future. A million men with rifles in their hands are always important. For the special purpose for which it was raised (static defence against an invader) it is already a fairly formidable army. It is better trained and slightly better armed than were most of the Spanish militias after a year of war. Unless it disintegrates or is disbanded, which is not likely, or unless Great Britain wins an easy victory in the near future, which is even less likely, it will have a big influence over political events

> **But what kind of influence? That depends upon whether it develops into a People's Army or into a kind of S.A.[2] commanded by the most reactionary section of the middle class. Both these developments are in the womb of time, and it is partly within our power to see that the right one comes out.**

We do not know what lies ahead of us. It is childish to suppose that the danger of invasion has passed. Childish, also, to suppose that there might not at some time be an attempt at treachery by an English equivalent of the Pétain Government;[3] or possibly post-war chaos in which it would be necessary to use violence to restore democracy and prevent some kind of reactionary *coup d'état*.

In any of those circumstances the existence of a popular militia, armed and politically conscious, and capable of influencing the regular forces, will be of profound importance. But we have got to see to it that the Home Guard has that character. And we shall not do so by standing outside and saying 'This is Fascism'. In the last twenty years the Left has suffered terribly for the 'Holier than thou' attitude which in practice has meant handing all real power to its opponents.

The Communists, I.L.P. and all their kind can parrot 'Arms for the Workers', but they cannot put a rifle into the workers' hands; the Home Guard can and does. The moral for any Socialist who is reasonably fit and can spare a certain amount of time (six hours a week, perhaps) is obvious. All over London and in many other parts of the country you will see the recruiting posters on the wall, telling you where to apply. But it is important to join *now*, for the particular opportunity which exists at this moment may not recur.[4]

When serving as a sergeant in the Home Guard, Orwell gave a number of lectures on such subjects as street fighting, static defence and field fortifications. His surviving notes are printed in XII/328–40. *See also his articles, 'Don't Let Colonel Blimp Ruin the Home Guard' (*XII/387–9*); Review of* Home Guard for Victory!, *by Hugh Slater (*XII/439–41*); Notes on the Home Guard (for Captain B. H. Liddell Hart⁵) (*XIII/483–6*); 'Three Years of Home Guard: Unique Symbol of Stability' (*XV/92–4*); and 'Home Guard Lessons for the Future' (*XVI/431–2*).*

1. The Independent Labour Party (ILP) was founded in 1893 by Keir Hardie (1856–1915). The Labour Party was formed by the ILP and trades unions in 1900. Orwell was a member of the ILP (see his 'Why I Join the I.L.P.', XI/457, reproduced in *Orwell and Politics* in this series) but he resigned owing to its pacifist stance when the Second World War started. At this time the ILP and Labour Party had split and they were separately represented in the House of Commons. Keir Hardie was the first Socialist to be elected a Member of Parliament (1892). He led the Labour Party in the House of Commons, 1906–15.

2. In German, S.A. stands for *Sturmabteilung*, the Nazi storm troopers. Orwell certainly regarded Blimpish officers with little favour, but this seems a little exaggerated.

3. Henri Philippe Pétain (1856–1951), successful defender of Verdun in 1916, which led to his becoming a national hero; created Marshal of France in 1918. He became Premier in 1940 and presided over the defeat and dismemberment of France by the Germans. From Vichy (hence 'the Vichy Government') he led the government of France until the end of the war. He was tried for collaboration with the Nazis and sentenced to death. President de Gaulle commuted his sentence to solitary confinement for life.

4. See David Fernbach, 'A New Look at Dad's Army', *New Statesman*, 24 October 1980. This makes plain the Labour Party's weak support for Wintringham and the Communist Party's attempt 'to sabotage the defence effort until Hitler invaded Russia in June 1941'. Henry (Tom) Wintringham (1898–1949) served in the Royal Flying Corps in World War 1, edited *Left Review*, 1934–6, went to Spain in 1936 as a war correspondent and commanded the British Battalion of the International Brigade near Madrid in 1937. He was a founder member of the Communist Party but left after serving in Spain. He was a founder, with Hugh Slater (1905–58), of Osterley Park Training School for the Home Guard.

5. Captain Sir Basil Henry Liddell Hart (1895–1970) wrote more than thirty books, including *History of the Second World War* (1970). He was military correspondent to the *Daily Telegraph*, 1925–35, and to *The Times*, 1935–9. In 1945, in a footnote to his 'Notes on Nationalism' (XVII/2668, printed in *Orwell and Politics* in this series), Orwell wrote that 'The two military critics most favoured by the intelligentsia are Captain Liddell Hart and Major-General [J.F.C.] Fuller [1876–1966], the first of whom teaches that the defence is stronger than the attack, and the second that the attack is stronger than the defence. This contradiction has not prevented both of them being accepted as authorities by the same public. The secret reason for their vogue in left-wing circles is that both of them are at odds with the War Office.'

[775]

'A Roadman's Day'
Picture Post, 15 March 1941

This little-known article was spread over four pages of Picture Post,' *dominated by ten illustrations and captions (which may not have been contributed by Orwell). It was written when Orwell was scraping a living from writing drama and film reviews and its ungainly style may have been a result of the need to fit the text to the many illustrations. The captions are not reprinted here; they can be found in* XII/451; *for the illustrations recourse must be had to* Picture Post.

Britain lives by her ocean traffic, but inland communications are also vitally important, most of all in time of war. Not enough is heard of the hundred thousands of men, employees of County Councils, who work day in, day out, in all weathers, to keep the winding roads of England in tip-top condition. Hear Mr. Ernest Short – shrewd, red-faced, twelve years in the Navy and sixteen years a roadman – on the conditions of his trade:

I work for the Mid-Surrey area. I'm what they call a ganger: that's a foreman, like. There's eight in my gang – nine, counting myself. Mostly we work a forty-eight-hour week, or forty-four hours in winter, when the days get very short. You can add on a couple of hours a day for travelling, because a chap may have to bike anything up to twelve miles to and from his work. They pay you for wet time nowadays – didn't used to, before we had the Union – but it's got to be pretty tough weather before we knock off. Of course, the work varies a lot. Asphalting's the hardest job of all. Why? Because you've got to spread the asphalt while it's still hot, and that means you've got to work quick. My gang, that's nine men, sometimes shift between forty and fifty tons of asphalt in a day. I draw three pounds ten a week, and another four bob war bonus. We're trying for an extra four bob now. Of course, that's a ganger's wage. Some of the others – the engine-driver's mate, for instance – only draw two pound twelve and six, and the bonus. A man has a job to get by on that, these days. But there's been a great improvement all the same. It's not so long back since some of the County Councils were paying as low as thirty-four bob a week, and no holidays or wet time either.

The Union's done a lot for us – worth the tanner a week, we always say. Stand it? Oh, yes, I can stand it. It's a healthy life, if you start healthy. But it's kind of tough sometimes, in winter, when you get up on a hog-back road with no cover, and a frozen surface to work on.

There is no doubt that Mr. Short underrates the toughness of his job, if anything. It is lighter labour than a coalminer's but – allowing for weather conditions – not much lighter. Most jobs on the road do not technically rank as skilled labour, but you have only to look at the accurate surfaces of the concrete by-pass roads to realise the skill and conscientiousness of the men who make them. Naturally the war has not made things any easier for them. New constructional work has almost ceased, but repair work is more urgent than ever, and it is done more and more by middle-aged men, for only a few road jobs count as reserved occupations. The volume of private traffic diminishes, but heavy Army lorries and, above all, tanks knock the road surfaces to pieces.

What are their grievances, these men who keep Britain's half-million miles of road in order? – for, of course, they have their grievances, like everyone else.

As soon as one even glances at the lives of ill-paid manual workers, one comes on the fact that the worst hardships are caused by very petty things which more comfortably situated people would never notice. Almost anyone can realise that breaking concrete in frosty weather is an unpleasant job. But not everyone would grasp that much hardship and resentment is caused by the practice of nearly all County Councils of paying their employees by cheque.

For years past an unsuccessful struggle has gone on against this practice, which is quite inexcusable and might come near to infringing the Truck Act.[2] Most County Councils pay their employees by cheque because by doing so they save the wages of a few clerks who would otherwise have to draw and count out the money. Now, men who earn two or three pounds a week do not have banking accounts, and men working a forty-eight-hour week (with perhaps another ten hours' travelling time) are not often at home during the hours when banks are open. What does the roadman do when he receives his weekly cheque? He can only get it cashed 'as a favour' by the local grocer or publican; and sometimes the

grocer or publican happens to be out of cash. Other grievances, incidental
to the war, are the wages, on which it is harder and harder to 'get by',
and the rationing, which undoubtedly hits the manual worker harder than
the sedentary. The shortage of bacon and the practical impossibility of
getting cheese are a bad blow to the roadman – as also to the farm
labourer and all others who take their dinner to work with them.

But Mr. Short spoke truly when he said that the Union had done a lot
for the roadmen. The energetic National Union of Public Employees has
jacked up the average weekly wage by a pound or thereabouts during the
past five years, and it has just scored a great victory which will have
far-reaching consequences. This is the setting up of a National Wage
Board which may make it possible to equalise Council employees' wages
all over Britain. Previously, each county followed its own devices, and
not only were wages often scandalously low – as low as thirty-one
shillings a week, in a few cases – but they varied so greatly that two men
in adjoining counties, doing identical work, might find that their wages
differed by nearly a pound a week. Under the new scheme the Government
takes over a bigger share of responsibility for the roads, including the
entire expenses of the main trunk roads.

In the fifty years since they were first established the County Councils
have not won themselves a good name as employers. They are too often
dominated by squires and retired colonels who have no conception of
how the working man lives. Struggling against this is the N.U.P.E.,
which aims at unionising every Council employee in England. Chief
difficulty is the scattered nature of the work, which makes even the
collection of delegates for a conference a costly business. As they fling the
concrete into the mixer, spread out the bomb-debris which nowadays
serves for drainage, and drive their fussy little engines to and fro, the
roadmen may be less picturesque than soldiers or airmen, but they are
hardly less necessary, and if they fell down on the job we should suffer
for it within a week. It is obvious enough that the importance of the roads
has increased in war-time and will increase even more.

In point of fact they have shown no sign of falling down on a job. It is
true that the number of men on this kind of work has fallen from the
figure of about half a million which it reached just before the war broke
out. But that is because new road works are practically non-existent. The

roadmen themselves are constant to their work and never look elsewhere
for a livelihood. They stick to their jobs in spite of the fact that machinery
has made the work harder through speeding it up prodigiously. A few
men have come in from other trades – mining for instance – but most
have been roadmen all their lives. We must see to it that they do not
become forgotten men in a war effort which will demand the last ounce
of energy from everyone, and which can be endangered by under-feeding
and the sense of grievance more seriously than by German bombs.

1. *Picture Post* was founded by Edward Hulton (1906–88; Kt., 1957) when he was only
thirty-two. It ran from October 1938 until May 1957, and within four months of its launch
had a circulation of 1,350,000. It was in a large format and presented serious issues and
entertaining features with many large illustrations. Its founder-editor was Stefan Lorant
(1901–97), a Hungarian refugee who had been imprisoned by the Nazis; Tom Hopkinson
(1905–90) was its editor in its 'great' years. Among those who were major contributors
were Anne Scott-James, Honor Balfour, Maurice Edelman, Kenneth Allsop and James
Cameron. It might be described as 'a picture magazine with a conscience' and it can be
claimed that it played a part in preparing the way for the Welfare State. Perhaps its most
memorable feature was that entitled 'Unemployed!' (21 January 1939), which, with its
statistics, family details and poignant illustrations, can be seen as an offspring of *The Road to
Wigan Pier*. In July of that year was a feature, 'Scotland and Home Rule', by Compton
Mackenzie. See the Penguin compilation, *Picture Post 1938–1950*, edited and with an
introduction by Tom Hopkinson (1970). This is fully illustrated (in reduced format).
2. The Truck Acts were passed in 1831, 1887 and 1896, and were designed to stop the
practice of paying employees' wages in goods instead of money, and of forcing employees
to use employers' shops in which goods were sold at inflated prices. For Disraeli's depiction
of this practice, see Joseph Diggs's 'tommy shop' in *Sybil*, Book III, ch. 3, and for the people's
revenge, Book VI, ch. 7; see also the review of *From One Generation to Another*, below.

[850]

'The Art of Donald McGill'
Horizon, *September 1941*[1]

Who does not know the 'comics' of the cheap stationers' windows, the
penny or twopenny coloured post cards with their endless succession of fat
women in tight bathing-dresses and their crude drawing and unbearable
colours, chiefly hedge-sparrow's egg tint and Post Office red?

This question ought to be rhetorical, but it is a curious fact that many people seem to be unaware of the existence of these things, or else to have a vague notion that they are something to be found only at the seaside, like nigger minstrels[2] or peppermint rock. Actually they are on sale everywhere – they can be bought at nearly any Woolworth's, for example – and they are evidently produced in enormous numbers, new series constantly appearing. They are not to be confused with the various other types of comic illustrated post card, such as the sentimental ones dealing with puppies and kittens or the Wendyish, sub-pornographic ones which exploit the love-affairs of children. They are a *genre* of their own, specialising in very 'low' humour, the mother-in-law, baby's nappy, policemen's boots type of joke, and distinguishable from all the other kinds by having no artistic pretensions. Some half-dozen publishing houses issue them, though the people who draw them seem not to be numerous at any one time.

I have associated them especially with the name of Donald McGill because he is not only the most prolific and by far the best of contemporary post-card artists, but also the most representative, the most perfect in the tradition. Who Donald McGill is, I do not know.[3] He is apparently a trade name, for at least one series of post cards is issued simply as 'The Donald McGill Comics', but he is also unquestionably a real person with a style of drawing which is recognisable at a glance. Anyone who examines his post cards in bulk will notice that many of them are not despicable even as drawings, but it would be mere dilettantism to pretend that they have any direct aesthetic value. A comic post card is simply an illustration to a joke, invariably a 'low' joke, and it stands or falls by its ability to raise a laugh. Beyond that it has only 'ideological' interest. McGill is a clever draughtsman with a real caricaturist's touch in the drawing of faces, but the special value of his post cards is that they are so completely typical. They represent, as it were, the norm of the comic post card. Without being in the least imitative, they are exactly what comic post cards have been any time these last forty years, and from them the meaning and purpose of the whole *genre* can be inferred.

Get hold of a dozen of these things, preferably McGill's – if you pick out from a pile the ones that seem to you funniest, you will probably find that most of them are McGill's – and spread them out on a table. What do you see?

Your first impression is of overpowering vulgarity. This is quite apart from the ever-present obscenity, and apart also from the hideousness of the colours. They have an utter lowness of mental atmosphere which comes out not only in the nature of the jokes but, even more, in the grotesque, staring, blatant quality of the drawings. The designs, like those of a child, are full of heavy lines and empty spaces, and all the figures in them, every gesture and attitude, are deliberately ugly, the faces grinning and vacuous, the women monstrously parodied, with bottoms like Hottentots. Your second impression, however, is of indefinable familiarity. What do these things remind you of? What are they so like? In the first place, of course, they remind you of the barely different post cards which you probably gazed at in your childhood. But more than this, what you are really looking at is something as traditional as Greek tragedy, a sort of sub-world of smacked bottoms and scrawny mothers-in-law which is a part of Western European consciousness. Not that the jokes, taken one by one, are necessarily stale. Not being debarred from smuttiness, comic post cards repeat themselves less often than the joke columns in reputable magazines, but their basic subject-matter, the *kind* of joke they are aiming at, never varies. A few are genuinely witty, in a Max Millerish[4] style. Examples:

'I like seeing experienced girls home.'
'But I'm not experienced!'
'You're not home yet!'

'I've been struggling for years to get a fur coat. How did you get yours?'
'I left off struggling.'

JUDGE: 'You are prevaricating, sir. Did you or did you not sleep with this woman?'
CO-RESPONDENT: 'Not a wink, my lord!'

In general, however, they are not witty but humorous, and it must be said for McGill's post cards, in particular, that the drawing is often a good deal funnier than the joke beneath it. Obviously the outstanding characteristic of comic post cards is their obscenity, and I must discuss that more fully later. But I give here a rough analysis of their habitual subject-matter, with such explanatory remarks as seem to be needed:

Sex. – More than half, perhaps three-quarters, of the jokes are sex jokes, ranging from the harmless to the all but unprintable. First favourite is probably the illegitimate baby. Typical captions: 'Could you exchange this lucky charm for a baby's feeding-bottle?' 'She didn't ask me to the christening, so I'm not going to the wedding.' Also newlyweds, old maids, nude statues and women in bathing-dresses. All of these are *ipso facto* funny, mere mention of them being enough to raise a laugh. The cuckoldry joke is very seldom exploited, and there are no references to homosexuality.

Conventions of the sex joke:
  (i) Marriage only benefits the women. Every man is plotting seduction and every woman is plotting marriage. No woman ever remains unmarried voluntarily.
  (ii) Sex-appeal vanishes at about the age of twenty-five. Well-preserved and good-looking people beyond their first youth are never represented. The amorous honeymooning couple reappear as the grim-visaged wife and shapeless, moustachioed, red-nosed husband, no intermediate stage being allowed for.

Home life. – Next to sex, the henpecked husband is the favourite joke. Typical caption: 'Did they get an X-ray of your wife's jaw at the hospital?' – 'No, they got a moving picture instead.'

Conventions:
  (i) There is no such thing as a happy marriage.
  (ii) No man ever gets the better of a woman in argument.

Drunkenness. – Both drunkenness and teetotalism are *ipso facto* funny.

Conventions:
  (i) All drunken men have optical illusions.
  (ii) Drunkenness is something peculiar to middle-aged men. Drunken youths or women are never represented.

W.C. jokes. – There is not a large number of these. Chamberpots are *ipso facto* funny, and so are public lavatories. A typical post card, captioned 'A Friend in Need', shows a man's hat blown off his head and disappearing down the steps of a ladies' lavatory.

Inter-working-class snobbery. – Much in these post cards suggests that they are aimed at the better-off working class and poorer middle class.

There are many jokes turning on malapropisms, illiteracy, dropped aitches and the rough manners of slum-dwellers. Countless post cards show draggled hags of the stage-charwoman type exchanging 'unladylike' abuse. Typical repartee: 'I wish you were a statue and I was a pigeon!' A certain number produced since the war treat evacuation from the anti-evacuee angle. There are the usual jokes about tramps, beggars and criminals, and the comic maidservant appears fairly frequently. Also the comic navvy, bargee, etc.; but there are no anti Trade-Union jokes. Broadly speaking, everyone with much over or much under £5 a week is regarded as laughable. The 'swell' is almost as automatically a figure of fun as the slum-dweller.

Stock figures. – Foreigners seldom or never appear. The chief locality joke is the Scotsman, who is almost inexhaustible. The lawyer is always a swindler, the clergyman always a nervous idiot who says the wrong thing. The 'knut' or 'masher' still appears, almost as in Edwardian days, in out-of-date-looking evening-clothes and an opera hat, or even with spats and a knobby cane. Another survival is the Suffragette, one of the big jokes of the pre-1914 period and too valuable to be relinquished. She has reappeared, unchanged in physical appearance, as the Feminist lecturer or Temperance fanatic. A feature of the last few years is the complete absence of anti-Jew post cards. The 'Jew joke', always somewhat more ill-natured than the 'Scotch joke', disappeared abruptly soon after the rise of Hitler.

Politics. – Any contemporary event, cult or activity which has comic possibilities (for example, 'free love', feminism, A.R.P.,[5] nudism) rapidly finds its way into the picture post cards, but their general atmosphere is extremely old-fashioned. The implied political outlook is a Radicalism appropriate to about the year 1900. At normal times they are not only not patriotic, but go in for a mild guying of patriotism, with jokes about 'God save the King', the Union Jack, etc. The European situation only began to reflect itself in them at some time in 1939, and first did so through the comic aspects of A.R.P. Even at this date few post cards mention the war except in A.R.P. jokes (fat woman stuck in the mouth of Anderson shelter,[6] wardens neglecting their duty while young woman undresses at window she has forgotten to black out, etc. etc.). A few express anti-Hitler sentiments of a not very vindictive kind. One, not McGill's, shows Hitler, with the usual hypertrophied backside, bending down to pick a flower. Caption: 'What would *you* do, chums?' This is about as high a flight of patriotism as any post card is likely to attain. Unlike the twopenny weekly papers, comic post cards are not the product of any great monopoly company, and eventually they are not regarded as having any importance in forming public opinion. There is no sign in them of any attempt to induce an outlook acceptable to the ruling class.

Here one comes back to the outstanding, all-important feature of comic post cards – their obscenity. It is by this that everyone remembers them, and it is also central to their purpose, though not in a way that is immediately obvious.

A recurrent, almost dominant motif in comic post cards is the woman with the stuck-out behind. In perhaps half of them, or more than half, even when the point of the joke has nothing to do with sex, the same female figure appears, a plump 'voluptuous' figure with the dress clinging to it as tightly as another skin and with breasts or buttocks grossly over-emphasised, according to which way it is turned. There can be no doubt that these pictures lift the lid off a very widespread repression, natural enough in a country whose women when young tend to be slim to the point of skimpiness. But at the same time the McGill post card – and this applies to all other post cards in this *genre* – is not intended as pornography but, a subtler thing, as a skit on pornography. The Hottentot figures of the women are caricatures of the Englishman's secret ideal, not portraits of it. When one examines McGill's post cards more closely, one notices that his brand of humour only has meaning in relation to a fairly strict moral code. Whereas in papers like *Esquire*, for instance, or *La Vie Parisienne*, the imaginary background of the jokes is always promiscuity, the utter breakdown of all standards, the background of the McGill post card is marriage. The four leading jokes are nakedness, illegitimate babies, old maids and newly married couples, none of which would seem funny in a really dissolute or even 'sophisticated' society. The post cards dealing with honeymoon couples always have the enthusiastic indecency of those village weddings where it is still considered screamingly funny to sew bells to the bridal bed. In one, for example, a young bridegroom is shown getting out of bed the morning after his wedding night. 'The first morning in our own little home, darling!' he is saying; 'I'll go and get the milk and paper and bring you up a cup of tea.' Inset is a picture of the front doorstep; on it are four newspapers and four bottles of milk. This is obscene, if you like, but it is not immoral. Its implication – and this is just the implication *Esquire* or the *New Yorker* would avoid at all costs – is that marriage is something profoundly exciting and important, the biggest event in the average human being's life. So also with jokes about nagging wives and tyrannous mothers-in-law. They do at least imply a stable society in which marriage is indissoluble and family loyalty taken for granted. And bound up with this is something I noted earlier, the fact that there are no pictures, or hardly any, of good-looking people beyond their first youth. There is the 'spooning' couple and the middle-aged, cat-and-dog couple, but nothing in between. The liaison, the illicit but more or less decorous love-affair which used to be the stock joke of French comic papers, is not a post-card subject. And this reflects, on a comic level, the working-class outlook which takes it as a matter of course that youth and adventure – almost, indeed, individual life – end with marriage. One of the few authentic class-differences, as opposed to class-distinctions, still existing in England is that the working classes age very much earlier. They do not live less long, provided that they survive their childhood, nor do they lose their physical activity earlier, but they do lose very early their youthful appearance. This fact is observable everywhere, but can be most easily verified by watching one of the higher age groups registering for military service; the middle- and upper-class members look, on average, ten years younger than the others. It is usual to attribute this to the harder lives that the working classes have to live, but it is doubtful whether any such difference now exists as would account for it. More probably the truth is that the working classes reach middle age earlier because they accept it earlier. For to look young after, say, thirty is largely a matter of wanting to do so. This generalisation is less true of the better-paid workers, especially those who live in council houses and labour-saving flats, but it is true enough even of them to point to a difference of outlook. And in this, as usual, they are more traditional, more in accord with the Christian past than the well-to-do women who try to stay young at forty by means of physical jerks, cosmetics and avoidance of child-bearing. The impulse to cling to youth at all costs, to attempt to preserve your sexual attraction, to see even in middle age a future for yourself and not merely for your children, is a thing of recent growth and has only precariously established itself. It will probably disappear again when our standard of living drops and our birth-rate rises. 'Youth's a stuff will not endure'[7] expresses the normal, traditional attitude. It is this ancient wisdom that McGill and his colleagues are reflecting, no doubt unconsciously, when they allow for no transition stage between the honeymoon couple and those glamourless figures, Mum and Dad.

I have said that at least half McGill's post cards are sex jokes, and a proportion, perhaps ten per cent., are far more obscene than anything else that is now printed in England. Newsagents are occasionally prosecuted for selling them, and there would be many more prosecutions if the broadest jokes were not invariably protected by double meanings. A single example will be enough to show how this is done. In one post card, captioned 'They didn't believe her', a young woman is demonstrating, with her hands held apart, something about two feet long to a couple of open-mouthed acquaintances. Behind her on the wall is a stuffed fish in a glass case, and beside that is a photograph of a nearly naked athlete. Obviously it is not the fish that she is referring to, but this could never be proved. Now, it is doubtful whether there is any paper in England that would print a joke of this kind, and certainly there is no paper that does so habitually. There is an immense amount of pornography of a mild sort, countless illustrated papers cashing in on women's legs, but there is no popular literature specialising in the 'vulgar', farcical aspect of sex. On the other hand, jokes exactly like McGill's are the ordinary small change of the revue and music-hall stage, and are also to be heard on the radio, at moments when the censor happens to be nodding. In England the gap between what can be said and what can be printed is rather exceptionally wide. Remarks and gestures which hardly anyone objects to on the stage would raise a public outcry if any attempt were made to reproduce them on paper. (Compare Max Miller's stage patter with his weekly column in the *Sunday Dispatch*.)[8] The comic post cards are the only existing exception to this rule, the only medium in which really 'low' humour is considered to be printable. Only in post cards and on the variety stage can the stuck-out behind, dog and lamp-post, baby's nappy type of joke be freely exploited. Remembering that, one sees what function these post cards, in their humble way, are performing.

What they are doing is to give expression to the Sancho Panza view of life, the attitude to life that Miss Rebecca West once summed up as 'extracting as much fun as possible from smacking behinds in basement kitchens'. The Don Quixote–Sancho Panza combination, which of course is simply the ancient dualism of body and soul in fiction form, recurs more frequently in the literature of the last four hundred years than can be explained by mere imitation. It comes up again and again, in endless variations, Bouvard and Pécuchet,[9] Jeeves and Wooster, Bloom and Dedalus, Holmes and Watson (the Holmes–Watson variant is an exceptionally subtle one, because the usual physical characteristics of two partners have been transposed). Evidently it corresponds to something enduring in our civilisation, not in the sense that either character is to be found in a 'pure' state in real life, but in the sense that the two principles, noble folly and base wisdom, exist side by side in nearly every human being. If you look into your own mind, which are you, Don Quixote or Sancho Panza? Almost certainly you are both. There is one part of you that wishes to be a hero or a saint, but another part of you is a little fat man who sees very clearly the advantages of staying alive with a whole skin. He is your unofficial self, the voice of the belly protesting against the soul. His tastes lie towards safety, soft beds, no work, pots of beer and women with 'voluptuous' figures. He it is who punctures your fine attitudes and urges you to look after Number One, to be unfaithful to your wife, to bilk your debts, and so on and so forth. Whether you allow yourself to be influenced by him is a different question. But it is simply a lie to say that he is not part of you, just as it is a lie to say that Don Quixote is not part of you either, though most of what is said and written consists of one lie or the other, usually the first.

But though in varying forms he is one of the stock figures of literature, in real life, especially in the way society is ordered, his point of view never gets a fair hearing. There is a constant world-wide conspiracy to pretend that he is not there, or at least that he doesn't matter. Codes of law and morals, or religious systems, never have much room in them for a humorous view of life. Whatever is funny is subversive, every joke is ultimately a custard pie, and the reason why so large a proportion of jokes centre round obscenity is simply that all societies, as the price of survival, have to insist on a fairly high standard of sexual morality. A dirty joke is not, of course, a serious attack upon morality, but it is a sort of mental rebellion, a momentary wish that things were otherwise. So also with all other jokes, which always centre round cowardice, laziness, dishonesty or some other quality which society cannot afford to encourage. Society has always to demand a little more from human beings than it will get in practice. It has to demand faultless discipline and self-sacrifice, it must expect its subjects to work hard, pay their taxes, and be faithful to their wives, it must assume that men think it glorious to die on the battlefield and women want to wear themselves out with child-bearing. The whole of what one may call official literature is founded on such assumptions. I never read the proclamations of generals before battle, the speeches of führers and prime ministers, the solidarity songs of public schools and Left-wing political parties, national anthems, Temperance tracts, papal encyclicals and sermons against gambling and contraception, without seeming to hear in the background a chorus of raspberries from all the millions of common men to whom these high sentiments make no appeal. Nevertheless the high sentiments always win in the end, leaders who offer blood, toil, tears and sweat[10] always get more out of their followers than those who offer safety and a good time. When it comes to the pinch, human beings are heroic. Women face childbed and the scrubbing brush, revolutionaries keep their mouths shut in the torture chamber, battleships go down with their guns still firing when their decks are awash. It is only that the other element in man, the lazy, cowardly, debt-bilking adulterer who is inside all of us, can never be suppressed altogether and needs a hearing occasionally.

The comic post cards are one expression of his point of view, a humble one, less important than the music halls, but still worthy of attention. In a society which is still basically Christian they naturally concentrate on sex jokes; in a totalitarian society, if they had any freedom of expression at all, they would probably concentrate on laziness or cowardice, but at any rate on the unheroic in one form or another. It will not do to condemn them on the ground that they are vulgar and ugly. That is exactly what they are meant to be. Their whole meaning and virtue is in their unredeemed lowness, not only in the sense of obscenity, but lowness of outlook in every direction whatever. The slightest hint of 'higher' influences would ruin them utterly. They stand for the worm's-eye view of life, for the music-hall world where marriage is a dirty joke or a comic disaster, where the rent is always behind and the clothes are always up the spout,[11] where the lawyer is always a crook and the Scotsman always a miser, where the newlyweds make fools of themselves on the hideous beds of seaside lodging-houses and the drunken, red-nosed husbands roll home at four in the morning to meet the linen-nightgowned wives who wait for them behind the front door, poker in hand. Their existence, the fact that people want them, is symptomatically important. Like the music halls, they are a sort of saturnalia, a harmless rebellion against virtue. They express only one tendency in the human mind, but a tendency which is always there and will find its own outlet, like water. On the whole, human beings want to be good, but not too good, and not quite all the time. For:

there is a just man that perishes in his righteousness, and there is a wicked man that prolongeth his life in his wickedness. Be not righteous over much; neither make thyself over wise; why shouldst thou destroy thyself? Be not overmuch wicked, neither be thou foolish: why shouldst thou die before thy time?[12]

In the past the mood of the comic post card could enter into the central stream of literature, and jokes barely different from McGill's could casually be uttered between the murders in Shakespeare's tragedies.[13] That is no longer possible, and a whole category of humour, integral to our literature till 1800 or thereabouts, has dwindled down to these ill-drawn post cards, leading a barely legal existence in cheap stationers' windows. The corner of the human heart that they speak for might easily manifest itself in worse forms, and I for one should be sorry to see them vanish.

1. The version given here is that reprinted in *Critical Essays*, second impression (May 1946). The first impression was published in February 1946. This contained a few verbal changes and a number of styling alterations from the version in *Horizon*. The consistency in changing word order suggests that the changes are intentional and are probably authorial. *Horizon* reproduced two of McGill's cards, but these have not been reprinted since. In one, a soap-box orator advocating temperance is concluding his oration with 'Now I have just one tract left. What shall I do with it?'. A wife is depicted with her hand over a fat man's mouth, stopping his answering, and the caption is: 'Don't say it George!' In the other, a vastly overweight man who might be a bookie, accompanied by a shapely young lady, is seen telling a hotel

receptionist, 'I and my daughter would like adjoining bedrooms!' A shortened version of the essay was published in *Strand Magazine*, August 1943 and a Polish version in *Kultura* (Paris), January 1950 (the month of Orwell's death).

2. The US edition (retitled *Dickens, Dali & Others*; 1946) changed 'nigger minstrels' to 'Negro minstrels'. The English usage, especially associated with 'minstrels', was not then repugnant. Orwell was later to demand a capital 'N' for Negro; see n.11 to 'Boys' Weeklies', above.

3. Donald McGill (1875–1962) *was* a real person (compare Orwell's doubts about the existence of a Frank Richards in his essay 'Boys' Weeklies', above). He began his career in 1904 when he sketched a drawing on the back of a postcard to cheer up a nephew in hospital. By December 1905, *Picture Postcard Magazine* 'picked him out as a designer whose cards would become "widely popular" '. One card, no. 1772, designed in 1916, sold over three million copies. It was not of the kind described by Orwell, but showed a little girl in a nightdress at which a puppy was tugging; the caption read: 'Please, Lord, excuse me a minute while I kick Fido!!' He fairly claimed that his cards were not obscene but depicted situations with honest vulgarity, and he was depressed by the way his art-form was allowed to degenerate. See Tonie and Valmai Holt, *Picture Postcards of the Golden Age* (1971), 91–3, and Arthur Calder Marshall, *Wish You Were Here* (1966). Orwell, in commenting that McGill was 'a clever draughtsman' could not have known that, from 1897 to 1907, McGill worked as an engineering draughtsman.

4. Max Miller (1895–1963) was one of the later music hall's great comics. He was billed as 'The Cheekie Chappie' and wore outrageously flamboyant suits. He would offer jokes from one of two books, one coloured blue and thus more suggestive. Much of his act depended on innuendo and, as he would reprimand audiences: 'It's all in your minds. You'll get me sent off.' He was brilliant at working an audience and at seemingly off-the-cuff (but carefully planned) ad libs. His act (with that of Tommy Trinder) underlies Archie Rice's in John Osborne's *The Entertainer* (1957).

5. Air Raid Precautions.

6. An air-raid shelter built in the gardens of individual houses, capable of holding four to six people in modest discomfort. It was designed by Sir William Paterson (1874–1956) at the instigation of Sir John Anderson (1882–1958; Viscount 1952; held various ministerial posts, 1938–45) in 1938. More than three million Andersons were built, and they are credited with saving many lives. A few have survived as makeshift garden sheds.

7. 'Youth's a stuff will not endure': Shakespeare, *Twelfth Night*, II.iii.

8. The column was banal and lacked all Miller's sparkle and innuendo.

9. *Bouvard and Pécuchet* by Gustave Flaubert (1881) recounts the adventures of two copy-clerks, one of whom, Bouvard, inherits a fortune. He and his friend, Pécuchet, seek an 'ideal retreat' in Normandy and explore intellectual, philosophical and practical worlds of experience for which they are educationally and temperamentally unfitted, with serio-comic results. The novel is unfinished. Associated with it is a *Dictionary of Received Ideas*, full of comic absurdities but with many satirical touches. For example: *Thicket*: Always 'dark and impenetrable'; *Tights*: Sexually exciting; *Toad*: Male of the frog. Its venom is very dangerous. Lives inside a stone (Penguin Books edition, translated by A. J. Krailsheimer (1976), 328).

10. Winston Churchill, in addressing the House of Commons, 13 May 1940, said: 'I would say to the House, as I said to those who have joined this Government, "I have nothing to offer but blood, toil, tears, and sweat" ' (*The Second World War* (1948–54), II, 24).

11. 'Up the spout' = in pawn.

12. Ecclesiastes 7:15–17. The Authorized Version (King James Version) differs slightly: perishes] perisheth; shouldst] shouldest (*twice*); overmuch wicked] over much wicked.

13. Orwell may have had especially in mind the Porter in *Macbeth* – his favourite of Shakespeare's plays.

---

[948]

'Rudyard Kipling'
Horizon, *February 1942*

This essay took as its starting point the publication of A Choice of Kipling's Verse, *made and introduced by T. S. Eliot (December 1941). The text reproduced below is that of* Critical Essays, *second impression, May 1946, with Orwell's emendations, and amended as indicated in the notes below. Orwell here, as elsewhere, does not always quote exactly. He doubtless relied on memory, having a good knowledge of what he was quoting. These errors are treated in two ways. The original is corrected if the error does not seem significant, however slightly, to Orwell's argument or to the impression the words might have made upon him. Thus 'Hosts' is given its initial capital, as in Kipling. If the form Orwell uses might have been important to him, it is left uncorrected; the proper reading is in the notes. Thus, Orwell substitutes 'thee' for 'you' in his quotation from W. E. Henley (see n. 15) and has 'What do they know of England' for 'What should they know of England' (see n. 25).*

The sources and page references of Kipling's poems quoted by Orwell are from Rudyard Kipling's Verse: Definitive Edition *(1940; abbreviated to* RKV*). Dates of poems are provided where given in* RKV*. Reference is also made to Kipling's posthumous autobiography,* Something of Myself *(1937), and to Charles Carrington's* Rudyard Kipling: His Life and Work *(1955; Penguin, 1970, to which edition reference is made as 'Carrington').*

Rudyard Kipling (1865–1936) was born in India and, like Orwell, returned to England for his education as a young child. Orwell's early experiences, described in 'Such, Such Were the Joys' (printed in Orwell's England *in this series), and Kipling's, reflected in 'Baa, Baa Black Sheep' (1891), have much in common. Kipling steadfastly refused the offer of the Order of Merit.*

It was a pity that Mr. Eliot should be so much on the defensive in the long essay with which he prefaces this selection of Kipling's poetry, but it was not to be avoided, because before one can even speak about Kipling one has to clear away a legend that has been created by two sets of people who have not read his works. Kipling is in the peculiar position of having been a by-word for fifty years. During five literary generations every enlightened person has despised him, and at the end of that time nine-tenths of those enlightened persons are forgotten and Kipling is in some sense still there. Mr. Eliot never satisfactorily explains this fact, because in answering the shallow and familiar charge that Kipling is a 'Fascist', he falls into the opposite error of defending him where he is not defensible. It is no use pretending that Kipling's view of life, as a whole, can be accepted or even forgiven by any civilised person. It is no use claiming, for instance, that when Kipling describes a British soldier beating a 'nigger' with a cleaning rod in order to get money out of him, he is acting merely as a reporter and does not necessarily approve what he describes. There is not the slightest sign anywhere in Kipling's work that he disapproves of that kind of conduct – on the contrary, there is a definite strain of sadism in him, over and above the brutality which a writer of that type has to have. Kipling *is* a jingo imperialist, he *is* morally insensitive and aesthetically disgusting. It is better to start by admitting that, and then to try to find out why it is that he survives while the refined people who have sniggered at him seem to wear so badly.

And yet the 'Fascist' charge has to be answered, because the first clue to any understanding of Kipling, morally or politically, is the fact that he was *not* a Fascist. He was further from being one than the most humane or the most 'progressive' person is able to be nowadays. An interesting instance of the way in which quotations are parroted to and fro without any attempt to look up their context or discover their meaning is the line from 'Recessional', 'Lesser breeds without the Law'.[1] This line is always good for a snigger in pansy-left circles. It is assumed as a matter of course that the 'lesser breeds' are 'natives' and a mental picture is called up of some pukka sahib in a pith helmet kicking a coolie. In its context the sense of the line is almost the exact opposite of this. The phrase 'lesser breeds' refers almost certainly to the Germans, and especially the pan-German writers, who are 'without the Law' in the sense of being lawless, not in the sense of being powerless. The whole poem, conventionally thought of as an orgy of boasting, is a denunciation of power politics, British as well as German. Two stanzas are worth quoting (I am quoting this as politics, not as poetry):

> If, drunk with sight of power, we loose
> Wild tongues that have not Thee in awe,
> Such boastings as the Gentiles use,
> Or lesser breeds without the Law –
> Lord God of Hosts, be with us yet,
> Lest we forget – lest we forget!
>
> For heathen heart that puts her trust
> In reeking tube and iron shard,
> All valiant dust that builds on dust,
> And guarding, calls not Thee to guard,
> For frantic boast and foolish word –
> Thy mercy on Thy People, Lord!

Much of Kipling's phraseology is taken from the Bible, and no doubt in the second stanza he had in mind the text from Psalm cxxvii: 'Except the Lord build the house, they labour in vain that build it: except the Lord keep the city, the watchman waketh but in vain.' It is not a text that makes much impression on the post-Hitler mind. No one, in our time, believes in any sanction greater than military power; no one believes that it is possible to overcome force except by greater force. There is no 'law', there is only power. I am not saying that that is a true belief, merely that it is the belief which all modern men do actually hold. Those who pretend otherwise are either intellectual cowards, or power-worshippers under a thin disguise, or have simply not caught up with the age they are living in. Kipling's outlook is pre-Fascist. He still believes that pride comes before a fall and that the gods punish *hubris*. He does not foresee the tank, the bombing plane, the radio and the secret police, or their psychological results.

But in saying this, does not one unsay what I said above about Kipling's jingoism and brutality? No, one is merely saying that the nineteenth-century imperialist outlook and the modern gangster outlook are two different things. Kipling belongs very definitely to the period 1885–1902. The Great War and its aftermath embittered him,[2] but he shows little sign of having learned anything from any event later than the Boer War. He was the prophet of British Imperialism in its expansionist phase (even more than his poems, his solitary novel, *The Light that Failed*,[3] gives you the atmosphere of that time) and also the unofficial historian of the British Army, the old mercenary army which began to change its shape in 1914. All his confidence, his bouncing vulgar vitality, sprang out of limitations which no Fascist or near-Fascist shares.

Kipling spent the later part of his life in sulking, and no doubt it was political disappointment rather than literary vanity that accounted for this. Somehow history had not gone according to plan. After the greatest victory she had ever known, Britain was a lesser world power than before, and Kipling was quite acute enough to see this. The virtue had gone out of the classes he idealised, the young were hedonistic or disaffected, the desire to paint the map red had evaporated. He could not understand what was happening, because he had never had any grasp of the economic forces underlying imperial expansion. It is notable that Kipling does not seem to realise, any more than the average soldier or colonial administrator, that an empire is primarily a money-making concern. Imperialism as he sees it is a sort of forcible evangelising. You turn a Gatling gun[4] on a mob of unarmed 'natives', and then you establish 'the Law', which includes roads, railways and a court-house. He could not foresee, therefore, that the same motives which brought the Empire into existence would end by destroying it. It was the same motive, for example, that caused the Malayan jungles to be cleared for rubber estates, and which now causes those estates to be handed over intact to the Japanese.[5] The modern totalitarians know what they are doing, and the nineteenth-century English did not know what they were doing. Both attitudes have their advantages, but Kipling was never able to move forward from one into the other. His outlook, allowing for the fact that after all he was an artist, was that of the salaried bureaucrat who despises the 'box-wallah'[6] and often lives a lifetime without realising that the 'box-wallah' calls the tune.

But because he identifies himself with the official class, he does possess one thing which 'enlightened' people seldom or never possess, and that is a sense of responsibility. The middle-class Left hate him for this quite as much as for his cruelty and vulgarity. All left-wing parties in the highly industrialised countries are at bottom a sham, because they make it their business to fight against something which they do not really wish to destroy. They have internationalist aims, and at the same time they struggle to keep up a standard of life with which those aims are incompatible. We all live by robbing Asiatic coolies, and those of us who are 'enlightened' all maintain that those coolies ought to be set free; but our standard of living, and hence our 'enlightenment', demands that the robbery shall continue. A humanitarian is always a hypocrite, and Kipling's understanding of this is perhaps the central secret of his power to create telling phrases. It would be difficult to hit off the one-eyed pacifism of the English in fewer words than in the phrase, 'making mock of uniforms that guard you while you sleep'.[7] It is true that Kipling does not understand the economic aspect of the relationship between the highbrow and the blimp. He does not see that the map is painted red chiefly in order that the coolie may be exploited. Instead of the coolie he sees the Indian Civil Servant; but even on that plane his grasp of function, of who protects whom, is very sound. He sees clearly that men can only be highly civilised while other men, inevitably less civilised, are there to guard and feed them.

How far does Kipling really identify himself with the administrators, soldiers and engineers whose praises he sings? Not so completely as is sometimes assumed. He had travelled very widely while he was still a young man, he had grown up with a brilliant mind in mainly philistine surroundings, and some streak in him that may have been partly neurotic led him to prefer the active man to the sensitive man. The nineteenth-century Anglo-Indians, to name the least sympathetic of his idols, were at any rate people who did things. It may be that all that they did was evil, but they changed the face of the earth (it is instructive to look at a map of Asia and compare the railway system of India with that of the surrounding countries), whereas they could have achieved nothing, could not have maintained themselves in power for a single week, if the normal Anglo-Indian outlook had been that of, say, E. M. Forster. Tawdry and shallow though it is, Kipling's is the only literary picture that we possess of nineteenth-century Anglo-India, and he could only make it because he was just coarse enough to be able to exist and keep his mouth shut in clubs and regimental messes. But he did not greatly resemble the people he admired. I know from several private sources that many of the Anglo-Indians who were Kipling's contemporaries did not like or approve of him. They said, no doubt truly, that he knew nothing about India, and on the other hand, he was from their point of view too much of a highbrow. While in India he tended to mix with 'the wrong' people, and because of his dark complexion he was wrongly suspected of having a streak of Asiatic blood. Much in his development is traceable to his having been born in India and having left school early. With a slightly different background he might have been a good novelist or a superlative writer of music-hall songs. But how true is it that he was a vulgar flag-waver, a sort of publicity agent for Cecil Rhodes?[8] It is true, but it is not true that he was a yes-man or a time-server. After his early days, if then, he never courted public opinion. Mr. Eliot says that what is held against him is that he expressed unpopular views in a popular style. This narrows the issue by assuming that 'unpopular' means unpopular with the intelligentsia, but it is a fact that Kipling's 'message' was one that the big public did not want, and, indeed, has never accepted. The mass of the people, in the 'nineties as now, were anti-militarist, bored by the Empire, and only unconsciously patriotic. Kipling's official admirers are and were the 'service' middle class, the people who read *Blackwood's*.[9] In the stupid early years of this century, the blimps, having at last discovered someone who could be called a poet and who was on their side, set Kipling on a pedestal, and some of his more sententious poems, such as 'If', were given almost Biblical status. But it is doubtful whether the blimps have ever read him with attention, any more than they have read the Bible. Much of what he says they could not possibly approve. Few people who have criticised England from the inside have said bitterer things about her than this gutter patriot. As a rule it is the British working class that he is attacking, but not always. That phrase about 'the flannelled fools at the wicket or the muddied oafs at the goals'[10] sticks like an arrow to this day, and it is aimed at the Eton and Harrow match as well as the Cup-Tie Final. Some of the verses he wrote about the Boer War have a curiously modern ring, so far as their subject-matter goes. 'Stellenbosch',[11] which must have been written about 1902, sums up what every intelligent infantry officer was saying in 1918, or is saying now, for that matter.

Kipling's romantic ideas about England and the Empire might not have mattered if he could have held them without having the class-prejudices which at that time went with them. If one examines his best and most representative work, his soldier poems, especially *Barrack-Room Ballads*, one notices that what more than anything else spoils them is an underlying air of patronage. Kipling idealises the army officer, especially the junior officer, and that to an idiotic extent, but the private soldier, though lovable and romantic, has to be a comic. He is always made to speak in a sort of stylised Cockney, not very broad but with all the aitches and final 'g's carefully omitted. Very often the result is as embarrassing as the humorous recitation at a church social. And this accounts for the curious fact that one can often improve Kipling's poems, make them less facetious and less blatant, by simply going through them and translating them from Cockney into standard speech. This is especially true of his refrains, which often have a truly lyrical quality. Two examples will do (one is about a funeral and the other about a wedding):

> So it's knock out your pipes and follow me!
> And it's finish up your swipes and follow me!
>   Oh, hark to the big drum calling,
>   Follow me – follow me home![12]

and again:

> Cheer for the Sergeant's wedding –
>   Give them one cheer more!
> Grey gun-horses in the lando,
>   And a rogue is married to a whore![13]

Here I have restored the aitches, etc. Kipling ought to have known better. He ought to have seen that the two closing lines of the first of these stanzas are very beautiful lines, and that ought to have overridden his impulse to make fun of a working-man's accent. In the ancient ballads the lord and the peasant speak the same language. This is impossible to Kipling, who is looking down a distorting class-perspective, and by a piece of poetic justice one of his best lines is spoiled – for 'follow me 'ome' is much uglier than 'follow me home'. But even where it makes no difference musically the facetiousness of his stage Cockney dialect is irritating. However, he is more often quoted aloud than read on the printed page, and most people instinctively make the necessary alterations when they quote him.

Can one imagine any private soldier, in the 'nineties or now, reading *Barrack-Room Ballads* and feeling that here was a writer who spoke for him? It is very hard to do so.[14] Any soldier capable of reading a book of verse would notice at once that Kipling is almost unconscious of the class war that goes on in an army as much as elsewhere. It is not only that he thinks the soldier comic, but that he thinks him patriotic, feudal, a ready admirer of his officers and proud to be a soldier of the Queen. Of course that is partly true, or battles could not be fought, but 'What have I done for thee, England, my England?' is essentially a middle-class query.[15] Almost any working man would follow it up immediately with 'What has England done for me?'. In so far as Kipling grasps this, he simply sets it down to 'the intense selfishness of the lower classes' (his own phrase).[16] When he is writing not of British but of 'loyal' Indians he carries the 'Salaam, sahib' motif to sometimes disgusting lengths. Yet it remains true that he has far more interest in the common soldier, far more anxiety that he shall get a fair deal, than most of the 'liberals' of his day or our own. He sees that the soldier is neglected, meanly underpaid and hypocritically despised by the people whose incomes he safeguards. 'I came to realise', he says in his posthumous memoirs, 'the bare horrors of the private's life, and the unnecessary torments he endured.'[17] He is accused of glorifying war, and perhaps he does so, but not in the usual manner, by pretending that war is a sort of football match. Like most people capable of writing battle poetry, Kipling had never been in battle,[18] but his vision of war is realistic. He knows that bullets hurt, that under fire everyone is terrified, that the ordinary soldier never knows what the war is about or what is happening except in his own corner of the battlefield, and that British troops, like other troops, frequently run away:

> I 'eard the knives be'ind me, but I dursn't face my man,
> Nor I don't know where I went to, 'cause I didn't stop to see,
> Till I 'eard a beggar squealin' out for quarter as 'e ran,
> An' I thought I knew the voice an' – it was me![19]

Modernise the style of this, and it might have come out of one of the debunking war books of the nineteen-twenties. Or again:

An' now the hugly bullets come peckin' through the dust,
An' no one wants to face 'em, but every beggar must;
So, like a man in irons, which isn't glad to go,
They moves 'em off by companies uncommon stiff an' slow.[20]

Compare this with:

Forward the Light Brigade!
Was there a man dismayed?
No! though the soldier knew
Someone had blundered. [21]

If anything, Kipling overdoes the horrors, for the wars of his youth were hardly wars at all by our standards. Perhaps that is due to the neurotic strain in him, the hunger for cruelty. But at least he knows that men ordered to attack impossible objectives *are* dismayed, and also that fourpence a day is not a generous pension.

How complete or truthful a picture has Kipling left us of the long-service, mercenary army of the late nineteenth century? One must say of this, as of what Kipling wrote about nineteenth-century Anglo-India, that it is not only the best but almost the only literary picture we have. He has put on record an immense amount of stuff that one could otherwise only gather from verbal tradition or from unreadable regimental histories. Perhaps his picture of army life seems fuller and more accurate than it is because any middle-class English person is likely to know enough to fill up the gaps. At any rate, reading the essay on Kipling that Mr. Edmund Wilson has just published or is just about to publish,[22] I was struck by the number of things that are boringly familiar to us and seem to be barely intelligible to an American. But from the body of Kipling's early work there does seem to emerge a vivid and not seriously misleading picture of the old pre-machine-gun army – the sweltering barracks in Gibraltar or Lucknow, the red coats, the pipeclayed belts and the pillbox hats, the beer, the fights, the floggings, hangings and crucifixions, the bugle-calls, the smell of oats and horse-piss, the bellowing sergeants with foot-long moustaches, the bloody skirmishes, invariably mismanaged, the crowded troopships, the cholera-stricken camps, the 'native' concubines, the ulti-mate death in the workhouse. It is a crude, vulgar picture, in which a patriotic music-hall turn seems to have got mixed up with one of Zola's gorier passages, but from it future generations will be able to gather some idea of what a long-term volunteer army was like. On about the same level they will be able to learn something of British India in the days when motorcars and refrigerators were unheard of. It is an error to imagine that we might have had better books on these subjects if, for example, George Moore, or Gissing, or Thomas Hardy, had had Kipling's opportunities. That is the kind of accident that cannot happen. It was not possible that nineteenth-century England should produce a book like *War and Peace*, or like Tolstoy's minor stories of army life, such as *Sebastopol* or *The Cossacks*, not because the talent was necessarily lacking but because no one with sufficient sensitiveness to write such books would ever have made the appropriate contacts. Tolstoy lived in a great military empire in which it seemed natural for almost any young man of family to spend a few years in the army, whereas the British Empire was and still is demilitarised to a degree which continental observers find almost incredible. Civilised men do not readily move away from the centres of civilisation, and in most languages there is a great dearth of what one might call colonial literature. It took a very improbable combination of circumstances to produce Kipling's gaudy tableau, in which Private Ortheris and Mrs. Hauksbee[23] pose against a background of palm trees to the sound of temple bells, and one necessary circumstance was that Kipling himself was only half civilised.

Kipling is the only English writer of our time who has added phrases to the language. The phrases and neologisms which we take over and use without remembering their origin do not always come from writers we admire. It is strange, for instance, to hear the Nazi broadcasters referring to the Russian soldiers as 'robots', thus unconsciously borrowing a word from a Czech democrat whom they would have killed if they could have laid hands on him.[24] Here are half a dozen phrases coined by Kipling which one sees quoted in leaderettes in the gutter press or overhears in saloon bars from people who have barely heard his name. It will be seen that they all have a certain characteristic in common:

> East is East, and West is West.
> The white man's burden.

What do they know of England who only England know?
The female of the species is more deadly than the male.
Somewhere East of Suez.
Paying the Dane-geld.[25]

There are various others, including some that have outlived their context by many years. The phrase 'killing Kruger with your mouth',[26] for instance, was current till very recently. It is also possible that it was Kipling who first let loose the use of the word 'Huns' for Germans;[27] at any rate he began using it as soon as the guns opened fire in 1914. But what the phrases I have listed above have in common is that they are all of them phrases which one utters semi-derisively (as it might be 'For I'm to be Queen o' the May, mother, I'm to be Queen o' the May'[28]), but which one is bound to make use of sooner or later. Nothing could exceed the contempt of the *New Statesman*, for instance, for Kipling, but how many times during the Munich period did the *New Statesman* find itself quoting that phrase about paying the Dane-geld? The fact is that Kipling, apart from his snack-bar wisdom and his gift for packing much cheap picturesqueness into a few words ('Palm and Pine' – 'East of Suez' – 'The Road to Mandalay'[29]), is generally talking about things that are of urgent interest. It does not matter, from this point of view, that thinking and decent people generally find themselves on the other side of the fence from him. 'White man's burden' instantly conjures up a real problem, even if one feels that it ought to be altered to 'black man's burden'. One may disagree to the middle of one's bones with the political attitude implied in 'The Islanders',[30] but one cannot say that it is a frivolous attitude. Kipling deals in thoughts which are both vulgar and permanent. This raises the question of his special status as a poet, or verse-writer.

Mr. Eliot describes Kipling's metrical work as 'verse' and not 'poetry', but adds that it is '*great* verse', and further qualifies this by saying that a writer can only be described as a 'great verse-writer' if there is some of his work 'of which we cannot say whether it is verse or poetry'. Apparently Kipling was a versifier who occasionally wrote poems, in which case it was a pity that Mr. Eliot did not specify these poems by name. The trouble is that whenever an aesthetic judgment on Kipling's work seems to be called for, Mr. Eliot is too much on the defensive to be able to speak plainly. What he does not say, and what I think one ought to start by saying in any discussion of Kipling, is that most of Kipling's verse is so horribly vulgar that it gives one the same sensation as one gets from watching a third-rate music-hall performer recite 'The Pigtail of Wu Fang Fu' with the purple limelight on his face, *and yet* there is much of it that is capable of giving pleasure to people who know what poetry means. At his worst, and also his most vital, in poems like 'Gunga Din' or 'Danny Deever',[31] Kipling is almost a shameful pleasure, like the taste for cheap sweets that some people secretly carry into middle life. But even with his best passages one has the same sense of being seduced by something spurious, and yet unquestionably seduced. Unless one is merely a snob and a liar it is impossible to say that no one who cares for poetry could get any pleasure out of such lines as:

> For the wind is in the palm-trees, and the temple-bells they say,
> 'Come you back, you British soldier; come you back to Mandalay!'[32]

and yet those lines are not poetry in the same sense as 'Felix Randal'[33] or 'When icicles hang by the wall' are poetry. One can, perhaps, place Kipling more satisfactorily than by juggling with the words 'verse' and 'poetry', if one describes him simply as a good bad poet. He is as a poet what Harriet Beecher Stowe was as a novelist.[34] And the mere existence of work of this kind, which is perceived by generation after generation to be vulgar and yet goes on being read, tells one something about the age we live in.

There is a great deal of good bad poetry in English, all of it, I should say, subsequent to 1790. Examples of good bad poems – I am deliberately choosing diverse ones – are 'The Bridge of Sighs', 'When all the World is Young, Lad', 'The Charge of the Light Brigade', Bret Harte's 'Dickens in Camp', 'The Burial of Sir John Moore', 'Jenny Kissed Me', 'Keith of Ravelston', 'Casabianca'.[35] All of these reek of sentimentality, and yet – not these particular poems, perhaps, but poems of this kind, are capable of giving true pleasure to people who can see clearly what is wrong with them. One could fill a fair-sized anthology with good bad poems, if it were not for the significant fact that good bad poetry is usually too well known to be worth reprinting. It is no use pretending that in an age like our own, 'good' poetry can have any genuine popularity. It is, and must be, the cult of a very few people, the least tolerated of the arts. Perhaps that statement needs a certain amount of qualification. True poetry can sometimes be acceptable to the mass of the people when it disguises itself as something else. One can see an example of this in the folk-poetry that England still possesses, certain nursery rhymes and mnemonic rhymes, for instance, and the songs that soldiers make up, including the words that go to some of the bugle-calls. But in general ours is a civilisation in which the very word 'poetry' evokes a hostile snigger or, at best, the sort of frozen disgust that most people feel when they hear the word 'God'. If you are good at playing the concertina you could probably go into the nearest public bar and get yourself an appreciative audience within five minutes. But what would be the attitude of that same audience if you suggested reading them Shakespeare's sonnets, for instance? Good bad poetry, however, can get across to the most unpromising audiences if the right atmosphere has been worked up beforehand. Some months back Churchill produced a great effect by quoting Clough's 'Endeavour'[36] in one of his broadcast speeches. I listened to this speech among people who could certainly not be accused of caring for poetry, and I am convinced that the lapse into verse impressed them and did not embarrass them. But not even Churchill could have got away with it if he had quoted anything much better than this.

In so far as a writer of verse can be popular, Kipling has been and probably still is popular. In his own lifetime some of his poems travelled far beyond the bounds of the reading public, beyond the world of school prize-days, Boy Scout singsongs, limp-leather editions, pokerwork and calendars, and out into the yet vaster world of the music halls. Nevertheless, Mr. Eliot thinks it worth while to edit him, thus confessing to a taste which others share but are not always honest enough to mention. The fact that such a thing as good bad poetry can exist is a sign of the emotional overlap between the intellectual and the ordinary man. The intellectual *is* different from the ordinary man, but only in certain sections of his personality, and even then not all the time. But what is the peculiarity of a good bad poem? A good bad poem is a graceful monument to the obvious. It records in memorable form – for verse is a mnemonic device, among other things – some emotion which very nearly every human being can share. The merit of a poem like 'When all the world is young, lad' is that, however sentimental it may be, its sentiment is 'true' sentiment in the sense that you are bound to find yourself thinking the thought it expresses sooner or later; and then, if you happen to know the poem, it will come back into your mind and seem better than it did before. Such poems are a kind of rhyming proverb, and it is a fact that definitely popular poetry is usually gnomic or sententious. One example from Kipling will do:

> White hands cling to the tightened rein,
> Slipping the spur from the booted heel,
> Tenderest voices cry 'Turn again',
> Red lips tarnish the scabbarded steel,
> High hopes faint on a warm hearth-stone –
> He travels the fastest who travels alone.[37]

There is a vulgar thought vigorously expressed. It may not be true, but at any rate it is a thought that everyone thinks. Sooner or later you will have occasion to feel that he travels the fastest who travels alone, and there the thought is, ready made and, as it were, waiting for you. So the chances are that, having once heard this line, you will remember it.

One reason for Kipling's power as a good bad poet I have already suggested – his sense of responsibility, which made it possible for him to have a world-view, even though it happened to be a false one. Although he had no direct connection with any political party, Kipling was a Conservative, a thing that does not exist nowadays. Those who now call themselves Conservatives are either Liberals, Fascists or the accomplices of Fascists. He identified himself with the ruling power and not with the opposition. In a gifted writer this seems to us strange and even disgusting, but it did have the advantage of giving Kipling a certain grip on reality. The ruling power is always faced with the question, 'In such and such circumstances, what would you *do*?', whereas the opposition is not obliged to take responsibility or make any real decisions. Where it is a permanent and pensioned opposition, as in England, the quality of its thought deteriorates accordingly. Moreover, anyone who starts out with a pessimistic, reactionary view of life tends to be justified by events, for Utopia never arrives and 'the gods of the copybook headings', as Kipling himself put it, always return.[38] Kipling sold out to the British governing class, not financially but emotionally. This warped his political judgment, for the British ruling class were not what he imagined, and it led him into abysses of folly and snobbery, but he gained a corresponding advantage from having at least tried to imagine what action and responsibility are like. It is a great thing in his favour that he is not witty, not 'daring', has no wish to *épater les bourgeois*.[39] He dealt largely in platitudes, and since we live in a world of platitudes, much of what he said sticks. Even his worst follies seem less shallow and less irritating than the 'enlightened' utterances of the same period, such as Wilde's epigrams or the collection of cracker-mottoes at the end of *Man and Superman*.

1. 'Recessional', *RKV*, 328–9, was written after Queen Victoria's Jubilee and published in *The Times*, 17 July 1897.

2. Kipling's son, John, was killed at the Battle of Loos in 1915. He was at first reported wounded and missing; it was two years before it was revealed that he had been shot through the head. Kipling had persuaded Lord Roberts to take John into the Irish Guards when he was seventeen, despite his having been rejected because of his poor sight. See Carrington, 498, 502–10. Kipling cannot but have felt a certain responsibility for his son's death, though he would, in any case, have been soon called into the services when medical standards became less demanding. John Kipling's body was only found quite recently.

3. London and Philadelphia, 1891. The US edition has a happy ending. Kipling maintained in his Preface that the English edition is 'as it was originally conceived and written'.

4. Patented by R. J. Gatling (1818–1903) in 1862, this was a crank-operated, ten-barrel antecedent of the single-barrel, automatic machine-gun. It saw service for fifty years. Orwell refers to 'the old pre-machine-gun army' later in his essay.

5. Although Singapore did not surrender until 15 February 1942, most of Malaya had already been overrun.

6. Strictly, a pedlar, but in the context applied derogatively to those working in commerce in India.

7. 'Tommy', *RKV*, 398–9.

8. Cecil Rhodes (1853–1902), South African politician and 'empire builder'. From 1890–96 he was Prime Minister of Cape Colony. He organized the defence of Kimberley in the Boer War. Rhodesia was named after him. (Northern Rhodesia is now Zambia and Southern Rhodesia Zimbabwe.) He endowed the Rhodes Scholarships at Oxford (where he had studied).

9. *Blackwood's Magazine* was founded by the Edinburgh publisher William Blackwood in 1817. In its early issues it attacked Coleridge, Keats and Shelley. The magazine survived until 1980. William Blackwood's great-great-great-grandson, Douglas (who, in the Battle of Britain, distinguished himself as a fighter pilot), was its Managing Director from 1948 to 1976, when he handed over to the journal's first non-Blackwood editor. It was popular in colonial circles, was rather staid and espoused traditional values; it was known familiarly as *The Maga*. Orwell refers to it in *Burmese Days*, II, 25.

10. 'The Islanders' (1902), *RKV*, 301–4; Orwell has 'and' for 'or' and 'goal' for 'goals'.

11. *RKV*, 477–8, which has this note: 'The more notoriously incompetent commanders used to be sent to the town of Stellenbosch, which name presently became a verb.' Kipling tells how the General 'got 'is decorations thick' and 'The Staff 'ad D.S.O.'s till we was sick/An' the soldier – 'ad the work to do again!'.

12. ' "Follow Me 'Ome" ', *RKV*, 446–7.

13. 'The Sergeant's Weddin' ', *RKV*, 447–9.

14. Contrast Sir George Younghusband (1859–1953), 'one of Kipling's archetypal subalterns', quoted from his memoirs (1917) by Michael Edwardes in 'Oh to Meet an Army Man: Kipling and the Soldiers' in *Rudyard Kipling, the Man, his Work and his World*, edited by John Gross (1972, 44): 'I myself had served for many years with soldiers, but had never heard the words or expressions that Rudyard Kipling's soldiers used. Many a time did I ask my brother Officers whether they had heard them. No, never. But sure enough, a few years after, the soldiers thought, and talked, and expressed themselves exactly like Rudyard Kipling had taught them in his stories . . . Rudyard Kipling made the modern soldier.'

15. From 'For England's Sake' by W. E. Henley (1849–1903), who has 'you' for Orwell's 'thee'. Kipling had 'the greatest admiration for Henley's verse and prose' (*Something of Myself*, 82), and it was Henley who encouraged Kipling by publishing his verse in the *Scots Observer*, beginning with 'Danny Deever', 22 February 1890.

16. 'Drums of the Fore and Aft' in *Wee Willie Winkie* (Centenary Edition, 1969, 331). It occurs in a story that is a parallel to the poem 'That Day' (see n. 18 below) and concerns an occasion when, contrary to popular belief, British soldiers fled in terror. Kipling teases out why soldiers don't follow 'their officers into battle' and why they refuse to respond to orders from 'those who had no right to give them' (330). The context of these words, which may be significant, is: 'Armed with imperfect knowledge, cursed with the rudiments of an imagination, hampered by the intense selfishness of the lower classes, and unsupported by any regimental associations . . .' It is not surprising, argues Kipling, that such soldiers falter before a native attack if surrounded only by similarly raw soldiers and if poorly and uncertainly led.

17. *Something of Myself*, 56. Kipling continued by saying he endured 'on account of Christian doctrine which lays down that "the wages of sin is death" ' (Romans 6.23).

18. He was, however, a close observer. See 11, ch. 6, 'South Africa', and his account of the (slightly ironically titled?) 'Battle of Kari Siding' (157–61).

19. 'That Day', *RKV*, 437–8.

20. 'The 'Eathen', *RKV*, 451–3. 'They' are the NCOs – 'the backbone of the Army is the Non-commissioned Man'.

21. Tennyson, 'The Charge of the Light Brigade'.

22. Orwell added a footnote when this essay was published in *Critical Essays* (1946): '1945: Published in a volume of Collected Essays, *The Wound and the Bow* (Secker & Warburg).' When *Critical Essays* was published in the USA (as *Dickens, Dali & Others*), 'or is just about to publish' was omitted. The collection was published in New York in 1941.

23. Private Stanley Ortheris appears in eighteen stories with his friends Privates Jock Learoyd and Terence Mulvaney; see, for example, 'The Madness of Private Ortheris' in *Plain Tales from the Hills* (1888). Lucy Hauksbee, a scheming woman, appears in eight stories. See for example, 'The Education of Otis Yeere' in *Under the Deodars* (1888).

24. Orwell probably refers to Karel Čapek (1890–1938), novelist and dramatist, whose play

R.U.R. (1920) features Rossum's Universal Robots and is usually thought to have introduced the word 'robot' into general use. However, according to William Harkins's *Karel Čapek* (1962), it was Karel's brother Josef (1887–1945) who introduced the word, in a story published in 1917. *OED* gives Czech *robota*, statute labour; *robotnik*, serf. Possibly 'forced labour' aptly conveys the sense.

25. 'East is East, and West is West': 'The Ballad of East and West' (1899), *RKV*, 234–8. 'The white man's burden': from the poem of that title (1899), *RKV*, 323–4, significantly subtitled 'The United States and the Philippine Islands'. The poem was first published in the United States, in *McClure's Magazine*. The appeal was initially to Americans, to take responsibility for the less fortunate, to assume a colonial burden. 'What do they know of England who only England know?': 'The English Flag' (1891), *RKV*, 221–4; Kipling has 'What should they know . . .'. 'The female of the species is more deadly than the male': from a poem of that title (1911), *RKV*, 367–9. 'Somewhere East of Suez': 'Mandalay', *RKV*, 418–20; Kipling has 'somewheres'. 'Paying the Dane-geld': 'Dane-geld', *RKV*, 712–13.

26. 'The Absent-Minded Beggar', *RKV*, 459–60. Published 31 October 1899 in the *Daily Mail*, with music composed by Sir Arthur Sullivan, it raised some £250,000 for servicemen and their dependants. Kipling refused to admit the poem to his collected verse for many years. See *Something of Myself* 150; Carrington, 363–4.

27. Orwell added the following note when this essay was published in *Critical Essays* 1945:

On the first page of his recent book, *Adam and Eve*, Mr. Middleton Murry quoted the well-known lines:

> There are nine and sixty ways
> > Of constructing tribal lays,
> > And every single one of them is right.

He attributes these lines to Thackeray. This is probably what is known as a 'Freudian error'. A civilised person would prefer not to quote Kipling – *i.e.* would prefer not to feel that it was Kipling who had expressed his thought for him.

In all editions and reprints this footnote has been keyed to 'Dane-geld', here, at the end of the second sentence below this note number. In the copy of *DD* Orwell annotated, he marked it to be keyed to 'Germans'. Page proof of the first impression of *Critical Essay* and *Dickens, Dali & Others* has 'nine and fifty', as does Murry; Kipling has 'nine and sixty' ('In the Neolithic Age', 1895, *RKV*, 342–3). The first two lines should be printed as one; each word of the last line is connected by a long dash. Murry's *Adam and Eve: An Essay towards a New and Better Society* was published in 1944.

'Hun' had been used derogatively for a German in the nineteenth century, but the immediate source of its twentieth-century usage was German: Kaiser Wilhelm II introduced the word when addressing his troops on 27 July 1900, in a much reported speech, just before they sailed for China. Kipling used the word in *The Times*, 22 December 1902: 'the Goth and the shameless Hun' (*OED*, Supplement, II, 1976).

28. Tennyson, 'The May-Queen'.

29. The line 'Dominion over palm and pine' appears in 'Recessional' (see n. 1, above); 'east of Suez' is in 'The *Mary Gloster*' (a ballad about a rich shipowner on his deathbed), published

in *The Seven Seas* (1896); 'On the road to Mandalay/Where the flyin' fishes play' is in the nostalgic ballad 'Mandalay', *Barrack-Room Ballads and Other Verses* (1892).

30. The poem concludes, in italic: '*No doubt but ye are the People . . . ! On your own heads, in your own hands, the sin and the saving lies!*' (*RKV*, 304). Kipling records in *Something of Myself* that 'after a few days' newspaper correspondence' these verses 'were dismissed as violent, untimely and untrue' (222).

31. *RKV*, 406–8 and 397–8.

32. 'Mandalay', *RKV*, 418–20 (hyphenation and punctuation corrected).

33. Orwell gave a series of four broadcasts on literary criticism in 1941 (before joining the BBC). The third, 'The Meaning of a Poem', was devoted to Gerald Manley Hopkins's 'Felix Randal' (see XII/800). Orwell told Stephen Spender on 2 April 1938 that he had said this poem to himself over and over when on sentry-go in the trenches in Spain 'to pass the time away in that bloody cold'. It was, he wrote, 'about the last occasion when I had any feeling for poetry' (XI/*434*).

34. Harriet Beecher Stowe (1811–96), ardent abolitionist, was the author of *Uncle Tom's Cabin* (1852), which brought her fame and aided the anti-slavery cause. She later started another storm, at home and in England, with her article 'The True Story of Lady Byron's Life'.

35. The authors of these poems are Thomas Hood ('The Bridge of Sighs'); Charles Kingsley ('When all the world is young, lad', from 'Young and Old'); Alfred, Lord Tennyson ('The Charge of the Light Brigade'); Charles Wolfe ('The Burial of Sir John Moore after Corunna'); Leigh Hunt ('Jenny kissed me', from 'Rondeau'); Sidney Dobell ('Keith of Ravelston', from 'A Nuptial Eve'); and Mrs Hemans ('Casabianca', which includes the line 'The boy stood on the burning deck').

36. Arthur Hugh Clough (1819–61) wrote no poem entitled 'Endeavour'. Churchill quoted the last two stanzas of his lyric 'Say not the struggle naught availeth' in his broadcast of 3 May 1941. The last line quoted was obviously directed at the United States, then providing much aid but still seven months away from becoming a combatant: 'But westward, look, the land is bright'; see Churchill, *The Second World War*, III, 209–10, and U.S.: *The Grand Alliance*, 237. It is possible that the title, 'Endeavour', comes from a reprint of the poem in an anthology.

37. When it was published in 1942 and reprinted in 1946, this verse, the second from 'The Winners' (July 1888), was conflated with the first, so the penultimate line read 'Down to Gehenna or up to the Throne'; in the first line, Orwell mistakenly had 'bridle rein'; and the punctuation at the ends of lines 2, 3 and 4 was, respectively, a semi-colon, an exclamation mark and a colon. When annotating his copy of *Dickens, Dali & Others*, he changed the text to the form found here, which is as first published, as L'Envoi, to *The Story of the Gadsbys* (Allahabad, 1889). *RKV* (530) introduced an exclamation mark at the end of line 3 and a full point at the end of line 4. Eliot did not include 'The Winners' in his selection. In the margin of the copy Orwell annotated is written, in black ink, 'Get correct version'; this is crossed out in blue ink – the colour used to make the emendation.

38. 'The Gods of the Copybook Headings' (1919), *RKV*, 793–5. In the last line Kipling has them 'with terror and slaughter return!'

39. To shake up the hidebound.

[1584]

'Answering You' [Tramps]

BBC, London, and Mutual Broadcasting System, New York; 18 October 1942

The extracts from this two-way broadcast give only Orwell's contributions, in context. There are gaps in the transcript (represented by ellipses) where, presumably, what was said could not be heard to be transcribed; there is no indication that the censor cut anything. The programme was purportedly repeated on 19 October in North American and Eastern Services, but this was not recorded in the official 'Programmes as Broadcast' details. The two Masters of Ceremonies were, in New York, Peter Donald (a radio raconteur of the US programme, 'Can you top this?') and Colin Wills (an Australian war commentator) in London. The speakers here other than Orwell were (in New York) Pat Mulhearne, editor of Hobo News, and (in London) George R. Strauss (1901–93), a Labour MP, made a Life Peer (as Baron Strauss) in 1979. He was a director of Tribune. He was expelled from the Labour Party in 1939–40 for supporting the Communist-inspired Popular Front. In 1968 he introduced the Theatres Bill for the abolition of stage censorship. This was the 65th edition of this two-way programme.

MULHEARNE: After the first war General Pershing[1] said that the American hobo was one of the best fighters under his command. He said that they can march further with a pack on their back, they could go for days without anything to eat, they could sleep in a 'bus, car or a trench – it didn't make any difference. And what is the British military opinion of this?

WILLS: Well Pat we haven't got any British military leaders right here in the studio but we've got a fellow who's a Sergeant in the Home Guard – you know what that is? This Sergeant is George Orwell. He's also a bit of a poet and he's been a bit of a hobo in the English way. So George, will you tell him how the British hobo – if you can define such a person – gets on in the war.

ORWELL: Well you've got to remember that in England the whole set-up is a bit different. There isn't that big hobo community here that you've got in America. The reason is at bottom that England's a very small country – I suppose it's only about as big as one of the smaller American States. It's very thickly populated, there's a policeman at every corner, you can't live that sort of wild, free life found in . . . novels and so on. Of course that type exists in England but they generally tend to emigrate to Australia or Canada or somewhere. You see, people going on the road – as they call it here in England – is generally a direct result of poverty, particularly unemployment. The time when that population on the road was biggest in England was during the slump years when I suppose there were not less than a hundred thousand people living that sort of life in England. But I'm afraid that by American standards you'd find it a very peaceful, harmless, dull existence. They're extremely law-abiding and their life really consists of going from one casual ward to another, eat a very unpleasant meal of bread and margarine, sleep on a hard bed and go on to the next.

MULHEARNE: But how about their fighting qualities?

ORWELL: Well it's quite true that some of the best regiments in the British Army, particularly the Highland regiments – the Scotch regiments – are recruited from very poor quarters of big towns such as Glasgow. But not, I should have thought, from what you could possibly call the derelict community.

DONALD: Well any more questions on that theme?

MULHEARNE: Question number two. The American hobo you know is basically a skilled migratory farm worker, or what you'd call an apple-knocker. Now are the English hobos skilled in farm work? And what part are the English hobos playing in this war? Are they digging up a lot of scrap over there and so forth?

WILLS: Well, George here will answer that one too I think.

ORWELL: Well I think the chief fact about them as a result of the war is that they've diminished in numbers very much – they have sort of got jobs or are in the army. There is in England that nucleus of skilled or semi-skilled migratory farm labour. For instance hop-picking, potato-picking, even sheep-shearing is done largely by that type of labour. But very largely by the gypsies. Or apart from the gypsies there's other people who are not gypsies by blood but have adopted that way of life. They travel around from farm to farm according to the seasons, working for rather low wages. They're quite an important section of the community.

But I think that's been somewhat interfered with by the war because now there's all sorts of voluntary labour, also Italian prisoners, schoolboys and whatnot.

> *Later, the American dramatist, Howard Dietz (1896–1983) asked about the democratizing effects of war. George Strauss replied at length on the theme that 'war is a great leveller', and he quoted figures given by the Chancellor of the Exchequer that, whereas in 1938 there were 7,000 people with an income of over $24,000 net per year, there were only 80 in 1942. He concluded, 'Those modifications will go on, and as the war goes on, will get more level.' Orwell was asked to respond.*

ORWELL: Well, I can't altogether agree with Strauss about the decrease in big incomes, I know that's what the statistics say but that's not what I see when on occasion I put my nose inside an expensive hotel.

WILLS: You ought to put your nose inside a British restaurant.[2]

ORWELL: . . . war, two years during which at any rate there has been a good . . . [3] in people's thoughts, is that people are still thinking in terms of what they call going back to normal after the war. For example, it's a fact that the average man working in a factory is afraid of mass unemployment after the war. I do agree with what you might call mechanical changes that have been brought about by war rationing and lack of consumption goods and so on, but that, to have any real deep effect without any structural changes, is dependent on the war going on for some years. I think we must conclude that a change is happening in England but it's happening in a very peaceful manner – sort of twilight sleep.

---

1. General John Joseph Pershing (1860–1948) was Commander-in-Chief of the American Expeditionary Force that fought in France in World War I.

2. He was referring to officially sponsored restaurants, often in temporary quarters, which provided a basic hot meal at a very modest price; see the extract from London Letter, 17 April 1944, below, for Orwell's first visit to a British Restaurant.

3. The transcript is defective here.

[1987]

'Not Enough Money: A Sketch of George Gissing'
Tribune, *2 April 1943*

All books worth reading 'date', and George Gissing,[1] perhaps the best novelist England has produced, is tied more tightly than most writers to a particular place and time. His world is the grey world of London in the 'eighties, with its gas lamps flickering in the everlasting fog, its dingy overcoats and high-crowned bowler hats, its Sunday gloom tempered by drunkenness, its unbearable 'furnished apartments', and, above all, its desperate struggle against poverty by a middle class which was poor chiefly because it had remained 'respectable'. It is hard to think of Gissing without thinking of a hansom cab. But he did much more than preserve an atmosphere which, after all, is also preserved in the early *Sherlock Holmes* stories, and it is as a novelist that he will be remembered, even more than as an interpreter of the middle-class view of life.

When I suggest that Gissing is the best novelist we have produced I am not speaking frivolously. It is obvious that Dickens, Fielding and a dozen others are superior to him in natural talent, but Gissing is a 'pure' novelist, a thing that few gifted English writers have been. Not only is he genuinely interested in character and in telling a story, but he has the great advantage of feeling no temptation to burlesque. It is a weakness of nearly all the characteristic English novelists, from Smollett to Joyce, that they want to be 'like life' and at the same time want to get a laugh as often as possible. Very few English novels exist throughout on the same plane of probability. Gissing solves this problem without apparent difficulty, and it may be that his native pessimism was a help to him. For though he certainly did not lack humour, he did lack high spirits, the instinct to play the fool which made Dickens, for instance, as unable to pass a joke as some people are to pass a pub. And it is a fact that *The Odd Women*, to name only one, is more 'like life' than the novels of bigger but less scrupulous writers.

At this date Gissing's best-known book is probably *The Private Papers of Henry Ryecroft*, written towards the end of his life when his worst struggles with poverty were over. But his real masterpieces are three novels, *The Odd Women*, *Demos* and *New Grub Street*, and his book on

Dickens. In an article of this length I cannot even summarise the plots of the novels, but their central theme can be stated in three words – 'not enough money'. Gissing is the chronicler of poverty, not working-class poverty (he despises and perhaps hates the working class) but the cruel, grinding, 'respectable' poverty of underfed clerks, downtrodden govern- esses and bankrupt tradesmen. He believed, perhaps not wrongly, that poverty causes more suffering in the middle class than in the working class. *The Odd Women*, his most perfect and also his most depressing novel, describes the fate of middle-class spinsters flung on to the world with neither money nor vocational training. *New Grub Street* records the horrors of free-lance journalism, even worse then than now. In *Demos* the money theme enters in a somewhat different way. The book is a story of the moral and intellectual corruption of a working-class Socialist who inherits a fortune. Writing as he was in the 'eighties, Gissing shows great presci- ence, and also a rather surprising knowledge of the inner workings of the Socialist movement. But the usual shabby-genteel motif is present in the person of the heroine, pushed into a hateful marriage by impoverished middle-class parents. Some of the social conditions Gissing describes have passed away, but the general atmosphere of his books is still horribly intelligible, so much so that I have sometimes thought that no professional writer should read *New Grub Street* and no spinster *The Odd Women*.

What is interesting is that with all his depth of understanding Gissing has no revolutionary tendency. He is frankly anti-Socialist and anti- democratic. Understanding better than almost anyone the horror of a money-ruled society, he has little wish to change it, because he does not believe that the change would make any real difference. The only worth-while objective, as he sees it, is to make a purely personal escape from the misery of poverty and then proceed to live a civilised, aesthetically decent life. He is not a snob, he does not wish for luxury or great wealth, he sees the spuriousness of the aristocracy and he despises beyond all other types the go-getting, self-made business man; but he does long for an untroubled, studious life, the kind of life that cannot be lived on less than about £400 a year.[2] As for the working class, he regards them as savages, and says so with great frankness. However wrong he may have been in his outlook, one cannot say of him that he spoke in ignorance, for he himself came of very poor parents, and circumstances forced him to live much of his life among the poorest of the working class. His reactions are worth studying, even at this date. Here was a humane, intelligent man, of scholarly tastes, forced into intimacy with the London poor, and his conclusion was simply this: these people are savages who must on no account be allowed political power. In a more excusable form it is the ordinary reaction of the lower-middle-class man who is near enough to the working class to be afraid of them. Above all, Gissing grasped that the middle classes suffer more from economic insecurity than the working class, and are more ready to take action against it. To ignore that fact has been one of the major blunders of the Left, and from this sensitive novelist who loved Greek tragedies, hated politics and began writing long before Hitler was born, one can learn something about the origins of Fascism.

1. George Gissing (1857–1903) was the son of a Wakefield pharmacist. He was educated at a Quaker school and won a scholarship to the precursor of Manchester University, but a brilliant academic career was cut short because he stole money in order to try to reform a prostitute, whom he later married after he had spent time in prison and in a failed attempt to make a new life in the United States. The marriage was a disaster and after his wife died he married again; that marriage failed but he could not obtain a divorce. He entered into a bigamous marriage in France four years before his death. His first novel, *Workers in the Dawn*, was published in 1880. Of the books Orwell mentions, *Demos: A Story of English Socialism* was published in 1886; *New Grub Street*, 1891; *The Odd Women*, 1893; *Charles Dickens: A Critical Study*, 1898; and *The Private Papers of Henry Ryecroft*, 1903. The last of these was not only often reprinted in England but also in the US, and it was translated many times, including into Dutch, Japanese, Swedish, Chinese and Korean.

2. If Orwell is thinking of £400 in 1943, that might be about £15,000 at the end of the twentieth century.

[2357]

'The Detective Story'
17 November 1943

Orwell's essay 'The Detective Story' (the title Orwell gives it in his 'Notes for My Literary Executor', 1949) was published in French in Fontaine, *Nos. 37–40, 1944, as 'Grandeur et décadence du roman policier anglais'. This cumulative issue of some 500 pages was devoted to English literature, 1918–40, and, though dated 1944, was published in Algiers in the spring of 1945. Because the delay in publication was so great, it is reproduced here under the date of its completion, given in Orwell's Payments Book (see 2831, XVII/466). The English original has not survived and this translation from the French text (which can be found in XV/310–15) is based on those by Dr Shirley E. Jones and Janet Percival, modified in the light of comments by Professor Patrick Parrinder, Ian Willison and the editor. For a comment on the essay, see Patrick Parrinder, 'George Orwell and the Detective Story',* Journal of Popular Culture, *6 (1972–3), reprinted in* Dimensions of Detective Fiction, *edited by L. N. Landrum and P. and R. B. Brown (Ohio, 1976). The Ministry of Information paid for Rights for this essay. It is possible that this was for a Russian translation that has not been traced. The English title, 'The Detective Story', was given by Orwell in his list of reprintable essays, (XX/229).*

It was between 1920 and 1940 that the majority of detective stories were written and read, but this is precisely the period that marks the decline of the detective story as a literary genre. Throughout these troubled and frivolous years, 'crime stories' as they were called (this title includes the detective story proper as well as the 'thriller' where the author follows the conventions of Grand Guignol[1]), were in England a universal palliative equal to tea, aspirins, cigarettes and the wireless. These works were mass-produced, and it is not without some surprise that we find that their authors include professors of political economy and Roman Catholics as well as Anglican priests. Any amateur who had never dreamed of writing a novel felt capable of tackling a detective story, which requires only the haziest knowledge of toxicology and a plausible alibi to conceal the culprit. Yet soon the detective story started to get more complicated; it demanded more ingenuity if its author were to satisfy the reader's constantly growing appetite for violence and thirst for bloodshed. The crimes became more sensational and more difficult to unravel. It is nevertheless a fact that in this multitude of later works there is hardly anything worth re-reading.

Things were not always like this. Entertaining books are not necessarily bad books. Between 1880 and 1920 we had in England three specialists in the detective novel who showed undeniably artistic qualities. Conan Doyle of course belonged to this trio, together with two writers who are not his equal, but who should not be despised: Ernest Bramah and

R. Austin Freeman.[2] The *Memoirs* and the *Adventures of Sherlock Holmes,*
Max Carrados and *The Eyes of Max Carrados* by Bramah, *The Eye of Osiris*
and *The Singing Bone* by Freeman are, together with the two or three short
stories of Edgar Allan Poe[3] which inspired them, the classics of English
detective fiction. We can find in each of these works a quality of style,
and even better an *atmosphere*, which we do not usually find in contemporary authors (Dorothy Sayers, for example, or Agatha Christie or Freeman
Wills Croft). The reasons for this are worth examining.

Even today, more than half a century after his first appearance, Sherlock
Holmes[4] remains one of the most popular characters in the English novel.
His slim, athletic build, his beaky nose, his crumpled dressing gown, the
cluttered rooms of his Baker Street flat with their alcoves and test tubes,
the violin, the tobacco in the Indian slipper, the bullet marks on the walls,
all this is part of the intellectual furniture of the Englishman who knows
his authors. Moreover the exploits of Sherlock Holmes have been translated into some twenty languages, from Norwegian to Japanese. The other
two authors I mentioned, Ernest Bramah and R. Austin Freeman, never
reached such a wide public, but both of them created unforgettable
characters. Freeman's Dr Thorndyke is the laboratory detective, the for-
ensic scientist who solves the mystery with his microscope and camera.
As for Ernest Bramah's Max Carrados, he is blind, but his blindness only
serves to sharpen his other senses, and he is all the better because of it. If
we seek to determine why we are drawn to these three authors, we are
led to a preliminary observation of a purely technical nature, one which
emphasizes the weakness of the modern detective story and of all English
short stories of the past twenty years.

We can see that the vintage detective story (from Poe to Freeman) is
much more *dense* than the modern novel. The dialogue is richer, the
digressions more frequent. If the stories of Conan Doyle or Poe had been
written yesterday, it is doubtful whether any editor would have accepted
them. They are too long for the compact magazines of today, and their
interminable opening scenes run counter to the current fad for economy.

Yet it is by accumulating details which at first seem superfluous that
Conan Doyle, like Dickens before him, gains his most striking effects. If
you set out to examine the Sherlock Holmes stories, you find that the
eccentricities and the perspicacity of a character are principally revealed

in episodes which do not form an integral part of the plot. Holmes is especially distinguished by his method of 'reasoning by deduction' which amazes the good Doctor Watson. We can see an example at the beginning of 'The Blue Carbuncle'. Holmes only has to examine a bowler hat found in the street to give a detailed – and, as subsequent events prove, exact – description of its owner. Yet the hat incident has only the vaguest connection with the main events; several episodes are preceded by six or seven pages of conversation which do not claim to be anything but digressions pure and simple. These conversations act as a vehicle to demonstrate Holmes's genius and Watson's naïvety.

Ernest Bramah and R. Austin Freeman also write with the same contempt for conciseness. It is largely thanks to their digressions that their stories are literary works and not mere 'puzzles'.

The vintage detective story is not necessarily founded on a mystery, and it is worth reading even if it does not end with a surprise or a sensational revelation. The most annoying thing about the writers of modern detective stories is their constant, almost painful effort to hide the culprit's identity – and this convention is doubly annoying because it soon palls on a reader, who eventually finds the intricacies of concealment grotesque. On the other hand, in several of Conan Doyle's stories and in Poe's famous story 'The Purloined Letter', the perpetrator of the crime is known at the outset. How will he react? How, in the end, will he be brought to justice? That is what is so intriguing. Austin Freeman sometimes has the audacity to describe the crime first in minute detail, then merely explains how the mystery was solved. In the earlier stories, the crime is not necessarily sensational or ingeniously contrived. In the modern detective story the key incident is almost always a murder (the formula hardly changes: a corpse, a dozen suspects, each with a watertight alibi); but the earlier stories often deal with petty crimes, perhaps the culprit is no more than a third-rate thief. There may even turn out to be neither culprit nor crime. Many of the mysteries investigated by Holmes fade away in the broad light of day. Bramah wrote ten or twenty stories, of which only two or three deal with a murder. The authors can indulge themselves like this because the success of their work depends, not on the unmasking of the criminal, but in the interest the reader finds in an account of the methods of detection so dear to Holmes, Thorndyke or Carrados. These characters appeal to the imagination, and the reader, if he reacts as he is meant to, transforms them into intellectual giants.

It is now possible for us to make a fundamental distinction between the two schools of detective story – the old and the new.

The earlier writers believed in their own characters. They made their detectives into exceptionally gifted individuals, demi-gods for whom they felt a boundless admiration. Against our present-day background of world wars, mass unemployment, famines, plague and totalitarianism, crime has lost much of its savour; we know far too much about its social and economic causes to look upon the ordinary detective as a benefactor of mankind. Nor is it easy for us to consider as an end in itself the mental gymnastics demanded of us by this kind of work. Sitting in the darkness that accompanies him everywhere, Poe's Dupin uses his mental faculties without ever thinking of action; because of this, he does not arouse in us quite the admiration which Poe feels for him. 'The Mystery of Marie Roget', a typical example of pure mental acrobatics, demanding from its reader the agility of a crossword-puzzle addict, could only have appeared in a more leisured age. In the Sherlock Holmes stories you catch the author taking evident pleasure in this display of virtuosity, which seems totally detached from the plot. It is the same with 'Silver Blaze', 'The Musgrave Ritual', 'The Dancing Men', or the sort of episode that allows Holmes to deduce the life-history of a passer-by from his appearance, or to astound Watson by guessing what he is thinking at that very moment. And yet the work which these detectives were striving to accomplish was obviously important for their creators. During the peaceful years at the close of the last century, Society seemed mainly composed of law-abiding people, whose security was disturbed only by the criminal. In his contemporaries' eyes, Dr Moriarty was as demoniac a figure as Hitler is today. The man who defeated Moriarty became a knight errant or a national hero. And when Conan Doyle, sending Holmes to his death at the end of *The Memoirs*,* allows Watson to echo the words of Plato's farewell to Socrates, there is no fear of his seeming ridiculous.[5]

---

* Doyle had intended to finish his Sherlock Holmes series with *The Memoirs*, but his readers protested so vehemently that he felt obliged to carry on. Letters poured in from all over the world, and some were said to threaten Doyle with violence if he did not carry on with

Among modern writers, there are only two who seem to us to believe in their detectives: G. K. Chesterton and Edgar Wallace. Yet their motives are not as disinterested as those of Doyle or Freeman. Wallace, an extraordinarily prolific and gifted writer in a morbid genre, was inspired by his own private form of sadism which there is no time to analyse here. Chesterton's hero, Father Brown, is a Catholic priest used by Chesterton as an instrument of religious propaganda. In the other detective stories, at least in those I have read, I can see either a comic side, or a rather unconvincing effort on the author's part to create an atmosphere of horror around crimes which he himself has great difficulty in finding horrific. And then, to achieve their aims, the detectives in contemporary novels rely first and foremost on luck and intuition. They are less intellectual than the heroes of Poe, Doyle, Freeman or Bramah. It is clear that for the earlier writers, Holmes, Thorndyke and many others are all the prototype of the man of science, or, rather, of omniscience, who owes everything to logic and nothing to chance. Chesterton's Father Brown possesses almost magical powers. Holmes is a nineteenth-century rationalist. In creating this character Conan Doyle faithfully reproduced his contemporaries' idea of a scientist.

In the last century the detective was always a bachelor. That must be taken as further proof of his superiority. The modern detective also has a marked taste for celibacy (a wife does rather complicate matters in a detective story), but the celibacy of Holmes and Thorndyke is of a particularly monkish kind. It is stated categorically that neither of them is interested in the opposite sex. It is felt that the wise man should not be married, just as the Saint must practise celibacy. The wise man should have a complementary character beside him – the fool. The contrast accentuates the wise man's good qualities. This role is reserved for the police chief whose problems are solved by Dupin in 'The Purloined Letter'. Jarvis, the fool who seconds Dr Thorndyke, lacks depth, but Mr Carlyle, Max Carrados's friend, is a well-rounded character. As for Watson, whose imbecility is almost chronic, he is a more lifelike character than Holmes himself. It is by design, and not accidental, that the early detectives

Holmes's adventures. So *The Memoirs* was followed by several more volumes. Yet the earlier ones are the best [Orwell's footnote].

are amateurs rather than police officers. It fell to Edgar Wallace to set the fashion for the professional Scotland Yard officer. This respect for the amateur is characteristically British. We can see in Sherlock Holmes a certain resemblance to one of his contemporaries, Raffles, the gentleman thief, the English counterpart of Arsène Lupin.[6] Yet the unofficial role of the early sleuth serves once again to reveal superior gifts. In the early Sherlock Holmes stories and in some Dr Thorndyke adventures, the police are clearly hostile to outside investigators. The professionals constantly make mistakes and do not hesitate to accuse innocent people. Holmes's analytical genius and Thorndyke's encyclopaedic knowledge only shine more brightly against the background of humdrum official routine.

In this brief study I have only been able to write at length about one group of writers and I have not discussed foreign writers or American novelists apart from Poe. Since 1920 the output of detective stories has been enormous and the war has not slowed it down, yet, for the reasons I have tried to stress, the magic wand of yesteryear has lost its power. There is more ingenuity in the modern novel, but the authors seem incapable of creating an atmosphere. First place among modern writers should probably go to the brooding Edgar Wallace, more likely to terrorize his reader than to guide him through a jungle of complex problems. Mention must be made of Agatha Christie, who handles dialogue elegantly and shows artistry in laying false trails. The much vaunted short stories of Dorothy Sayers would probably have attracted little attention if the author had not had the bright idea of making her detective the son of a Duke. As for the works of the other contemporary writers, Freeman Wills Croft, G. D. H. and Margaret Cole, Ngaio Marsh and Philip Macdonald, they have scarcely more relevance to literature than a crossword puzzle.

It is not difficult to imagine that a novel conceived as a pure intellectual exercise, like 'The Gold Bug', might appear again one day. But it is unlikely to reappear as a detective story. I have already said, and this seems to me a significant fact, that the best detective story writers could exploit small-scale crimes. It is hard to believe that the game of cops and robbers could still inspire writers of the stature of Conan Doyle, let alone Poe. The detective story as we know it belonged to the nineteenth century, above all to the end of the nineteenth century. It belonged to the London of the eighties and nineties, to that gloomy and mysterious London where men in high-domed bowler hats slipped out into the flickering light of the gaslamps, where the bells of hansom cabs jingled through perpetual fogs; it belonged to the period when English public opinion was more deeply stirred by the exploits of Jack the Ripper* than by the problems of Irish Home Rule or the Battle of Majuba.[7]

1. Grand Guignol derives from the name of an eighteenth-century French marionette, Guignol, which originated in Lyons, and which grafted local peasant humour onto a Polichinelle puppet-character. The puppet was particularly violent. It migrated to Parisian cabarets, especially at what came to be called Le Théâtre du Grand Guignol. That specialized in short plays delighting in murder, rape, ghosts, blood and violence. It crossed the Channel in 1908 but is best known in England as a description of drama and films of excess.

2. Ernest Bramah Smith (1869?–1942) published under a shortened name, dropping 'Smith'. His detective, Max Carrados, was blind. Orwell briefly reviewed *The Wallet of Kai Lung* in 1936 (X/321) and *The Secret of the League* more fully in 1940 (XII/655). Richard Austin Freeman (1862–1943) wrote many novels and short stories. The first, *The Red Thumb Mark* (1907), was written after his enforced retirement as a physician and surgeon in what is now Ghana. This established Freeman (and his pathologist-detective, John Thorndyke). His novels were characterized by their scientific accuracy.

3. Edgar Allan Poe (1809–49), poet and short-story writer. In addition to the detective stories ('tales of ratiocination') Orwell mentions ('The Mystery of Marie Roget', 1842, and 'The Purloined Letter', 1844), he also wrote 'The Murders in the Rue Morgue' (1841), in all of which his detective, C. Auguste Dupin, featured. Dupin was marked by his analytical abilities deriving from his being a poet and mathematician (as was Poe). 'The Gold Bug' combined cryptography and buried treasure and won a prize of $100 in 1843.

4. Sherlock Holmes and Dr Watson were created by Arthur Conan Doyle (1859–1930; Kt., 1902, for his books defending British policy in the Boer War). Doyle studied medicine at Edinburgh University and practised as a physician. Holmes's deductive powers were suggested by the practice of one of Doyle's teachers at Edinburgh, Dr Joseph Bell. Doyle also wrote adventure stories. Following the death of his son in Flanders in World War I (Doyle wrote *The British Campaign in Flanders*, 6 vols., 1916–19), he turned to spiritualism, about which he also wrote.

5. In the last paragraph of 'The Final Problem', at the end of *The Memoirs of Sherlock Holmes*, Watson, who is looking for Holmes, finds a 'small square of paper' held down by Holmes's cigarette case at 'the fall of Reichenbach'. The note asks Watson to 'tell Inspector Patterson that the papers which he needs to convict the gang are in a pigeon-hole, done up in a blue envelope and inscribed "Moriarty" '. Holmes continues: 'I have made every disposition of my property before leaving England, and handed it to my brother Mycroft', and asks Watson to give his greetings to Mrs Watson. Holmes says that these few lines have been written 'through the courtesy of Mr. Moriarty' before they engaged in their final struggle which, in this story, seems to end with both their deaths in the chasm below. Dr Watson's final words

* The London counterpart of Landru who was loose in the English capital at the time, and who struck terror into the whole nation [Orwell's foonote].

describing Holmes as 'him whom I shall ever regard as the best and the wisest man whom I have ever known', echo Plato's on Socrates in the *Phaedo*: 'Such was the end, Echecrates, of our friend, whom I may truly call the wisest, and justest, and best of all men whom I have ever known' (private communication from L. J. Hunt). Orwell similarly links the classical and contemporary in *Burmese Days*. Flory's complaint that the British 'build a prison and call it progress' alludes to the *Agricola* by Tacitus. The British leader at the Battle of Mons Graupius declares that those who created the Roman Empire, 'when they make a desert, call it peace', an allusion Flory fears Dr Veraswami 'would not recognise' (see *CW*, II/41).

6. A series of books by Ernest William Hornung (1866–1921) featured Raffles, an elegant, socially-acceptable, cricket-playing 'amateur cracksman'. Orwell discusses Raffles in his essay 'Raffles and Miss Blandish', reprinted below. Arsène Lupin was the hero of Maurice Leblanc's crime novels, which included *Wanton Venus* and *Man of Miracles*.

7. At the Battle of Majuba, 1881, General Pietrus Jacobus Joubert (1831–1900) routed the British forces in the First Boer War.

[2454]

Extracts from London Letter, 17 April 1944 [The coal industry]
Partisan Review, *Summer 1944*

Orwell contributed fifteen 'London Letters' to the most influential of US left-wing journals, Partisan Review, *from January 1941 to early May 1946. Clement Greenberg (1909–94), on behalf of the editors, told Orwell on 9 December 1940 what they were seeking:*

What's happening under the surface in the way of politics? Among labor groups? What is the general mood, if there is such a thing, among writers, artists and intellectuals? What transmutations have their lives and their preoccupations suffered? You can be as gossipy as you please and refer to as many personalities as you like. The more the better.

Payment was to be $2.00 per printed page – $11.00 a letter (approximately £2.75 at the then rate of exchange, perhaps £90–100 at today's values), Orwell's predecessor as contributor of these Letters was Desmond Hawkins, who, when he was no longer in a position to continue this work, suggested Orwell to the editors. (For Hawkins, see the Discussion 'Proletarian Writers,' n. 1, above.) The second paragraph from this extract (which Orwell starts with 'There isn't a great deal of political news') has been omitted.

Spring is here, a late spring after a mild winter, and there is universal expectation that 'It' (I don't have to tell you what 'It' is)[1] will begin some time next month. The streets swarm with American troops. In the expensive quarters of the town British soldiers, who are not allowed to spend their leave in London unless they have their homes there, are hardly to be seen. The air raids began to hot up about the beginning of February and there have been one or two biggish ones – nothing like 1940 but still very trying because of the deafening noise of the ack-ack.[2] On the other hand, the scenic effects are terrific. The orange-colored flares dropped by the German planes drift slowly down, making everything almost as light as day, and carmine-colored tracer shells sail up to meet them: and as the flares get lower the shadows on the window pane move slowly upwards. The food situation is as always. I am ashamed to say that only very recently I had my first meal in a British Restaurant[3] and was amazed to find that food quite good and very cheap. (These places are run by the public authorities on a non-profit basis.) Various kinds of manufactured goods are now almost unprocurable. It is almost impossible to buy a watch or clock, new or secondhand. A typewriter which before the war would have cost twelve pounds now costs at least thirty pounds secondhand, supposing that you can get hold of one at all. Cars are scarcer than ever on the roads. On the other hand the bourgeoisie are coming more and more out of their holes, as one can see by the advertisements for servants quite in the old style, e.g., this one from *The Times*: 'Countess of Shrewsbury requires experienced Head Housemaid of three.' There were several years during which one did not see advertisements of that kind. Evening dress (for men) is said to be reappearing though I haven't seen anyone wearing it yet.

. . . The big event of the last few months has been the large-scale coal strikes, which are the culmination of a long period during which coal production has been behind schedule and – coming on the eve of the Second Front – obviously indicate very serious grievances. The immediate trouble is over money, but the root cause is the unbearable conditions in the British mines, which naturally seem worse in wartime when unemployment hardly enters into the picture. I don't know a great deal about the technical side of mining, but I have been down a number of mines and I know that the conditions are such that human beings simply will not stand them except under some kind of compulsion. (I described all this years ago in a book called *The Road to Wigan Pier*.) Most of the British mines are very old, and they belong to a multitude of comparatively small owners who often haven't the capital to modernize them even if they wanted to. This means not only that they often lack up-to-date machinery, but that the 'travelling' may be almost more exhausting than the work itself. In the older mines it may be more than three miles from the shaft to the coal face (a mile would be a normal distance) and most of the way the galleries will be only four feet high or less. This means that the miner has to do the whole journey bent double, sometimes crawling on all fours for a hundred yards or so, and then on top of this do his day's work, which may have to be done kneeling down if it is a shallow seam. The exertion is so great that men who come back to work after a long go of unemployment sometimes fall by the wayside, unable even to get as far as the coal face. Added to this there are the ghastly hovels that most of the miners have to live in, built in the worst period of the Industrial Revolution, the general lack of pithead baths, the dullness of the mining towns compared with the newer towns that have sprung up round the light industries, and, of course, very poor wages. In peace time, when the dole is the alternative, people will just put up with this, but now every miner is aware that if he could only get out of the mines (which he isn't allowed to, of course) he could be earning twice the money for easy work in some hygienic factory. It has been found impossible to recruit enough miners and for some time past they have had to be conscripted. This is done by ballot, and it is an index of how mining is regarded that to be drawn as a miner (instead of, say, being put in a submarine) is looked on as a disaster. The conscripted youths, who include public-school boys, have been to the fore in the strikes. On top of all the other causes for discontent, it is said that the coal owners, while reading the miners sermons on patriotism, are doing jiggery-pokery by working uneconomic seams, saving up the good seams for after the war when the demand for coal will have dropped again.[4]

Everyone except the interested minority is aware that these conditions can't be cured without nationalization of the mines, and public opinion is entirely ready for this step. Even the left-wing Tories, though not facing up to nationalization, talk of compelling the coal-owners to amalgamate into larger units. It is, in fact, obvious that without centralizing the industry it would be impossible to raise the enormous sums needed to bring the mines up to date. But nationalization would solve the short-term problem as well, for it would give the miners something to look forward to, and in return they would certainly undertake to refrain from striking for the duration of the war. Needless to say there is no sign of any such thing happening. Instead there has been a hue and cry after the Trotskyists, who are alleged to be responsible for the strikes. Trotskyism, which not one English person in a hundred had heard of before the war, actually got the big headlines for several days. In reality the English Trotskyists only number, I believe, about five hundred, and it is unlikely they have a footing among the full-time miners, who are very suspicious of anyone outside their own community.

1. 'It' was D-Day, 6 June 1944, the invasion of Normandy to liberate France, leading to the defeat of Germany. Orwell had commented in his War-time Diary on the expectation of a Second Front being opened exactly two years earlier, 6 June 1942 (X/*1209*). Stalin was then demanding that a Second Front be opened to relieve pressure on Soviet forces. The first 'new front' was opened on 8 November 1942 in North Africa, but that was not widely regarded as *the* Second Front.

2. Anti-aircraft guns; army signallers once called the letter 'A' ack.

3. See n. 2 to 'Answering You', above.

4. 'Total British coal output dropped by 12 per cent between 1938 and 1944, while German output rose by 7.2 per cent. Even though nearly a third of German coalminers had been drafted into the forces by 1944 and replaced by foreign workers with barely more than half their productivity, German production per wage-earner per annum at 298.7 metric tons remained significantly more impressive than the 1944 British figure of 252.2 tons. In the Ruhr, and despite Allied bombing, total production dropped by only 1.18 per cent from 1938/9 to 1943/4' (Correlli Barnett, *The Audit of War*, 1986, 60–61).

[2498]

Review of From One Generation to Another by Hilda Martindale, CBE

Manchester Evening News, *29 June 1944*

To become a factory inspector does not sound a very thrilling achievement, but its unusualness depends partly on the sex of the person in question, and also on the date. Miss Hilda Martindale[1] was one of the first women factory inspectors to be appointed in this country, and afterwards held one of the highest posts in her department. Behind that rather prosaic statement there lies a story of feminine struggle stretching far back into the nineteenth century – for Miss Martindale is almost more interested in her mother's history than her own.[2]

At the beginning of her book there is a photograph of her mother in old age; a grim but handsome face, belonging obviously to a woman of character. Miss Spicer (as her maiden name was) had been born into a wealthy nonconformist family, and like her near-contemporary, Florence Nightingale, she became dissatisfied in early adult life with the idle meaningless existence that a woman of the richer classes was then expected to lead.

This dissatisfaction persisted in spite of a happy marriage and the birth of two children, and she became one of the pioneers of the women's suffrage movement. Her great aim in life was to see men and women regarded as the same kind of animal – once, when approached by a clergyman who was opening a home for fallen women, she told him that if he opened a home for fallen men she would subscribe to it – and to make it possible for girls to follow any profession that suited them instead of being tied down to a few 'ladylike' pursuits.

Among the innumerable girls to whom she gave help and advice was an eager, intelligent, overworked shop assistant of 16 named Margaret Bondfield.[3] Mrs. Martindale did not live long enough to see female suffrage become a reality, but unlike some of her fellow-workers she did not lose her faith in the Liberal party.

The Liberals, from Gladstone onwards, tended to be tepid or evasive on the subject of female emancipation, and it was out of disappointment with the behaviour of the Liberal Government that the 'militant' suffragette movement arose. It is interesting to learn that as early as the 'nineties female suffrage was opposed inside the Liberal party on the ground that if women were given votes they would vote Conservative.

Miss Hilda Martindale's official career began about 1895. Much the most interesting thing in her book is the revelation that the kind of sweating and child labour that we associate with the early days of the Industrial Revolution persisted in England till almost the beginning of the last war. At different times she was investigating conditions in the pottery trade, the textile industries, the dressmaking trade, and many others, both in England and in Ireland, and everywhere she found atrocious things happening.

In the Potteries, for instance, children as young as 12 worked long hours carrying lumps of clay weighing 60 or 70 pounds, while among adults lead poisoning was extremely common and was regarded as something unavoidable, like the weather. In Ireland the highly skilled lacemakers earned round about a penny an hour, and the Truck Act which had been passed 70 years earlier[4] was flagrantly disregarded. Lace-making was a cottage industry, and orders were farmed out to an 'agent' who in most cases was also the local shopkeeper and publican. As far as possible he paid his work people in goods instead of money, grossly overcharging for everything, and kept them permanently in debt to him.

The prosecutions which Miss Martindale instituted generally failed, because no one dared to give evidence against the 'agent'. But the worst sweating of all seems to have happened in the workshops of 'court' dressmakers in London. When some urgent order, for a wedding or something of the kind, had to be completed the sempstresses might be kept on the job for 60 or 70 hours continuously. The laws against Sunday work and child labour were a dead letter. If a factory inspector arrived unexpectedly the girls were simply bundled into an attic, or anywhere else where they would be out of sight, and the employer was able to declare that no law was being infringed.

The enormous supplies of cheap female labour that were available made it very difficult to combat these conditions. Any girl who complained against her employer knew that she would be dismissed, and Miss Martindale had to proceed chiefly on the evidence of anonymous letters.

On one occasion she received information that the girls in a certain shop were being kept at work on Sunday. When she arrived there she was assured that the girls were all at their homes, and was shown round the empty workrooms. She promptly jumped into a hansom cab and made a tour of all the girls' homes, the addresses of which she had procured beforehand.

They were, in fact, all at work, and had been hidden somewhere or other while Miss Martindale made her visit. Miss Martindale is convinced that industrial conditions have enormously improved over the last 40 years, and when one reads of her experiences – especially when one reads the pathetic ill-spelt letters she used to receive from working girls – it is impossible not to agree.

Wages, working hours, protection against accident and industrial diseases and also the treatment of children are very different from what they were 40 years ago, although there has been no basic change in the economic system. Miss Martindale thinks that the improvement, at any rate so far as women are concerned, dates from the last war, when women for the first time were employed in large numbers in industry including trades previously reserved for men, and made their first acquaintance with trade unions.

It was, incidentally, the Boer War that had first made the Government realise that the national physique was deteriorating as a result of industrial conditions, and the present war has probably worked another improvement in the status of labour.

Evidently war has its compensations since military efficiency is not compatible with underfeeding, overwork, or even illiteracy.

Parts of this book are rather slow going, but it is an informative book, and a remarkably good-tempered one. Herself a feminist and the daughter of an even more ardent feminist, Miss Martindale has none of that bitter anti-masculine feeling that feminist writers used to have. Her own career, and the self-confidence and independence of outlook that she evidently showed from the very start, bear out her claim that women are the equals of men in everything except physical strength.

1. Hilda Martindale (1875–1952), a civil servant, was born into a great Liberal-Nonconformist family, but her father and one sister died before she was born. (In fact there were three children, not two, as Orwell says; the surviving sister, Louisa, became one of the first women surgeons.) She was appointed deputy chief inspector after years of devoted work against opposition and with little support from the magistracy. She also fought for equal opportunities for women in the Civil Service. When, some years after her retirement in 1937, a woman became principal assistant secretary in charge of all general establishment work, she wrote, 'Now indeed my desire was fulfilled.' She also did much to establish the Home Office Industrial Museum (*DNB*).

2. Louisa Spicer, Hilda Martindale's mother, was the daughter of a wealthy paper manufacturer from a leading Liberal and Nonconformist family. She was William Martindale's second wife and had two children by him, Louisa and Hilda. Hilda's father died before she was

born and her mother brought up both girls with tireless energy, which she also devoted to Liberal politics, women's suffrage and nonconformism. It was she who directed Hilda towards social service (*DNB*).

3. Margaret Bondfield (1873–1953), trade union leader and first woman cabinet minister, as Minister of Labour in Ramsay MacDonald's second administration, 1929. She was the first woman Privy Councillor. She said that Hilda Martindale's mother was 'a most vivid influence in my life' (*DNB*).

4. For the Truck Acts, see n. 2 to 'A Roadman's Day', above.

[2521]

Extract from 'As I Please', 35 [Women's Twopenny Papers]
Tribune, *28 July 1944*

Although Orwell had contributed to Tribune *on a couple of dozen occasions from 8 March 1940, he contributed regularly (with some breaks in order to concentrate on other activities) from 29 November 1943 to 4 April 1947. Initially Orwell served as literary editor. One of his principal contributions was a series of personal columns, 'As I Please', of which he wrote eighty. The title had been used briefly by Raymond Postgate (1896–1971; editor of* Tribune, *1940–41, an economist and a writer on food and wine) for a short series in the journal,* Controversy, *in 1939. The use of this title was suggested to Orwell by his friend Jon Kimche (1909–94). Kimche and Orwell worked together at Booklovers' Corner in Hampstead (see X/212), he went to Spain to meet Orwell, and he became acting editor and editor of* Tribune, *1942–6. See* Remembering Orwell, *54–6, 88–9, 94–5, 139–41, 215.*

Some years ago, in the course of an article about boys' weekly papers,[1] I made some passing remarks about women's papers – I mean the twopenny ones of the type of *Peg's Paper*, often called 'love books.' This brought me, among much other correspondence, a long letter from a woman who had contributed to and worked for the *Lucky Star*, the *Golden Star*, *Peg's Paper*, *Secrets*, the *Oracle*, and a number of kindred papers. Her main point was that I had been wrong in saying that these papers aim at creating wealth fantasy. Their stories are 'in no sense Cinderella stories' and do not exploit the 'she married her boss' motif. My correspondent adds:

Unemployment is mentioned – quite frequently . . . The dole and the trade union are certainly never mentioned. The latter may be influenced by the fact that the largest publishers of these women's magazines are a non-union house. One is never allowed to criticise the system, or to show up the class struggle for what it really is, and the word Socialist is *never* mentioned – all this is perfectly true. But it might be interesting to add that class feeling is not altogether absent. The rich are often shown as mean, and as cruel and crooked money-makers. The rich and idle beau is nearly always planning marriage without a ring, and the lass is rescued by her strong, hard-working garage hand. Men with cars are generally 'bad' and men in well-cut, expensive suits are nearly always crooks. The ideal of most of these stories is *not* an income worthy of a bank manager's wife, but a life that is 'good'. A life with an upright, kind husband, however poor, with babies and a 'little cottage'. The stories are conditioned to show that the meagre life is not so bad really, as you are at least honest and happy, and that riches bring trouble and false friends. The poor are given moral values to aspire to as something within their reach.

There are many comments I could make here, but I choose to take up the point of the moral superiority of the poor being combined with the non-mention of trade unions and Socialism. There is no doubt that this is deliberate policy. In one woman's paper I actually read a story dealing with a strike in a coal-mine, and even in that connection trade unionism was not mentioned. When the U.S.S.R. entered the war one of these papers promptly cashed in with a serial entitled *Her Soviet Lover*, but we may be sure that Marxism did not enter into it very largely.

The fact is that this business about the moral superiority of the poor is one of the deadliest forms of escapism the ruling class have evolved. You may be downtrodden and swindled, but in the eyes of God you are superior to your oppressors, and by means of films and magazines you can enjoy a fantasy existence in which you constantly triumph over the people who defeat you in real life. In any form of art designed to appeal to large numbers of people, it is an almost unheard of thing for a rich man to get the better of a poor man. The rich man is usually 'bad', and his machinations are invariably frustrated. 'Good poor man defeats bad rich man' is an accepted formula, whereas if it were the other way about we should feel that there was something very wrong somewhere. This is as noticeable in films as in the cheap magazines, and it was perhaps most noticeable of all in the old silent films, which travelled from country to country and had to appeal to a very varied audience. The vast majority of the people who will see a film are poor, and so it is politic to make a poor man the hero. Film magnates, Press lords and the like amass quite a lot of their wealth by pointing out that wealth is wicked.

The formula 'good poor man defeats bad rich man' is simply a subtler version of 'pie in the sky'. It is a sublimation of the class struggle. So long as you can dream of yourself as a 'strong, hard-working garage hand' giving some moneyed crook a sock on the jaw, the *real* facts can be forgotten. That is a cleverer dodge than wealth fantasy. But, curiously enough, reality does enter into these women's magazines, not through the stories but through the correspondence columns, especially in those papers that give free medical advice. Here you can read harrowing tales of 'bad legs' and hemorrhoids, written by middle-aged women who give themselves such pseudonyms as 'A Sufferer', 'Mother of Nine', and 'Always Constipated'. To compare these letters with the love stories that lie cheek by jowl with them is to see how vast a part mere day-dreaming plays in modern life.

1. See 'Boys' Weeklies', above, especially p. 265 for the letter from Denise Ruthers.

[2532]

Review of Branch Street *by Marie Paneth*[1]
Observer, *13 August 1944*

A valuable piece of sociological work has been done by Mrs. Marie Paneth, the Austrian authoress, whose book, *Branch Street*, recently published by Allen and Unwin, brought to light some rather surprising facts about the slum conditions still existing here and there in the heart of London.

For nearly two years Mrs. Paneth has been working at a children's play centre in a street which she chooses to conceal under the name of Branch Street. Though not far from the centre of London it happens to be a 'bad' quarter, and it is quite clear from her descriptions that when she first went there the children were little better than savages. They did, indeed, have homes of sorts, but in behaviour they resembled the troops of 'wild children' who were a by-product of the Russian civil war. They were not only dirty, ragged, undernourished and unbelievably obscene in language and corrupt in outlook, but they were all thieves, and as intractable as wild animals.

A few of the girls were comparatively approachable, but the boys simply smashed up the play centre over and over again, sometimes breaking in at night to do the job more thoroughly, and at times it was even dangerous for a grown-up to venture among them single-handed.

It took a long time for this gentle, grey-haired lady, with her marked foreign accent, to win the children's confidence. The principle she went on was never to oppose them forcibly if it could possibly be avoided, and never to let them think that they could shock her. In the end this seems to have worked, though not without some very disagreeable experiences. Mrs. Paneth believes that children of this kind, who have had no proper home life and regard grown-ups as enemies, are best treated on the 'libertarian' principles evolved by Homer Lane, Mr. A. S. Neill,[2] and others.

Though not a professional psychologist, Mrs. Paneth is the wife of a doctor, and has done work of this kind before. During the last war she worked in a children's hospital in Vienna and later in a children's play centre in Berlin. She describes the *Branch Street* children as much the worst she has encountered in any country. But, speaking as a foreign observer, she finds that nearly all English children have certain redeeming traits: she instances the devotion which even the worst child will show in looking after a younger brother or sister.

It is also interesting to learn that these semi-savage children, who see nothing wrong in stealing and flee at the very sight of a policeman, are all deeply patriotic and keen admirers of Mr. Churchill.

It is clear from Mrs. Paneth's account that *Branch Street* is simply a forgotten corner of the nineteenth century existing in the middle of a comparatively prosperous area. She does not believe that the conditions in which the children live have been made much worse by the war. (Incidentally, various attempts to evacuate these children were a failure: they all came under the heading of 'unbilletable'.[3])

It is impossible to talk to her or read her book without wondering how many more of these pockets of corruption exist in London and other big towns. Mrs. Paneth has managed to keep in touch with some of the children who were previously under her care and have now gone to work. With such a background they have neither the chance of a worth-while job nor, as a rule, the capacity for steady work. At best they find their way into some blind-alley occupation, but are more likely to end up in crime or prostitution.

The surprise which this book caused in many quarters is an indication of how little is still known of the under side of London life. The huge slum areas that existed within living memory have been cleared up, but in a smaller way there is obviously still a great deal to do. Mrs. Paneth was astonished and gratified that her book, which casts a very unfavourable light on this country, received no hostile criticism.

Probably that is a sign that public opinion is becoming more sensitive to the problem of the neglected child. In any case it would be difficult to read the book without conceiving an admiration for its author, who has carried out a useful piece of civilising work with great courage and infinite good-temper.

But *Branch Street* still exists, and it will go on creating wild and hopeless children until it has been abolished and rebuilt along with the other streets that have the same atmosphere.

1. The article was originally headed (presumably by a sub-editor at the *Observer*) 'The Children Who Cannot be Billeted'.

2. Homer Tyrell Lane (1876–1925), author of *Talking to Parents and Teachers* (1928). The 1949 edition had a preface by A. S. Neill. Alexander Sutherland Neill (1883–1973), Scottish educationalist, who reacted against what he regarded as his own repressive education. He argued, and put into practice through his school, Summerhill, a libertarian education for children in which there was complete freedom for children to do what they liked, and no discipline. The titles of many of his books indicate his line of thought: *The Problem Child* (1926), *The Problem Parent* (1932), *The Dreadful School* (1937), *The Problem Teacher* (1939) and *The Problem Family* (1948). Among his other books are *Is Scotland Educated?* (1936) and *Summerhill: A Compilation* (1962).

3. Elisaveta Fen (1899–1983; she also worked as Lydia Jackson), a close friend of Orwell's wife, Eileen, and also of Orwell (see XI/534A, 542A, 542B) worked for a time as assistant matron of a home for 'unbilletable children' in Oxford, June 1941 (see her *A Russian's England*, 1976, 465). Unaffected comments on the reception of evacuees will be found in Joyce Grenfell's letters to her mother in *Darling Ma*: 4 and 18 September and 2 October 1939.

[2538]

'Raffles and Miss Blandish'

28 August 1944; Horizon, *October 1944;* Politics, *November 1944*

> *Orwell's Payments Book records that this essay was completed on 28 August*
> *1944 (see 2831,* XVII/470*). It was published in* Horizon *(edited by*
> *Orwell's friend, Cyril Connolly) in the issue for October 1944 and Orwell was*
> *paid a fee of £13. Its title was then 'The Ethics of the Detective Story from*
> Raffles *to* Miss Blandish*'. The text was modified in three ways: changes were*
> *made to make the text more accurate (see notes 7, 12, 17 and 18); for fear of*
> *libel (see notes 13 and 14); and to ensure that offence was not given to the Soviet*
> *Union (see notes 21, 22 and 24). Orwell seems to have initiated or approved of*
> *the changes to make the text more accurate. He was unhappy about the other*
> *changes (see his letters to Dwight Macdonald, editor of the US journal* Politics,
> XVI/2545 *and* 2550*). When Macdonald published the essay in November*
> *1944, he not only ignored all the attempts at censorship but wrote a note in the*
> *'Comment' feature of the journal stating that 'This kind of panicky self-*
> *censorship is evidence of the degree to which the English intelligentsia has*
> *succumbed to Russomania'; he referred also to the way Orwell had suffered at*
> *the hands of the* Manchester Evening News *because of what Orwell called*
> *'the supposed Russomania of the general public and also because of complaints*
> *which the Soviet government is constantly raising about the British press' (see*
> *Orwell to Macdonald, 23 July 1944,* X/2518, *and headnote to 'Raffles and*
> *Miss Blandish' for fuller details,* X/2538, *which, with its footnotes, record*
> *all stylistic and other changes). A Polish version of this article was published*
> *in* Kultura *(Paris), Nos. 9–10, Sept–Oct 1948. See 'The Detective Story'*
> *above for details of many of the authors and characters.*

Nearly half a century after his first appearance, Raffles, 'the amateur cracksman', is still one of the best-known characters in English fiction. Very few people would need telling that he played cricket for England, had bachelor chambers in the Albany[1] and burgled the Mayfair houses which he also entered as a guest. Just for that reason he and his exploits make a suitable background against which to examine a more modern crime story such as *No Orchids for Miss Blandish*.[2] Any such choice is necessarily arbitrary – I might equally well have chosen *Arsène Lupin*,[3] for instance – but at any rate *No Orchids* and the Raffles books* have the common quality of being crime stories which play the limelight on the criminal rather than the policeman. For sociological purposes they can be compared. *No Orchids* is the 1939 version of glamorised crime, *Raffles* the 1900 version. What I am concerned with here is the immense difference in moral atmosphere between the two books, and the change in the popular attitude that this probably implies.

At this date, the charm of *Raffles* is partly in the period atmosphere, and partly in the technical excellence of the stories. Hornung was a very conscientious and, on his level, a very able writer. Anyone who cares for sheer efficiency must admire his work. However, the truly dramatic thing about Raffles, the thing that makes him a sort of by-word even to this day (only a few weeks ago, in a burglary case, a magistrate referred to the prisoner as 'a Raffles in real life'), is the fact that he is *a gentleman*. Raffles is presented to us – and this is rubbed home in countless scraps of dialogue and casual remarks – not as an honest man who has gone astray, but as a public-school man who has gone astray. His remorse, when he feels any, is almost purely social: he has disgraced 'the old school', he has lost his right to enter 'decent society', he has forfeited his amateur status and become a cad. Neither Raffles nor Bunny appears to feel at all strongly that stealing is wrong in itself, though Raffles does once justify himself by the casual remark that 'the distribution of property is all wrong anyway'. They think of themselves not as sinners but as renegades, or simply as outcasts. And the moral code of most of us is still so close to Raffles's own that we do feel his situation to be an especially ironical one. A West End clubman who is really a burglar! That is almost a story in itself, is it not? But how if it were a plumber or a greengrocer who was really a burglar? Would there be anything inherently dramatic in that? No – although the theme of the 'double life', of respectability covering crime, is still there. Even Charles Peace[5] in his clergyman's dog-collar seems somewhat less of a hypocrite than Raffles in his Zingari[6] blazer.

---

* *Raffles, A Thief in the Night* and *Mr. Justice Raffles*, by E. W. Hornung. The third of these is definitely a failure, and only the first has the true Raffles atmosphere. Hornung wrote a number of crime stories, usually with a tendency to take the side of the criminal. A successful book in rather the same vein as *Raffles* is *Stingaree* [Orwell's footnote].[4]

Raffles, of course, is good at all games, but it is peculiarly fitting that his chosen game should be cricket. This allows not only of endless analogies between his cunning as a slow bowler and his cunning as a burglar, but also helps to define the exact nature of his crime. Cricket is not in reality a very popular game in England – it is nowhere near so popular as football, for instance – but it gives expression to a well-marked trait in the English character, the tendency to value 'form' or 'style' more highly than success. In the eyes of any true cricket-lover it is possible for an innings of ten runs to be 'better' (i.e. more elegant) than an innings of a hundred runs: cricket is also one of the very few games in which the amateur can excel the professional. It is a game full of forlorn hopes and sudden dramatic changes of fortune, and its rules are so ill-defined that their interpretation is partly an ethical business. When Larwood, for instance, practised body-line bowling in Australia[7] he was not actually breaking any rule: he was merely doing something that was 'not cricket'. Since cricket takes up a lot of time and is rather expensive to play, it is predominantly an upper-class game,[8] but for the whole nation it is bound up with such concepts as 'good form', 'playing the game', etc., and it has declined in popularity just as the tradition of 'don't hit a man when he's down' has declined. It is not a twentieth-century game, and nearly all modern-minded people dislike it. The Nazis, for instance, were at pains to discourage cricket, which had gained a certain footing in Germany before and after the last war. In making Raffles a cricketer as well as a burglar Hornung was not merely providing him with a plausible disguise; he was also drawing the sharpest moral contrast that he was able to imagine.

Raffles, no less than *Great Expectations* or *Le Rouge et le Noir*, is a story of snobbery, and it gains a great deal from the precariousness of Raffles's social position. A cruder writer would have made the 'gentleman burglar' a member of the peerage, or at least a baronet. Raffles, however, is of upper-middle-class origin and is only accepted by the aristocracy because of his personal charm. 'We were in Society but not of it,' he says to Bunny towards the end of the book; and 'I was asked about for my cricket'. Both he and Bunny accept the values of 'Society' unquestioningly, and would settle down in it for good if only they could get away with a big enough haul. The ruin that constantly threatens them is all the blacker because they only doubtfully 'belong'. A duke who has served a prison sentence is still a duke, whereas a mere man-about-town if once disgraced, ceases to be 'about town' for evermore. The closing chapters of the book, when Raffles has been exposed and is living under an assumed name, have a twilight-of-the-gods feeling, a mental atmosphere rather similar to that of Kipling's poem, 'Gentlemen-Rankers':

> A trooper of the forces –
> I, who kept my own six horses! etc.[9]

Raffles now belongs irrevocably to the 'cohorts of the damned'.[10] He can still commit successful burglaries, but there is no way back into Paradise, which means Piccadilly[11] and the M.C.C. According to the public-school code there is only one means of rehabilitation: death in battle. Raffles dies fighting against the Boers (a practiced reader would foresee this from the start), and in the eyes of both Bunny and his creator this cancels his crimes.

Both Raffles and Bunny, of course, are devoid of religious belief, and they have no real ethical code, merely certain rules of behaviour which they observe semi-instinctively. But it is just here that the deep moral difference between *Raffles* and *No Orchids* becomes apparent. Raffles and Bunny, after all, are gentlemen, and such standards as they do have are not to be violated. Certain things are 'not done', and the idea of doing them hardly arises. Raffles will not, for example, abuse hospitality. He will commit a burglary in a house where he is staying as a guest, but the victim must be a fellow-guest and not the host. He will not commit murder,* and he avoids violence wherever possible and prefers to carry out his robberies unarmed. He regards friendship as sacred, and is chivalrous though not moral in his relations with women. He will take extra risks in the name of 'sportsmanship', and sometimes even for aesthetic reasons. And above all he is intensely patriotic. He celebrates the Diamond Jubilee ('For sixty years, Bunny, we've been ruled over by absolutely the finest

---

* 1945. Actually Raffles does kill one man and is more or less consciously responsible for the death of two others. But all three of them are foreigners and have behaved in a very reprehensible manner. He also, on one occasion, contemplates murdering a blackmailer. It is, however, a fairly well-established convention in crime stories that murdering a blackmailer 'doesn't count' [Orwell's footnote].[12]

sovereign the world has ever seen') by despatching to the Queen, through the post, an antique gold cup which he has stolen from the British Museum. He steals, from partly political motives, a pearl which the German Emperor is sending to one of the enemies of Britain, and when the Boer War begins to go badly his one thought is to find his way into the fighting line. At the front he unmasks a spy at the cost of revealing his own identity, and then dies gloriously by a Boer bullet. In this combination of crime and patriotism he resembles his near-contemporary Arsène Lupin, who also scores off the German Emperor and wipes out his very dirty past by enlisting in the Foreign Legion.

It is important to note that by modern standards Raffles's crimes are very petty ones. Four hundred pounds' worth of jewelry seems to him an excellent haul. And though the stories are convincing in their physical detail, they contain very little sensationalism – very few corpses, hardly any blood, no sex crimes, no sadism, no perversions of any kind. It seems to be the case that the crime story, at any rate on its higher levels, has greatly increased in bloodthirstiness during the past twenty years. Some of the early detective stories do not even contain a murder. The Sherlock Holmes stories, for instance, are not all murders, and some of them do not even deal with an indictable crime. So also with the John Thorndyke stories, while of the Max Carrados stories only a minority are murders. Since 1918, however, a detective story not containing a murder has been a great rarity, and the most disgusting details of dismemberment and exhumation are commonly exploited. Some of the Peter Wimsey stories, for instance, seem to point to definite necrophilia.[13] The Raffles stories, written from the angle of the criminal, are much less anti-social than many modern stories written from the angle of the detective. The main impression that they leave behind is of boyishness. They belong to a time when people had standards, though they happened to be foolish standards. Their key phrase is 'not done'. The line that they draw between good and evil is as senseless as a Polynesian taboo, but at least, like the taboo, it has the advantage that everyone accepts it.

So much for *Raffles*. Now for a header into the cesspool. *No Orchids for Miss Blandish*, by James Hadley Chase, was published in 1939 but seems to have enjoyed its greatest popularity in 1940, during the Battle of Britain and the blitz. In its main outlines its story is this:

Miss Blandish, the daughter of a millionaire, is kidnapped by some gangsters who are almost immediately surprised and killed off by a larger and better organised gang. They hold her to ransom and extract half a million dollars from her father. Their original plan had been to kill her as soon as the ransom-money was received, but a chance keeps her alive. One of the gang is a young man named Slim whose sole pleasure in life consists in driving knives into other people's bellies. In childhood he has graduated by cutting up living animals with a pair of rusty scissors. Slim is sexually impotent, but takes a kind of fancy to Miss Blandish. Slim's mother, who is the real brains of the gang, sees in this the chance of curing Slim's impotence, and decides to keep Miss Blandish in custody till Slim shall have succeeded in raping her. After many efforts and much persuasion, including the flogging of Miss Blandish with a length of rubber hosepipe, the rape is achieved. Meanwhile Miss Blandish's father has hired a private detective, and by means of bribery and torture the detective and the police manage to round up and exterminate the whole gang. Slim escapes with Miss Blandish and is killed after a final rape, and the detective prepares to restore Miss Blandish to her family. By this time, however, she has developed such a taste for Slim's caresses* that she feels unable to live without him, and she jumps out of the window of a skyscraper.

Several other points need noticing before one can grasp the full implications of this book. To begin with its central story is an impudent plagiarism[14] of William Faulkner's novel, *Sanctuary*. Secondly it is not, as one might expect, the product of an illiterate hack, but a brilliant piece of writing, with hardly a wasted word or a jarring note anywhere. Thirdly, the whole book, *récit* as well as dialogue, is written in the American language. The author, an Englishman who has (I believe) never been in the United States, seems to have made a complete mental transference to the American underworld. Fourthly, the book sold, according to its publishers, no less than half a million copies.

I have already outlined the plot, but the subject-matter is much more

---

* 1945. Another reading of the final episode is possible. It may mean merely that Miss Blandish is pregnant. But the interpretation I have given above seems more in keeping with the general brutality of the book [Orwell's footnote].

sordid and brutal than this suggests. The book contains eight full-dress murders, an unassessable number of casual killings and woundings, an exhumation (with a careful reminder of the stench), the flogging of Miss Blandish, the torture of another woman with redhot cigarette ends, a strip-tease act, a third-degree scene of unheard-of cruelty, and much else of the same kind. It assumes great sexual sophistication in its readers (there is a scene, for instance, in which a gangster, presumably of masochistic tendency, has an orgasm in the moment of being knifed), and it takes for granted the most complete corruption and self-seeking as the norm of human behaviour. The detective, for instance, is almost as great a rogue as the gangsters, and actuated by nearly the same motives. Like them, he is in pursuit of 'five hundred grand'. It is necessary to the machinery of the story that Mr. Blandish should be anxious to get his daughter back, but apart from this such things as affection, friendship, good-nature or even ordinary politeness simply do not enter. Nor, to any great extent, does normal sexuality. Ultimately only one motive is at work throughout the whole story: the pursuit of power.

It should be noticed that the book is not in the ordinary sense pornography. Unlike most books that deal in sexual sadism, it lays the emphasis on the cruelty and not on the pleasure. Slim, the ravisher of Miss Blandish, has 'wet, slobbering lips': this is disgusting, and it is meant to be disgusting. But the scenes describing cruelty to women are comparatively perfunctory. The real high-spots of the book are cruelties committed by men upon other men: above all the third-degreeing of the gangster, Eddie Schultz, who is lashed into a chair and flogged on the windpipe with truncheons, his arms broken by fresh blows as he breaks loose. In another of Mr. Chase's books, *He Won't Need It Now*, the hero, who is intended to be a sympathetic and perhaps even noble character, is described as stamping on somebody's face, and then, having crushed the man's mouth in, grinding his heel round and round in it. Even when physical incidents of this kind are not occurring, the mental atmosphere of these books is always the same. Their whole theme is the struggle for power and the triumph of the strong over the weak. The big gangsters wipe out the little ones as mercilessly as a pike gobbling up the little fish in a pond; the police kill off the criminals as cruelly as the angler kills the pike. If ultimately one sides with the police against the gangsters it is merely because they are better organised and more powerful, because, in fact, the law is a bigger racket than crime. Might is right: *vae victis.*[15]

As I have mentioned already, *No Orchids* enjoyed its greatest vogue in 1940, though it was successfully running as a play till some time later. It was, in fact, one of the things that helped to console people for the boredom of being bombed. Early in the war the *New Yorker* had a picture of a little man approaching a news-stall littered with papers with such headlines as GREAT TANK BATTLES IN NORTHERN FRANCE, BIG NAVAL BATTLE IN THE NORTH SEA, HUGE AIR BATTLES OVER THE CHANNEL, etc. etc. The little man is saying, '*Action Stories*, please'. That little man stood for all the drugged millions to whom the world of the gangsters and the prize-ring is more 'real', more 'tough' than such things as wars, revolutions, earthquakes, famines and pestilences. From the point of view of a reader of *Action Stories*, a description of the London blitz, or of the struggles of the European underground parties, would be 'sissy stuff'. On the other hand some puny gun-battle in Chicago, resulting in perhaps half a dozen deaths, would seem genuinely 'tough'. This habit of mind is now extremely widespread. A soldier sprawls in a muddy trench, with the machine-gun bullets crackling a foot or two overhead and whiles away his intolerable boredom by reading an American gangster story. And what is it that makes that story so exciting? Precisely the fact that people are shooting at each other with machine-guns! Neither the soldier nor anyone else sees anything curious in this. It is taken for granted that an imaginary bullet is more thrilling than a real one.

The obvious explanation is that in real life one is usually a passive victim, whereas in the adventure story one can think of oneself as being at the centre of events. But there is more to it than that. Here it is necessary to refer again to the curious fact of *No Orchids* being written – with technical errors, perhaps, but certainly with considerable skill – in the American language.

There exists in America an enormous literature of more or less the same stamp as *No Orchids*. Quite apart from books, there is the huge array of 'pulp magazines', graded so as to cater for different kinds of fantasy but nearly all having much the same mental atmosphere. A few of them go in for straight pornography but the great majority are quite plainly aimed at sadists and masochists. Sold at threepence a copy under the title of Yank

Mags* these things used to enjoy considerable popularity in England, but when the supply dried up owing to the war, no satisfactory substitute was forthcoming. English imitations of the 'pulp magazine' do now exist, but they are poor things compared with the original. English crook films, again, never approach the American crook film in brutality. And yet the career of Mr. Chase shows how deep the American influence has already gone. Not only is he himself living a continuous fantasy-life in the Chicago underworld, but he can count on hundreds of thousands of readers who know what is meant by a 'clipshop' or the 'hotsquat', do not have to do mental arithmetic when confronted by 'fifty grand', and understand at sight a sentence like 'Johnnie was a rummy and only two jumps ahead of the nut-factory'.[16] Evidently there are great numbers of English people who are partly Americanised in language and, one ought to add, in moral outlook. For there was no popular protest against *No Orchids*. In the end it was withdrawn,[17] but only retrospectively, when a later work, *Miss Callaghan comes to Grief*,[18] brought Mr. Chase's books to the attention of the authorities. Judging by casual conversations at the time, ordinary readers got a mild thrill out of the obscenities in *No Orchids*, but saw nothing undesirable in the book as a whole. Many people, incidentally, were under the impression that it was an American book reissued in England.

The thing that the ordinary reader *ought* to have objected to – almost certainly would have objected to, a few decades earlier – was the equivocal attitude towards crime. It is implied throughout *No Orchids* that being a criminal is only reprehensible in the sense that it does not pay. Being a policeman pays better, but there is no moral difference, since the police use essentially criminal methods. In a book like *He Won't Need It Now* the distinction between crime and crime-prevention practically disappears. This is a new departure for English sensational fiction, in which till recently there has always been a sharp distinction between right and wrong and a general agreement that virtue must triumph in the last chapter. English books glorifying crime (modern crime, that is – pirates

---

* They are said to have been imported into this country as ballast, which accounted for their low price and crumpled appearance. Since the war the ships have been ballasted with something more useful, probably gravel [Orwell's footnote].

and highwaymen are different) are very rare. Even a book like *Raffles*, as I have pointed out, is governed by powerful taboos, and it is clearly understood that Raffles's crimes must be expiated sooner or later. In America, both in life and fiction, the tendency to tolerate crime, even to admire the criminal so long as he is successful, is very much more marked. It is, indeed, ultimately this attitude that has made it possible for crime to flourish upon so huge a scale. Books have been written about Al Capone[19] that are hardly different in tone from the books written about Henry Ford, Stalin, Lord Northcliffe and all the rest of the 'log cabin to White House' brigade. And switching back eighty years, one finds Mark Twain adopting much the same attitude towards the disgusting bandit Slade, hero of twenty-eight murders, and towards the Western desperadoes generally. They were successful, they 'made good', therefore he admired them.

In a book like *No Orchids* one is not, as in the old-style crime story, simply escaping from dull reality into an imaginary world of action. One's escape is essentially into cruelty and sexual perversion. *No Orchids* is aimed at the power-instinct which *Raffles* or the Sherlock Holmes stories are not. At the same time the English attitude towards crime is not so superior to the American as I may have seemed to imply. It too is mixed up with power-worship, and has become more noticeably so in the last twenty years. A writer who is worth examining is Edgar Wallace, especially in such typical books as *The Orator* and the Mr. J. G. Reeder stories. Wallace was one of the first crime-story writers to break away from the old tradition of the private detective and make his central figure a Scotland Yard official. Sherlock Holmes is an amateur, solving his problems without the help and even, in the earlier stories, against the opposition of the police. Moreover, like Dupin,[20] he is essentially an intellectual, even a scientist. He reasons logically from observed fact, and his intellectuality is constantly contrasted with the routine methods of the police. Wallace objected strongly to this slur, as he considered it, on Scotland Yard, and in several newspaper articles he went out of his way to denounce Holmes by name. His own ideal was the detective-inspector who catches criminals not because he is intellectually brilliant but because he is part of an all-powerful organisation. Hence the curious fact that in Wallace's most characteristic stories the 'clue' and the 'deduction' play no part. The criminal is always defeated either by an incredible coincidence, or because in some unexplained manner the police know all about the crime before-hand. The tone of the stories makes it quite clear that Wallace's admiration for the police is pure bully-worship. A Scotland Yard detective is the most powerful kind of being that he can imagine, while the criminal figures in his mind as an outlaw against whom anything is permissible, like the condemned slaves in the Roman arena. His policemen behave much more brutally than British policemen do in real life – they hit people without provocation, fire revolvers past their ears to terrify them, and so on – and some of the stories exhibit a fearful intellectual sadism. (For instance, Wallace likes to arrange things so that the villain is hanged on the same day as the heroine is married.) But it is sadism after the English fashion: that is to say it is unconscious, there is not overtly any sex in it, and it keeps within the bounds of the law. The British public tolerates a harsh criminal law and gets a kick out of monstrously unfair murder trials: but still that is better, on any count, than tolerating or admiring crime. If one must worship a bully, it is better that he should be a policeman than a gangster. Wallace is still governed to some extent by the concept of 'not done'. In *No Orchids* anything is 'done' so long as it leads on to power. All the barriers are down, all the motives are out in the open. Chase is a worse symptom than Wallace, to the extent that all-in wrestling is worse than boxing, or Fascism is worse than capitalist democracy.

In borrowing from William Faulkner's *Sanctuary*, Chase only took the plot; the mental atmosphere of the two books is not similar. Chase really derives from other sources, and this particular bit of borrowing is only symbolic. What it symbolises is the vulgarisation of ideas which is con-stantly happening, and which probably happens faster in an age of print. Chase has been described as 'Faulkner for the masses', but it would be more accurate to describe him as Carlyle for the masses. He is a popular writer – there are many such in America, but they are still rarities in England – who has caught up with what it is now fashionable to call 'realism', meaning the doctrine that might is right. The growth of 'realism' has been the great feature of the intellectual history of our own age. Why this should be so is a complicated question. The interconnection between sadism, masochism, success-worship, power-worship, nationalism and totalitarianism is a huge subject whose edges have barely been scratched, and even to mention it is considered somewhat indelicate. To take merely the first example that comes to mind, I believe no one has ever pointed out the sadistic and masochistic element in Bernard Shaw's work, still less suggested that this probably has some connection with Shaw's admiration for dictators.

Fascism is often loosely equated with sadism, but nearly always by people who see nothing wrong in the most slavish worship of Stalin. The truth is, of course, that the countless English intellectuals who kiss the arse of Stalin[21] are not different from the minority who give their allegiance to Hitler or Mussolini, nor from[22] the efficiency experts who preached 'punch', 'drive', 'personality' and 'learn to be a Tiger Man' in the nineteen-twenties, nor from the older generation of intellectuals, Carlyle, Creasey[23] and the rest of them, who bowed down before German militarism. All of them are worshipping power and successful cruelty. It is important to notice that the cult of power tends to be mixed up with a love of cruelty and wickedness *for their own sakes*. A tyrant is all the more admired if he happens to be a bloodstained crook as well, and 'the end justifies the means' often becomes, in effect, 'the means justify themselves provided they are dirty enough'. This idea colours the outlook of all sympathisers with totalitarianism, and accounts, for instance, for the positive delight with which many English intellectuals greeted the Nazi-Soviet pact. It was a step only doubtfully useful to the U.S.S.R. but it was entirely unmoral, and for that reason to be admired: the explanations of it, which were numerous and self-contradictory, could come afterwards.[24]

Until recently the characteristic adventure stories of the English-speaking peoples have been stories in which the hero fights *against odds*. This is true all the way from Robin Hood to Popeye the Sailor. Perhaps the basic myth of the Western world is Jack the Giant Killer. But to be brought up to date this should be renamed Jack the Dwarf Killer, and there already exists a considerable literature which teaches, either overtly or implicitly, that one should side with the big man against the little man. Most of what is now written about foreign policy is simply an embroidery on this theme, and for several decades such phrases as 'play the game', 'don't hit a man when he's down' and 'it's not cricket' have never failed to draw a snigger from anyone of intellectual pretensions. What is comparatively new is to find the accepted pattern according to which (a) right is right and wrong is wrong, whoever wins, and (b) weakness must be respected, disappearing from popular literature as well. When I first read D. H. Lawrence's novels, at the age of about twenty, I was puzzled by the fact that there did not seem to be any classification of the characters into 'good' and 'bad'. Lawrence seemed to sympathise with all of them about equally, and this was so unusual as to give me the feeling of having lost my bearings. Today no one would think of looking for heroes and villains in a serious novel, but in lowbrow fiction one still expects to find a sharp distinction between right and wrong and between legality and illegality. The common people, on the whole, are still living in the world of absolute good and evil from which the intellectuals have long since escaped. But the popularity of *No Orchids* and the American books and magazines to which it is akin shows how rapidly the doctrine of 'realism' is gaining ground.

Several people, after reading *No Orchids*, have remarked to me, 'It's pure Fascism.' This is a correct description, although the book has not the smallest connection with politics and very little with social or economic problems. It has merely the same relation to Fascism as, say, Trollope's novels have to nineteenth-century capitalism. It is a daydream appropriate to a totalitarian age. In his imagined world of gangsters Chase is presenting, as it were, a distilled version of the modern political scene, in which such things as mass bombing of civilians, the use of hostages, torture to obtain confessions, secret prisons, execution without trial, floggings with rubber truncheons, drownings in cesspools, systematic falsification of records and statistics, treachery, bribery and quislingism are normal and morally neutral, even admirable when they are done in a large and bold way. The average man is not directly interested in politics, and when he reads he wants the current struggles of the world to be translated into a simple story about individuals. He can take an interest in Slim and Fenner as he could not in the G.P.U.[25] and the Gestapo. People worship power in the form in which they are able to understand it. A twelve-year-old boy worships Jack Dempsey.[26] An adolescent in a Glasgow slum worships Al Capone. An aspiring pupil at a business college worships Lord Nuffield. A *New Statesman* reader worships Stalin. There is a difference in intellectual maturity, but none in moral outlook. Thirty years ago the heroes of popular fiction had nothing in common with Mr. Chase's gangsters and detectives, and the idols of the English liberal intelligentsia were also comparatively sympathetic figures. Between

Holmes and Fenner on the one hand, and between Abraham Lincoln and Stalin on the other, there is a similar gulf.

One ought not to infer too much from the success of Mr. Chase's books. It is possible that it is an isolated phenomenon, brought about by the mingled boredom and brutality of war. But if such books should definitely acclimatise themselves in England, instead of being merely a half-understood import from America, there would be good grounds for dismay. In choosing *Raffles* as a background for *No Orchids*, I deliberately chose a book which by the standards of its time was morally equivocal. Raffles, as I have pointed out, has no real moral code, no religion, certainly no social consciousness. All he has is a set of reflexes – the nervous system, as it were, of a gentleman. Give him a sharp tap on this reflex or that (they are called 'sport', 'pal', 'woman', 'king and country' and so forth), and you get a predictable reaction. In Mr. Chase's book there are no gentlemen, and no taboos. Emancipation is complete, Freud and Macchiavelli have reached the outer suburbs. Comparing the schoolboy atmosphere of the one book with the cruelty and corruption of the other, one is driven to feel that snobbishness, like hypocrisy, is a check upon behaviour whose value from a social point of view has been underrated.

1. Albany (not 'The Albany') in Piccadilly, London W1, is composed of a mansion, built as Melbourne House in the early 1770s, and two wings of chambers built in 1802–3. Melbourne, facing heavy debts, sold out to the Duke of York and Albany ('the Grand Old Duke of York') and the house was renamed. In 1802, he in turn sold out to a consortium that constructed the world's first purpose-built apartments (the two wings to the rear of the house) on what had been a fine garden. From 1803 to the present they have been governed by elected, residential Trustees. There are sixty-nine sets of chambers and one flat. Many famous authors, actors and prime ministers have lived there. Charles Egremont, the hero of Disraeli's *Sybil*, supposedly had a set of chambers there (K1). Although its fortunes have varied, Albany has generally been regarded as a particularly desirable place to live. Penguin Books was launched from Albany (1935; see plaque in Vigo Street).

2. *No Orchids for Miss Blandish* was James Hadley Chase's first novel and was written when he was working for a book wholesaler. It was published in 1939 and by the time Orwell wrote his essay had sold over a million copies. Chase's real name was René Brabazon Raymond (1906–85). He wrote some eighty books using various pseudonyms.

3. The hero of Maurice Leblanc's crime novels. Orwell sometimes confuses Lupin and Dupin; see n. 20, below, and p. 343, n. 6, above.

4. The correct title of *Raffles* by E. W. Hornung (1868–1921) was *The Amateur Cracksman* (1899). *Stingaree* and *A Thief in the Night* were both published in 1905, four years before his *Mr. Justice Raffles*.

5. Charles Peace (1832–79), petty criminal and murderer. In 1876 he killed Police Constable Cook, but another man was charged with the murder and found guilty. In 1878 Peace murdered Alfred Dyson. He was arrested committing a burglary, was tried for Dyson's murder and found guilty. He confessed to having killed Cook, and the man originally charged, William Habron, was given a free pardon. Peace was executed. His exploits entered popular myth and he was the subject of an early, and quite famous, silent film.

6. Properly 'I Zingari' (Italian for 'The Gypsies'), an exclusive English cricket club founded in 1845. It has no ground of its own so travels away to all its matches.

7. 'practised body-line bowling in Australia': *Horizon* and *Politics* had 'left a trail of broken bones up and down Australia'. This was altered in the page-proofs of *Critical Essays* (1946; a collection of Orwell's essays) by one of the directors of Secker & Warburg, Roger Senhouse (c. 1900–1965), doubtless on the grounds of accuracy. Although Larwood inspired terror in the Australians he did not litter Australia with broken bones.

8. Had Orwell stayed in Wigan beyond March 1936 he would have realized that cricket is anything but a game reserved to the upper classes. The leagues of Lancashire and Yorkshire were not, and are not, their preserves.

9. 'A trooper . . . kept' is given in *Critical Essays*, also incorrectly, as 'Yes, a trooper of the forces – / Who has kept'. These lines, from Rudyard Kipling's *Barrack-Room Ballads* (1892) should be printed as a single line: 'Yes a trooper of the forces who has run his own six horses' (without exclamation point). Orwell was doubtless quoting (as he often did) from memory.

10. 'To the legion of the lost ones, to the cohorts of the damned' is the first line of 'Gentleman-Rankers'. They are damned 'from here to Eternity' because they have 'done with Hope and Honour' and are 'lost to Love and Truth'.

11. Raffles allegedly lived in Albany (see n. 1, above) although the author of *The Amateur Cracksman*, in which he appears, gets the topography of Albany wrong. The reference to 'Paradise' is because Albany is sometimes referred to as 'Paradise in Piccadilly' owing to its remarkable peacefulness despite its location, and the supposed selectivity of its occupants. For Raffles at Albany see Harry Furniss, *Paradise in Piccadilly* (1925), 163–71.

12. This note originally read, 'He does once contemplate murdering a blackmailer. It is, however, a fairly well established convention in crime stories that murdering a blackmailer "doesn't count".'

13. Orwell originally wrote 'seem to point to definite necrophilia' (so printed in *Politics*) but this was changed to 'centre round macabre practical jokes played with corpses' in *Horizon*, and 'display an extremely morbid interest in corpses' in *Critical Essays*. Dwight Macdonald, editor of *Politics*, chose what Orwell wrote, although Orwell suggested he might like to change the text to avoid a libel action (XVI/*2545*). The Lord Peter Wimsey stories were written by Dorothy L. Sayers (1893–1957). In addition to many detective stories, she also wrote a play-cycle for the BBC on the life of Christ, *The Man Born to be King* (1941–2), and translated Dante's *Inferno* and *Purgatorio* (1949, 1955).

14. It was feared that the description, 'an impudent plagiarism', might be libellous. *Politics* retained this but *Horizon* and *Critical Essays* changed it to 'bears a very marked resemblance to'.

15. Woe to the vanquished.

16. In case contemporary readers are not so familiar with some of these words: clipshop (or

clip-joint): club, sometimes illegal, which charged exorbitant prices and where customers were likely to be cheated (perhaps from the practice of clipping the edges of precious metal coinage, reducing the value of the coins and allowing the clipper to sell the clippings); hotsquat: electric chair; fifty grand: $50,000; rummy: excessive drinker; two jumps: very little distance; nut-factory: lunatic asylum.

17. Orwell originally wrote 'suppressed' (which *Politics* printed) but he thought 'withdrawn' was more accurate.

18. *Miss Callaghan Comes to Grief* appeared in *Horizon* and *Critical Essays* and also in the proofs for the latter. *Politics* has, instead, *Lady – Don't Turn Over*, which is not by Chase but by Darcy Glinto (Harold Ernest Kelly) and was published in May 1940, eighteen months after *No Orchids for Miss Blandish*.

19. Al(fonso) Capone (1899–1947), American gang leader of Italian origin. His mob terrorized Chicago in the 1920s.

20. Dupin was the detective in Edgar Allan Poe's stories (see n. 3 to 'The Detective Story', above). In the US edition of *Critical Essays* (entitled *Dickens, Dali & Others: Studies in Popular Culture*, 1946), Dupin was printed 'Lupin'. Orwell annotated his copy with the correct reading. 'Lupin' also appears in the Penguin compilation, *Decline of English Murder and Other Essays* (1965), 74.

21. In *Horizon* and *Critical Essays*, 'who kiss the arse of Stalin' was modified to 'who worship dictators' for fear of offending the Soviets; *Politics* has Orwell's original, as here.

22. 'the minority . . . nor from' was omitted from *Horizon*.

23. Edward Creasy (no second 'e'), 1812–78. He and Thomas Carlyle (1795–1881) saw the growth of German nationalism under Bismarck in the nineteenth century. Frederick the Great (1712–86) was idolized by Carlyle, whose six-volume biography was published 1858–65.

24. 'This idea colours the outlook . . . could come back afterwards': these half-dozen lines were reduced in *Horizon* to 'This idea colours the outlook of all sympathizers with totalitarianism in any of its forms' to avoid offending English intellectuals (who might well be readers of *Horizon*) sympathetic to the Soviet Union.

25. Soviet security and intelligence service. Originally the Cheka, December 1917 to February 1922, when it was incorporated in the NKVD (the People's Commissariat for Internal Affairs); from July 1923 to July 1934 it was known as the OGPU and was then again incorporated in the NKVD. It had various other manifestations and from March 1954 to December 1991 was known as the KGB.

26. Jack (William Harrison) Dempsey (1895–1983), American boxer who won the heavyweight championship from Jess Willard in 1919; he was defeated by Gene Tunney in 1926 and 1927 (a fight involving a controversial 'long count').

[2624]

'In Defence of P. G. Wodehouse'
Recorded in Payments Book 20 February 1945
The Windmill, No. 2, [July] 1945

Orwell records in his Payments Book the completion of this essay on 20 February 1945 and that he was paid a fee of £10. When the essay was printed in The Windmill *a few sentences were not included or were slightly modified;* Critical Essays *published the full text except for the references to Lloyd George and Bernard Shaw (see n. 11, below) and they are included here. (Details of all changes can be found in the notes to XVII/2624.)*

When the Germans made their rapid advance through Belgium in the early summer of 1940, they captured, among other things, Mr. P. G. Wodehouse,[1] who had been living throughout the early part of the war in his villa at Le Touquet, and seems not to have realised until the last moment that he was in any danger. As he was led away into captivity, he is said to have remarked, 'Perhaps after this I shall write a serious book.' He was placed for the time being under house arrest, and from his subsequent statements it appears that he was treated in a fairly friendly way, German officers in the neighbourhood frequently 'dropping in for a bath or a party'.[2]

Over a year later, on 25th June 1941, the news came that Wodehouse had been released from internment and was living at the Adlon Hotel in Berlin. On the following day the public was astonished to learn that he had agreed to do some broadcasts of a 'non-political' nature over the German radio. The full texts of these broadcasts are not easy to obtain at this date, but Wodehouse seems to have done five of them between 26th June and 2nd July,[3] when the Germans took him off the air again. The first broadcast, on 26th June, was not made on the Nazi radio but took the form of an interview with Harry Flannery, the representative of the Columbia Broadcasting System, which still had its correspondents in Berlin. Wodehouse also published in the *Saturday Evening Post* an article which he had written while still in the internment camp.

The article and the broadcasts dealt mainly with Wodehouse's experiences in internment, but they did include a very few comments on the war. The following are fair samples:

I never was interested in politics. I'm quite unable to work up any kind of belligerent feeling. Just as I'm about to feel belligerent about some country I meet a decent sort of chap. We go out together and lose any fighting thoughts or feelings.

A short time ago they had a look at me on parade and got the right idea; at least they sent us to the local lunatic asylum. And I have been there forty-two weeks. There is a good deal to be said for internment. It keeps you out of the saloon and helps you to keep up with your reading. The chief trouble is that it means you are away from home for a long time. When I join my wife I had better take along a letter of introduction to be on the safe side.

In the days before the war I had always been modestly proud of being an Englishman, but now that I have been some months resident in this bin or repository of Englishmen I am not so sure ... The only concession I want from Germany is that she gives me a loaf of bread, tells the gentlemen with muskets at the main gate to look the other way, and leaves the rest to me. In return I am prepared to hand over India, an autographed set of my books, and to reveal the secret process of cooking sliced potatoes on a radiator. This offer holds good till Wednesday week.

The first extract quoted above caused great offence. Wodehouse was also censured for using (in the interview with Flannery) the phrase 'whether Britain wins the war or not', and he did not make things better by describing in another broadcast the filthy habits of some Belgian prisoners among whom he was interned. The Germans recorded this broadcast and repeated it a number of times. They seem to have supervised his talks very lightly, and they allowed him not only to be funny about the discomforts of internment but to remark that 'the internees at Trost camp all fervently believe that Britain will eventually win'. The general upshot of the talks, however, was that he had not been ill treated and bore no malice.

These broadcasts caused an immediate uproar in England. There were questions in Parliament, angry editorial comments in the press, and a stream of letters from fellow-authors, nearly all of them disapproving, though one or two suggested that it would be better to suspend judgment, and several pleaded that Wodehouse probably did not realise what he was doing. On 15th July, the Home Service of the B.B.C. carried an extremely violent Postscript by 'Cassandra'[4] of the *Daily Mirror*, accusing Wodehouse of 'selling his country'. This postscript made free use of such expressions as 'Quisling'[5] and 'worshipping the Führer'. The main charge was that Wodehouse had agreed to do German propaganda as a way of buying himself out of the internment camp.

'Cassandra's' Postscript caused a certain amount of protest, but on the whole it seems to have intensified popular feeling against Wodehouse. One result of it was that numerous lending libraries withdrew Wodehouse's books from circulation. Here is a typical news item:

Within twenty-four hours of listening to the broadcast of Cassandra, the *Daily Mirror* columnist, Portadown (North Ireland) Urban District Council banned P. G. Wodehouse's books from their public library. Mr. Edward McCann said that Cassandra's broadcast had clinched the matter. Wodehouse was funny no longer. (*Daily Mirror*.)

In addition the B.B.C. banned Wodehouse's lyrics from the air and was still doing so a couple of years later. As late as December 1944 there were demands in Parliament that Wodehouse should be put on trial as a traitor.

There is an old saying that if you throw enough mud some of it will stick, and the mud has stuck to Wodehouse in a rather peculiar way. An impression has been left behind that Wodehouse's talks (not that anyone remembers what he said in them) showed him up not merely as a traitor but as an ideological sympathiser with Fascism. Even at the time several letters to the press claimed that 'Fascist tendencies' could be detected in his books, and the charge has been repeated since. I shall try to analyse the mental atmosphere of those books in a moment, but it is important to realise that the events of 1941 do not convict Wodehouse of anything worse than stupidity. The really interesting question is how and why he could be so stupid. When Flannery met Wodehouse (released, but still under guard) at the Adlon Hotel in June 1941, he saw at once that he was dealing with a political innocent, and when preparing him for their broadcast interview he had to warn him against making some exceedingly unfortunate remarks, one of which was by implication slightly anti-Russian. As it was, the phrase 'whether England wins or not' did get through.[6] Soon after the interview Wodehouse told him that he was also going to broadcast on the Nazi radio, apparently not realising that this action had any special significance. Flannery comments:*

By this time the Wodehouse plot was evident. It was one of the best Nazi publicity stunts of the war, the first with a human angle . . . Plack (Goebbels's assistant) had gone to the camp near Gleiwitz to see Wodehouse, found that the author was completely without political sense, and had an idea. He suggested to Wodehouse that in return for being released from the prison camp he write a series of broadcasts about his experiences; there would be no censorship and he would put them on the air himself. In making that proposal Plack showed that he knew his man. He knew that Wodehouse made fun of the English in all his stories and that he seldom wrote in any other way, that he was still living in the period about which he wrote and had no conception of Nazism and all it meant. Wodehouse was his own Bertie Wooster.

The striking of an actual bargain between Wodehouse and Plack seems to be merely Flannery's own interpretation. The arrangement may have been of a much less definite kind, and to judge from the broadcasts themselves, Wodehouse's main idea in making them was to keep in touch with his public and – the comedian's ruling passion – to get a laugh. Obviously they are not the utterances of a Quisling of the type of Ezra Pound[7] or John Amery[8] nor, probably, of a person capable of understanding the nature of Quislingism. Flannery seems to have warned Wodehouse that it would be unwise to broadcast, but not very forcibly. He adds that Wodehouse (though in one broadcast he refers to himself as an Englishman) seemed to regard himself as an American citizen. He had contemplated naturalisation, but had never filled in the necessary papers. He even used, to Flannery, the phrase, 'We're not at war with Germany.'

I have before me a bibliography of P. G. Wodehouse's works. It names round about fifty books, but is certainly incomplete. It is as well to be honest, and I ought to start by admitting that there are many books by Wodehouse – perhaps a quarter or a third of the total – which I have not read. It is not, indeed, easy to read the whole output of a popular writer who is normally published in cheap editions. But I have followed his

---

* *Assignment to Berlin*, by Harry W. Flannery. (Michael Joseph, 1942) [Orwell's footnote].

work fairly closely since 1911, when I was eight years old, and am well acquainted with its peculiar mental atmosphere – an atmosphere which has not, of course, remained completely unchanged, but shows little alteration since about 1925. In the passage from Flannery's book which I quoted above there are two remarks which would immediately strike any attentive reader of Wodehouse. One is to the effect that Wodehouse 'was still living in the period about which he wrote', and the other that the Nazi Propaganda Ministry made use of him because he 'made fun of the English'. The second statement is based on a misconception to which I will return presently. But Flannery's other comment is quite true and contains in it part of the clue to Wodehouse's behaviour.

A thing that people often forget about P. G. Wodehouse's novels is how long ago the better-known of them were written. We think of him as in some sense typifying the silliness of the nineteen-twenties and nineteen-thirties, but in fact the scenes and characters by which he is best remembered had all made their appearance before 1925. Psmith first appeared in 1909, having been foreshadowed by other characters in earlier school-stories. Blandings Castle, with Baxter and the Earl of Emsworth both in residence, was introduced in 1915. The Jeeves-Wooster cycle began in 1919, both Jeeves and Wooster having made brief appearances earlier. Ukridge appeared in 1924. When one looks through the list of Wodehouse's books from 1902 onwards, one can observe three fairly well-marked periods. The first is the school-story period. It includes such books as *The Gold Bat*, *The Pothunters*, etc., and has its high-spot in *Mike* (1909). *Psmith in the City*, published in the following year, belongs in this category, though it is not directly concerned with school life. The next is the American period. Wodehouse seems to have lived in the United States from about 1913 to 1920, and for a while showed signs of becoming Americanised in idiom and outlook. Some of the stories in *The Man with Two Left Feet* (1917) appear to have been influenced by O. Henry, and other books written about this time contain Americanisms (*e.g.* 'highball' for 'whisky and soda') which an Englishman would not normally use *in propria persona*. Nevertheless, almost all the books of this period – *Psmith, Journalist*; *The Little Nugget*; *The Indiscretions of Archie*; *Piccadilly Jim* and various others – depend for their effect on the *contrast* between English and American manners. English characters appear in an American setting, or *vice versa*: there is a certain number of purely English stories, but hardly any purely American ones. The third period might fitly be called the country-house period. By the early nineteen-twenties Wodehouse must have been making a very large income, and the social status of his characters moved upwards accordingly, though the Ukridge stories form a partial exception. The typical setting is now a country mansion, a luxurious bachelor flat or an expensive golf club. The schoolboy athleticism of the earlier books fades out, cricket and football giving way to golf, and the element of farce and burlesque becomes more marked. No doubt many of the later books, such as *Summer Lightning*, are light comedy rather than pure farce, but the occasional attempts at moral earnestness which can be found in *Psmith, Journalist*; *The Little Nugget*; *The Coming of Bill*; *The Man with Two Left Feet* and some of the school stories, no longer appear. Mike Jackson has turned into Bertie Wooster. That, however, is not a very startling metamorphosis, and one of the most noticeable things about Wodehouse is his *lack* of development. Books like *The Gold Bat* and *Tales of St. Austin's*, written in the opening years of this century, already have the familiar atmosphere. How much of a formula the writing of his later books had become one can see from the fact that he continued to write stories of English life although throughout the sixteen years before his internment he was living at Hollywood and Le Touquet.

Mike, which is now a difficult book to obtain in an unabridged form, must be one of the best 'light' school stories in English. But though its incidents are largely farcical, it is by no means a satire on the public-school system, and *The Gold Bat*, *The Pothunters*, etc., are even less so. Wodehouse was educated at Dulwich, and then worked in a bank and graduated into novel-writing by way of very cheap journalism. It is clear that for many years he remained 'fixated' on his old school and loathed the unromantic job and the lower-middle-class surroundings in which he found himself. In the early stories the 'glamour' of public-school life (house matches, fagging, teas round the study fire, etc.) is laid on fairly thick, and the 'play the game' code of morals is accepted with not many reservations. Wrykyn, Wodehouse's imaginary public school, is a school of a more fashionable type than Dulwich, and one gets the impression that between *The Gold Bat* (1904) and *Mike* (1909) Wrykyn itself has become more expensive and moved farther from London. Psychologically the most revealing book of

Wodehouse's early period is *Psmith in the City*. Mike Jackson's father has suddenly lost his money, and Mike, like Wodehouse himself, is thrust at the age of about eighteen into an ill-paid subordinate job in a bank. Psmith is similarly employed, though not from financial necessity. Both this book and *Psmith, Journalist* (1915) are unusual in that they display a certain amount of political consciousness. Psmith at this stage chooses to call himself a Socialist – in his mind, and no doubt in Wodehouse's, this means no more than ignoring class distinctions – and on one occasion the two boys attend an open-air meeting on Clapham Common and go home to tea with an elderly Socialist orator, whose shabby-genteel home is described with some accuracy. But the most striking feature of the book is Mike's inability to wean himself from the atmosphere of school. He enters upon his job without any pretence of enthusiasm, and his main desire is not, as one might expect, to find a more interesting and useful job, but simply to be playing cricket. When he has to find himself lodgings he chooses to settle at Dulwich, because there he will be near a school and will be able to hear the agreeable sound of the ball striking against the bat. The climax of the book comes when Mike gets the chance to play in a county match and simply walks out of his job in order to do so. The point is that Wodehouse here sympathises with Mike: indeed he identifies himself with him, for it is clear enough that Mike bears the same relation to Wodehouse as Julien Sorel to Stendhal. But he created many other heroes essentially similar. Through the books of this and the next period there passes a whole series of young men to whom playing games and 'keeping fit' are a sufficient life-work. Wodehouse is almost incapable of imagining a desirable job. The great thing is to have money of your own, or, failing that, to find a sinecure. The hero of *Something Fresh* (1915) escapes from low-class journalism by becoming physical-training instructor to a dyspeptic millionaire: this is regarded as a step up, morally as well as financially.

In the books of the third period there is no narcissism and no serious interludes, but the implied moral and social background has changed much less than might appear at first sight. If one compares Bertie Wooster with Mike, or even with the rugger-playing prefects of the earliest school stories, one sees that the only real difference between them is that Bertie is richer and lazier. His ideals would be almost the same as theirs, but he fails to live up to them. Archie Moffam, in *The Indiscretions of Archie* (1921), is a type intermediate between Bertie and the earlier heroes: he is an ass, but he is also honest, kind-hearted, athletic and courageous. From first to last Wodehouse takes the public-school code of behaviour for granted, with the difference that in his later, more sophisticated period he prefers to show his characters violating it or living up to it against their will:

'Bertie! You wouldn't let down a pal?'

'Yes, I would.'

'But we were at school together, Bertie.'

'I don't care.'

'The old school, Bertie, the old school!'

'Oh, well – dash it!'

Bertie, a sluggish Don Quixote, has no wish to tilt at windmills, but he would hardly think of refusing to do so when honour calls. Most of the people whom Wodehouse intends as sympathetic characters are parasites, and some of them are plain imbeciles, but very few of them could be described as immoral. Even Ukridge is a visionary rather than a plain crook. The most immoral, or rather un-moral, of Wodehouse's characters is Jeeves, who acts as a foil to Bertie Wooster's comparative high-mindedness and perhaps symbolises the widespread English belief that intelligence and unscrupulousness are much the same thing. How closely Wodehouse sticks to conventional morality can be seen from the fact that nowhere in his books is there anything in the nature of a sex joke. This is an enormous sacrifice for a farcical writer to make. Not only are there no dirty jokes, but there are hardly any compromising situations: the horns-on-the-forehead motif is almost completely avoided. Most of the full-length books, of course, contain a 'love interest' but it is always at the light-comedy level: the love affair, with its complications and its idyllic scenes, goes on and on, but, as the saying goes, 'nothing happens'. It is significant that Wodehouse, by nature a writer of farces, was able to collaborate more than once with Ian Hay,[9] a serio-comic writer and an exponent (vide *Pip*, etc.) of the 'clean-living Englishman' tradition at its silliest.

In *Something Fresh* Wodehouse had discovered the comic possibilities of the English aristocracy, and a succession of ridiculous but, save in a

very few instances, not actually contemptible barons, earls and what-not
followed accordingly. This had the rather curious effect of causing Wodehouse to be regarded, outside England, as a penetrating satirist of English
society. Hence Flannery's statement that Wodehouse 'made fun of the
English', which is the impression he would probably make on a German
or even an American reader. Some time after the broadcasts from Berlin I
was discussing them with a young Indian Nationalist who defended
Wodehouse warmly. He took it for granted that Wodehouse *had* gone
over to the enemy, which from his own point of view was the right thing
to do. But what interested me was to find that he regarded Wodehouse
as an anti-British writer who had done useful work by showing up the
British aristocracy in their true colours. This is a mistake that it would be
very difficult for an English person to make, and is a good instance of the
way in which books, especially humorous books, lose their finer nuances
when they reach a foreign audience. For it is clear enough that Wodehouse
is *not* anti-British, and not anti-upper class either. On the contrary, a
harmless old-fashioned snobbishness is perceptible all through his work.
Just as an intelligent Catholic is able to see that the blasphemies of
Baudelaire or James Joyce are not seriously damaging to the Catholic
faith, so an English reader can see that in creating such characters as
Hildebrand Spencer Poyns de Burgh John Hanneyside Coombe-Crombie,
12th Earl of Dreever, Wodehouse is not really attacking the social hierarchy. Indeed, no one who genuinely despised titles would write of them
so much. Wodehouse's attitude towards the English social system is the
same as his attitude towards the public-school moral code – a mild
facetiousness covering an unthinking acceptance. The Earl of Emsworth
is funny because an earl ought to have more dignity, and Bertie Wooster's
helpless dependence on Jeeves is funny partly because the servant ought
not to be superior to the master. An American reader can mistake these
two, and others like them, for hostile caricatures, because he is inclined
to be Anglophobe already and they correspond to his preconceived ideas
about a decadent aristocracy. Bertie Wooster, with his spats and his cane,
is the traditional stage Englishman. But, as any English reader would see,
Wodehouse intends him as a sympathetic figure, and Wodehouse's real
sin has been to present the English upper classes as much nicer people
than they are. All through his books certain problems are consistently

avoided. Almost without exception his moneyed young men are unassuming, good mixers, not avaricious: their tone is set for them by Psmith, who retains his own upper-class exterior but bridges the social gap by addressing everyone as 'Comrade'.

But there is another important point about Bertie Wooster: his out-of-dateness. Conceived in 1917 or thereabouts, Bertie really belongs to an epoch earlier than that. He is the 'knut'[10] of the pre-1914 period, celebrated in such songs as 'Gilbert the Filbert' or 'Reckless Reggie of the Regent's Palace'. The kind of life that Wodehouse writes about by preference, the life of the 'clubman' or 'man about town', the elegant young man who lounges all the morning in Piccadilly with a cane under his arm and a carnation in his buttonhole, barely survived into the nineteen-twenties. It is significant that Wodehouse could publish in 1936 a book entitled *Young Men in Spats*. For who was wearing spats at that date? They had gone out of fashion quite ten years earlier. But the traditional 'knut', the 'Piccadilly Johnny', *ought* to wear spats, just as the pantomime Chinese ought to wear a pigtail. A humorous writer is not obliged to keep up to date, and having struck one or two good veins, Wodehouse continued to exploit them with a regularity that was no doubt all the easier because he did not set foot in England during the sixteen years that preceded his internment. His picture of English society had been formed before 1914, and it was a naïve, traditional and, at bottom, admiring picture. Nor did he ever become genuinely Americanised. As I have pointed out, spontaneous Americanisms do occur in the books of the middle period, but Wodehouse remained English enough to find American slang an amusing and slightly shocking novelty. He loves to thrust a slang phrase or a crude fact in among Wardour Street English ('With a hollow groan Ukridge borrowed five shillings from me and went out into the night'), and expressions like 'a piece of cheese' or 'bust him on the noggin' lend themselves to this purpose. But the trick had been developed before he made any American contacts, and his use of garbled quotations is a common device of English writers running back to Fielding. As Mr. John Hayward has pointed out,* Wodehouse owes a good deal to his knowledge of English literature and

---

* *P. G. Wodehouse*, by John Hayward. (*The Saturday Book*, 1942.) I believe this is the only full-length critical essay on Wodehouse [Orwell's footnote].

especially of Shakespeare. His books are aimed, not, obviously, at a highbrow audience, but at an audience educated along traditional lines. When, for instance, he describes somebody as heaving 'the kind of sigh that Prometheus might have heaved when the vulture dropped in for its lunch', he is assuming that his readers will know something of Greek mythology. In his early days the writers he admired were probably Barry Pain, Jerome K. Jerome, W. W. Jacobs, Kipling and F. Anstey, and he has remained closer to them than to the quick-moving American comic writers such as Ring Lardner or Damon Runyon. In his radio interview with Flannery, Wodehouse wondered whether 'the kind of people and the kind of England I write about will live after the war', not realising that they were ghosts already. 'He was still living in the period about which he wrote,' says Flannery, meaning, probably, the nineteen-twenties. But the period was really the Edwardian age, and Bertie Wooster, if he ever existed, was killed round about 1915.

If my analysis of Wodehouse's mentality is accepted, the idea that in 1941 he consciously aided the Nazi propaganda machine becomes untenable and even ridiculous. He *may* have been induced to broadcast by the promise of an earlier release (he was due for release a few months later, on reaching his sixtieth birthday), but he cannot have realised that what he did would be damaging to British interests. As I have tried to show, his moral outlook has remained that of a public-school boy, and according to the public-school code, treachery in time of war is the most unforgivable of all the sins. But how could he fail to grasp that what he did would be a big propaganda score for the Germans and would bring down a torrent of disapproval on his own head? To answer this one must take two things into consideration. First, Wodehouse's complete lack – so far as one can judge from his printed works – of political awareness. It is nonsense to talk of 'Fascist tendencies' in his books. There are no post-1918 tendencies at all. Throughout his work there is a certain uneasy awareness of the problem of class distinctions, and scattered through it at various dates there are ignorant though not unfriendly references to Socialism. In *The Heart of a Goof* (1926) there is a rather silly story about a Russian novelist, which seems to have been inspired by the factional struggle then raging in the U.S.S.R. But the references in it to the Soviet system are entirely frivolous and, considering the date, not markedly hostile. That is about

the extent of Wodehouse's political consciousness, so far as it is dis-
coverable from his writings. Nowhere, so far as I know, does he so much
as use the word 'Fascism' or 'Nazism'. In left-wing circles, indeed in
'enlightened' circles of any kind, to broadcast on the Nazi radio, to have
any truck with the Nazis whatever, would have seemed just as shocking
an action before the war as during it. But that is a habit of mind that had
been developed during nearly a decade of ideological struggle against
Fascism. The bulk of the British people, one ought to remember, remained
anaesthetic to that struggle until late into 1940. Abyssinia, Spain, China,
Austria, Czechoslovakia – the long series of crimes and aggressions had
simply slid past their consciousness or were dimly noted as quarrels
occurring among foreigners and 'not our business'. One can gauge the
general ignorance from the fact that the ordinary Englishman thought of
'Fascism' as an exclusively Italian thing and was bewildered when the
same word was applied to Germany. And there is nothing in Wodehouse's
writings to suggest that he was better informed, or more interested in
politics, than the general run of his readers.

The other thing one must remember is that Wodehouse happened to
be taken prisoner at just the moment when the war reached its desperate
phase. We forget these things now, but until that time feelings about the
war had been noticeably tepid. There was hardly any fighting, the
Chamberlain government was unpopular, eminent publicists like Lloyd
George and Bernard Shaw[11] were hinting that we should make a
compromise peace as quickly as possible, trade union and Labour Party
branches all over the country were passing anti-war resolutions. Afterwards, of course, things changed. The Army was with difficulty extricated
from Dunkirk, France collapsed, Britain was alone, the bombs rained on
London, Goebbels announced that Britain was to be 'reduced to degradation and poverty'. By the middle of 1941 the British people knew what
they were up against and feelings against the enemy were far fiercer than
before. But Wodehouse had spent the intervening year in internment, and
his captors seem to have treated him reasonably well. He had missed the
turning-point of the war, and in 1941 he was still reacting in terms of
1939. He was not alone in this. On several occasions about this time the
Germans brought captured British soldiers to the microphone, and some
of them made remarks at least as tactless as Wodehouse's. They attracted

no attention, however. And even an outright Quisling like John Amery was afterwards to arouse much less indignation than Wodehouse had done.

But why? Why should a few rather silly but harmless remarks by an elderly novelist have provoked such an outcry? One has to look for the probable answer amid the dirty requirements of propaganda warfare.

There is one point about the Wodehouse broadcasts that is almost certainly significant – the date. Wodehouse was released two or three days before the invasion of the U.S.S.R., and at a time when the higher ranks of the Nazi party must have known that the invasion was imminent. It was vitally necessary to keep America out of the war as long as possible, and in fact, about this time, the German attitude towards the U.S.A. did become more conciliatory than it had been before. The Germans could hardly hope to defeat Russia, Britain and the U.S.A. in combination, but if they could polish off Russia quickly – and presumably they expected to do so – the Americans might never intervene. The release of Wodehouse was only a minor move, but it was not a bad sop to throw to the American isolationists. He was well known in the United States, and he was – or so the Germans calculated – popular with the Anglophobe public as a caricaturist who made fun of the silly-ass Englishman with his spats and his monocle. At the microphone he could be trusted to damage British prestige in one way or another, while his release would demonstrate that the Germans were good fellows and knew how to treat their enemies chivalrously. That presumably was the calculation, though the fact that Wodehouse was only broadcasting for about a week suggests that he did not come up to expectations.

But on the British side similar though opposite calculations were at work. For the two years following Dunkirk, British morale depended largely upon the feeling that this was not only a war for democracy but a war which the common people had to win by their own efforts. The upper classes were discredited by their appeasement policy and by the disasters of 1940, and a social levelling process appeared to be taking place. Patriotism and left-wing sentiments were associated in the popular mind, and numerous able journalists were at work to tie the association tighter. Priestley's 1940 broadcasts, and 'Cassandra's' articles in the *Daily Mirror*, were good examples of the demagogic propaganda flourishing at that time. In this atmosphere, Wodehouse made an ideal whipping-boy. For it was generally felt that the rich were treacherous, and Wodehouse – as 'Cassandra' vigorously pointed out in his broadcast – was a rich man. But he was the kind of rich man who could be attacked with impunity and without risking any damage to the structure of society. To denounce Wodehouse was not like denouncing, say, Beaverbrook. A mere novelist, however large his earnings may happen to be, is not *of* the possessing class. Even if his income touches £50,000 a year he has only the outward semblance of a millionaire. He is a lucky outsider who has fluked into a fortune – usually a very temporary fortune – like the winner of the Calcutta Derby Sweep. Consequently, Wodehouse's indiscretion gave a good propaganda opening. It was a chance to 'expose' a wealthy parasite without drawing attention to any of the parasites who really mattered.

In the desperate circumstances of the time, it was excusable to be angry at what Wodehouse did, but to go on denouncing him three or four years later – and more, to let an impression remain that he acted with conscious treachery – is not excusable.[12] Few things in this war have been more morally disgusting than the present hunt after traitors and Quislings. At best it is largely the punishment of the guilty by the guilty. In France, all kinds of petty rats – police officials, penny-a-lining journalists, women who have slept with German soldiers – are hunted down while almost without exception the big rats escape. In England the fiercest tirades against Quislings are uttered by Conservatives who were practising appeasement in 1938 and Communists who were advocating it in 1940. I have striven to show how the wretched Wodehouse – just because success and expatriation had allowed him to remain mentally in the Edwardian age – became the *corpus vile* in a propaganda experiment, and I suggest that it is now time to regard the incident as closed. If Ezra Pound is caught and shot by the American authorities, it will have the effect of establishing his reputation as a poet for hundreds of years; and even in the case of Wodehouse, if we drive him to retire to the United States and renounce his British citizenship, we shall end by being horribly ashamed of ourselves. Meanwhile, if we really want to punish the people who weakened national morale at critical moments, there are other culprits who are nearer home and better worth chasing.[13]

The Times Literary Supplement, *29 October 1999, published an article by Iain Sproat, 'In all innocence: The truth about P. G. Wodehouse and the Nazis'. This was based on the MI5 documents at last released in October 1999. He concludes:*

The British Foreign Office and Ministry of Defence papers, contained in the MI5 file, show that by 1947 the British authorities had concluded that Wodehouse had no case to answer either over the broadcasts or the money [he had received], and, in the words of the Foreign Office, contained in the file: 'Mr Wodehouse made the celebrated broadcasts in all innocence and without any evil intent' (pp. 14–15).

Orwell took the Wodehouses for a meal in a restaurant near Les Halles when he was in Paris for the Observer. He had, presumably, wished to follow up the writing of his article with a small, direct gesture of kindness. P. G. Wodehouse was anxious to reciprocate if Orwell returned to Paris, for he felt he owed him 'a Grade A lunch'. In a letter to his friend William Townend, 29 April 1945, Wodehouse said that Orwell's 'criticism of my stuff was masterly' and he praised Orwell for writing such an article 'at a time when it was taking a very unpopular view. He really is a good chap.' This seems to indicate that Orwell had sent Wodehouse an advance copy of his article, in typescript or proof. After Orwell's death, Wodehouse wrote to Denis MacKail (biographer of J. M. Barrie) on 11 August 1951 in rather different terms. He described the essay as 'practically one long roast of your correspondent. Don't you hate the way these critics falsify the facts in order to make a point?' His complaint was directed particularly at what Orwell had described as Wodehouse's out-of-touchness. This, Wodehouse claimed, was caused by his living in America where he couldn't write American stories and 'the only English characters the American public would read about were exaggerated dudes'. These two letters were published in a special feature, 'Yours, Plum' ('Plum' being Wodehouse's pet name), Sunday Telegraph Review, *19 August 1990. See* XVII/2625.

In 2000, Beyond a Joke, *a play on Wodehouse's involvement in making broadcasts for the Germans was written by Roger Milner and performed at Richmond Theatre and then toured. Wodehouse was played by Anton Rogers.*

1. P. G. Wodehouse (1881–1975), author, dramatist and lyricist. Although best remembered for his outstanding series of humorous novels (of which those featuring Jeeves are probably the best examples of his fantasy, language, wit and story construction), he also had considerable success in the theatre on both sides of the Atlantic, collaborating with, among others, Jerome Kern and Ira and George Gershwin, and wrote scripts for some two dozen films. Oxford University awarded him a D. Litt. in 1939. A year later, when France was overrun by the Germans, he was interned. In the summer of 1941 he gave an interview in Berlin for the CBS network to be broadcast to the United States (then neutral), and recorded five talks which were broadcast to the United States and to Britain (see n. 3 below). He was immediately vilified in Britain as a traitor. As Iain Sproat explains in *Wodehouse at War* (1981), the campaign was led by the Ministry of Information under Duff Cooper against the advice of the Governors of the BBC. Duff Cooper overruled them and insisted that a vitriolic attack be broadcast by the popular journalist William Connor, 'Cassandra' of the *Daily Mirror* (105). It is now remarkable that the *content* of these broadcasts should have caused such anger, though, given the circumstances in which Britain was then placed, it is not surprising that Wodehouse's motives were suspect. A full analysis, with the MI5 (secret service) report of 28 September 1944, which 'found no acceptable evidence of Wodehouse's guilt', is given in *Wodehouse at War* (12). When Orwell wrote his essay, he did not have access to the MI5 report. The texts of the broadcasts were published by *Encounter*, reprinted in *Performing Flea: A Self-Portrait in Letters* (Penguin, 1961), which also includes details of his time as an internee, ironically titled 'Wodehouse in Wonderland', and included by Sproat. After the war Wodehouse lived in virtual self-exile in the United States, but his work remained very popular, even during the war (Sproat, 28). In 1975, six weeks before he died, he was knighted. For Wodehouse's immediate and later reactions to Orwell's defence, see XVII/ 2625.

2. Wodehouse denied this; see Sproat, 42–3.

3. The BBC provided Major E. J. P. Cussen, the MI5 officer who interrogated Wodehouse, with the details known to them of the broadcasts. The interview with Flannery was broadcast to the United States from Berlin on 27 June 1941, and it was in June that Wodehouse recorded his five talks. The first was broadcast to America on 28 June, repeated to the Far East on 1 July and again to America the next day. Talks two to five were broadcast from 9 July to 6 August 1941. The five talks were broadcast to Britain from 9 to 14 August 1941 (Sproat, 160). Orwell's uncertainty here is indicative of the general lack of knowledge of precisely what had happened.

4. 'Cassandra' was the pseudonym of William Connor (1900–1967; Kt., 1966), a well-known radical journalist who wrote a personal column in the *Daily Mirror* under this name. (Cassandra was a Trojan prophetess whose predictions were fated not to be believed, though they invariably came to pass.) His *English at War* (April 1941) was the most popular of the Searchlight Books edited by T. R. Fyvel and Orwell; it was reprinted three times.

5. Vidkun Quisling (1887–1945), Norwegian Fascist who led the puppet government of Norway under the Germans. He was executed for treason. His name has been applied generally to collaborators.

6. In an interview with British journalist Hubert Cole (*Illustrated,* 7 December 1946) Wodehouse maintained that this statement, which appeared in his interview, was written by Flannery: 'He wrote the whole script, including the words you mention, and I read them without realising their intention. I did not even notice them at the time' (Sproat, 58).

7. Ezra Pound (1885–1972), American poet who supported Mussolini in the 1930s. During World War II he lived in Italy and from 1941 broadcast in support of the Fascist powers. He was arrested by US forces in 1945 and tried for treason, but was declared insane. He was confined in St Elizabeths [*sic*] Hospital in Washington until 1958. On 14 February 1949 he was awarded the Bollingen Prize for Poetry. Orwell wrote a defence of this award, 'A Prize for Ezra Pound', *Partisan Review*, May 1949 (XX/*3612*). It was one of his last writings.

8. John Amery (1912–45), right-wing politician and son of Leo Amery, who was a Conservative and patriotic MP and Secretary of State for India, 1940–45. John Amery, an ardent admirer of Hitler, broadcast from Germany during the war urging British subjects in captivity to fight for Germany against England and Russia, and also made public speeches throughout occupied Europe on behalf of the German regime. He was executed for treason by the British in December 1945.

9. Ian Hay (John Hay Beith, 1876–1952), novelist and dramatist. Wodehouse and Hay collaborated on the plays *A Damsel in Distress* (1928) and *Baa, Baa, Black Sheep* (1929).

10. A 'Knut' is a variant of 'Nut' (perhaps slang for the head) and, with a 'K', dates from 1911. It refers to a smart man-about-town and, in the music-hall song sung by Basil Hallam which Orwell mentions, 'Gilbert the Filbert' (picking up the reference to 'nut'), the 'K' was pronounced: 'I'm Gilbert the Filbert, the Colonel of the K-nuts'.

11. 'like Lloyd George and Bernard Shaw' was not included in *The Windmill* and, though set in proof for *Critical Essays*, was marked to be omitted. This cut may have been a result of in-house censorship for fear of libel. Lloyd George, World War I Prime Minister, died in 1945 but Bernard Shaw was alive until 1950 and, until then, a libel action could have been launched.

12. For thirty-five years, successive British governments kept Wodehouse's file under seal as an 'official secret'. This included the MI5 interrogation report. The suspicion of Wodehouse's treachery was allowed to stand unanswered authoritatively (Sproat, 104). See Afterword.

13. When Evelyn Waugh reviewed *Critical Essays*, he referred to Wodehouse's 'pacifist strain'. This prompted Orwell to look up 'a rare early book', *The Gold Bat* (1904), where he found passages suggesting that 'Wodehouse had had some kind of connection with the Liberal Party, about 1908, when it was the anti-militarist party'. (Orwell has slightly mistaken the date.) He told Waugh in his letter to him of 16 May 1948 (see XIX/*3401*), 'I will add a footnote to this effect if I ever reprint the essays.' Orwell died before the essays were reprinted, so this reference has been added here.

[*2818*]

'The Sporting Spirit'
Tribune, *14 December 1945*

Now that the brief visit of the Dynamo football team[1] has come to an end, it is possible to say publicly what many thinking people were saying privately before the Dynamos ever arrived. That is, that sport is an unfailing cause of ill-will, and that if such a visit as this had any effect at all on Anglo-Soviet relations, it could only be to make them slightly worse than before.

Even the newspapers have been unable to conceal the fact that at least two of the four matches played led to much bad feeling. At the Arsenal match, I am told by someone who was there, a British and a Russian player came to blows and the crowd booed the referee. The Glasgow match, someone else informs me, was simply a free-for-all from the start.[2] And then there was the controversy, typical of our nationalistic age, about the composition of the Arsenal team. Was it really an all-England team, as claimed by the Russians, or merely a league team, as claimed by the British? And did the Dynamos end their tour abruptly in order to avoid playing an all-England team? As usual, everyone answers these questions according to his political predilections. Not quite everyone, however. I noted with interest, as an instance of the vicious passions that football provokes, that the sporting correspondent of the Russophile *News Chronicle* took the anti-Russian line and maintained that Arsenal was *not* an all-England team. No doubt the controversy will continue to echo for years in the footnotes of history books. Meanwhile the result of the Dynamos' tour, in so far as it has had any result, will have been to create fresh animosity on both sides.

And how could it be otherwise? I am always amazed when I hear people saying that sport creates goodwill between the nations, and that if only the common peoples of the world could meet one another at football or cricket, they would have no inclination to meet on the battlefield. Even if one didn't know from concrete examples (the 1936 Olympic Games, for instance) that international sporting contests lead to orgies of hatred, one could deduce it from general principles.

Nearly all the sports practised nowadays are competitive. You play to win, and the game has little meaning unless you do your utmost to win. On the village green, where you pick up sides and no feeling of local patriotism is involved, it is possible to play simply for the fun and the exercise: but as soon as the question of prestige arises, as soon as you feel that you and some larger unit will be disgraced if you lose, the most savage combative instincts are aroused. Anyone who has played even in a school football match knows this. At the international level sport is frankly mimic warfare. But the significant thing is not the behaviour of the players but the attitude of the spectators: and, behind the spectators, of the nations who work themselves into furies over these absurd contests, and seriously believe – at any rate for short periods – that running, jumping and kicking a ball are tests of national virtue.

Even a leisurely game like cricket, demanding grace rather than strength, can cause much ill-will, as we saw in the controversy over body-line bowling and over the rough tactics of the Australian team that visited England in 1921. Football, a game in which everyone gets hurt and every nation has its own style of play which seems unfair to foreigners, is far worse. Worst of all is boxing. One of the most horrible sights in the world is a fight between white and coloured boxers before a mixed audience. But a boxing audience is always disgusting, and the behaviour of the women, in particular, is such that the Army, I believe, does not allow them to attend its contests. At any rate, two or three years ago, when Home Guards and regular troops were holding a boxing tournament, I was placed on guard at the door of the hall, with orders to keep the women out.

In England, the obsession with sport is bad enough, but even fiercer passions are aroused in young countries where games-playing and nationalism are both recent developments. In countries like India or Burma, it is necessary at football matches to have strong cordons of police to keep the crowd from invading the field. In Burma, I have seen the supporters of one side break through the police and disable the goalkeeper of the opposing side at a critical moment. The first big football match that was played in Spain, about fifteen years ago, led to an uncontrollable riot. As soon as strong feelings of rivalry are aroused, the notion of playing the game according to the rules always vanishes. People want to see one side on top and the other side humiliated, and they forget that victory gained through cheating or through the intervention of the crowd is meaningless. Even when the spectators don't intervene physically, they try to influence the game by cheering their own side and 'rattling' opposing players with boos and insults. Serious sport has nothing to do with fair play. It is bound up with hatred, jealousy, boastfulness, disregard of all rules and sadistic pleasure in witnessing violence: in other words it is war minus the shooting.

Instead of blah-blahing about the clean, healthy rivalry of the football field and the great part played by the Olympic Games in bringing the nations together, it is more useful to inquire how and why this modern cult of sport arose. Most of the games we now play are of ancient origin, but sport does not seem to have been taken very seriously between Roman times and the nineteenth century. Even in the English public schools the games cult did not start till the later part of the last century. Dr. Arnold, generally regarded as the founder of the modern public school, looked on games as simply a waste of time. Then, chiefly in England and the United States, games were built up into a heavily-financed activity, capable of attracting vast crowds and rousing savage passions, and the infection spread from country to country. It is the most violently combative sports, football and boxing, that have spread the widest. There cannot be much doubt that the whole thing is bound up with the rise of nationalism – that is, with the lunatic modern habit of identifying oneself with large power units and seeing everything in terms of competitive prestige. Also, organised games are more likely to flourish in urban communities where the average human being lives a sedentary or at least a confined life, and does not get much opportunity for creative labour. In a rustic community a boy or young man works off a good deal of his surplus energy by walking, swimming, snowballing, climbing trees, riding horses, and by various sports involving cruelty to animals, such as fishing, cock-fighting and ferreting for rats. In a big town one must indulge in group activities if one wants an outlet for one's physical strength or for one's sadistic impulses. Games are taken seriously in London and New York, and they were taken seriously in Rome and Byzantium: in the Middle Ages they were played, and probably played with much physical brutality, but they were not mixed up with politics nor a cause of group hatreds.

If you wanted to add to the vast fund of ill-will existing in the world at this moment, you could hardly do it better than by a series of football matches between Jews and Arabs, Germans and Czechs, Indians and British, Russians and Poles, and Italians and Jugoslavs, each match to be watched by a mixed audience of 100,000 spectators. I do not, of course, suggest that sport is one of the main causes of international rivalry; big-scale sport is itself, I think, merely another effect of the causes that have produced nationalism. Still, you do make things worse by sending forth a team of eleven men, labelled as national champions, to do battle against some rival team, and allowing it to be felt on all sides that whichever nation is defeated will 'lose face'.

I hope, therefore, that we shan't follow up the visit of the Dynamos by sending a British team to the USSR If we must do so, then let us send a second-rate team which is sure to be beaten and cannot be claimed to represent Britain as a whole. There are quite enough real causes of trouble already, and we need not add to them by encouraging young men to kick each other on the shins amid the roars of infuriated spectators.

> *'The Sporting Spirit' produced quite a lively correspondence in* Tribune *(see XVII/443–6). One letter, from E. S. Fayers, said, 'It is obvious from the article that George'* – *the familiar style is indicative of Orwell's relationship with many of his readers* – *'has never played football for the love of it* – *and nobody, except perhaps a few schoolboys and professionals, ever plays for any other reason. Let me assure George that football does not consist of two young men kicking one another's shins.' He went on to argue that football crowds were not 'ignorant mobs of sadistic morons' but 'a pretty good mixture of just ordinary men'. Orwell had, of course, played football (and the Wall Game) with some success and with evident enjoyment, especially at Eton; see X/40 for his poem 'Wall Game'* – *a parody of Kipling's 'If' and 40, n. 1 for a brief account of his prowess. For his own experience of 'international football', see the first paragraph of 'Shooting an Elephant' (see* Orwell and Politics *in this series, or XI/326), describing the animosity between Burmese and British players and the attitude of spectators. Orwell played football for the police in Burma so he had personal experience of games between British and local players.*

1. The Moscow Dynamos, a Russian soccer team, toured Britain in the autumn of 1945 and played a number of leading British clubs. 'Guest players' were allowed into teams at this time because of wartime conditions, but, even allowing for that, it was claimed that Britain's Arsenal team had been unduly strengthened.

2. The editor was present at Ibrox Park, Glasgow, for this match. There was an enormous crowd, and memory suggests that it was orderly and that the game was not unduly 'robust' – but Orwell was pointing accurately to the way sport, especially international contact sport, would develop.

[2983]

Review of The Ragged-Trousered Philanthropists by Robert Tressall

Manchester Evening News, 25 April 1946

When *The Ragged-Trousered Philanthropists*, which was reprinted as a Penguin about a year ago, was first published the term 'proletarian literature' had hardly been coined. In the last 15 years, on the other hand, we have heard rather too much of it and usually in a specialised and unsatisfactory sense.

A 'proletarian' book has come to mean not necessarily a book written by a member of the working class, and still less the kind of book that the average working man would willingly read, but the kind of book which in the opinion of middle-class intellectuals every right-minded worker ought to read. 'Proletarian literature' means books about industrial life written from an orthodox Marxist angle, and its most successful practitioners are people who have either never done any manual work or have long since abandoned it.

The Ragged-Trousered Philanthropists seldom gets a mention when this school of literature is discussed, though it has been reprinted often enough to make it describable as a popular book.

Robert Tressall, its author, was a house painter, who died prematurely (he is said to have committed suicide) in 1914 before his book was published.[1] He thus never left the ranks of the working class, and it is interesting to speculate whether he would have wished to do so if he had lived on with the opportunity of becoming a successful writer.

Although his book is cast in story form it is in effect a day-to-day account of life in the building trade at a time (1913 or thereabouts) when sevenpence an hour was an accepted wage for a skilled man. One cannot say that it is a strictly 'objective' book – it does indeed contain a good deal of Socialist propaganda of a naïve idealistic kind – but it is essentially an honest book and valuable above all for the exactness of its observation.

Without sensationalism and almost without plot it sets out to record the actual detail of manual work and the tiny things almost unimaginable to any comfortably situated person which make life a misery when one's income drops below a certain level.

Here is a typical extract – a description of a workman stripping the walls and ceiling of a room before distempering it.

Although it was only a small room Joe had to tear into the work pretty hard all the time, for the ceiling seemed to have had two or three coats of whitewash which had never been washed off, and there were several thicknesses of paper on the walls. The difficulty of removing these papers was increased by the fact that the dado had been varnished. In order to get this off it had been necessary to soak it several times with strong soda water, and, although Joe was as careful as possible, he had not been able to avoid getting some of this stuff on his fingers. The result was that his nails were all burnt and discoloured and the flesh round them cracked and bleeding. However, he had got it all off at last and he was not sorry, for his right arm and shoulder were aching from the prolonged strain and in the palm of his right hand there was a blister as large as a shilling caused by the handle of the stripping knife.

It is pedestrian enough, and yet the accumulation of authentic details of this kind produces in the long run an extraordinarily vivid effect. Tressall is especially good at bringing out the importance of very small disasters.

He knows, for instance, all about the loss of sleep that can be entailed by not possessing a clock. But he also has another kind of realism which makes his book especially interesting and marks it off sharply from the 'proletarian literature' of today.

In the last twenty years or so books written from a Left-wing angle have usually idealised the working class. Tressall, although he pities his fellow-workers, also despises them and says so plainly. The word 'philanthropists' in the title of the book is ironical. The workers are 'philanthropists' because they are fools enough to support – out of charity, as it were – a worthless class of property-owners. They not only accept their fate like cattle but 'oppose and ridicule any suggestion of reform'. This last is the main theme of the book.

All the way through the thoughtful Socialistic workman Frank Owen (who is, no doubt, a portrait of Tressall himself) is shown arguing with his mates trying to make them see that the capitalist system is responsible for their miseries and being met not merely with apathy and ignorance but with downright ill-will.

With few exceptions they regard the social system as reasonably just and the division into rich and poor as inevitable, believe unemployment to be due to 'this here labour-saving machinery', and are resentful when someone proposes – as they see it – to rob them of their chance of making a fortune by private enterprise.

Although the likeliest end for all of them is to die in the work-house, their outlook is essentially capitalistic, and Owen's private comment on them is, 'No wonder the rich despised them and looked upon them as dirt. They were despicable. They were dirt.'

The unfortunate Owen, discouraged by their ignorance and hostility, assails them with arguments taken out of penny tracts, using pedantic language, which irritates them all the more. These conversations make very pathetic reading. They remind one of the years of patient, unrewarded work by obscure people that has to be done before any new idea can get a footing among the great masses.

The pathos lies in the fact that nearly everything Owen says would now be regarded as a commonplace. When he says that machinery increases wealth and does not diminish it or that money is merely a token which has no value in itself he is greeted with jeers. Today such ideas are accepted by almost everyone, thanks precisely to the efforts of thousands of unhonoured people like Owen himself.

Although the book ends with Owen, who is suffering from tuberculosis and sees no hope for his wife and child after he is gone, contemplating murder and suicide its effect is in some sense encouraging. For, after all, the particular kind of folly against which he struggled so unsuccessfully is no longer dominant. The 'Conservative working man' is almost a vanished type.

Tressall died before completing the book and the manuscript was afterwards put in order by Miss Jessie Pope. It is a book that everyone should read. Quite apart from its value as a piece of social history it leaves one with the feeling that a considerable novelist was lost in this young working-man whom society could not bother to keep alive.

1. Tressall's real name was Robert Noonan; 'Tressall' is properly spelt 'Tressell' (born 1870, died of tuberculosis 1911). Jessie Pope's edition was abridged. The complete text was not published until 1955, edited by F. C. Ball. Ball wrote two excellent biographies of Tressell: *Tressell of Mugsborough* (1951) and *One of the Damned: The Life and Times of Robert Tressell* (1973).

[3104]

'How the Poor Die'
Now, *[n.s.] No. 6, [November 1946]*

*It is not known when this article was written. Orwell describes his experiences
in the Hôpital Cochin, rue Faubourg Saint-Jacques, Paris, when taken ill
with 'une grippe' (influenza) in March 1929. The article was intended for
Horizon but rejected. George Woodcock (editor of Now, which published
the article in 1946) told Ian Angus in 1991 that he understood from Orwell
that Connolly had rejected the article on medical advice that claimed the
essay was highly exaggerated and libelled the medical profession. It is a little
surprising if Connolly found such reasons convincing although, if the rejection
came shortly after Orwell's wife's beloved brother was killed attending the
wounded at Dunkirk, Orwell might have been sympathetic to such suggestions.
I conjecture that the essay was intended for Horizon for December 1940.
The Germans were then carrying out heavy bombing and it was pretty plain
'how the poor (and others) died'. That issue contains what looks rather like
a stop-gap, a six-page extract from Orwell's forthcoming book, The Lion
and the Unicorn (Part I is included in Orwell's England, and Parts II
and III in Orwell and Politics, both in this series). The article in Now
takes eight pages. This may be too neat a solution (especially as 'The Ruling
Class' might have appealed to Connolly in its own right in the light of what
he was writing in the Comment columns of Horizon from July to December
1940). In August 1946, Woodcock wrote to Orwell in Jura asking him to
write something for Now; Orwell agreed but added, 'God knows when I'll
write anything' (XVIII/3048). He returned from Jura on 13 October and,
following Woodcock's request, he may have resorted to the article he had
written some time earlier. At a time when the National Health Service
(established 1948) was being proposed, it must have seemed far more timely
than in 1940. There is one further oddity about the genesis of this article.
The hospital records show Orwell's date of birth as 1902, not 1903. This
must have been taken from his passport. Records show that between 1928
and 1949 (when he applied for a passport with his correct date of birth)
Orwell's passports were dated 1902. The error seems to stem from that of a
clerk in Burma. In itself this is of little moment were it not that it may have
been this that drew his attention to the falsification of dates for political*

purposes (see, for example, Maurice Thorez, XVI/*2579, and* Nineteen
Eighty-Four, *81). For a much fuller account of both matters, see* XVIII/
3103.

In the year 1929 I spent several weeks in the Hôpital X, in the fifteenth
Arrondissement of Paris.[1] The clerks put me through the usual third-
degree at the reception desk, and indeed I was kept answering questions
for some twenty minutes before they would let me in. If you have ever
had to fill up forms in a Latin country you will know the kind of questions
I mean. For some days past I had been unequal to translating Réaumur
into Fahrenheit, but I know that my temperature was round about 103,
and by the end of the interview I had some difficulty in standing on my
feet. At my back a resigned little knot of patients, carrying bundles done
up in coloured handkerchiefs, waited their turn to be questioned.

After the questioning came the bath – a compulsory routine for all
newcomers, apparently, just as in prison or the workhouse. My clothes
were taken away from me, and after I had sat shivering for some minutes
in five inches of warm water I was given a linen nightshirt and a short
blue flannel dressing-gown – no slippers, they had none big enough for
me, they said – and led out into the open air. This was a night in February
and I was suffering from pneumonia.[2] The ward we were going to was
200 yards away and it seemed that to get to it you had to cross the
hospital grounds. Someone stumbled in front of me with a lantern. The
gravel path was frosty underfoot, and the wind whipped the nightshirt
round my bare calves. When we got into the ward I was aware of a strange
feeling of familiarity whose origin I did not succeed in pinning down till
later in the night. It was a long, rather low, ill-lit room, full of murmuring
voices and with three rows of beds surprisingly close together. There was
a foul smell, faecal and yet sweetish. As I lay down I saw on a bed nearly
opposite me a small, round-shouldered, sandy-haired man sitting half
naked while a doctor and a student performed some strange operation on
him. First the doctor produced from his black bag a dozen small glasses
like wine glasses, then the student burned a match inside each glass to
exhaust the air, then the glass was popped on to the man's back or chest
and the vacuum drew up a huge yellow blister. Only after some moments
did I realise what they were doing to him. It was something called

cupping, a treatment which you can read about in old medical textbooks but which till then I had vaguely thought of as one of those things they do to horses.

The cold air outside had probably lowered my temperature, and I watched this barbarous remedy with detachment and even a certain amount of amusement. The next moment, however, the doctor and the student came across to my bed, hoisted me upright and without a word began applying the same set of glasses, which had not been sterilised in any way. A few feeble protests that I uttered got no more response than if I had been an animal. I was very much impressed by the impersonal way in which the two men started on me. I had never been in the public ward of a hospital before, and it was my first experience of doctors who handle you without speaking to you, or, in a human sense, taking any notice of you. They only put on six glasses in my case, but after doing so they scarified the blisters and applied the glasses again. Each glass now drew out about a dessert-spoonful of dark-coloured blood. As I lay down again, humiliated, disgusted and frightened by the thing that had been done to me, I reflected that now at least they would leave me alone. But no, not a bit of it. There was another treatment coming, the mustard poultice, seemingly a matter of routine like the hot bath. Two slatternly nurses had already got the poultice ready, and they lashed it round my chest as tight as a strait jacket while some men who were wandering about the ward in shirt and trousers began to collect round my bed with half-sympathetic grins. I learned later that watching a patient have a mustard poultice was a favourite pastime in the ward. These things are normally applied for a quarter of an hour and certainly they are funny enough if you don't happen to be the person inside. For the first five minutes the pain is severe, but you believe you can bear it. During the second five minutes this belief evaporates, but the poultice is buckled at the back and you can't get it off. This is the period the onlookers most enjoy. During the last five minutes, I noted, a sort of numbness supervenes. After the poultice had been removed a waterproof pillow packed with ice was thrust beneath my head and I was left alone. I did not sleep, and to the best of my knowledge this was the only night of my life – I mean the only night spent in bed – in which I have not slept at all, not even a minute.

During my first hour in the Hôpital X I had had a whole series of different and contradictory treatments, but this was misleading, for in general you got very little treatment at all, either good or bad, unless you were ill in some interesting and instructive way. At five in the morning the nurses came round, woke the patients and took their temperatures, but did not wash them. If you were well enough you washed yourself, otherwise you depended on the kindness of some walking patient. It was generally patients, too, who carried the bedbottles and the grim bedpan, nicknamed *la casserole*. At eight breakfast arrived, called army-fashion *la soupe*. It was soup, too, a thin vegetable soup with slimy hunks of bread floating about in it. Later in the day the tall, solemn, black-bearded doctor made his rounds, with an interne and a troop of students following at his heels, but there were about sixty of us in the ward and it was evident that he had other wards to attend to as well. There were many beds past which he walked day after day, sometimes followed by imploring cries. On the other hand if you had some disease with which the students wanted to familiarise themselves you got plenty of attention of a kind. I myself, with an exceptionally fine specimen of a bronchial rattle, sometimes had as many as a dozen students queuing up to listen to my chest. It was a very queer feeling – queer, I mean, because of their intense interest in learning their job, together with a seeming lack of any perception that the patients were human beings. It is strange to relate, but sometimes as some young student stepped forward to take his turn at manipulating you he would be actually tremulous with excitement, like a boy who has at last got his hands on some expensive piece of machinery. And then ear after ear – ears of young men, of girls, of negroes – pressed against your back, relays of fingers solemnly but clumsily tapping, and not from any one of them did you get a word of conversation or a look direct in your face. As a non-paying patient, in the uniform nightshirt, you were primarily *a specimen*, a thing I did not resent but could never quite get used to.

After some days I grew well enough to sit up and study the surrounding patients. The stuffy room, with its narrow beds so close together that you could easily touch your neighbour's hand, had every sort of disease in it except, I suppose, acutely infectious cases. My right-hand neighbour was a little red-haired cobbler with one leg shorter than the other, who used to announce the death of any other patient (this happened a number of times, and my neighbour was always the first to hear of it) by whistling to me, exclaiming 'Numero 43!' (or whatever it was) and flinging his arms above his head. This man had not much wrong with him, but in most of the other beds within my angle of vision some squalid tragedy or some plain horror was being enacted. In the bed that was foot to foot with mine there lay, until he died (I didn't see him die – they moved him to another bed), a little weazened man who was suffering from I do not know what disease, but something that made his whole body so intensely sensitive that any movement from side to side, sometimes even the weight of the bedclothes, would make him shout out with pain. His worst suffering was when he urinated, which he did with the greatest difficulty. A nurse would bring him the bedbottle and then for a long time stand beside his bed, whistling, as grooms are said to do with horses, until at last with an agonised shriek of '*Je pisse!*' he would get started. In the bed next to him the sandy-haired man whom I had seen being cupped used to cough up blood-streaked mucus at all hours. My left-hand neighbour was a tall, flaccid-looking young man who used periodically to have a tube inserted into his back and astonishing quantities of frothy liquid drawn off from some part of his body. In the bed beyond that a veteran of the war of 1870 was dying, a handsome old man with a white imperial,[3] round whose bed, at all hours when visiting was allowed, four elderly female relatives dressed all in black sat exactly like crows, obviously scheming for some pitiful legacy. In the bed opposite me in the further row was an old baldheaded man with drooping moustaches and greatly swollen face and body, who was suffering from some disease that made him urinate almost incessantly. A huge glass receptacle stood always beside his bed. One day his wife and daughter came to visit him. At sight of them the old man's bloated face lit up with a smile of surprising sweetness, and as his daughter, a pretty girl of about twenty, approached the bed I saw that his hand was slowly working its way from under the bedclothes. I seemed to see in advance the gesture that was coming – the girl kneeling beside the bed, the old man's hand laid on her head in his dying blessing. But no, he merely handed her the bedbottle, which she promptly took from him and emptied into the receptacle.

About a dozen beds away from me was Numero 57 – I think that was his number – a cirrhosis of the liver case. Everyone in the ward knew him by sight because he was sometimes the subject of a medical lecture. On two afternoons a week the tall, grave doctor would lecture in the ward to a party of students, and on more than one occasion old Numero 57 was wheeled on a sort of trolley into the middle of the ward, where the doctor would roll back his nightshirt, dilate with his fingers a huge flabby protuberance on the man's belly – the diseased liver, I suppose – and explain solemnly that this was a disease attributable to alcoholism, commoner in the wine-drinking countries. As usual he neither spoke to his patient nor gave him a smile, a nod or any kind of recognition. While he talked, very grave and upright, he would hold the wasted body beneath his two hands, sometimes giving it a gentle roll to and fro, in just the attitude of a woman handling a rolling-pin. Not that Numero 57 minded this kind of thing. Obviously he was an old hospital inmate, a regular exhibit at lectures, his liver long since marked down for a bottle in some pathological museum. Utterly uninterested in what was said about him, he would lie with his colourless eyes gazing at nothing, while the doctor showed him off like a piece of antique china. He was a man of about sixty, astonishingly shrunken. His face, pale as vellum, had shrunken away till it seemed no bigger than a doll's.

One morning my cobbler neighbour woke me by plucking at my pillow before the nurses arrived. 'Numero 57!' – he flung his arms above his head. There was a light in the ward, enough to see by. I could see old Numero 57 lying crumpled up on his side, his face sticking out over the side of the bed, and towards me. He had died some time during the night, nobody knew when. When the nurses came they received the news of his death indifferently and went about their work. After a long time, an hour or more, two other nurses marched in abreast like soldiers, with a great clumping of sabots, and knotted the corpse up in the sheets, but it was not removed till some time later. Meanwhile, in the better light, I had had time for a good look at Numero 57. Indeed I lay on my side to look at him. Curiously enough he was the first dead European I had seen. I had seen dead men before, but always Asiatics and usually people who had died violent deaths. Numero 57's eyes were still open, his mouth also open, his small face contorted into an expression of agony. What most impressed me however was the whiteness of his face. It had been pale before, but now it was little darker than the sheets. As I gazed at the tiny, screwed-up face it struck me that this disgusting piece of refuse, waiting to be carted away and dumped on a slab in the dissecting-room, was an example of 'natural' death, one of the things you pray for in the Litany.[4] There you are, then, I thought, that's what is waiting for you, twenty, thirty, forty years hence: that is how the lucky ones die, the ones who live to be old. One wants to live, of course, indeed one only stays alive by virtue of the fear of death, but I think now, as I thought then, that it's better to die violently and not too old. People talk about the horrors of war, but what weapon has man invented that even approaches in cruelty some of the commoner diseases? 'Natural' death, almost by definition, means something slow, smelly and painful. Even at that, it makes a difference if you can achieve it in your own home and not in a public institution. This poor old wretch who had just flickered out like a candle-end was not even important enough to have anyone watching by his deathbed. He was merely a number, then a 'subject' for the students' scalpels. And the sordid publicity of dying in such a place! In the Hôpital X the beds were very close together and there were no screens. Fancy, for instance, dying like the little man whose bed was for a while foot to foot with mine, the one who cried out when the bedclothes touched him! I dare say '*Je pisse!*' were his last recorded words. Perhaps the dying don't bother about such things – that at least would be the standard answer: nevertheless dying people are often more or less normal in their minds till within a day or so of the end.

In the public wards of a hospital you see horrors that you don't seem to meet with among people who manage to die in their own homes, as though certain diseases only attacked people at the lower income levels. But it is a fact that you would not in any English hospitals see some of the things I saw in the Hôpital X. This business of people just dying like animals, for instance, with nobody standing by, nobody interested, the death not even noticed till the morning – this happened more than once. You certainly would not see that in England, and still less would you see a corpse left exposed to the view of the other patients. I remember that once in a cottage hospital in England a man died while we were at tea, and though there were only six of us in the ward the nurses managed things so adroitly that the man was dead and his body removed without our even hearing about it till tea was over. A thing we perhaps underrate in England is the advantage we enjoy in having large numbers of well-trained and rigidly-disciplined nurses. No doubt English nurses are dumb enough, they may tell fortunes with tealeaves, wear Union Jack badges and keep photographs of the Queen on their mantelpieces, but at least they don't let you lie unwashed and constipated on an unmade bed, out of sheer laziness. The nurses at the Hôpital X still had a tinge of Mrs. Gamp about them, and later, in the military hospitals of Republican Spain, I was to see nurses almost too ignorant to take a temperature. You wouldn't, either, see in England such dirt as existed in the Hôpital X. Later on, when I was well enough to wash myself in the bathroom, I found that there was kept there a huge packing case into which the scraps of food and dirty dressings from the ward were flung, and the wainscotings were infested by crickets.

When I had got back my clothes and grown strong on my legs I fled from the Hôpital X, before my time was up and without waiting for a medical discharge. It was not the only hospital I have fled from, but its gloom and bareness, its sickly smell and, above all, something in its mental atmosphere stand out in my memory as exceptional. I had been taken there because it was the hospital belonging to my arrondissement, and I did not learn till after I was in it that it bore a bad reputation. A year or two later the celebrated swindler, Madame Hanaud, who was ill while on remand, was taken to the Hôpital X, and after a few days of it she managed to elude her guards, took a taxi and drove back to the prison, explaining that she was more comfortable there. I have no doubt that the Hôpital X was quite untypical of French hospitals even at that date. But the patients, nearly all of them working-men, were surprisingly resigned. Some of them seemed to find the conditions almost comfortable, for at least two were destitute malingerers who found this a good way of getting through the winter. The nurses connived because the malingerers made themselves useful by doing odd jobs. But the attitude of the majority was: of course this is a lousy place, but what else do you expect? It did not seem strange to them that you should be woken at five and then wait three hours before starting the day on watery soup, or that people should die with no one at their bedside, or even that your chance of getting medical attention should depend on catching the doctor's eye as he went past. According to their traditions that was what hospitals were like. If you are seriously ill, and if you are too poor to be treated in your own home, then you must go into hospital, and once there you must put up with harshness and discomfort, just as you would in the army. But on top of this I was interested to find a lingering belief in the old stories that have now almost faded from memory in England – stories, for instance, about doctors cutting you open out of sheer curiosity or thinking it funny to start operating before you were properly 'under'. There were dark tales about a little operating-room said to be situated just beyond the bathroom. Dreadful screams were said to issue from this room. I saw nothing to confirm these stories and no doubt they were all nonsense, though I did see two students kill a sixteen-year-old boy, or nearly kill him (he appeared to be dying when I left the hospital, but he may have recovered later) by a mischievous experiment which they probably could not have tried on a paying patient. Well within living memory it used to be believed in London that in some of the big hospitals patients were killed off to get dissection subjects. I didn't hear this tale repeated at the Hôpital X, but I should think some of the men there would have found it credible. For it was a hospital in which not the methods, perhaps, but something of the atmosphere of the nineteenth century had managed to survive, and therein lay its peculiar interest.

During the past fifty years or so there has been a great change in the relationship between doctor and patient. If you look at almost any literature before the later part of the nineteenth century, you find that a hospital is popularly regarded as much the same thing as a prison, and an old-fashioned, dungeon-like prison at that. A hospital is a place of filth, torture and death, a sort of antechamber to the tomb. No one who was not more or less destitute would have thought of going into such a place for treatment. And especially in the early part of the last century, when medical science had grown bolder than before without being any more successful, the whole business of doctoring was looked on with horror and dread by ordinary people. Surgery, in particular, was believed to be no more than a peculiarly gruesome form of sadism, and dissection, possible only with the aid of bodysnatchers, was even confused with necromancy. From the nineteenth century you could collect a large horror-literature connected with doctors and hospitals. Think of poor old George III, in his dotage, shrieking for mercy as he sees his surgeons approaching to 'bleed him till he faints'! Think of the conversations of

Bob Sawyer and Benjamin Allen, which no doubt are hardly parodies, or the field hospitals in *La Débâcle* and *War and Peace*, or that shocking description of an amputation in Melville's *White-Jacket*![5] Even the names given to doctors in nineteenth-century English fiction, Slasher, Carver, Sawyer, Fillgrave and so on, and the generic nickname 'sawbones', are about as grim as they are comic. The anti-surgery tradition is perhaps best expressed in Tennyson's poem, 'The Children's Hospital', which is essentially a pre-chloroform document though it seems to have been written as late as 1880.[6] Moreover, the outlook which Tennyson records in this poem had a lot to be said for it. When you consider what an operation without anaesthetics must have been like, what it notoriously *was* like, it is difficult not to suspect the motives of people who would undertake such things. For these bloody horrors which the students so eagerly looked forward to ('A magnificent sight if Slasher does it!') were admittedly more or less useless: the patient who did not die of shock usually died of gangrene, a result which was taken for granted. Even now doctors can be found whose motives are questionable. Anyone who has had much illness, or who has listened to medical students talking, will know what I mean. But anaesthetics were a turning point, and disinfectants were another. Nowhere in the world, probably, would you now see the kind of scene described by Axel Munthe in *The Story of San Michele*,[7] when the sinister surgeon in top hat and frock coat, his starched shirtfront spattered with blood and pus, carves up patient after patient with the same knife and flings the severed limbs into a pile beside the table. Moreover, national health insurance has partly done away with the idea that a working-class patient is a pauper who deserves little consideration. Well into this century it was usual for 'free' patients at the big hospitals to have their teeth extracted with no anaesthetic. They didn't pay, so why should they have an anaesthetic – that was the attitude. That too has changed.

And yet every institution will always bear upon it some lingering memory of its past. A barrack-room is still haunted by the ghost of Kipling, and it is difficult to enter a workhouse without being reminded of *Oliver Twist*. Hospitals began as a kind of casual ward for lepers and the like to die in, and they continued as places where medical students learned their art on the bodies of the poor. You can still catch a faint suggestion of their history in their characteristically gloomy architecture.

I would be far from complaining about the treatment I have received in any English hospital, but I do know that it is a sound instinct that warns people to keep out of hospitals if possible, and especially out of the public wards. Whatever the legal position may be, it is unquestionable that you have far less control over your own treatment, far less certainty that frivolous experiments will not be tried on you, when it is a case of 'accept the discipline or get out'. And it is a great thing to die in your own bed, though it is better still to die in your boots. However great the kindness and the efficiency, in every hospital death there will be some cruel, squalid detail, some thing perhaps too small to be told but leaving terribly painful memories behind, arising out of the haste, the crowding, the impersonality of a place where every day people are dying among strangers.

The dread of hospitals probably still survives among the very poor, and in all of us it has only recently disappeared. It is a dark patch not far beneath the surface of our minds. I have said earlier that when I entered the ward at the Hôpital X I was conscious of a strange feeling of familiarity. What the scene reminded me of, of course, was the reeking, pain-filled hospitals of the nineteenth century, which I had never seen but of which I had a traditional knowledge. And something, perhaps the black-clad doctor with his frowsy black bag, or perhaps only the sickly smell, played the queer trick of unearthing from my memory that poem of Tennyson's, 'The Children's Hospital', which I had not thought of for twenty years. It happened that as a child I had had it read aloud to me by a sick-nurse whose own working life might have stretched back to the time when Tennyson wrote the poem. The horrors and sufferings of the old-style hospitals were a vivid memory to her. We had shuddered over the poem together, and then seemingly I had forgotten it. Even its name would probably have recalled nothing to me. But the first glimpse of the ill-lit, murmurous room, with the beds so close together, suddenly roused the train of thought to which it belonged, and in the night that followed I found myself remembering the whole story and atmosphere of the poem, with many of its lines complete.

1. The admission records of the Hôpital Cochin show that Orwell was admitted to the Salle Lancereaux 'pour une grippe' on 7 March 1929 and discharged on 22 March. This essay, therefore, though based on experience, is not strictly autobiographical. See n. 2. (Information supplied to Sonia Orwell by le Directeur-Adjoint. Hôpital Cochin, 25 November 1971.)

2. Orwell was evidently seriously ill with a bad attack of influenza – *une grippe* – rather than pneumonia; and the month was March, not February. Had Orwell been ill with pneumonia he would hardly have recovered in two weeks after the treatment he described – if he recovered at all. The essay, as indicated in n. 1, is a literary rather than a documentary account.

3. A white tuft on the lower lip, so named because Emperor Napoleon III sported such a tuft in 1839.

4. In the Anglican Church's *Book of Common Prayer*, 'The Litany, or General Supplication' is a sequence of requests and responses for priest and congregation. It is ordained that it should follow Morning Prayer on Sundays, Wednesdays and Fridays, and at other times as directed, but this instruction is infrequently carried out in most parish churches nowadays. The requests that Orwell probably has in mind are: 'From lightning and tempest; from plague, pestilence, and famine; from battle and murder, and from sudden death', and 'In all time of our tribulation; in all time of our wealth; in the hour of death, and in the day of judgement'. The response to each is 'Good Lord, deliver us'.

5. *La Débâcle* (1892) by Émile Zola describes the Franco-Prussian War of 1870, the disastrous defeat of the French at Sedan and the violent uprising in Paris in 1871, the Commune. *War and Peace* (1865–9), by Leo Tolstoy, is an epic account, from a Russian standpoint, of Napoleon's invasion of Russia in 1812. *White-Jacket* (1850), by Herman Melville, describes life on an American frigate in the Pacific.

6. Tennyson's 'In the Children's Hospital: Emmie' was published in 1880. Tennyson said it was a 'true story told me by Mary Gladstone'. It would fit perfectly into Orwell's category of 'good-bad poetry'; see p. 323, above. Although the reader is aware that his or her feelings are being manipulated (especially because the poem is concerned with the death of a little child), and the poem is undeniably sentimental, it is an extraordinarily moving poem, and essential reading to a full understanding of 'How the Poor Die'.

7. *The Story of San Michele* (1929) was written in English by the Swedish physician Axel Munthe, based on his experiences when practising in Paris, Rome and Capri, where he lived at the Villa San Michele. It was translated into many languages and proved immensely popular in the 1930s.

Further Reading

The principal source for this volume is *The Complete Works of George Orwell*, edited by Peter Davison, assisted by Ian Angus and Sheila Davison, 20 vols. (1998; paperback edn, from September 2000). Reference might also usefully be made to *The Collected Essays, Journalism and Letters of George Orwell*, edited by Sonia Orwell and Ian Angus, 4 vols. (1968; Penguin, 1970) and to the volume *Orwell's England* in this series.

Volumes of *CW* in which items will be found are as follows:

X 1–355	XIV 1435–1915	XVIII 2832–3143
XI 355A–582	XV 1916–2377	XIX 3144–3515
XII 583–843	XVI 2378–2596	XX 3516–3715A
XIII 844–1434	XVII 2597–2831	

Vol. XX also includes in Appendix 15 the following supplementary items: 2278A, 2278B, 2420A, 2451A, 2563B, 2593A, 2625A, 3351A and 3715A. Each volume is indexed and vol. XX has a Cumulative Index, indexes of topics, and an index of serials in which Orwell's work appeared.

The following highly selective list might also prove helpful:

Matthew Arnold, *Culture and Anarchy* (1869 and 1875), ed. J. Dover Wilson (1932); see especially chapter 3, 'Barbarians, Philistines, Populace'
Audrey Coppard and Bernard Crick, eds., *Orwell Remembered* (1984)
Bernard Crick, *George Orwell: A Life* (1980; 3rd edn 1992)
Peter Davison, *George Orwell: A Literary Life* (1996)
Benjamin Disraeli, *Sybil, or The Two Nations* (1845), ed. Sheila M. Smith (1981; 1998)

Tosco Fyvel, *George Orwell: A Personal Memoir* (1982)

Miriam Gross, ed., *The World of George Orwell* (1971)

Rayner Heppenstall, *Four Absentees* (1960)

Graham Holderness, Bryan Loughrey and Nahem Yousaf, *George Orwell, Contemporary Critical Essays* (1998)

Peter Lewis, *George Orwell: The Road to 1984* (1981)

Jeffrey Meyers, ed., *George Orwell: The Critical Heritage* (1975)

—, *Orwell: Wintry Conscience of a Generation* (2000)

John Newsinger, *Orwell's Politics* (1999)

Christopher Norris, ed., *Inside the Myth: Orwell: Views from the Left* (1984)

Alok Rai, *Orwell and the Politics of Despair* (1988)

Sir Richard Rees, *For Love or Money* (1960)

—, *George Orwell: Fugitive from the Camp of Victory* (1961)

Patrick Reilly, *George Orwell: The Age's Adversary* (1986)

John Rodden, *The Politics of Literary Reputation: The Making and Claiming of 'St George Orwell'* (1989)

Michael Shelden, *Orwell: The Authorised Biography* (1991)

Ian Slater, *Orwell: The Road to Airstrip One: The Development of George Orwell's Political and Social Thought from* Burmese Days *to* 1984 (1985)

Peter Stansky and William Abrahams, *The Unknown Orwell* (1974)

—, *Orwell: The Transformation* (1979)

John Thompson, *Orwell's London* (1984)

Richard J. Voorhees, *The Paradox of George Orwell* (1961)

Stephen Wadhams, ed., *Remembering Orwell* (1984)

George Woodcock, *The Crystal Spirit: A Study of George Orwell* (1967)

David Wykes, *A Preface to Orwell* (1987)

Selective Index

To index every reference to every topic, title and person, directly and indirectly, would overwhelm the user. Thus, characters mentioned in 'Boys' Weeklies' are not indexed, and usually comics, books and authors are only indexed if Orwell comments upon them. References to Britain, England and poverty are pervasive and thus there are no dedicated entries to these topics except for one title involving poverty and Germany's intention to reduce Britain to degradation and poverty (p. 382). The 'story' and the characters of *Down and Out in Paris and London* are not indexed but Orwell's discussion of social issues within the book (e.g., the Embankment as a place to sleep, casual wards, and tramps' slang and swearing) are indexed. Discussion of 'class' is important in this volume and very frequent. A fairly generous selection of references is indexed, all under 'Class' but with subheadings, such as 'Working Class'. Some references may seem insignificant and appear only once or twice, but their appearance can be related to Orwell's other works. Thus, Lambeth Cut (p. 41) appears in *A Clergyman's Daughter* (148) and in *Keep the Aspidistra Flying* (226); the weekly, *Cage Birds*, appears in the former novel (149 and 150) and in this volume on pp. 240 and 288. Bracketed explanations are sometimes provided after line references to books and authors (e.g., 'rev.' for Orwell's reviews) to give additional guidance. Where it might be helpful, dates are occasionally added to index entries. Sources within footnotes are not usually indexed although there are exceptions if it is thought these would help the user. The various forms of the Soviet secret police (e.g., OGPU, KGB) are listed under GPU, the form used in this volume. Page numbers for the text are given in roman type (e.g., 57, 168); footnotes are in italic (e.g., *33*, *284*); bold italic is used for biographical and fuller details (e.g., *44*, *357*).